PRAISE FOR *THE COACH'S CASEBOOK*

'A comprehensive toolkit for coaches looking to deepen their skills and help their clients achieve meaningful transformation. It covers the importance of self-awareness, self-management, supervision and well-being, along with neuroscience, enabling energy shifts, building strong habits and working with clients' systems to create lasting change. Highly recommended!'
Katherine Tulpa, Group CEO, Association for Coaching and Executive Director, Wisdom8

'An outstanding resource for beginner coaches, with insights and chapters to also engage the more experienced coach. Full of witty and insightful examples, the contributors have brought coaching alive, showcasing the key attributes needed by every coach and explorations of the prime issues facing coaches in the 2020s. This book will be the place to start for every new coach.'
Jonathan Passmore, Professor of Coaching and Behavioural Change, Henley Business School

'A remarkable coaching manual that provides practical tools and techniques for both novice and experienced coaches. Highly recommended for anyone looking to take their coaching practice to the next level.'
Andrea Giraldez-Hayes, Clinical Director, Department of Professional Psychology. University of East London

'Provides a treasure trove of tools, techniques, approaches and strategies that are vital for novice and experienced coaches' professional development. Written by experienced practitioners, the book is a fresh and welcome addition to professional guidebooks on coaching.'
Ioanna Iordanou, Reader in Human Resource Management, Oxford Brookes Business School

'A comprehensive volume, which will be an excellent resource for both new and seasoned coaches. It combines theory, practice and topical issues such as mental health and coaches' own self-care, which should be considered by all working in this field.'
Ana Paula Nacif, Lecturer, Department of Professional Psychology, University of East London

The Coach's Casebook

Skills, tools and techniques for effective coaching

Edited by
Joan Swart and Christine Guirguis

First published in Great Britain and the United States in 2023

2nd Floor, 45 Gee Street
London
EC1V 3RS
United Kingdom
www.koganpage.com

8 W 38th Street, Suite 902
New York, NY 10018
USA

4737/23 Ansari Road
Daryaganj
New Delhi 110002
India

Kogan Page books are printed on paper from sustainable forests.

ISBNs

Hardback	978 1 3986 1049 1
Paperback	978 1 3986 1047 7
Ebook	978 1 3986 1048 4

British Library Cataloguing-in-Publication Data
A CIP record for this book is available from the British Library.

Library of Congress Cataloging-in-Publication Data
Names: Swart, Joan, editor. | Guirguis, Christine, editor.
Title: The coach's casebook : skills, tools and techniques for effective
    coaching / edited by Joan Swart and Christine Guirguis.
Description: London ; New York, NY : Kogan Page, 2023. | Includes
    bibliographical references and index.
Identifiers: LCCN 2023015457 (print) | LCCN 2023015458 (ebook) | ISBN
    9781398610477 (paperback) | ISBN 9781398610491 (hardback) | ISBN
    9781398610484 (ebook)
Subjects: LCSH: Employees–Coaching of. | Executive coaching. | Personal
    coaching. | BISAC: BUSINESS & ECONOMICS / Mentoring & Coaching |
    BUSINESS & ECONOMICS / Training
Classification: LCC HF5549.5.C53 C6365 2023 (print) | LCC HF5549.5.C53
    (ebook) | DDC 658.3/124–dc23/eng/20230406
LC record available at https://lccn.loc.gov/2023015457
LC ebook record available at https://lccn.loc.gov/2023015458

Typeset by Integra Software Services, Pondicherry
Print production managed by Jellyfish
Printed and bound by CPI Group (UK) Ltd, Croydon CR0 4YY

CONTENTS

FOREWORD

When Joan first approached me to write the foreword for this book, my first thought was, 'Who am I to do this?' You can imagine my palpable relief when I discovered a chapter devoted to imposter syndrome! I quickly realized that in my practice as a master executive coach, trainer, mentor and supervisor and in my previous role as Director of Accreditation with the Association for Coaching (AC), I should be asking myself, 'Why not me?'

I have been coaching and working with coaches since 1997. All aspects of my professional life touch coaching in some way, shape or form. I select, train and performance-manage coaches in all industry sectors. I support training providers to create coach training programmes that fulfil the rigorous and robust requirements for AC Coach Training Accreditation and educate, advise and supervise coaches working through their accreditation. I have also contributed as an author to *Excellence in Coaching*, *The Trainee Coach Handbook*, *Coaching Supervision Groups* and *Leader Coach at Work*.

How I wish this book had been available to support me at the beginning of my journey. These authors are each hands-on practitioners in their respective fields – not just theorists! This publication satisfies the need to impart the critical information that coaches need to meet their clients where they are.

The book is divided into seven sections, covering models and frameworks, competencies, approaches, techniques and tools, application and implementation, execution, and special niches and target groups. Some will read eagerly from cover to cover, wanting to absorb the gems within each chapter. Others will dip in and out as their clients' (or their own) needs determine. Structuring the format in this way enables the reader to use it in the way that works best for them.

This reference book is vital for new and experienced coaches wanting to develop their coaching skills and knowledge. It supports coaches in practical ways, covering many of the themes that arise in coaching sessions. Illustrated throughout with client stories and challenges – we are invited to join Carlos on his journey to be a restaurateur, George with his desire to be a guru, and Katra in her quest to recognize and increase her feminine energy.

Included in various chapters is a detailed consideration of the core coaching skills of active listening, powerful questioning, goal setting, committing to action and structuring sessions (or not!). In addition, there is information on the much-feared discovery call with crucial guidance on connecting and closing that coaching conversation. The chapter on coaching 'difficult' clients does much to reassure coaches (novice or experienced) in identifying the 'coachability' of clients. Knowing when to continue working with a client and when to refer them to a professional trained in other interventions is linked directly to the three Cs of coaching and professional practice. If these subjects resonate with you, then Chapters 3, 4 and 5 are a must-read – along with all the other chapters too!

Other topics include misconceptions in coaching, holistic transformation, ikigai, empowering women to overcome cultural barriers, goal setting, and the power of intention, to name a few.

One of the many highlights is focusing on the coach's self-care, not only on the clients. Chapters include:

- Coaching presence – offering practical steps and structured techniques.
- Importance of self-management for a coach – allowing coaches to be objective, present and curious.
- Preventing burnout by attaining a healthy work and personal life balance – cultivating awareness of available interventions.

This publication contains topical issues prevalent when working with clients, such as mental health, mindfulness and psychological flexibility. More importantly, they cover the fundamental knowledge, practical application and summaries of techniques to be successfully incorporated into your coaching practice. Exploration of embodiment, the power of intention and transformation versus focusing on solutions all serve to take a holistic approach when working with clients.

It is essential in a non-regulated industry to ensure that standards are underpinned by practising ethically and having supervision. Delivered in a clear, practical and implementable way, this book contains a wealth of information on these specific topics, which will elevate the standards of excellence in coaching.

This will become the 'go-to' book for all coaches, irrespective of their levels of expertise. It delivers not just the theory but serves to enlighten the reader with clear examples of the practical application. In reading this book so that I could write the foreword, I do not doubt that I have increased my knowledge, which has enhanced my practice and the service I deliver to my clients.

The proof of a book's calibre is whether I would want this to be on my bookshelf. *The Coach's Casebook: Skills, Tools and Techniques for Effective Coaching* will have pride of place!

Jeannette Marshall
CEO, Marshall Vere Associates
and former Director of Accreditation, Assocation for Coaching

LIST OF CONTRIBUTORS

Anna Allgäuer, based in Feldkirch, Austria, is an accredited coach, coach supervisor and embodiment trainer who has taken a particular interest in combining knowledge of positive psychology and embodiment approaches in her work.

Marisabel Becker is a certified life coach, whose passion is to help and support young women break down barriers, reach their dreams and live the life they were meant to live.

Mirjam Blank is an emotion and energy coach, based in Kirschberg, Austria.

Frida Bruhn guides clients to uncover some significant blind spots and enables them to thrive by guiding her clients through them.

Donna Burfield is a fully licensed, certified and accredited coach with the International Coaching Federation (ICF) and European Mentoring and Coaching Council (EMCC). She is the founder of Joy and Purpose Coaching, Coaches Supporting Coaches Dubai and CSC Certified Coaches Group.

Bernice Fabi is a life and success coach and NLP practitioner.

Marie Faire is co-founder of The Beyond Partnership Ltd. She is an accredited master executive coach, an accredited master coach supervisor and an ANLP recognized master NLP trainer.

Vijaya Gowrisankar is based in Mumbai, India and is a transformation coach and a business leader in an IT organization. She has completed the EMCC Accredited Coaching Certification Programme from Coaching Minds.

Rob Hallott is an accredited executive coach with the Association for Coaching, and a qualified NLP practitioner. He has 20 years' experience in management and leadership, at both operational and strategic levels.

Mondana Hamniaz is a certified universal consciousness master, and a Jay Shetty certified integration and transformational coach.

Chris Hawkins has been a mentor, leader, trainer and change maker for over 30 years, and has earned accreditation as an associate certified coach through the ICF.

Sharon Hooper draws on decades of direct business experience, in addition to coaching hundreds of individuals in multiple fields.

Narina Hovhannisyan is a master certified coach, and the president of the International Coaching Federation, Armenia Chapter.

Lucian Lo is a life purpose coach, trained in NLP, EQ (emotional intelligence), PQ (positive intelligence), growth mindset, neuroscience peak performance and positive psychology.

Christopher Mitra is a certified executive leadership coach, tech entrepreneur, author and mentor.

Anjali Nankani is a Jay Shetty certified wellness coach based in Toronto, Canada. Her holistic approach brings confidence and perspective for her clients.

Daniel Noh is an entrepreneur and a Jay Shetty certified life coach, based in Calgary, Canada.

Kassandra Parker is a Jay Shetty certified life and success coach, coaching people to connect with the life they deeply desire by unravelling limiting beliefs.

Neela Pirwitz is a Jay Shetty certified performance and well-being coach, focusing on burnout prevention, based in Groningen, the Netherlands.

Natalia Pivovarova is an accredited foundation coach (Association for Coaching) and a member of the International Association of NeuroGestalt.

Isabel Rechberg is a management professor, a researcher in organizational behavior and an Association for Coaching accredited coach.

Jana Siedenhans, based in Heidelberg, Germany, is a multi-accredited coach, including by the Association for Coaching and the German Association for Systemic Coaching, and certified as an EQ Profiler.

Ryan Sipes, based in Denver, Colorado, graduated from the Jay Shetty Certification School in 2020, where he earned his accreditation from the Association for Coaching.

Paul Smith is an accredited senior practitioner with the EMCC, and Managing Director of Coaching Minds, an organization which offers industry-accredited coach training programmes.

Louise Sockett is a coach and HR consultant with 20 years' experience.

Madhvi Tailor is a certified women's empowerment coach, a 2022 TechWomen100 award winner and UN Women UK delegate.

Amaya Toland is a human resources professional and life coach. She obtained her Life and Success Certification from the Jay Shetty Certification School.

Martijn van Eijk is a certified mindfulness trainer, life and success coach and meditation teacher based in Amsterdam.

1

Introduction and misconceptions of coaching

RYAN SIPES

ABSTRACT

Although coaching has already come a long way out of the building dock, we are still just getting started on its maiden journey. With uncertain times and social engineering creeping into every crevice on earth, consistent and responsible care is more important than ever. With the right foundations, coaching can provide a reset and stimulus forward to many people in many places and situations.

Introduction

It is true that coaching, as an approach or technique, can be applied in many contexts, settings and populations. As such, there are heaps of 'thoughts' or 'ideas' of what it is that an individual expects when talking about coaching or when exploring the opportunity to be coached. There is a caveat, though. When the act, intention or potential of coaching is misapplied and misunderstood, negative results are possible. In support of the acquisition of knowledge, and development of coaching as a personal professional endeavour and collective undertaking, this chapter aims to clarify the differences of what coaching is and is not; when, where and how to best apply coaching skills and techniques; and when other solutions may be more suitable.

Coaching is seen in many different forms whether it be a sports coach, getting coached by a manager at your day job, or from the different relationships in your life such as a friend or a parent. Coaching has become such a broadly used term and it is not for any bad reason. This earth is just filled with folks wanting to help their loved ones and those closest to them!

The global coaching industry

A Global Coaching Study by the International Coaching Federation (ICF) and PricewaterhouseCoopers (2020) valued coaching as a $2.85 billion global industry, $1.3 billion in North America alone with about 71,000 certified coaches active in the field. What is even more astonishing is that the number of professional coaches increased by 33 per cent between 2014 and 2019 (ICF, 2020)! Come to think of it, if you are reading this book, you may be the potential addition to this year's increase of active certified coaches.

We like to think that there is always room in today's society for more people seeking to help and understand those who may feel helpless, downtrodden and misunderstood. But when any industry becomes this big, and continues to grow, the jostling for competition becomes fierce and may distract coaches from their original intention of helping others. They may take professional shortcuts or opt out of training, accreditation and supervision, for instance, or focus too much on marketing and social media, compromise on ethical issues, and forget their roots, so to speak. Education and training are lifelong endeavours without which coaching (and a coach) will not thrive and survive. They may also drift between approaches and modalities, such as coaching, consulting, mentoring, therapy, education and training. While this may be perfectly fine, conditions involving competence, clients' interest and contracting must be combined to set the appropriate foundations, essentially putting on another similar hat with intention (see Chapter 2).

Misconceptions of coaching

The misconceptions of coaching that continue to hold the profession back from realizing full potential are 1) confusion and uncertainty of the difference between coaching and other helping roles, 2) that a coach will impart their answers to tell and show clients how to achieve their goals, and 3) that a good coach has personal expertise in the area a client needs help with. First, understanding how coaching differs from other helping professions helps clients make the best help-seeking decisions and manage their expectations.

Distinguishing coaching, consulting/advising, training, mentoring and therapy

As stated by iPEC (nd), coaching is commonly confused with other forms of personal support such as consulting, mentoring, training or therapy. The reason is that there tends to be so much crossover because if you were to ask someone 'What does x personal support help their client achieve?', they may answer 'The coach shows the client from Point A to Point B.' At first glance, circling back to the opening statement, this is why this notion of coaching as a guide is so exciting as the service provider may feel that they have multiple avenues to help their client arrive at Point B!

Although, when we focus only on the result that is attained for the client, many subtle disparities appear, almost like parallel universes. There are different levels of empowerment, satisfaction, durability, stability and so forth in each journey and arrival. It not only depends on where the client was at the beginning, but the process of their journey and relationship with their coach, which is how each of these services tend to blend in with another.

However, what differentiates each of these personal support methods is how to get the client to the result – the 'HOW' in moving the client from Point A to Point B. This specific key is of strong significance to the impact the client can expect to receive, depending on the specific service and their context, situation and needs.

Therefore, when looking at each orientation, the easiest way is to depict how each service is delivered and with what focus. Differentiating these methods will also give a greater understanding of the 'Point B' or 'future state' that the client can expect to experience when working with each of the services.

Let's say the client is inexperienced in what they are seeking help for. There are many different services that seem to cross over when serving the client. For the purpose of this discussion, I focus on coaching, consulting, training, mentoring and therapy.

COACHING

Whitmore argues that 'the essence of coaching is unlocking a person's potential to maximize their performance. It is helping them to learn rather than teaching them' (2002: 8). In other words, how can a coachee (or even employee), rather than a service provider, learn x to show, teach or do x? With coaching, the coachee creates their own path to succeed. The coach accepts that a coachee has the potential to discover their unique solutions on their own to reach the goals that they set.

The value of a coach is to facilitate and accelerate the client's ability to create their path by giving them additional tools they may not have on their own. With many issues, clients need guidance in the process and a safe professional space to reflect to find their answers. As such, the coach does not position themselves as an expert. Instead, they focus on the coachee being the expert in their own life and they deliver the structure, process and space for the client to be creative, open-minded and vulnerable, if needed. A coach focuses on listening and asking questions to help clients discover the best (unique) way for them to get to their destination. Accordingly, the cornerstone and most widely accepted premise of coaching is that the client is 'naturally creative, resourceful, and whole' (ICF, 2020, para 5).

Therefore, coaches are not providing a service with the answers, or know the answers for their coachee. They have process skills (listening, questioning, showing empathy, building trust, encouraging, knowing which tools and methods to use, etc) to guide the coachee to find their own answers.

CONSULTING AND ADVISING

Clients hire a consultant to help them define their problems and formulate solutions (iPEC, nd). Here, the client is wanting to get the answers from someone with expertise, to receive the solution rather than being guided to find answers themselves. The consultant, or expert, provides the answers, solutions and any opinions on smaller, shorter-term situations the client needs to progress forward. The client is inexperienced and is looking for an expert on a short-term basis to resolve an issue that is impeding their progress or results at the moment. Different from a consultant, people do not (or should not) seek a coach because of the subject expertise a coach has. A good coach withholds any opinions based on their experience and, instead, focuses on exploring the opinions and experience of the client.

Advisors are similar to consultants, as organizations and individuals get an advisor to tackle and find answers to their problems or challenges. Advisors often work with clients on a longer-term (retainer) basis, providing ongoing advice, while continuing to identify new problems and solutions. Whereas a consultant is most suited to solve granular problems on a short-term basis, an advisor works consistently with the company to facilitate decision making that preempts or prevents organic problems arising due to growth, strategy or other changes (Maister, 2018).

So, clients go to a consultant or an advisor to seek answers based on their experience. In contrast, a coach looks at the client as the expert to seek the answers from within themselves.

TRAINING

Training is sometimes mixed with coaching as they both involve creating solutions for their clients, but in different ways. A client of either a coach or trainer can receive actionable solutions that will then be implemented into their own lives or practice. Again, the key difference is that the coaching client comes up with their own solutions and action plans while a trainer prescribes these for their clients. As such, a trainer gives advice or instructions based on personal expertise to work towards the desired results for the client.

Coaching creates solutions by asking the coachee questions that guide them not only to find solutions but build the confidence to overcome their challenges in their own unique way. As a result, a coach guides the client to create their own solutions while a trainee relies on the trainer to provide the solutions for them.

MENTORING

iPEC (nd) writes that *mentoring* is like serving as a wise role model. Mentees want to emulate the success of the mentor. This is well suited for people who want to follow the same path and reach a similar outcome as their preferred mentor.

Therefore, mentoring is different as mentors rely heavily on their experience to give advice that points the mentee in their desired direction. Also, the mentor is not necessarily curating new solutions for the client. Rather they are using solutions that worked for them in a similar instance.

With coaching, the coachee is not looking to follow the path of their coach. The coach assists the coachee in formulating their own path with their knowledge, expertise and process experiences to launch clients forward. It is about the process and not the expert topic.

THERAPY

The last comparison is to *therapy*. A therapist seeks to understand the client's dysfunctions in the present by understanding underlying issues and past roots. Whereas, in coaching, the client is typically at a balanced and functional level but needs a collaborative space where they can find and explore ways to move forward (iPEC, nd).

A coach should be extremely intentional in portraying that they are working on progressing forward and that they are not equipped to work on past trauma if they are not trained and experienced otherwise. This is not just because the coachee needs to understand they are working from the present towards a future goal and know the objective of the relationship. A coach is empowered by watching their coachee build their own path and find their own solutions. It is this process, and the skills needed to guide the client forward, that makes the coach an expert, and not their knowledge of a topic or the client's life and circumstances.

Therefore, treating the client as the expert is the key that separates coaching from the other four services. This by no means makes the other services any less of a benefit to a person's life. But, in the appropriate context and circumstances, coaching is very powerful as clients are acknowledged as the experts of their own lives. Distinguishing coaching from other helping approaches and services is important to ensure that the potential of coaching is realized in a responsible and ethical way, that the coach stays within the limits of their competence, and that the context and situation are suitable to coaching.

This gives a great baseline for how coaching can be separated from some of the other 'solution providers'. Now, with these key differentiators in mind, let's explore what seems to be the misunderstanding of why or why not people think they need to seek a coach.

As you or other individuals seek growth opportunities, it is imperative you distinguish the differences as you align your goals to what benefits each service works

FIGURE 1.1 Different approaches in helping professions

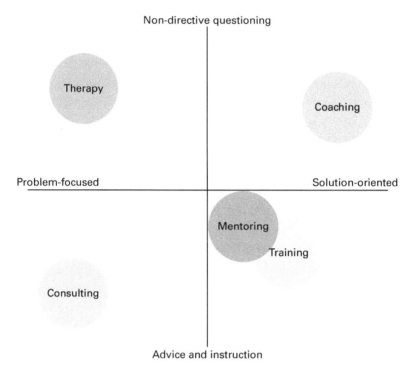

towards. Figure 1.1 broadly illustrates the main differences in orientation between coaching, consulting, training, mentoring and therapy.

Unlike the other services, coaching avoids giving advice and instructions and focuses on the client's strengths to support their goal achievement rather than a diagnosis of their problems and dysfunctions. If prospective clients understand these differences, they will be more informed and clearer about the service that most suits their needs.

Why seek coaching?

Sir John Whitmore, the co-creator of the GROW Model, defines coaching as primarily being concerned with the type of relationship between a coach and a coachee, and the means and style of communication used (Whitmore, 2002). Let's consider two separate examples here.

Think about something as simple as learning to walk. A parent, in most cases, cannot necessarily teach or tell their child how to walk. They are left to help them learn how to walk because they are unable to communicate this to the child. This is why one would seek a coach. To learn how to do something themselves that no one can do for them.

Another good example to consider is identifying blind spots. A blind spot is an area in which one fails to exercise informed, objective judgement but is usually not aware of it. In other words, you cannot see what is holding you back or preventing you from achieving your goals. Similar to blind spots when driving a vehicle, your blind spots can only be seen with the help of someone else. Coaches guide their clients to uncover and identify blind spots that cannot be seen by the coachee on their own, thereby creating the awareness to challenge their existence.

Does this mean you have to be at rock bottom to seek this type of help? No. Would someone need to feel lost in getting to their ideal future state? They could, but not necessarily. Many people feel if they are doing well a coach would not be beneficial. But this is actually where coaching could be the most powerful. If you are at the 'top of your game', but there is an opportunity to go even higher than the supposed 'top', why would that not be enticing?

The misconceptions about whether coaching can be effective can be directly tied to humans having a fixed or growth mindset of their own abilities in different situations in their lives (Dweck, 2006). In other words, when one has a growth mindset, they believe that their intelligence and talents can evolve, grow and develop over time. Whereas with a fixed mindset, one believes their intelligence and other abilities are fixed. This means that if you are not good at something, you will never be good at it, or if you are good at something, that is as good as you will ever be. Therefore, a person with a fixed mindset is less likely to seek to better themselves with a coach as they believe that they are the way that they are, and nothing can change that or the situation that they are in, or, alternatively, they may expect the coach to tell them what to do. With a growth mindset established, coaching can present a life-altering outlook when challenges arise in the present. Whether the coach and/or client realizes it or not, the client is learning to relieve the pressure of achieving the end result because they are focusing on the smaller steps to get to where they eventually want to be. With a growth mindset their sole focus is not on the outcome, but on what needs to be done for the outcome to be reached. They believe the outcome is achievable and there is a path. Focusing on the growth to navigate through each step on the path is what they can expect to gain when working with a coach. In the fixed mindset, you can be stuck with no path forward and reliant on just receiving an immediate solution from someone outside you. Instead, coaching shows the client that they are capable of creating their own solutions by using questions to guide the client in the best direction.

Therefore, coaching is a powerful way of helping clients to develop a growth mindset, which, once it becomes a strong muscle, can lead to continued success in many areas of a person's life.

While understanding the difference between coaching, consulting, training, mentoring and therapy, and appreciating that anyone who can use a growth mindset and creative ways to move forward towards goals can benefit from an effective coach, let's reiterate that a good coach does not have to be an expert in the client's world.

Coaching is not about expertise

Coaching is not a last resort answer but an ongoing process of exploring, reflecting and finding answers that is suitable at any time a person seeks to move forward. If you're halfway to reaching the top of a mountain where you discover tools that could either accelerate your time or improve the safety of reaching the peak, would you use them? The answer, almost 100 per cent of the time, will be yes! Coaching, for any client, can be a great tool implemented at any given point in your life. There is no wrong time to start with a coach.

Coaches do not need to be experts to help a client achieve their goals. A coach is not measured by their past experiences because accredited/certified coaches do not focus their training based on a field of expertise, although they may, perhaps later on, develop a niche that requires specialized knowledge and training. Coach training involves learning, practising and refining process-related skills and techniques. For example, the Association for Coaching (AC), one of the most prominent coach representation bodies, requires coaches to acquire certain core competencies. None of these are related to being a subject matter expert. The following is a summary of the official AC core competencies required to earn your coaching accreditation or certification (AC, 2022: 1):

1 **Meeting ethical, legal and professional guidelines** – including a coach distinguishing themselves from the other support professions.
2 **Establishing the coaching agreement and outcomes** – contract clearly for the objective(s) of the client, competencies, and practices of the coach, in an ethical framework.
3 **Establishing a trust-based relationship with the client** – seek to understand the client within their context in an empathetic and accepting way.
4 **Maintaining self and a coaching presence** – create a safe and accepting space including demonstrating curiosity during the coaching process.
5 **Communicate effectively** – practise focusing on what the client is and is not saying to fully understand what is being communicated in the context of the client systems and ask non-leading questions deliberately to gain information, raise awareness, encourage creativity and motivate action.

6 **Raising awareness and insight** – facilitate client insight with techniques such as powerful questioning and silence.

7 **Designing strategies and actions** – supports and inspires the client to find and try new solutions, commit to actions and be accountable for their own outcomes.

8 **Maintain forward momentum and evaluation** – partner with your client to transform learning into action (promotes client autonomy in the coaching process).

9 **Undertaking continuous coach development** – apply feedback, reflection, supervision and learning consistently to improve your coaching practice.

The International Coaching Federation is considered by many to be the world's leading accrediting and credentialling of trained coaches, so this clearly exemplifies what you should search for when identifying the correct coach for you. ICF does not train its students to be subject matter experts but to be coaches whose practices are in line with their core competencies. Also, the required core competencies coaches are held to in their practice serve as quality assurance in the accreditation process.

This includes business coaches working with clients to earn a promotion, make a job transition, or gain confidence to network in their respective industries, and coaches in other areas, such as athletics. This does not mean an athletic performance coach can take the place of a life coach to lead their team to become world champions, or vice versa. Rather, the idea is getting to that specific accolade may take a life coach to get past roadblocks that a technical expert is not experienced to help their people overcome.

One of the highest-quality examples to conclude this final point as to why coaches do not need to be experts to be effective is a story of the world-renowned high-performance coach, Brendon Burchard.

In Burchard's book, *High-Performance Habits* (2022), he gives an example of an Olympic sprinter who was already at the top of his game that year. But in prior years his performance was often erratic. Sometimes he would win a competition; other times he did not make the qualifying cut. In fact, when the sprinter called Burchard to work together, he was on a year-long winning streak.

Burchard goes on to describe what the Olympic sprinter and he worked on together in their first session. They did not discuss physical performance. Rather than the key to the sprinter's success in that year, after having a spotty previous year, he described his success in three words to be 'Feeling, feeling, feeling' (Burchard, 2022: 84).

Most people would view a winning Olympic sprinter to be at the peak of their career. So why would they need a coach if they've already reached the top? The Olympic sprinter saw an opportunity to go beyond his highest of achievements by working with a coach to go further. He did not define his success as an end, but rather as a stepping stone to develop a growth mindset and reach new heights. How could someone of that calibre seek a coach that has no expertise, nor been a sprinter himself, in a quest to become a world-class sprinter? Hats off to Burchard's coachee for understanding that it takes more than physical performance to succeed. But successful coach–client relationships like these show that people looking for coaches still can find the right coach who does not have experience in their field.

Not only that – this should also encourage any aspiring coaches that they can expand their reach in any direction they desire to work with. Yes, this Olympic sprinter had athletic experts and trainers who helped him find consistency in his craft. Using a combination of technical experts, trainers and life coaches the athlete could achieve something far greater than his current success by engaging in a coaching relationship with Burchard.

Conclusion

Coaching roughly fulfils a similar purpose to therapy, mentoring, consulting and training, but has a uniquely powerful approach of collaborative, non-directional discovery that empowers the client to find their own unique solutions. A coach does not show and tell you what to do to solve a problem or achieve a goal. They do not offer answers and quick fixes. And, as they are the experts in the process of change management, they do not have to be a specialist in the field the client needs help with.

This understanding is intended to provide an objective foundation to the knowledge and practices throughout this book that is backed by scientific evidence and meant to expand and deepen coaches' skills and techniques to deliver a successful coaching process. As you read the upcoming sections analysing the models and frameworks, competencies, approaches, techniques and tools, and transforming theory into practice – you will learn in greater depth about how effective coaches apply their trade in rigorous and proven ways.

References

AC (2022) AC Coaching Competency Framework, Association for Coaching, www.associationforcoaching.com/resource/resmgr/Accreditation/Accred_General/Coaching_Competency_Framewor.pdf (archived at https://perma.cc/KJ47-YA8L)
Burchard, B (2022) *High Performance Habits: How extraordinary people become that way*, Hay House, London
Dweck, C (2006) *Mindset: The new psychology of success*, Random House, New York

ICF (2020) 2020 ICF Global Coaching Study, International Coaching Federation, coachingfederation.org/research/global-coaching-study (archived at https://perma. cc/9JJ8-98Y7)

iPEC (nd) What is coaching? www.ipeccoaching.com/ resources/faq (archived at https:// perma.cc/C65Q-MJXF)

Maister, D (2018) Professionalism in consulting, in *Management Consulting Today and Tomorrow: Perspectives and advice from leading experts*, 2nd edn, ed F Poulfelt and T H Olson, pp 37–50, Routledge, New York

Whitmore, J (2002) *Coaching for Performance: Growing human potential and purpose*, 3rd edition, Nicholas Brealey, London

PART ONE

Models and frameworks

2

The three Cs of coaching
and professional practice

MARIE FAIRE

ABSTRACT

The coaching profession has gone to great efforts to define itself and there is extensive literature on the boundaries between coaching, mentoring, counselling and therapy. In this chapter the author will challenge how useful this is, and offer what she considers to be a more fruitful model to ensure ethical and best practice.

Introduction

In the last 30 years, the professional coaching community has become somewhat obsessed with defining itself. At a time of ever-impending legislation and increasing requirements for accreditation, there appear to be heightened sensibilities, and competition between varying professions that offer 'interpersonal, talking help'. It is not surprising therefore, that those engaged in coaching, the newest of those professions, have succumbed to the search for the Holy Grail – a definitive definition of what coaching is and is not.

Definitions

The coaching profession, like others, has spent enormous energy in developing a definitive definition that separates it from other professions. It is interesting to note that prior to its formation, BACP (British Association for Counselling and Psychotherapy) gave up trying to distinguish between counselling and psychotherapy.

Much has been written about the distinctions between coaching and mentoring; between coaching and counselling; and between coaching and therapy. If we google 'definition of coaching' we find 250 million options. Of course, many may well be the same and taken from one or the other of the professional bodies or academic texts, but it makes the point that that number of sites feel the need to define the activity in an absolute way.

Any accreditation with which I am familiar will at some point test for the applicant's knowledge and practice of coaching as opposed to any other helping strategy.

Certainly, in the initial stages of training people how to coach, it is a challenge for most not to teach, mentor, problem solve or direct. As a trainer and supervisor of coaches I have spent many hours exploring with students and supervisees 'but is it coaching?'

Wilson (2005) offers the metaphor of driving a car:

- A therapist will explore what is stopping you driving your car.
- A counsellor will listen to your anxieties about the car.
- A mentor will share tips from their experience of driving cars.
- A consultant will advise you on how to drive the car.
- A coach will encourage and support you in driving the car.

Clearly there are some situations that would be better suited to a particular helping strategy. However, the search for precise definition of what any given practitioner does presupposes that we could produce definitions that would be isolated and separate.

Although it is a 'buyer beware' market and the public do not know that, in most countries, anyone can declare themselves a coach without any training, let alone accreditation, I believe by far most of our clients could not care less. They may want to know we can assist them to get from where they are now to where they want to be, but all too often they do not even seem to check that out.

The attempt to draw distinct lines between consulting, mentoring, coaching, counselling and therapy is of primary interest to those who are the practitioners.

Famously, John Whitmore, when asked 'What is the difference between coaching and counselling?' replied 'They are spelt differently'.

All the helping professions use the same core interpersonal skills and require some of the same competencies. There is far more overlap than there is difference, both in what we do and the issues that can be usefully supported.

To be perfectly frank, in my less-considered moments there is a part of me that does ask 'who cares what we call what we do, if it works?'

Furthermore, the coaching field has grown and differentiated. If one were to compare the practice of an executive coach, a career coach, a public speaking coach, a mental health coach, a life coach, a therapeutic coach, we might find that some have more in common with counsellors or consultants, etc, than they do with their colleagues who are engaged in 'pure' coaching.

A different perspective

I would like to suggest that a more fruitful discussion is concerning how we determine professional practice rather that *what* it is.

I propose that the three vital ingredients in the process to decide whether to work with a client could be the three Cs of coaching professional practice: contracting, competency and client's interest.

The best metaphor that I have for this is the legs of a three-legged stool (see Figure 2.1). Without any one of those, the thing falls over.

Contract

Much has been written about the importance of getting the contract right and then delivering what has been agreed (Block, 1981; Bluckert, 2006; Fielder and Starr, 2008).

QUESTIONS

- Is what we are working on what we agreed we would work on?
- If not, is it appropriate and in our gift to renegotiate the contract?

It may be that you have the professional competency to do what is needed and it would be in the client's interest – but if it is not contracted (or recontracted) for, then we have no business going there.

FIGURE 2.1 Professional coaching practice as a three-legged stool

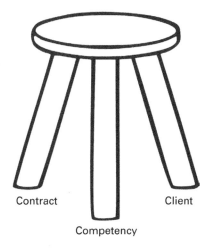

Contract   Client

Competency

Competency

Every professional body at some time defines the competencies for that profession. This is turning this on its head and asking the professional to use their 'internal supervisor' (Murdoch, 2006) to check their own competency and capacity for doing the work.

QUESTIONS

- Am I competent to deal with this issue?
- Do I have the capacity to address this issue appropriately?

If I am not competent (skill) or do not have the resources (time, energy) then I need to refer.

Client's best interest (and world)

Every client is part of a system, and we need to ensure that what we do attends to the client's best interest in the 'ecology' of that system.

QUESTIONS

- Is it appropriate for this client to work on this issue with me?
- Is it appropriate for this client to work on this issue in this context?

Just because I can doesn't mean I should.

This may be the contracted issue and I am competent, but it may not be right to proceed. For example, this may occur when both parties work for the same organization and the issue is of a deeper or personal nature.

CASE STUDIES

Case 1

Ray is a new coach and had previously been a manager of an L&D team. She has recently won a contract to coach first-time managers.

When she meets with the first three clients, she discovers that her coachees are very inexperienced and have had no training to enable them to manage effectively. She can help them explore how they want to be seen as a manager and the reality is they don't know how to do it.

At supervision

Although she has the competency to mentor (as well as coach) and this would be in the interest of her coachees, this is not what she has been contracted to do. In this case she would need to renegotiate her contract with the HR director who brought her in.

Case 2

Sal is a newly trained coach on a short programme. She was previously a sales director. Her first client has come for support, as she has just started her own business. At their second session the coachee bursts into tears and says that she feels like a fraud and that she believes she isn't good enough.

At supervision

Sal says she feels out of her depth. This issue may be within contract and is also clearly addressing a need and is in the best interest of her client. The issue is whether Sal has the competence to work at this depth. If not, then it may be appropriate to refer to someone who is and then offer to continue the coaching at a later date.

Case 3

Ed is an internal coach. He also sees private clients and has recently been accredited as an executive coach. His interest is in extending his competency and this year he is attending a programme on being a trauma-sensitive coach. One of his internal clients is a 'rising star' whose manager has referred him for coaching as he seems to have 'lost his mojo'. On their first meeting the coachee explains that he is still very motivated at work, it is just that his marriage is 'on the rocks' and he is devastated as his parents divorced when he was young, and he doesn't want 'to do the same thing' to his kids.

At supervision

Ed's contract is to deal with performance issues and the client has clearly identified that the cause is his personal situation. Ed is also a very experienced and competent coach and with support, could deal with this situation. The question is whether this is in the interest of the coachee. Would it be better for the coachee to work with someone outside the organization?

Conclusion

In summary, I advocate that any coach (new or experienced) may wish to consider:

- Contracting for the breadth and depth of your current competency.
- It is OK to be a 'hybrid' coach. A coach at core and able to do what the client needs, just check you are not mentoring, counselling, advising because that's what you want to do.
- Commit to do the continuous professional development (CPD) that increases your competency in the area that you want to work.
- Always consider the ecology of your client.
- If in doubt about any of the three Cs, take the dilemma to your supervisor.

Like the stool, we need all three in place if we are not to fall over and are to be professional practitioners of whatever we call ourselves.

References

Block, P (1981) *Flawless Consulting: A guide to getting your expertise used*, 3rd edn, Jossey-Bass, San Francisco, CA

Bluckert, P (2006) *Psychological Dimensions of Executive Coaching*, Open University Press, Maidenhead

Fielder, J H and Starr, L M (2008) What's the big deal about coaching contracts? *International Journal of Coaching in Organizations,* 6 (4), 15–27

Murdoch, E (2006) Building the internal supervisor, internal CSA paper, unpublished

Wilson, S (2005) It's all in the contract: A guide to getting it right first time, unpublished manuscript

3

Awareness and accountability in coaching

ANJALI NANKANI

ABSTRACT

Self-awareness is linked to the ability to overcome external factors while accountability empowers clients to manage and track their progress in the coaching process. The coach's job is to establish an honest relationship with the client, which facilitates these processes in a safe and encouraging space by recognizing that each client is their own best expert.

Introduction

Two of the most important steps in any coaching approach are to increase the client's level of self-awareness and hold them accountable for their own actions. By reflecting more on oneself and being more self-aware, one can develop the capacity to withstand and bounce back from external stressors and understand where change is needed. The coach's job is to keep the relationship genuine, concentrate on the client as a whole person, and increase the client's awareness. The coach engages in the coaching with the conviction that the client is their own best expert and with an attitude of acceptance, empathy and commitment.

This chapter reveals the importance of self-awareness and accountability and what it has to offer in the client's coaching experience.

Self-awareness

Why is it important to be self-aware? By evaluating yourself, you are better able to manage your emotions, align your behaviour with your values, and understand correctly how others perceive you (Duval and Wickland, 1972).

What you observe and process is awareness. Self-awareness is the act of observing oneself and analysing information. Observing your actions and their reasons, as well as your emotions, triggers, aspirations and sources of happiness, are all important. It is important because once you are aware of what motivates you to follow a certain behaviour pattern then you will be able to modify, add or remove your habits. You might start by becoming more conscious of your emotions and asking yourself why you feel the way you do. Self-reflection enables a coach to be more aware of their client too, as well as the coach–client relationship and coaching processes. The coach also extends their ability to become self-aware and continues to practise self-awareness to their clients. To assist clients in developing self-awareness, you can utilize a variety of questions and tools or exercises, such as the 'Every Picture Tells a Sstory' tool and the ORACLE model. Therefore, awareness is a key pillar (and starting point) of the coaching process.

Creating client awareness involves two approaches. First and foremost, a coach needs to be aware of the capabilities, goals and intents of their clients. Through skilful listening, questioning and analysing techniques, this skill can be mastered. A deeper knowledge of the client is helpful to generate self-awareness as deeper issues are exposed to the client in the process. As such, you apply this knowledge to assist clients in developing their own sense of awareness by shining a light onto thoughts, beliefs, emotion, and other inner experiences that were previously hidden.

Additionally, if your client is aware of who they are and how they are seen, they will be better able to recognize their strengths and respond to their surroundings, which will contribute to accomplishing desired outcomes. They have more supportive relationships, are better leaders, have greater personal and social control, act with more empathy – all aspects associated with satisfaction and happiness while negatively linked to stress and depression (Eurich, 2018).

Accountability

Accountability helps the client to be responsible and answerable for their own actions. Accountability involves both parties having a responsibility to each other and themselves. It is a way for the coach to know how the client is doing and for the client to be accountable for their own actions. Real change is hard enough and even more challenging unless your client is prepared to hold themselves accountable. Setting goals is fantastic but often futile if not backed up by accountability. For each of a client's potential outcomes, they must decide on their own level of priority and commitment.

It is imperative to keep in mind that a client who does not commit to or believe in the process will not do the work necessary to create the change. It is therefore helpful for clients to have a reward system and internal motivation to find the solution to stimulate their attempts to achieve the desired result. Clients who are more likely to attribute blame elsewhere, place a low value on the desired result or think they have no control over it are more likely to fail (Liddy et al, 2015).

Three primary care clinics in Ottawa, Ontario, began a health coaching trial programme in 2012. All of the interviews in this coaching programme emphasized the value of patient accountability and shared responsibility. Working with a coach seemed to assist patients in realizing the need of taking charge of their own health management and improvement. Through the coaching process, patients also appeared to develop a sense of shared responsibility for their care. The initiative encouraged patients to take charge of their health.

Some patients found that being monitored motivated them and increased their personal accountability. 'It's important to be able to sit with somebody and talk about it and to be monitored. If I know that I'm being monitored, I'm gonna be acting upon it' (Patient 4) (Liddy et al, 2015).

So, encourage the client to think they are capable of making the necessary changes, as mentioned above by the patients. In essence, responsibility is a crucial element that motivates clients to move towards accomplishing their objectives. The client would probably not finish the coaching journey or make a full attempt to change without this buy-in. For example, the buy-in for a patient is to get positive feedback after introducing new habits during coaching, which also keeps them accountable as they can track their progress through the feedback reports. As such, the patient can achieve this buy-in by seeing the results of their actions.

As a result, one of a coach's most crucial duties, especially in the beginning, is to advance the awareness and auditing results by leveraging their knowledge and skills to strengthen the client's accountability.

Theory and literature review

A review of the literature confirms that awareness and accountability are essential components of coaching (Gazelle, Liebschutz and Riess, 2014; Liddy et al, 2015). The best starting point and foundation is to help clients broaden self-awareness and to take responsibility for their own actions.

Gazelle, Liebschutz and Riess (2014) explain that an iterative process of questioning ideas and situations is at the core of the coaching process. Clients have the ability to challenge subconscious thoughts, beliefs and perceptions and distinguish between assumptions, facts and interpretations. People can go from reactive to intentional response by taking control of their thoughts and beliefs. The ability to tolerate and recover from outside pressures can be improved by increasing self-reflection and self-awareness.

A study by Liddy et al (2015) found that patients were greatly helped by coaches in understanding how diabetes affects their health. Patients who reflected on their circumstances and linked their actions (or inactivity) to their health, increased their health literacy, which frequently inspired them to take real action to better their health. In this study, patients mentioned how coaches assisted them in becoming more conscious of their behaviour, which motivated them to make the required adjustments to enhance their health. For instance, one participant said, 'It opened my eyes, actually, to what I'm eating and how it's affecting me, that's for sure.' (Liddy et al, 2015: e162)

This study also throws some light on accountability. The interviews emphasized the value of patient accountability and shared responsibility. Working with a coach seemed to assist patients in realizing the need of taking charge of their own health management and improvement. Patients thanked coaches for holding them accountable for their choices or inactions and the repercussions that followed during the biweekly meetings.

Two approaches that can help to enhance self-awareness and build accountability for the clients in the coaching programme are the gestalt coaching approach and the person-centred coaching approach.

Gestalt coaching approach

Gestalt coaching is an approach to coaching that focuses on the whole person (Allan and Whybrow, 2018). Gestalt psychology is a theory of mind and personality that emphasizes the importance of the whole, not just individual parts. Gestalt psychology believes that people are shaped by their relationships with others, their environment and their experiences. Gestalt coaching takes this premise into account and helps people identify what they want to change in themselves or in their lives, while also looking at how they can change these things within their environment or relationships. The goal is to support the client in broadening their options and utilizing their abilities to the fullest extent possible as they explore the world around them. The coach's role is to bring honesty to the connection, focus on the client as a whole person and raise the client's consciousness. The coach makes the client accountable by challenging them to respond to questions about their lack of commitment. These enquiries can also show patterns of self-sabotage, which is the first step in taking responsibility for one's behaviour. For example: What is holding them back from living their values? What can they do today that will bring them closer to self-acceptance?

Person-centred coaching approach

A person-centred approach puts the person's needs first and supports them in taking charge of their own self-care. Instead of the person's weaknesses, the emphasis is on what they are capable of and that helps them to create accountability for themselves as mentioned above in the patient example. Therefore, support should be targeted to the individual's requirements and specific situation with an emphasis on helping them achieve their goals. For example: If I am not afraid of rejection by my mother, what will I do that makes me feel self-loved?

The goal for coaches is to build an honest, accepting relationship with the client in order to create a 'social environment' where the client is confident they won't be criticized or pressured to do any particular action (Joseph and Bryant-Jefferies, 2018). Because person-centred approaches maintain that the client already possesses the solutions needed to attain goals and function at their peak, the authentic connection and social environment are produced (Joseph and Bryant Jefferies, 2018; Stoltzfus, 2005). As a result, in person-centred coaching, the coach acts with the belief that the client is their own best expert and with an attitude of affirmation, empathic understanding and expectation.

From the literature we see that increasing self-awareness and holding your clients responsible for their own behaviours contribute to their success. For example: A coach may ask the client what beliefs they are clinging to that result in low self-esteem. Also, where these beliefs stem from and what is the challenge for them to replace or eliminate these beliefs. It is essential to use evidence-based approaches in coaching that can help clients to progress in their coaching journey.

CASE STUDY

In the beginning of the session, the client struggled to identify the goal of the session. She kept saying that she had the awareness that she had self-sabotage behaviour, but she was struggling to keep the commitment to her plans and had the tendency to procrastinate. In that case, I as a coach had to ask her a few times to be very specific about her goal for the session in order to get what she really wanted.

The client defined self-sabotage as knowing what is right and not doing it. Getting in your own way. Here, I applied a gestalt coaching approach from the review above where I asked some difficult questions to expand the client's horizon and analyse what actually happened. The questions were the following:

- When did this pattern of self-sabotage start?
- How was it impacting the relationship with herself?
- What was making her still hold on to this pattern?

Through this approach, the client revealed some difficult truths.

Self-sabotage has been part of the client's behaviour from a very young age. Specifically, when she was 12 years old, she started to lean towards bad behaviour. For example, if her parents asked her to return home by 9 pm, she would return home at 10 pm. The client realized that she had been doing it on purpose because she wanted to get the attention of her parents, who were always busy with a full-time job and taking care of her sister, who had special needs. She remembered this when these difficult questions were asked, and she also remembered that there had been no consequences to her bad behaviour, which had then encouraged her to break the rules and become fearless. Moreover, the parents expected her to take responsibility as an elder child and be independent. The client acknowledged that she felt like 20 at the age of 12, as she was cooking for the family, cleaning the house, and acting as an adult already.

As a coach, I challenged my client to dig a little deeper into the needs of the 12-year-old self. The question was, what did she think that her 12-year-old version needed the most? In answer to that question, the client recalled that she was desperate for attention and tended to say yes to what was required of her though she wanted to say no. Consequently, she developed the habit of soothing herself via self-sabotage behaviour such as over-eating, drinking or smoking cigarettes.

As a second part of the coaching, I introduced principles of person-centred coaching that reassures the client that they are safe and won't be judged. Person-centred coaching is based on the idea that the coachee is in control of the process. It is goal-oriented coaching. The client decides and creates a goal for themselves. The coach works with the client to help them identify their goals and discover strategies to help them achieve those goals. During our coaching call, questions like how she managed her education, work and personal life made her realize that she is capable of breaking the self-sabotage pattern. In regard to this approach, it helped the client to reaffirm that she is resourceful and has everything that she needs to break this self-sabotage pattern.

To come full circle, the client reflected on why she is still holding on to this self-sabotage pattern. This question helped her to give closure to herself as it made her sensitive towards her children's emotional needs and receptive to their emotional cues. She is a proud mother of two children. The client feels that she is a self-aware mother and has avoided the mistakes that her parents made while she was growing up.. She also shared that her children are fully fledged human beings who are thriving in their college/career, finances and relationships.

Once the client found peace with this narrative, she decided to have an open-hearted conversation with her mother, and she didn't want to wait any longer. She believed it would help her to resolve the inner conflicts with herself that she had with her mother.

To incorporate accountability in this session, the client chose her husband as an accountability partner who would make sure that she was having an open-hearted conversation with her mother. He would remind and encourage her to have this conversation for the sake of her peace of mind and resolve inner conflicts with her mother. If she didn't, she would lose the chance to resolve this inner conflict and this inner battle would continue to show in her behaviour as self-sabotage.

In the end, the client was happy to see that she was able to accomplish the goal of the session, which was to explore the cause of her self-sabotage behaviour. This coaching call raised her self-awareness and made her accountable to decide what she wants to do with her self-sabotage behaviour. As a result, she was able to make small shifts gradually that helped her to break these subconscious patterns.

The key takeaway for the client from her childhood was that she did not fully acknowledge her feelings about her self-sabotaging behaviour. She was doing it as an act of rebellion. Once she embraced her feelings, it was not a problem. Then, nobody stopped her from doing what she needed and wanted to do.

Practical recommendations

Your coaching success is greatly impacted by the exercises you use. The following coaching tools can be readily included in your coaching practice to help clients with self-awareness and hold them accountable for their actions.

Every Picture Tells a Story

This method is for bringing subconscious thoughts and beliefs to the conscious surface. It helps to reflect on the stories and meaning you assign to visual images. One way to do this is to interpret tarot card images with strong visuals (you can also use any series of stock photos, oracle card decks or illustrations – images with a subjective emotional content or ambiguous interpretation work best) (Swart, 2022).

INSTRUCTIONS

1 Select a picture at random. Alternatively, have the client pick the one that causes the strongest emotions and most vivid memories, or resonates with them the most. The second option involves subjectivity in the selection process but is more meaningful to the client, which can give the coach additional information and enrich the exploration.
2 Ask the client to create a narrative/story around the image in five minutes.
3 Have them describe the following factors in their story: the scene's current circumstance, the character(s) in it, their thoughts and feelings, the events that preceded it and the scene's eventual resolution.

Every person sees an image differently depending on their personality, world view and life experiences. In the end, help your client to examine together or in self-reflection what their interpretation reveals by going as deep as they can to reach underlying feelings, beliefs, fears and expectations.

The ORACLE model

This practice is helpful for a client if they are having trouble moving towards a goal or maintaining momentum. It is intended to inspire the development of fresh concepts that will give their goals additional momentum. ORACLE stands for Outcome, Real issue, Alternatives, Creative ideas, Likelihood of success and Execute your new plan (Jones and Gorell, 2009).

INSTRUCTION

Identify your ORACLE for this exercise and be as detailed as you can by asking the following questions:

QUESTIONS FOR REFLECTION

Start the exercise by identifying the desired outcome and formulate the true problem that underlies the gap between your current reality and outcome.

- What specific issue do you actually wish to address?
- What motivation do you have for wanting to achieve this goal?
- Describe the resolutions that you have already tried.
- Can you come up with any less obvious or other untried solutions to accomplish this?
- Can you come up with any innovative ideas by modifying current strategies or techniques or by utilizing any from different areas of study or theory?

Then, ask your client to consider the balance of risks, repercussions, and rewards and advantages for each of their ideas. Help the client to create an action plan based on the concept they think is best and stipulate any assistance or resources required to carry it out.

Life events

If your client sometimes struggles to comprehend why they feel or act the way they do, it is possible that these issues have their roots in a traumatic experience from their past. This activity is meant to assist your client in methodically reviewing significant experiences so that they may better understand recurring patterns that still have an impact on them today (Jones and Gorell, 2009).

INSTRUCTIONS

1 Ask the client to pick the most memorable, significant or pivotal incidents they can recall from their childhood, both good and bad.

2   Analyse if they can spot any trends or recurring themes in the events, the people involved, their actions and decisions at the time, and their beliefs, thoughts, feelings and behaviour at present.

QUESTIONS FOR REFLECTION

- What have you learnt from your reflection – if anything?
- How did your behaviour and choices at the time serve you?
- What personal traits or abilities did you employ?

Guide your client to evaluate whether they can use any of these suggestions right now to help them appreciate their circumstances, responses and choices at the time.

Final thoughts

In any coaching strategy, raising the client's degree of self-awareness and holding them accountable for their own behaviours are two of the most crucial aspects. One can build the ability to withstand and recover from external pressures as well as recognize where change is required by reflecting more on oneself and being more self-aware using the tools and approaches discussed. The role of the coach is to maintain an authentic relationship, focus on the client as a whole person, and raise the client's level of awareness. With the belief that each client is their own best expert, and with an attitude of acceptance, empathy and commitment, the coach begins the coaching process with the best possible effect.

References

Allan, J and Whybrow, A (2018) Gestalt coaching, in *Handbook of Coaching Psychology: A guide for practitioners*, 2nd edn, eds S Palmer and A Whybrow, pp 180–94, Routledge, New York

Duval, S and Wickland, R A (1972) *A Theory of Objective Self Awareness*, Academic Press, New York

Eurich, T (2018) What self-awareness really is (and how to cultivate it), *Harvard Business Review*, 4 January, hbr.org/2018/01/what-self-awareness-really-is-and-how-to-cultivate-it (archived at https://perma.cc/2RBJ-PYCW)

Gazelle, G, Liebschutz, J M and Riess, H (2014) Physician burnout: Coaching a way out, *Journal of General Internal Medicine*, 30, 508–13, doi.org/10.1007/s11606-014-3144-y (archived at https://perma.cc/9YGN-JP3U)

Jones, G and Gorell, R (2009) *50 Top Tools for Coaching: A complete toolkit for developing and empowering people*, Kogan Page, Philadelphia, PA

Joseph, S and Bryant-Jefferies, R (2018) Person-centered coaching psychology, in *Handbook of Coaching Psychology: A guide for practitioners*, 2nd edn, eds S Palmer and A Whybrow, pp 131–43, Routledge, New York

Liddy, C, Johnston, S, Irving, H, Nash, K and Ward, N (2015) Improving awareness, accountability, and access through health coaching: Qualitative study of patients' perspectives, *Canadian Family Physician*, 61 (3), e158–64

Stoltzfus, T (2005) *Leadership Coaching: The disciplines, skills and heart of a Christian coach*, Tony Stoltzfus, Virginia Beach, VA

Swart, J (2022) 'Every Picture Tells a Story' as a coaching tool to explore personality and motivations, *ResearchGate*, doi.org//10.13140/RG.2.2.31890.12480 (archived at https://perma.cc/84QT-FNWP)

4

Building habits

DANIEL NOH

ABSTRACT

The purpose of this chapter is to give readers an understanding of what a habit is and how it is different from goal-directed behaviours. A step-by-step guide is provided for coaches and their clients to create new habits, including tools to help bring awareness for clients so that proper plans and strategies are implemented in support.

Introduction

Knowing what habits are and how they are formed is an important part of any coaching practice; life coaching, business coaching, even coaching a sports team. The value of knowing how to add new habits and remove unwanted ones is critical to change. With this skill we are able to shape our lives and the lives of our clients in a more meaningful way.

This chapter helps you understand what habits are and the fundamental ways they function. By understanding the three parts of a habit as well as the neurology behind them, you learn how to guide your client through behavioural changes. Creating awareness through the habit of journalling gives clients an effective tool to see the bigger picture in their lives and create plans that stick. At the end of the chapter there are practical steps on how a coach can help their client implement new habits in their lives.

The 3 Rs of habits

To begin, we must first ask, what is a habit? The Oxford dictionary defines a habit as a settled tendency or usual manner of behaviour that is often hard to give up. But there is more to habits than this basic description.

Habits are made up of three distinct parts, the *reminder* (also referred to as the trigger, cue or stimulus), the *response* (the behaviour), and the *reward* (implicit or explicit in the outcome) or the 3 Rs (Clear, 2015):

1 The **reminder** creates the initial spark of a habit that triggers our behaviour, which, with a fully formed habit, is not usually in our conscious mind. By identifying the reminder, we can start to see our habits more clearly and have more awareness of what they are.

2 The **response** to this reminder is typically an action and will require us to do something. It could be a nervous tic when reminded by stress or always taking the path to the right thing when you hit a fork in the road. Whatever this action step may be, in a habit, the reminder is always followed by a response.

3 The union of reminder–response leads to a **reward,** which is the last part of the cycle – it is the reason a behaviour is constantly repeated to form a habit. When the alarm goes off in the morning (reminder), our eyes open and we press the snooze button (response), we get to sleep an extra 10 minutes (reward). The reward of sleeping an extra 10 minutes is a positive result so we want to repeat the response. These typically lead to behavioural tendencies and by recognizing these patterns, we can make significant steps in our desired direction. Therefore, habits directly impact our behaviour, which ultimately determines our outcomes. However, when forming a habit through repetition, the goal or outcome is the driver of our decision-making process that leads to a goal-directed behaviour. With an existing habit, the reward is secondary as the behaviour is routine.

Habits are hard to give up because of the strong, automatic reminder–response pairing. Next, we will see how this pattern works on a neurological level.

The neurobiology of habits

The three-part cycle of a habit is reinforced by neurobiological processes in the brain. Research identified two distinct processes – one when a person is developing a new habit (including changing or trying to eliminate an existing one), and the other sustaining a habit that is fully formed (Mendelsohn, 2019).

Developing a new habit

Initially, when repeating a behaviour (response) following the cue (reminder), the reward is the driving force. An outcome that is (consciously) valuable motivates goal-directed behaviour that is expected to lead to that outcome (Figure 4.1).

FIGURE 4.1 Habitual behaviour versus goal-directed behaviour in habit processes

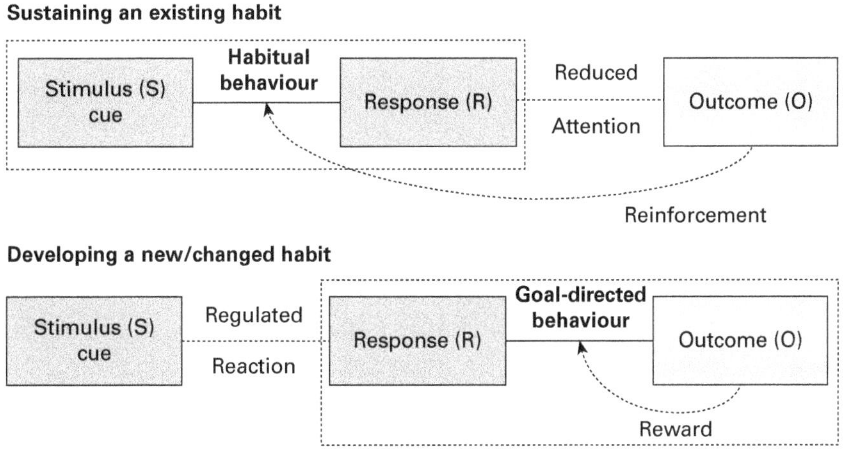

Sustaining an existing habit

Stimulus (S) cue — **Habitual behaviour** → Response (R) — Reduced Attention — Outcome (O) — Reinforcement

Developing a new/changed habit

Stimulus (S) cue — Regulated / Reaction — Response (R) — **Goal-directed behaviour** → Outcome (O) — Reward

SOURCE Adapted from Binz (2021)

The prefrontal cortex (PFC) plays a significant role in this process. As the centre for higher-level cognitive functions, such as decision making, attention and impulse inhibition, the PFC, together with the natural chemical dopamine, enables goal-directed behaviour. Dopamine activates the brain's reward system, which creates a pleasant feeling in anticipation of a reward and motivates us to obtain it.

However, the PFC is energy-intensive and human brains have developed to take shortcuts. A fully formed habit 'bypasses' the PFC to a significant degree because the cue-response is automatic. Conscious thought processes, including reward expectations, play a diminished role, which makes sustaining a habit easier and energy efficient. However, the same process also creates a resistance to building a new habit (or changing one) while favouring slipping back into an unwanted old one.

Enacting a fully formed habit

Repetition is critical when forming a new habit. The parts of the brain that recognize the cue (reminder) and react in a specific way (response) activate together, which forms new connections. Carla Shatz (1992: 64) summarized this principle of Hebbian learning as neurons that 'fire together, wire together', which means, in this case, that higher thinking functions of the PFC are bypassed, and the cue-following action becomes automated.

A major area of the brain that helps sustain existing habits is the basal ganglia. This area of the brain is primarily responsible for motor control as well as motor learning and behaviour. Within the basal ganglia is the dorsolateral striatum (DLS) (Seger and Spiering, 2011). The DLS is an input structure within the basal ganglia that promotes habit sustainability. DLS activation – strengthened in the habit-building process of repetition – supports acquiring or using action–outcome associations, forcing reliance on the habit strategy with a diminished reliance on reward expectations (Figure 4.1).

Goal-directed behaviour versus habitual behaviour

Therefore, habits are behaviours that have become so imbedded that we do them almost automatically, independent of the outcome (Gillan et al, 2015; Lipton, Gonzales and Citri, 2019). Goal-directed behaviours are performed with the deliberate intent and purpose of fulfilling a desired outcome. When the desired outcome is repeatedly met, the cue-response becomes automatic and the conscious motivation for the goal-directed behaviour ceases to exist. Understanding that the desired outcome does not play a vital role in sustaining a habit is pivotal in the way we think about them. The reward or outcome becomes a secondary reinforcer (after the fact), meaning that conscious thought and intent to accomplish a task are largely bypassed when engaging in a fully formed habit.

In other words, goal-directed behaviour dissipates once the desired outcome has been fulfilled repeatedly and a high level of motivation is not required to drive the cue-response any more. This is why habits persist even when there is no conscious thought about the desired outcome. This tells us that habits are driven by repeated experiences linked to positive emotional states and are usually inflexible, whereas goal-directed behaviour is driven by deliberate intent and motivation to reach a goal, which is what is needed to change a habit (Amaya and Smith, 2018).

The benefits to habits and their automaticity are that it can free up decision-making resources within the brain, allowing us to spend energy and resources elsewhere. However, in an extreme form, habits can become compulsions or even addictions (Gillan et al, 2015; Lipton, Gonzales and Citri, 2019). According to Lipton, Gonzales and Citri (2019: 2), 'The central characteristic of compulsions and addictions is the continued pursuit of a previously rewarding stimulus, despite its clear current association with adverse consequences.' They go on to explain that 'This hallmark of addiction, action performance in spite of punishment, can be viewed as an extreme of habitual behavior.' Knowing that habits can be good (e.g. healthy lifestyle) or bad (e.g. drug use) allows us to redirect our energy accordingly to create the habits that are more meaningful to what we want to accomplish.

Finding awareness

Self-monitoring behaviour is a great way for us to learn about the habits in our lives (good or bad). This awareness is crucial for us as coaches to come up with unique strategies and plans with our clients.

CASE STUDY
The power of journalling and reflection

One of the most effective tools to help clients find awareness is reflective journalling. Journalling allows the writer to see habits more clearly through daily reflections. This is also a good way to help the client understand and explore the 3 Rs – reminder, routine and reward. Once your client can clearly see when, what and why everything is happening, then, with your support, they can make a plan to swap the old routine with another that is more in alignment with their goals, sometimes often by getting the same reward and using the same reminder!

Using the Kolb method of learning serves as a great foundation for reflective journalling with clients. Kolb's four stages of learning include concrete experiences, reflective observation, abstract conceptualization and active experimentation.

1   **First stage – concrete experiences** Bob had no idea that he had a diet problem until he started to journal about each of his meals. He wrote down the specifics of each meal as well as any snacks he would eat throughout the day.

2   **Second stage – reflective observation** After writing a brief description of his meals, I asked him to reflect on each one and to really think about his environment and how each meal made him feel. In this stage, we broke down the 3Rs by identifying what was the reminder (hunger), the routine (fast food) and the reward (getting back to work quickly).

3   **Third stage – abstract conceptualization** In this stage, we looked at how we could change Bob's routine. By asking Bob questions about his meal choices and what made him eat what he was eating. He realized that he was consuming a lot of fast food, primarily because he was not planning his meals and more or less just reacting to his hunger by getting what was easy and fast. Guiding him to look at why he was consuming fast food twice a day, he realized it was not good for him.

4   **Fourth stage - active experimentation** Through his realization, Bob came to understand that he had to plan his meals better. He was so busy at work that he would usually grab anything convenient and sit at his desk. By journalling and seeing a clearer picture of his daily food habits, we were able to create a plan for him to do meal preparation and create meals at home that he could eat at his desk. Through this exploration we both realized that being busy should not mean forgoing healthy choices while still getting back to work quickly.

Having clarity in terms of what habits we want to change allows us to begin the process of forming new habits.

The process of forming habits

The process of achieving habit change is essential to know as a coach to help clients change their long-term behaviour in alignment with their goals. Most clients seek coaching because they want to change something in their life. Whether it is a paradigm or a behaviour, learning about habits allows us to support our clients more effectively.

Four steps to creating a new habit

The steps start with 1) a decision to change; 2) the decision is converted to action; 3) the action then needs to be repeated; 4) the repeated action 'must be repeated in a fashion conducive to the development of automaticity' (Lally and Gardner, 2013: S139–40).

STEP 1 – MAKING THE DECISION

The first step to creating a habit is making the decision to change, which can be a process in itself. It takes time and thoughtful discussion with your clients to figure out what needs to be changed and how to get there. Here are four steps to guide your clients through the decision-making process (Lunenburg, 2010):

1 **Identify the problem** The question is, 'What is the problem?' We want to clearly define what the client's problem is and what their intended solution is. Journalling could help to answer this question. My client Martin identified his problem as not being present with his family at home because he was bringing his work home with him. With the problem clearly stated we were able to move through the next steps.

2 **Generate alternatives** Once the problem has been identified we want to help our client figure out some alternatives to the problem. We want them to keep the alternatives as diverse as possible in order to find a good range of solutions. Depending on the scale of the problem, we want them to create as many alternative solutions as possible. For Martin, we came up with three alternative solutions – leaving work earlier, shutting his phone off at home and scheduling undisturbed time for his family.

3 **Evaluate alternatives** The third step has our client looking at the alternatives and evaluating them using the following three questions: 1) Is the alternative feasible? 2) Is it a satisfactory alternative? 3) What impact will it have on people? (Grant, 2021). We asked these questions for each of Martin's alternatives, which allowed him to see clearly which alternative would work best for him.

4 **Choosing the alternative** Once alternatives are evaluated, we need to have the client choose which one they want to pursue. While evaluating the alternatives for Martin we figured out the one that made the most sense. The third option, schedule time with his family, was the winner. It was the most feasible as his work schedule was sporadic, and it was also satisfactory for him and his family because they all knew the expectation to have.

STEP 2 – TAKING ACTION

The second stage of habit formation is converting the decision into action. This involves creating a plan that your client will (and can) stick to. Planning for action allows you to think of any obstacles or challenges that could get in the way. Have your client list what challenges they could face when implementing their plan. It is important to remind them that it's not about *if* a challenge arises, it's about *when*. Challenges and obstacles are a part of the journey so when they arise, we want our clients to be prepared. Here are some questions to help guide your clients through the process:

- What are obstacles that you have faced in the past regarding this problem?
- How do you usually overcome challenges in your life?
- What are the three worst-case scenarios that you can think of happening? Now what are three solutions for each of those scenarios?

Being prepared for future challenges increases success rates. My client made the decision to quit smoking. He knew one of the biggest challenges he would face was when getting into his car. This was a reminder of his habit and the response to getting in his car was lighting up a cigarette and his reward was relieving his boredom. Because we were able to foresee this potential stumbling block, he planned ahead by posting a 'no smoking' sticker on his rear-view mirror. This new reminder helped him create a new habit of chewing gum on his drive home or putting on music that he enjoyed singing along with. By acknowledging the challenges, your client can start creating a plan to tackle each one with a more focused approach.

Following on from the example in the previous section, Martin started to schedule out blocks of time with his family. He would ensure that his phone was not near him during this time and he would be able to give his wife and kids his full attention. It is important to know that when you are implementing a new decision, especially when others are involved, there must be clear communication. For Martin, he explained the criteria to his wife and kids that he would block out two hours each night to ensure they had their quality time. After the scheduled time was complete, he would be able to work freely if needed without any resentment or criticism from his family. He gauged the effectiveness of his new action by asking his family for feedback.

Now, for both clients, the outcome was promising and formed a solid foundation for the motivation needed to repeat the behaviour and form a habit.

STEP 3 – REPETITION

The third stage of creating a habit is all about consistency – we want to repeat the pattern until it has been ingrained and turns into automaticity. Consistent repetition is needed to rewire the brain and break past the goal-directed behaviour to form a habit. Much like muscle memory, consistency is key – repetitive action is fundamental to creating a new habit (Lally et al, 2010).

When it comes to consistency, it is important to focus on the small things and build from there. The micro habits may seem to be doing nothing but, little by little, they are moving mountains. Staying consistent can also be tough on motivation. By creating smaller tasks, it is easier for us to stay motivated and, in turn, to stay on track.

STEP 4 – REPETITION LEADING TO AUTOMATICITY

While the first three stages are generic principles to behaviour change (Lally and Gardner, 2013), this fourth stage is exclusive to habit creation. Repetition of an action needs to break past the goal-directed behaviour in order to become a habit. This is where having a coach is very helpful. Breaking past goal-directed behaviours can be quite difficult, especially when a goal has already been met. For example, if your goal was to lose 10 pounds and you accomplish that, it will be harder to continue with your new diet (new habit) because the motivation has been taken away. If the habit has not fully formed yet, a coach can help by exploring new goals and reinforcing the benefits the client received. As a coach, we also want to help our clients monitor their progress and hold them accountable for the new habits they have decided to create. Monitoring our clients' progress and tracking it vigorously will allow us to stay ahead, watch for new patterns and help keep our clients on course to creating the habits they want.

Monitoring and tracking are done by journalling, getting feedback from others who are affected by the change, and reflecting on the process with a coach. Although the outcome does not have a direct effect on habitual behaviour, as when building a new habit with goal-directed motivation, it nevertheless reinforces the behaviour subconsciously to sustain the habit. The coach can help with the reinforcement process by reminding the client of the benefits, thereby bringing it more into the client's awareness.

Conclusion

Habits are a part of who we are and the way we operate. They can come up in the most unlikely ways or are created with deliberate intent. By recognizing our own habits in our coaching practice, we can better serve our clients. The experience we gain from our own trials and tribulations will allow us to create the right strategies for our clients. For example, I took some time away from coaching to reflect on my practice and to see if there were any habits that needed updating. This exercise allowed me to recognize habits in the way I responded to clients when I had been in similar situations as them. I found myself suggesting rather than coaching and not allowing them to come up with their own answers. This profoundly shaped the way that I guided my sessions with clients. It also helped me realize that, sometimes, I just needed a moment to collect my thoughts and form the responses that would be the most beneficial for my clients.

Now that you have a good understanding of what a habit is and what it takes to form new ones, you are armed and ready to challenge yourself and your clients. By knowing the 3 Rs of habits as well as the four stages of habit formation, you can begin to create plans with your clients that will elicit real change. Using tools like journalling to help with self-awareness and pros-and-cons list for decision making, you can help your clients rewrite their days. Knowing that habits must stay consistent past goal-directed behaviour will allow you and clients to be prepared to push past comfort zones and be prepared for any and all obstacles.

References

Amaya, K A and Smith, K S (2018) Neurobiology of habit formation, *Current Opinion in Behavioral Sciences*, 20, 145–52, doi.org/10.1016/j.cobeha.2018.01.003 (archived at https://perma.cc/8CFL-AMAQ)

Binz, K (2021) Habit as action chunking, 13 August, kevinbinz.com/2021/08/13/hierarchical-behavior/ (archived at https://perma.cc/78MH-KX52)

Clear, J (2015) *Transform Your Habits*, 2nd edn, James Clear, jamesclear.com/wp-content/uploads/2013/09/habits-v2.pdf (archived at https://perma.cc/N7DT-QX98)

Gillan, C M, Otto, A R, Phelps, E A and Daw, N D (2015) Model-based learning protects against forming habits, *Cognitive, Affective & Behavioral Neuroscience*, 15 (3), 523–36, doi.org/10.3758/s13415-015-0347-6 (archived at https://perma.cc/KT4W-ZC5L)

Grant, R M (2021) *Contemporary strategy analysis*, 11th edn, Wiley, New York

Lally, P and Gardner, B (2013) Promoting habit formation, *Health Psychology Review*, 7 (S1), S137–58, doi.org/10.1080/17437199.2011.603640 (archived at https://perma.cc/K4XV-5YA5)

Lally, P, van Jaarsveld, C H M, Potts, H W W and Wardle, J (2010) How are habits formed: Modelling habit formation in the real world, *European Journal of Social Psychology*, 40 (6), 998–1009, doi.org/10.1002/ejsp.674 (archived at https://perma.cc/4362-8GRV)

Lipton, D M, Gonzales, B J and Citri, A (2019) Dorsal striatal circuits for habits, compulsions and addictions, *Frontiers in Systems Neuroscience*, 13, 28, doi.org/10.3389/fnsys.2019.00028 (archived at https://perma.cc/6ST5-YA82)

Lunenburg, F C (2010) The decision making process, *National Forum of Educational Administration and Supervision Journal*, 27 (4), 1–11

Mendelsohn, A I (2019) Creatures of habit: The neuroscience of habit and purposeful behavior, *Biological Psychiatry*, 85 (11), e49–51, doi.org/10.1016/j.biopsych.2019.03.978 (archived at https://perma.cc/7CXQ-D98Y)

Seger, C A and Spiering, B J (2011) A critical review of habit learning and the basal ganglia, *Frontiers in Systems Neuroscience*, 5, 66, doi.org/10.3389/fnsys.2011.00066 (archived at https://perma.cc/D9ZA-J6QA)

Shatz, C J (1992) The developing brain, *Scientific American*, 267 (3), 60–7, doi.org/10.1038/scientificamerican0992-60 (archived at https://perma.cc/526M-X93R)

PART TWO

Competencies

5

Coach supervision – who needs it?

MARIE FAIRE

ABSTRACT

Supervision is increasingly recognized as best practice and several of the professional coaching organizations require supervision as part of the eligibility for accreditation. There are many coaches, including those new to coaching, who do not have supervision. In this chapter, the author explores what supervision is, the rationale for supervision, and finally offers her own insights into what to look for in a supervisor and why she loves being a supervisor.

Out beyond ideas of wrongdoing and rightdoing, there is a field. I'll meet you there.

RUMI

Definitions

There are many definitions and in essence: supervision provides a collaborative and trusting relationship that creates a safe, confidential, compassionate, supportive and challenging space to reflect, explore and learn.

DEFINITIONS OFFERED BY THE MAIN GLOBAL PROFESSIONAL BODIES

'Coaching supervision is a formal and protected time for facilitating a coach's in-depth reflection on their practice with a Coaching Supervisor. Supervision offers a confidential framework within a collaborative working relationship in which the practice, tasks, process, and challenges of the coaching work can be explored.' (Association for Coaching (AC), nd)

'A safe space for reflective dialogue with a practicing supervisor, supporting the supervisee's practice, development and well-being.' (European Mentoring and Coaching Council (EMCC), nd)

'A collaborative learning practice to continually build the capacity of the coach through reflective dialogue for the benefit of both coaches and clients.' (International Coaching Federation (ICF), nd)

Functions of supervision

There are three primary functions of supervision, although they have been given various names by different authors and professional bodies.

Development

The coach supervisor facilitates the coach's development, which may include reflecting on the coach's work, the appropriate sharing of the supervisor's own coaching experiences and offering new perspectives. This function is also referred to as formative (Proctor, 1986), educative (Hawkins and Shohet, 2012) or developmental (Hawkins and Smith, 2007; Kadushin, 1992).

Support

Support includes offering personal as well as professional, psychological and emotional support. This function is also referred to as restorative (Proctor 1986), supportive (Hawkins and Shohet, 2012; Hay, 2007; Kadushin, 1992) or resourcing (Hawkins and Smith, 2007).

Professional assurance

Professional assurance includes exploring what is best practice and helping the coach to adhere to the Global Code of Ethics for Coaches, Mentors and Supervisors. This function is also referred to as normative (Proctor, 1986), managerial (Hawkins and Shohet, 2012), administrative (Kadushin, 1992) or qualitative (Hawkins and Smith, 2007).

Reasons to have regular coaching supervision

There are many reasons that coaches value regular supervision. It:

- is a safe space to reflect and learn from what works and what doesn't
- increases knowledge and skill through learning from another's experiences, approaches, theories, models and techniques
- challenges thinking, bias, blind spots, habits and patterns
- offers feedback on the content and process of their work from more than one perspective
- develops competence
- enhances self-worth and self-belief as a coach
- increases self-awareness and confidence
- reduces feelings of isolation
- offers a sense of belonging
- differentiates practice
- maintains quality standards and ethics
- protects all the stakeholders – the coach, the client and, where relevant, their organization
- satisfies professional requirements

WHAT YOU MIGHT TAKE TO SUPERVISION

In my view you can bring anything to supervision. Some examples are:

- They have had a call from their client's boss who asks you to give them feedback about your client to include in the performance review process.
- You agreed to work with a particular client on helping to restore their falling motivation. Several sessions later, they tell you that they are feeling depressed and 'can't really see much point in anything any more'.
- You've had an initial meeting with your client who talks about coaching as supporting their hoped-for promotion. You meet with their boss (about another matter), and you are told that your client is underperforming (i.e., heading towards a disciplinary) but the boss hasn't told your client this.
- You have been working with a client for several months and you seem to be going around in circles. They are stuck, and you are too.
- You are questioning whether you are adding value as a coach and experiencing 'imposter syndrome'.

- You are concerned that personal issues you are experiencing are impinging on your coaching and you are wondering if you are fit to practise.

- As time goes by you realize that you really don't like this particular client, and it is affecting your work. But you are aware that they are very senior in the business and could easily jeopardize your work in that organization.

- Your client books another six sessions with you and says they wouldn't know what to do without you. You are concerned about your client's dependency.

- A great session that was a significant breakthrough for the client.

- The challenges of working with multiple stressed people from one organization.

- You are asked to coach a second person and discover that they are the manager of your existing client.

- You have contracted to work with someone who wants to change their career. At the third session they tell you that what they really need is help to leave their partner.

- A client asks if you will work with their spouse.

- You want to refresh your website and need to think through what you say about yourself and your practice.

- You want to apply for accreditation.

WHAT COACHES SAY ABOUT INDIVIDUAL AND GROUP SUPERVISION

'Not only does supervision help us process the more challenging aspects of our work but also provides the opportunity to receive CPD (continuous professional development) from a more experienced colleague; ruminate, discuss and clarify our thinking, as well as develop our own skills so that we continue to progress on our coaching journey.' *Ben Tucker (Executive Coach)*

'To me, supervision is not an option; it's a must. It's like the lighthouse in the sea, the anchor for the ships, and the control tower for the planes. It supports and helps us keep grounded and focused when we drift or need direction. It's part of our growth and development. It helps us not just DO coaching but BE coaching.' *Roula Salman (Relationship Coach)*

'I was initially hesitant to seek out coaching supervision due to feelings of inadequacy surrounding my new honed coaching skills. I would have robbed myself of a tremendous growing experience and in turn, my clients. Supervision has allowed me to be present, intuitive and creative in ways I couldn't otherwise imagine.' *Bernice Fabi (Life Coach)*

'Group supervision is a beautiful experience to grow in consciousness. The supervisor creates a space to be connected, challenged, supported, and stretched into new levels of awareness. It exponentially led me towards more inner work, discoveries, healing, and really getting to know myself. Understanding this creative process of coaching allows me to guide clients to experience this magic of self-growth for themselves.' *Julie Cremoux (Mindset and Transformation Coach)*

'Supervision is an amazing experience. There is not one session where I walk away without learning something new about myself, my clients and how to be a better coach. Learning from the various scenarios brought to the group by the other members is invaluable, even if I have not yet come across this in my own practice. Like learning from a book, only much, much, much, much better.' *Liz Cresci*

'For me, Coach supervision allows me to gain new insights and learning: I can explore and discuss challenges; the process provides alternative perspectives that add to my way of thinking about my practice, allowing me to identify new ways to proceed with a client.' *I Clough-Brown*

On being a supervisor – some reflections

I started this chapter with the quote by Rumi (nd). And it is to the same quote that I return at the end. Supervision is not about wrong and right (in the 15 years I have been supervising, I can count on one hand the number of times I have said 'No' to a supervisee, and they were in extreme situations).

I am a coach supervisor (not a coaching supervisor). I supervise the whole person, not just the activity. The way I hold supervision is relational, collaborative, compassionate and trusting, and therefore I am able to be both supportive and challenging. I care for my supervisees. I want them to be looking forward to supervision – indeed, I would suggest that if you don't, you are with the wrong supervisor.

A professional, qualified supervisor will embrace multiple roles: a facilitator, supporter and safety net, a confidante, sounding board and reflective partner; a teacher, mentor and advisor; and sometimes simply a coach to a coach.

Find a supervisor who you can relate to, who you feel you can trust and will be what you need them to be.

It is fair to say that I get paid for doing something that I truly love, and I am aware what a privilege it is to be able to say that. Working with new coaches and getting delight from watching them grow in confidence and skill, or equally, getting as much pleasure from working with those with many years of experience and who are supervisors themselves – I am always a 'fellow traveller' and learn every bit as much as my supervisees.

In my opinion having a supervisor is some of the very best CPD you can have. So why would you possibly be without one?

References

AC (nd) Coaching defined, Association for Coaching, www.associationforcoaching.com/page/CoachingDefined (archived at https://perma.cc/G5ST-2MW7)

EMCC (nd) Glossary, European Mentoring and Coaching Council, www.emccglobal.org/accreditation/glossary/ (archived at https://perma.cc/JW3X-H5XH)

Hawkins, P and Shohet, R (2012) *Supervision in the Helping Professions*, 4th edn, Open University Press, London

Hawkins, P and Smith, N (2007) *Coaching, Mentoring, and Organizational Consultancy: Supervision and development*, Open University Press, Maidenhead

Hay, J (2007) *Reflective Practice and Supervision for Coaches*, Open University Press, Maidenhead

ICF (nd) All things coaching, International Coaching Federation, coachingfederation.org/about (archived at https://perma.cc/CNR3-CBQW)

Kadushin, A (1992) *Supervision in Social Work*, 3rd edn, Columbia University Press, New York

Proctor, B (1986) Supervision: A cooperative exercise in accountability, in *Enabling and Ensuring: Supervision in practice*, eds M Marken and M Payne, pp 21–34, National Youth Bureau and Council for Education and Training in Youth and Community Work, Leicester

Rumi (nd) 'A great wagon', *On Being*, onbeing.org/poetry/a-great-wagon/ (archived at https://perma.cc/SB6X-2HEP)

6

Coaching presence

AMAYA TOLAND

ABSTRACT

Coaching presence is a required competency in regulatory organizations. In practice it exists as a multidimensional phenomenon critical to the coaching session. Examination of coaching presence uncovers the roles coach and client play towards the creation of this phenomenon. Coaches hold the lead role in creating and maintaining presence, which can be achieved through either practical steps or structured techniques.

Introduction

As a new coach, my understanding of coaching presence took on new meaning when I started to write about it. My first attempts to pin down coaching presence on paper stumped me. I felt like the nuns in the abbey from the musical *The Sound of Music*, explaining the impossible task of solving the problem they have with one of their novices, Maria. They sing that solving the riddle of Maria is like asking, 'How do you catch a cloud and pin it down?' or 'How do you hold a moonbeam in your hand?' Similarly, I find the same riddle in describing and defining coaching presence. How does one pin down coaching presence on paper? How do we hold it in our hands so others can read and understand the depth and breadth of its meaning?

Looking back to the time when I was a student, my definition of maintaining a coaching presence mirrored what I learnt in coaching school. I realized that was the definition that anchored me and kept me grounded during sessions at the time. Similar to what one would find in a book of etiquette on how to conduct oneself during dinner, I followed the list of expected behaviours described for coaching presence like a checklist. Am I putting all of my attention on my client? Check. Am I remaining neutral and non-judgemental? Check. Am I ensuring a safe space that reflects integrity? Check. However, with more research I have learnt that coaching presence is much more complex in practice, going beyond a checklist of expected behaviours. Understanding coaching presence is more than just what accredited organizations like the International Coaching Federation and the Association for Coaching list as part of the core coaching competencies. It is a phenomenon experienced individually by the coach and shared with the client. It comes alive through mindfulness and through removal of the self. These elements come together to create a powerful space where greater insight emerges, acting as a catalyst for clients to take action.

Defining presence

For this chapter I examined the definitions supplied by accredited coaching organizations, researched the work of coaches who conducted studies on coaching presence, and digested the work of those skilled in attaining the state of being present.

I first examined the 'textbook' definitions of coaching presence provided by two of the largest global industry bodies, the International Coaching Federation (ICF) and the Association for Coaching (AC). Their descriptions define coaching presence as actions initiated by the coach involving deliberate and present interaction with the client.

While these definitions provide a solid platform towards understanding the requirements of a coaching presence, the attempt to describe it as practised and experienced in the 'real world' remains elusive. The word 'presence' itself is difficult to articulate because presence is an ephemeral phenomenon in which one person enters a state of being that emits a particular type of energy that another person experiences. Using words limits the full scope of the experience, and many times the use of similes and imagery are the best way to capture its elusive quality (Noon, 2018). Several studies use words such as 'nebulous' (p 14), 'numinous' and 'elusive' (Dängeli and Geldenhuys, 2018: 106) in an attempt to explain the transient quality of coaching presence.

Yet despite the varying interpretations, researchers agree that the phenomenon of coaching presence involves a co-creation between coach and client. This co-creation adds differing levels of reality, which happen simultaneously. Concordia University researchers call it a 'multidimensional construct' (Abravanel and Gavin, 2021: 39) that contains four dimensions: 1) the coach's internal thoughts, emotions and feelings; 2) the coach's physical sensations and actions; 3) the developing interaction between coach and client; and 4) the results of the coaching session. One executive coach writes of a 'relational dimension' (Noon, 2018: 11) in which the interconnected, symbiotic level of awareness between coach and client bolsters coaching presence, thereby reinforcing the concept of a co-created event.

Lastly, we see researchers define the resulting outcomes from an effective coaching presence as 'an open spacious container' (Abravanel and Gavin, 2021: 45) or a 'held space' (Dängeli and Geldenhuys, 2018: 107) from which a deepening level of trust between coach and client arises. According to Noon (2018), it is from here where the client's inner guidance and awareness awakens.

Presence as a coaching competency

To deepen our discussion on coaching presence, let's take a look at a side-by-side comparison of coaching presence as defined by the ICF and the AC. The ICF Core Competencies include coaching presence as one of the eight competencies a coach is expected to demonstrate, falling under the section of Co-Creating the Relationship (ICF, 2019: 4).

Maintaining presence

Is fully conscious and present with the client, employing a style that is open, flexible, grounded and confident:

- Remains focused, observant, empathetic and responsive to the client
- Demonstrates curiosity during the coaching process
- Manages one's emotions to stay present with the client
- Demonstrates confidence in working with strong client emotions during the coaching process
- Is comfortable working in a space of not knowing
- Creates or allows space for silence, pause or reflection

The AC Coaching Competency Framework lists nine competencies for coaches with an additional three pertaining to the practice of executive coaches (AC, 2021: 3).

Managing self and maintaining coaching presence

Indicators of competence:

- Pays close attention to the client, staying fully present and engaged
- Remains focused on the agreed client agenda outcomes
- Acts flexibly whilst staying aligned to own coaching approach
- Stays aligned to personal values whilst respecting the values of the client
- Works to ensure interventions get the best outcome for the client

Easy to understand, these definitions act as an anchor and guide for new and seasoned coaches. Action verbs are prominent, acting as directions, or steps from which one follows. Both definitions use the concept 'fully present', indicating the importance of mindfulness, as an 'awareness that arises through paying attention, on purpose, in the present moment, non-judgmentally' (Kabat-Zinn, 1994: 4). Both descriptions also mention interactions with the client, emphasizing that coaching presence involves both the coach and the client. These major points form a solid foundation from which to practise and build a coaching presence.

The four dimensions of simultaneous realities between coach and client

We now move into the more complex aspect of coaching presence, namely the nature of being a 'multidimensional construct' (Abravanel and Gavin, 2021: 39). As mentioned before, coaching presence requires the interaction of coach and client. This bilateral exchange results in the creation of a session flowing in and out of differing levels of reality simultaneously. The seasoned coaches interviewed by the Concordia University researchers described their experience and behaviour during coaching sessions (Abravanel and Gavin, 2021). From these interviews, researchers determined that coaching presence develops within four dimensions.

In the first dimension the coach becomes fully present. This state enables them to enter the second dimension, where the coach's actions flow freely and purposefully. The coach remains physically aware of themselves and their behaviour becoming like an open receptacle, untethered by judgements or triggers. Deeply meaningful interactions can begin to take place between coach and client constituting the third dimension. The awareness and insight arising from these interactions transforms the

FIGURE 6.1 Wilbert's quadrant model of coaching presence

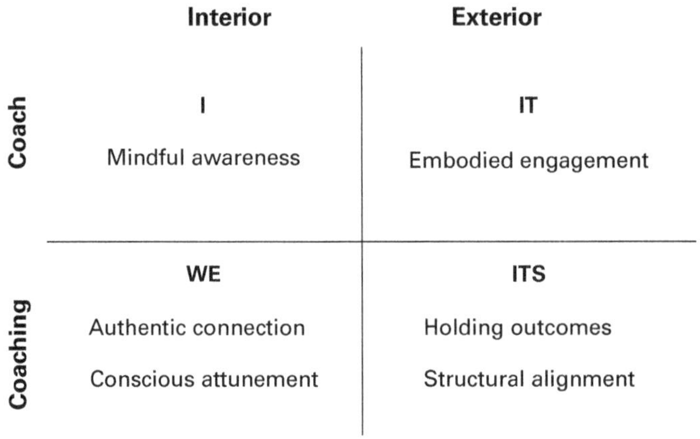

	Interior	Exterior
Coach	**I** Mindful awareness	**IT** Embodied engagement
Coaching	**WE** Authentic connection Conscious attunement	**ITS** Holding outcomes Structural alignment

SOURCE Abravanel and Gavin (2021: 49)

TABLE 6.1   Dimensional elements of coaching presence

Dimension of Presence	Action	Manifestation
First dimension	Mindful awareness	Coach becomes present
Second dimension	Embodied engagement	Coach and client become present to each other
Third dimension	Authentic connection	Coach and client develop deeply meaningful interaction
Fourth dimension	Holding space	Coach holds space from which client insight emerges

SOURCE Abravanel and Gavin (2021: 49)

process, entering the fourth dimension, where the coach holds a space allowing for burgeoning results (Abravanel and Gavin, 2021). Figure 6.1 and Table 6.1 present a visual view of the separation of the dimensions into their respective interior (as self-management)/exterior (as interaction) and coach (as a person with influence)/coaching (as a process) elements.

The first dimension

BEING PRESENT BEGINS WITH THE COACH

The multilayered experience of simultaneous realities cannot arise unless the coach initiates it by becoming fully present, and while this can occur naturally, it must occur intentionally (Siminovitch and Van Eron, 2008). Referring back to the definitions from the regulatory organizations, we mentioned the use of action verbs. These not only direct a coach towards a particular behaviour but indicate that the coaches are the initiators of that behaviour. For example, we see ICF's direction in 'Is fully conscious and present... Remains focused, observant' (ICF, 2019). The AC instructs with 'Pays close attention to the client, staying fully present... Remains focused' (AC, 2021). Moving into practice, the feedback from coaches in the Concordia University study include the importance of consciously showing up in a 'coach role' (Abravanel and Gavin, 2021: 42), emphasizing the need to present themselves to their clients 'with their whole self' (p 43). Establishing that being present begins first with the coach themselves, we can continue towards further understanding how it is defined.

MINDFUL AWARENESS

The coach enters the first dimension when they become fully present, which requires an internal observation of their thoughts and feelings. Further identifying what being present means as a coach holds similar challenges to identifying coaching presence itself, because both exist as transient experiences. Some researchers point to the understanding of presence originating from Buddhist and Taoist traditions which depict being present as a state of being that is mindful and awake (Abravanel and Gavin, 2021). There is irony in the term mindful, as mindfulness requires an emptying of the mind, where one acts as the observer of the mind's activity, not a consumer of it. Instead of believing the thoughts as true and getting carried away by the emotions they trigger, one witnesses them without judgement or commentary. Eckhart Tolle (1999) writes in *The Power of Now*, 'observation of the mind opens up the dimension of the timeless. The energy that is withdrawn from the mind turns into presence' (p 46). The energy used to fuel or identify with the thoughts and feelings is instead redirected to a state of conscious awareness. In this state there is no past or future, only the present moment.

With the complexity behind deciphering and describing coaching presence, one could conclude that obtaining this present state is an equally complex task. However becoming present is a task that can be achieved whether one is a novice or an expert. For individuals unaware of the concept of being present, Eckhart Tolle (2022) offers the concept of comparing presence to listening. For example, one could take a child outside into nature and ask them to become very still, and ask what they hear. Tolle points out that when one is listening intently trying to capture the subtlest of sounds, one is not thinking in that moment. 'You cannot carefully listen and think at the same time.... Consciousness needs to be reclaimed from the thinking function... and flows into auditory perception' (2:06). In one's concentration on listening for something, the energy used for thinking gets redirected instead towards becoming quiet and listening, resulting in a heightened state of awareness. One experiences a choice of where one wants to place one's attention instead of passively and unknowingly following one's 'stream of thinking' (2:42).

Some coaches describe being present as plainly as 'being silent, being quiet' (Noon, 2018: 43). Others take simple actions such as making time before a session to be quiet, helping to clear one's mind. Before a session, one coach reported taking deep breaths, making note of how their body is positioned, looking for a posture that is 'open and welcoming and... alert' (Subirana, 2016). Still others equate being present with meditation, using various forms to guide one towards silencing inner chatter, observing one's breath and remaining alert (Subirana, 2016).

Coaches can take the following steps towards becoming present (Tolle, 1999):

- Bring your attention to the inner body and try to feel the energy or the life within your hands, arms, legs, and so forth.
- Notice in the periphery of your awareness other people, your surroundings, etc.
- Notice any mental activity, or emotional reactions that exist or arise.
- Try to notice these things without absorbing them.
- Bring your attention back to the inner body and feel the 'whole body from within, as a single field of energy. It is almost as if you were listening or reading with your whole body' (p 97).

- 'Do not give all your attention away to the mind and the external world. By all means focus on what you are doing but feel the inner body at the same time whenever possible. Stay rooted within. Then observe how this changes your state of consciousness and the quality of what you are doing' (p 98).

The second dimension

EMBODIED ENGAGEMENT

After reaching a fully present state, the coach then enters the second dimension, maintaining an internal awareness while connecting with the client at the same time. According to Noon (2018), such awareness includes having an 'open, calm, clear mind and a sensitivity to somatic and emotional feelings' (p 11). When the coach is in this awakened state, they are able to truly see and hear their client. The are able to 'act as a mirror' (Subirana, 2016: 5), enabling the client to also reach a heightened state of awareness. Coach and client become fully present to each other and a bilateral resonance takes place. One appreciative inquiry coach describes this as a vibrational space that reverberates between themselves and their client as they interact, creating a vessel that enables their client to enter a fully awakened state of consciousness that allows them to discover a truer version of themselves (Subirana, 2016). In short, presence begets presence.

Techniques similar to meditation, such as those used in transcendence are helpful in cultivating this resonating presence. Transcendence coaching encourages first grounding the physical body with breath or paying attention to the physical sensations generated by the body (Uijen and Volz, 2016). With continued breathing and an attitude filled with empathy and care, transcendence coaching then directs to 'expand from the point of our attention to include everything, including the space between and around breaths or sensations' (p 6). A description of this exercise follows:

TRANSCENDENTAL EXERCISE

1 **Present moment** First, come to the present moment. Our body is anchored in the present moment, so in some way our attention needs to go to something related to the body. This could be sensing the breath, sensing sensations of the body or attending to any other sense.

2 **Open focus** Second, we need to let our awareness expand from the point of our attention to include everything, including the space between and around breaths or sensations, or things in our attention. At this point a person who has learnt to recognize presence would likely begin to sense it again unless a triggered subconscious pattern blocks them.

3 **Compassion** Because most people have subconscious patterns that might be triggered from time to time, the third useful hint is to bring compassion to all

experiences that arise in the first two steps. In compassion and kindness, consciously experienced experiences feel safer and are less likely to be resisted. When they are not resisted, they cannot block the experience of transcendent presence. When compassion is present, patterns have the opportunity to heal naturally. In compassion we can experience wellbeing independent of circumstance (Uijen and Volz, 2016: 6).

Another similar technique, open awareness, is also effective. Open awareness begins with observing one's current state of mind, concentrating through one's sensory perceptions. From there one witnesses the mind's activity and arising emotions. Attention is then drawn to the meaning of and the space in which the session is held. The attention expands to include the energy reverberating between the individuals and the objects in the room. Compassion plays a key role in this exercise, as an 'intentional attitude of unconditional acceptance and beneficence' is needed (Dängeli and Geldenhuys, 2018: 109). As the awareness deepens, the concept of objects and people existing as solid and distinct entities shifts to the background and the experience of separateness begins to dissolve. In this space, the client is able to witness concepts related to their issues and eventually is able to disengage from identifying with limiting beliefs. This exercise does not aim to create a particular result, but rather works to condition the mind so that what is unconscious or unrecognized has the chance to emerge and be seen (Dängeli and Geldenhuys, 2018).

AN EXAMPLE OF AN OPEN AWARENESS METHOD TO HOLD
THE SPACE IN COACHING AND THERAPY

1   Start by focusing on the space between you and the other(s).

2   Access peripheral vision (180 degrees left and right).

3   Expand your field of awareness all around you and the other(s).

4   Sense the entire volume of space that your whole awareness occupies.

5   Notice how everything that you experience, including the other(s), is within the extended space of your awareness.

6   Have the intention to embrace and gently hold the other(s) within the space of your expanded awareness.

7   Bring into the space your intention to be of unconditional support and service to the other(s) who are being held in your open awareness.

8   End by focusing your breath for at least 30 seconds (Dängeli and Geldenhuys, 2018: 115).

The third dimension – authentic connection

REMOVAL OF SELF TO BE IN SERVICE TO THE CLIENT

The grounding effect from being fully present allows a coach to let go of their ego, positioning them to be 'in the service of the client' (Noon, 2018: 11). This allows the session to transition to the third dimension where an exchange of deeply meaningful interactions takes place. Coaches interviewed reinforced the concept of a mindfully present interaction between themselves and their clients, while at the same time keeping the client as the centre of their attention (Abravanel and Gavin, 2021: 45). To achieve this focus, however, the coach must let go of any attachments to a particular outcome. Not to do so would pull them away from the coaching process and entice them to give advice, which tends to hamper the possibility of 'welcome[ing] what emerges from the conversation' (p 47). Letting go of attachments requires a coach to set aside their ego, an act often found in therapeutic settings, where identification with ego diminishes and a feeling of mutual presence is cultivated (Siegel, 2013). Detachment of a coach's personal identification to the session generates an atmosphere of non-judgement, of equal footing and of vulnerability, enabling an even deeper conscious exchange between coach and client.

The fourth dimension

A CONTAINED SPACE THAT HOUSES TRUST

From here we find that an established coaching presence also creates the fourth dimension. This realm is a contained space that houses trust between coach and client, giving the client liberty to delve into undiscovered areas and reveal limiting beliefs without fear of judgement or pity. This has also been referred to as 'holding the space' where the client not only feels safe to freely examine and entertain new ways of thinking but encouraged to do so (Dängeli and Geldenhuys, 2018: 106). Focus groups of coaches and clients shared that coaching presence includes 'enabling safety and trust; feeling connected with the other person' (Noon, 2018: 12).

It is no wonder then that after engendering this trust, an inner guidance arises organically (Abravanel and Gavin, 2021), leading to insight and personal transformation (Noon, 2018). In this setting, the client feels safe enough to allow thought-provoking questions from a coach to be received with less and less resistance. The client knows that responses will be heard without judgement, allowing room for honest introspection. From here intuition or 'the sensing of a solution' (Bennett, 2022: 138) comes alive, leading towards the discovery of that solution.

Managing obstacles to creating and maintaining presence

Threaded throughout the four dimensions discussed previously is the existence of obstacles, which one could argue as another realm that weaves in and out of coaching presence. Becoming present is achievable with practice, but maintaining the present state is more of a challenge, especially with the arrival of obstacles. These obstacles can take the form of external interruptions or distractions such as a flickering light or an unexpected sound. Other obstacles take on more subtle forms such as the mind wandering, a lack of connection between coach and client, or superficial listening where the coach's focus remains on themselves instead of the client (Abravanel and Gavin, 2021).

Coaches in the Concordia University study acknowledge that distractions will inevitably occur, and the solution is for the coach to find a way to recalibrate and anchor themselves again, bringing them back to the present moment (Abravanel and Gavin, 2021). This can be done with minor physical adjustments such as sitting up straight, bringing awareness to the breath or making eye contact with the client (Noon, 2018). Transcendence coaches recommend a coach go through another round of breathing and expansion exercises, delving further into their own present state (Uijen and Volz, 2016). Regardless of the tools used, it is the commitment towards realignment to presence that remains important.

Yet interruptions such as a loud noise or a flickering lamp are easier to manage than the distraction of an emotional trigger. Clients will eventually trigger unconscious thoughts and feelings in a coach. These in turn may cause a coach to shut down emotionally, to stop listening to the client and instead become attached to their own internal dialogue. This creates the perfect setting to unintentionally allow the ego to take over, and perhaps default to a familiar role of fixing or giving advice, for example. A coach who does not examine their own shortcomings, therefore, will be limited in their ability to help a client. Coaches who take time for personal reflection, self-examination into their psychological makeup, and display a willingness to understand and accept all aspects of themselves – the good and the bad – become better guides to their clients as they create and sustain a deeper presence (Bennett, 2022). For instance, how can a coach assist with examining a limiting belief, if they do not know how to do it themselves?

Conclusion

As human beings, coaches bring their own history, psychology, emotions and shortcomings to each session. The better a coach knows themselves, the better they are able to help others. Coaches are as unique as their clients, and it follows then that the coaching presence they obtain and maintain is also unique. Acknowledging the critical element of coaching presence in a coaching session becomes equally critical for coaches – new and seasoned – to examine their own definition of coaching presence, how they obtain it, what gets in the way of obtaining it, and how it can be nurtured and developed.

References

Abravanel, M and Gavin, J (2021) An integral quadrants perspective of coaching presence: A qualitative study of professional coaches, *International Journal of Evidence Based Coaching and Mentoring*, 19 (2), 38–53, doi.org/10.24384/mmhg-f721 (archived at https://perma.cc/TFQ3-LKVZ)

AC (2021) AC Coaching Competency Framework, Association for Coaching, www.associationforcoaching.com/resource/resmgr/Accreditation/Accred_General/Coaching_Competency_Framewor.pdf (archived at https://perma.cc/WXB7-NDBB)

Bennett, V (2022) Towards understanding that coaches' knowledge of themselves is the enabler of client insight, *International Journal of Evidence Based Coaching and Mentoring*, S16, 137–48, doi.org/10.24384/jdz5-jb45 (archived at https://perma.cc/NK7E-2CRP)

Dängeli, J and Geldenhuys, H (2018) Open awareness: Holding the liminal space in transpersonal coaching and therapy, *Integral Transpersonal Journal*, 10 (1), 105–17, jevondangeli.com/wp-content/uploads/2020/11/OA_Holding_Space_Dangeli_Geldenhuys_ITJ.pdf (archived at https://perma.cc/9TJY-SW72)

ICF (2019) ICF Core competencies, International Coaching Federation, coachfederation.org/credentials-and-standards/core-competencies (archived at https://perma.cc/DVJ9-CC8Z)

Kabat-Zinn, J (1994) *Wherever You Go There You Are: Mindfulness meditation for everyday life*, Hyperion, New York

Noon, R (2018) Presence in executive coaching conversations – The C² Model, *International Journal of Evidence Based Coaching and Mentoring*, 16, S12, 4–20, doi.org/10.24384/000533 (archived at https://perma.cc/VU78-PEBA)

Siegel, I R (2013) Therapist as a container for spiritual resonance and client transformation in transpersonal psychotherapy: An exploratory heuristic study, *The Journal of Transpersonal Psychology*, 45 (1), 49–74

Siminovitch, D and Van Eron, A (2008) The power of presence and intentional use of self: Coaching for awareness, choice and change, *International Journal of Coaching in Organizations*, 3, 90–111

Subirana, M (2016) Coaching to flourish, *AI Practitioner*, 18 (4), 24–30, doi.org/10.12781/978-1-907549-29-8-5 (archived at https://perma.cc/7XNB-TRRJ)

Tolle, E (1999) *The Power of Now*, New World Library, Novato, CA

Tolle, E (2022) How to enter a different state of consciousness, (online video) 21 July, youtu.be/uNyhYTVZu0w (archived at https://perma.cc/LJD4-GFNA)

Uijen, H and Volz, M (2016) Induction to transcendence and genuine wellbeing, *AI Practitioner*, 18 (4), 42–47, doi.org/10.12781/978-1-907549-29-8-8 (archived at https://perma.cc/4WJK-J5PH)

7

The importance of self-management for a coach

MARISABEL BECKER

ABSTRACT

Self-management is the ability to set aside personal opinions, judgements, emotions and actions. Self-management is a vital skill life coaches must develop not only for their personal growth, but also for the success of their clients. Self-management allows coaches to be objective, present, curious and supportive of the client's desired outcomes. Here are a few approaches and steps to help build self-management skills.

Introduction

Self-management is an important part of helping others. It is the skill that allows us to self-regulate and self-control our own thoughts, emotions and actions while coaching clients, and outside of coaching when we are preparing and managing our attitude and energy. As life coaches we develop self-management skills to set aside personal opinions and judgements, to become aware of topics that would trigger our own emotions, and to avoid the tendency to rescue the client by providing unsolicited advice or solutions. As Travis Kemp (2008: 29) so eloquently described it, 'self-management can be most succinctly defined as a developmental process in which coaches become increasingly aware of their unique cognitive, behavioural, perceptual and emotional systems and, through this process, develop an increasing capability to effectively manage their use in service to the client's development process within the coaching relationship'. Increasing awareness of our own natural dispositions and emotional reactions should be part of our growth process as a coach. Having the mindset of continuous self-awareness and self-management benefits us but ultimately benefits our clients even more. Since our goal is to help clients have a deeper understanding and self-awareness of themselves, we have the responsibility to 'walk the walk' and have the same goal for ourselves. Therefore, self-management is a vital skill in the life coaching profession.

Managing personal opinions and judgements

Effective coaches have a strong awareness of their own personal opinions, biases and judgements while in a coaching interaction with a client. Social psychology's theory of attribution explains our natural tendency as human beings to explain other people's behaviour by attributing it to their internal dispositions or to their external circumstances (Heider, 1958). For instance, when someone does not reply to our email or text, we might attribute it to a dispositional attribute like a lack of respect or lack of consideration and we might fail to consider that the person is unaware of the message because they are busy doing something else.

Many times, people make judgements or assumptions of another person based on their own cultural practices and beliefs. Some examples of assumptions based on cultural practices are the idea of punctuality, personal attire or styles, body gestures and eye contact, among others. If unchecked assumptions and judgements hinder us from being present, curious and objective when helping our clients it could lead us to misunderstand the client and lead them the wrong way, which, in turn, can be very frustrating and discouraging to them. Not being curious about their motives but assuming their intent is counteractive to helping them reach their desired goals. Clients could also sense judgement and feel misunderstood by the coach, which can lead to a breakdown and termination of the coaching relationship.

Being aware when we start making assumptions or judgements, and what would help us manage it, is important. During the discovery session or first session, we start getting to know the client's personal characteristics like the tone of voice, accent, physical appearance, mannerisms, physical and emotional states, likes and dislikes. At this point we need to be careful not to start associating the client with a particular group of people or set of attributes based on what we perceive they are. It is important that we make it a point to keep ourselves in check during our first encounter with the client, so we don't assign characteristics or behaviours based on stereotypes and personal beliefs. Things to pay attention to, along with some helpful questions to keep us in check during interactions with the clients, are:

- **Judgement:** Am I having any bias, assumption or judgement about this client?
- **Respect:** Am I respecting my client's individual characteristics and beliefs?
- **Trust:** Do I believe my client is the expert on their own life and has the answers to their questions within them?

- **Autonomy:** Am I acting and thinking in a way that benefits my client's individuality and ability to make independent decisions?
- **Space:** In what way does my use of interpersonal space potentially hinder my client's feelings of safety, growth and self-awareness?
- **Curiosity:** Am I staying curious and asking questions or am I assuming things about my clients?

We could stop ourselves from making assumptions and judgements by leaving reminder notes or quotes near our desk or monitor for easy access before and during a session. New concepts are not so heavily ingrained in our memory. Reverting to old habits or patterns of thinking can easily show up in a session. By writing down a note and keeping it visible during a session, we can create a conscious reminder that this new concept is important and in alignment with the type of coach we want to be.

By self-managing our attribution tendencies, we can actively and objectively listen to our clients with curiosity, which helps us ask revealing questions to help them discover their unique truths. Kemp (2011: 169) perfectly describes the benefits of self-managing in a coaching relationship in his research. He says: 'In short, the coach is able to listen, hear and respond to the client and his unique goals and aspirations in a way that reduces the subjective influence of the coach's life experiences and personal values, opinions and judgements on these responses'.

Managing emotional triggers

Experienced coaches also have a strong awareness of their own emotional triggers. Emotional triggers are events that cause emotions to spark automatically, and they are connected to our thoughts, experiences and memories. They can be associated with a variety of things, like a place, a particular situation, an uncomfortable topic, smells, and more. They are also automatic responses to the way others express emotions, like anger or sadness. For example, an emotion might be automatically triggered by watching a sad situation on television and we unconsciously start crying because of it. It is important to self-evaluate and learn how to manage our emotional triggers as coaches in the event that we get triggered in a coaching session by what the client is saying. This awareness will help us recognize when we are no longer being present in a session, projecting false judgement onto our client, or misunderstanding the situation.

Once we identify which thoughts trigger our emotional reactions, we can be prepared to follow a corrective action. For instance, if a client brings up a topic, situation or anything that would cause our emotions to rise and become self-focused, we could practise the following:

- Take a minute, breathe deeply, and check in with your emotions to see what you are feeling.

- Recognize the triggered feeling and what caused it to arise.

- Jot it down, and put it aside so you can reflect on it later.

- Have a statement or affirmation ready to help you focus your attention back on the client.

- Depending on the level of the emotion, you could end the session and reschedule.

- After a coaching session, work on writing a list of possible triggering scenarios and have a plan of action to help you regain focus. Here is a typical plan of action that has proven effective.

  o Define and recognize the trigger.

  o Recognize the emotions associated with the trigger.

  o Synchronize body and mind with a breathing technique.

  o Acknowledge the passing thought.

  o Mentally verbalize a statement to bring you back to the present moment. 'This is not about me right now. I am here to listen and support my client.'

- Discuss the situation with another coach or supervisor to help you understand and manage the situation and keep you accountable.

Failing to become aware of our emotional triggers could impact the client in a bad way. As an example of this, a fellow coach and I were having a practice coaching session and it was my turn to coach her. It happened to be that her topic was about dealing with her children and the emotions that she had about a difficult situation. I got emotionally triggered by her situation because it reminded me of a similar situation that I had. Unknowingly, I had started leading her with questions, trying to 'help' her to see where the pain point was and how to think about it. This was a great learning opportunity for me when my coaching supervisor brought to my attention that I was leading my client to the result I thought would be her solution. I then realized I had been triggered and had started to want to solve her issue myself. Seeking to understand how we react and behave in a difficult situation that might appear in coaching will help us manage the impact of these responses in the moment.

Managing trying to be the rescuer

Responsible coaches also self-manage their (often natural) tendencies to try to rescue the client from what they are feeling or not feeling. It is our role as coaches to believe in our client's capacity to find the answers to create change in their lives within themselves. We need to empower them instead of rescuing them. Based on the Karpman Drama Triangle, David Emerald (2015: 65) described a rescuer as any person or activity (such as an addiction) that serves to help a victim relieve the 'pain' of victimhood. As an activity, the rescuer helps the victim 'numb out'. Despite having helpful intentions, the rescuer, as a person, reinforces the victim's 'poor me' by adopting a 'poor you' attitude, which (often) unintentionally increases the victim's sense of powerlessness.

A form of rescuing our clients is giving them advice about what we think they should do. Even though in our heart as coaches we want to help the client get unblocked to move forward, we have to practise self-management and be respectful, patient and supportive until the client gets to that 'aha' moment on their own. There is a huge difference when the client sees the problem and works on the solution themselves, supported by the coach, than when being given the quick and easy answers that might not be the right answers for them. We can think back to when we were children, and our teachers or parents would make us come up with the correct maths solution instead of just giving it to us.

As coaches, we also want our clients to go through mental processes and do the inner work necessary to become more aware of who they are, and their limiting beliefs. That inner work will facilitate their growth, their self-confidence, their security and their determination to take on future situations.

Think of a butterfly's metamorphosis. Metamorphosis is the necessary process for them to become beautiful butterflies. The process seems long and difficult for a person looking from the outside, and one might be tempted to 'help' the butterfly break free from its cocoon, but for a butterfly those 21 days are very important for their complete development. Without this struggle, the butterfly fails to strengthen its wings and does not survive. As coaches, in the same way, we need to allow our clients to break free of their limiting beliefs in their own time and with their own effort in order for them to become their true self and live with full potential. Rescuing them by providing solutions and advice will only hinder their growth. Instead, we ask them powerful questions that help them dig inside themselves.

The following are some helpful questions:

- What is standing in the way of solving your situation?
- What do you really want to do?
- Can you tell me more?
- Can you think of a simple step in the direction of your goal that you could take today to move closer to it?
- What would happen if you didn't take this step?

We can support managing our rescuing tendencies by examining our need to rescue others and getting to the root of it. Martin (2018: 8, para 6) explains:

> Usually, our compulsion to help can be traced back to our childhoods. It tends to be the result of dysfunctional family dynamics, cultural roles, and societal expectations. Rescuing, of course, can also be a mindset that we were taught. Perhaps a family member modeled being a martyr. Or maybe you were praised for being self-sacrificing or taking care of others was a way to feel needed or get attention. These behaviors get reinforced the more we do them.

In any case, taking time to self-examine, get to know ourselves better and know what situations make us jump into rescue mode is important. Have a statement or affirmation nearby to read and redirect our thoughts when we are tempted to rescue the client. For instance I would say something like: 'My clients are whole, resourceful and complete, and they don't need rescuing'. Also, seeking the help of a fellow coach or a supervisor is optimal to get to the root of our behavioural impulses and heal our inner child, that part of our subconscious that formed mental and emotional messages when we were young that are triggered by memories or distress in adulthood.

Final thoughts

In conclusion, self-management is a practice that is a vital part of every responsible and ethical coach. Make it a part of your lifestyle by constantly noticing and being increasingly aware of your judgements, emotional triggers and rescuing tendencies. Reflect and identify where the roots of these tendencies are and work on healing them. This allows us to come up with a plan of action to help us reframe our beliefs, tendencies and reactions whenever we encounter a triggering situation. It also helps to keep in mind who our clients are and how we need to view them.

According to Jarosz (2016), life coaching operates on a few assumptions that are necessary for a successful coaching endeavour: 1) In general, clients are mentally healthy and do not suffer from mental health issues that obstruct their ability to achieve their goals. 2) Clients are not empty receptacles for the coach's knowledge and experience but are creative, resourceful, adaptive, and whole in and of themselves. 3) Clients possess the ability to change their thinking, belief systems and behaviours in pursuing growth. Working in partnership with our clients, and respecting their individuality and uniqueness as human beings, are necessary components to the success of the coaching relationship, which requires self-management as a vital skill.

References

Emerald, D (2015) *The Power OF TED (The Empowerment Dynamic)*, 3rd edn, Polaris Publishing, Edinburgh

Heider, F (1958) *The Psychology of Interpersonal Relations*, Wiley, New York

Jarosz, J (2016) What is life coaching? An integrative review of the evidence-based literature, *International Journal of Evidence Based Coaching and Mentoring*, 14 (1), 34–56

Kemp, T (2008) Coach self-management: The foundation of coaching effectiveness, in *The Philosophy and Practice of Coaching: Insights and issues for a new era*, eds D B Drake, D Brennan and K Gørtz, pp 27–50, Wiley, New York

Kemp, T (2011) Building the coaching alliance: Illuminating the phenomenon of relationship in coaching, in *Advancing Executive Coaching: Setting the course for successful leadership coaching*, eds G Hernez-Broome and L A Boyce, pp 151–76, Wiley, New York

Martin, S (2018) Rescuing, resenting, and regretting: A codependent pattern, *PsychCentral*, 8 June, psychcentral.com/blog/imperfect/2018/06/rescuing-resenting-and-regretting-a-codependent-pattern (archived at https://perma.cc/XU2P-25ZE)

8

Are you listening to listening?

The art of listening

CHRIS HAWKINS

ABSTRACT

Clients will have an expectation that you as the coach will be present and have an open mind to what they are saying. As the coach, you must do more than listen to what is being said by the client, as the greatest discoveries may happen. Hear beyond the verbal cues to take the coaching process to the next level. Active listening is an act of compassion as it addresses the basic human need to understand and be understood.

Introduction

The art of listening – or as some call it, active, reflective, attentive or empathetic listening – takes time to master. Homing in on the subtle difference between these terms becomes a part of your deeper acquisition of knowledge to take your mastery to another level. This chapter helps you to understand the difference between hearing and listening, gain knowledge of the areas of consideration far beyond that of just listening as it relates to the coaching relationship, learn actionable questions for reflection, take steps you can employ to improve your active listening skills, and review a success story through a case study.

In our youth, we were told to listen and learn, which then changed to 'tell me what you have to say'. As adults, we have things to say, and we need not force people to assume what we mean when we talk. As it relates to coaching, there is a need for the client to say what they have to say and not hold back due to fear or embarrassment, as a coach cannot help a client who holds back. Now, as coaches, we must listen and REALLY listen so that we can learn what our clients want out of life, how they discover and explore their obstacles, how they solve their struggles, and finally inherently know which questions to ask next... if any.

From aspects of coaching, patient care and even music, one central theme stands out and that is listening is something that you do deliberately rather than allow to happen passively. With practice, your reaction time reduces in how you apply the skills that you have learnt or will learn as you continue to fine-tune your skills. Let's take for example the intense training that military fighter pilots undergo. They do various exercises and drills to hone their skills and reduce their reaction time to respond to events or even threats. This ability to react and automatically take action quickly vice having to think things through saves time. Now imagine what your coaching skill set and communication will look like if you master a few of the steps that will be presented in this chapter. Rather than fiddling through your notes or lists of questions that you might ask your client, you will inherently be able to react accordingly when you realize that you stray from what we call actively listening.

'Active listening is more than just gathering information; it is about fully concentrating on what is being said to achieve shared understanding' (Grossman, 2022: 2). As such, active (or reflective) listening is all about observation that taps into the feelings as well as emotions of others as they express what they have to say (Nelsen, Erwin and Duffy, 2019). As a person listens in this manner, they will be able to clearly reflect back what they have heard or observed rather than come up with an assumed interpretation.

From explaining what coaching is to listening to what a client needs or wants

Years ago, we would take our kayaks out on the lake and paddle away from shore. Then we would place our paddles across our laps and play the 'what do you hear?' game. The usual responses were the birds chirping, wind rustling through the leaves in the trees, and cars off in the distance, or even other people on the lake enjoying themselves. As I was creating this chapter, modifying my notes, and having conversations with others about it, I began to realize that within the context of listening, it is not always what you hear; just as important is what you do not hear.

Reflecting back to the beginning of my coaching business and career in how I answered the 'are you a coach and can you help me?' questions, how I conducted the discovery sessions, as well as actually coached people when they became clients, things have changed. In the beginning, out of excitement, I was more eager to tell people what I was and what I could do as a coach, as I did not know how to truly listen. As time passed and through reflection of this chapter, I have realized that I have learnt to listen for what I do not hear with my clients. Now, when they ask what a coach is and what I can do as a coach, I ask them what they need. I will continue to take this to the next level and practise listening for what is not being said. The client will tell you that they want to improve this and that, or fix this and that, all in the name of seeking a solution. Sometimes, the best approach is to focus on what you are not hearing them say.

Many times, pain points are avoided with the simple thought 'If I fix this today, I am good', as many people do not understand the importance of exploring what is getting in the way. We know as coaches that the reality is that a simple fix may not solve their struggles long term. As coaches, we are too often focused on getting to the heart of the struggle that is the root cause and that is best accomplished by active listening with an open mind.

The art of listening goes deeper in areas that we may not consider

Listening and the study to enhance it comes from a much wider area than coaching. There was a Caltech professor by the name of Hugo Benioff whose speciality was in seismology (the study of earthquakes) (Dörries, 2021), and what stood out the most was how he phrased what listening is. In using his instruments, he was not using a passive search but rather an active search. Through his detailed exploration, he was able to understand the difference of the signal of the instruments to findings that were relative to the data capture and the noise. His role required that he collect an immense amount of data, analyse it, and be able to use the data, so that through experience he was able to see trends and know intuitively what to do. Relating this to a coaching relationship, mastering or understanding the art of listening better, we are able to decipher what it is the client is and is not saying. As we look at separating the signal from the noise, we as coaches need to be able to hear the signal the clients give when they need help, but also listen past the noise that will in many instances just be frustrations or what has not worked. With the ability to separate the signal and the noise, we listen for what is not being said.

Hearing and listening

We often hear or see written the two words – hearing and listening. For some, they are interchangeable but for coaches, they are very different in meaning. According to author and psychologist Richard Nelson-Jones (2005: 81), 'Hearing involves the capacity to be aware of and to receive sound. Listening involves not only receiving sounds but, as much as possible, accurately understanding their meaning'. It is important to stress that our focus on serving as a coach and working with our clients is to seek to understand. With intent in our listening and a more active approach, we will align with what the client is saying as we are focused on understanding vice trying to be understood. An inexperienced coach tends to want to be in a fixer mode as that is their comfort zone. As they become more seasoned, they shift from a fixer to a fellow traveller of sorts to walk alongside the client. As they walk alongside the client, they ask more clarifying questions to understand what the client is saying. With this possibly being a new focus for you as a coach, here is an exercise to help you discover where you might be with your listening skills.

ACTION REFLECTION MOMENT

Take a moment and write down on a scale of 1 to 10 how 'actively' you currently listen when your clients are talking. Before you write the number, take into consideration how focused you are on your clients and not thinking about anything else, even the next question.

Now, write down three reasons why you may have scored yourself the way that you did. There is no right or wrong answer, or number that is too high or too low. As you read this chapter, my hope is that you will be doing some critical reflection of where you are and why, along with where you want to be. We all grow at various speeds and for various reasons.

Steps you can take to improve your active listening

In her book, *Active Listening Techniques* (2020), Nixaly Leonardo suggests that we make effective use of silence. This means that after we ask the client a question, we must step back and not say anything for a short amount of time. This was one of the hardest things that I had to learn to be comfortable with. Working at a coaching school with my students, I would mention the 'wait ten seconds' trick. It is difficult for new coaches to understand that giving silence is affording the client time to reflect on the question that was asked. In many instances they are hearing a question for the first time. For example, what would your life look like if... ? Some people have never heard that question or even considered it, so they need time to think things through. A new coach might get uncomfortable or doubt themselves so they will start to just throw questions at the client, as they feel their coaching abilities are not working. As you stack or compound more questions, it can disrupt the client's reflection and responding.

Furthermore, a good coach has the goal that they will learn something new. I look at my clients as subject matter experts about whatever they are coming to me with in each session. I have the privilege of learning from them and literally being a student of their topic. Having a neutral mindset allows me to simply be there to ask questions through natural curiosity and the drive to learn.

Financial advisor Christopher Hayden (2022) suggests that we open our minds and focus on understanding what the client is saying and needing from us to get where they want to be, as well as what is holding them back. As a coach, we ask questions to understand what it is that the client desires, sees and wants to achieve, along with where they are in the process. Remaining neutral and not just focused on just learning something BUT also understanding the client's point of view paints another picture that we may have not even considered. Here are a few steps that will assist you in growing your skill set as a listener:

1 Write down any shortfalls that you may have with active listening.

2 Look for additional sources of improving active listening.

3 PRACTISE, PRACTISE, PRACTISE your active listening.

4 On a regular basis, complete a self-evaluation on where you feel you are with active listening.

5 Ask a friend or family member to tell you something and you repeat back what they said. Have them provide feedback to you.

CASE STUDY
Success story

My reflection on my lifelong journey to work towards mastery is simply that I find ways to learn more of what I am *not* doing, which impacts my ability to actively listen. At the same time, I shut out all of the other influences so that I can be more aware of what I am not hearing. I feel that is what our clients want most from us. It has been said time and time again that clients have all the answers within them, and it is our role as a coach to bring the insights out. If we focus only on what we hear, we are more likely to miss the biggest 'aha' moment opportunities for the client, as we do not listen for what we are not hearing. In many cases, that simply might just be not hearing hope in the voice of the client.

As a case in point, I want to share an experience that I had with one of my coaches. She was asking me various questions to help explore a struggle that I was having in marketing my coaching practice and things that I might want to do. After a period of time, she mentioned a theme that she heard in my wording. When asked what I was doing or could do, I would say that 'I just', which implied that I felt that I only needed five minutes or so for each of the items that I wanted to do. I felt under pressure as I tried to add more of those items to my list, which never seemed to end. Rather than take the route to see what I could do to accomplish these ever-growing tasks, the coach went in another direction. In the end, we discovered that my struggle was not trying to do all of these things. The time I needed to do everything was actually being eaten up as I was overcommitting myself with volunteering, trying to read the numerous emails for the organizations that I joined, and so forth. If I could not read the emails, I created folders to store them, which consumed even more time. I was actually trying to do too many things, which added stress and a continual shuffling of my agenda. Long story short, I had an 'aha' moment – I actually had time to do things and needed to give myself permission to no longer do those volunteer opportunities and unsubscribe from email lists for things that I would never read. A coach who did not pick up on that might be more focused on solutions to fixing my projects with me than realizing that I had actually overcommitted myself.

My coach and I discussed the discovery that I had, and it was eye opening. Now as I reflect on this, two thoughts come to mind in how I can improve my coaching abilities:

- I will listen for what I am not hearing. This includes pain points being avoided.
- I will listen for words that are constantly being said in a way to cover up or disguise underlying issues, beliefs or feelings, such as 'just' vice 'I am doing'.

Conclusion

What action steps are in the future for my coaching and personal abilities based on what I have learnt in writing this chapter? I will continue my reading to learn of ways to level up my listening skills and remove the shortfalls that impact my listening. I will centre myself or meditate more before a coaching session so as to remove the outside influences that might creep in, and finally take my kayak out to the lake and listen for what I do not hear, and see what happens. I believe that I will be amazed, as I will not focus on the things that are normal for me to hear but the things that I least expect, which might be silence. The hearing of silence might open my mind to deeper reflections of self, purpose, and more.

In closing, I ask you to reflect on this quote by Thich Nhat Hanh (2012) and how it reflects on your current practice as a coach, and what it might do for you moving forward. 'Deep listening is the kind of listening that can help relieve the suffering of another person. You can call it compassionate listening. You listen with only one purpose: to help him or her to empty his heart.'

This chapter has provided you with lots of what, why and how, as well as an exercise of 'where am I right now' with my active listening. It is time to go to the next level and discover what has changed in you by reading this chapter.

ACTION REFLECTION MOMENT

Now that you have read this chapter, take a moment, and write down on a scale of 1 to 10 of how you feel better prepared to enhance your growth in active listening. What actions step are you going to take or put into practice so that you can master the art of listening?

References

Dörries, M (2021) The art of listening: Hugo Benioff, seismology, and music, *Historical Studies in the Natural Sciences*, 51 (4), 468–506

Grossman, D (2022) 8 steps to become a better active listener, *Business Credit*, 124 (7), 2–4

Hanh, T N (2012) Oprah talks to Thich Nhat Hanh, Oprah Winfrey Network, www.oprah.com/spirit/oprah-talks-to-thich-nhat-hanh/5 (archived at https://perma.cc/YRG2-3ZAZ)

Hayden, C (2022) 7 Principles for becoming a better listener, *CPA Practice Advisor*, 32 (2), 20

Leonardo, N (2020) *Active Listening Techniques: 30 Practical tools to hone your communication skills*, Rockridge Press, Emeryville, CA

Nelsen, J, Erwin, C and Duffy, R (2019) *Positive Discipline for Preschoolers: For their early years – raising children who are responsible, respectful, and resourceful*, 4th edn, Harmony Books, New York

Nelson-Jones, R (2005) *Practical Counselling and Helping Skills: Text and activities for the lifeskills counselling model*, 5th edn, Sage, Thousand Oaks, CA

9

The power of non-directive questioning

ISABEL RECHBERG

NARINA HOVHANNISYAN

ABSTRACT

Allowing clients to take ownership over the direction of their growth and development is essential for a successful coaching relationship. Adopting the power of non-directive questions during coaching sessions will allow the coach to guide the client to learn and change through the client's own initiation. In order to adopt non-directive questioning in a coaching relationship the coach may develop their listening skills and presence and create a safe space to help clients reach a powerful outcome.

Introduction

Powerful questions are the cornerstones of a successful coaching session, triggering the client's thinking and reflection, encouraging them to observe their mental and emotional processes, and helping them find alternative ways to finding a solution. Non-directive questioning is a coaching competency that allows the client to take ownership over the direction of their growth and development. Grant and Stober (2006: 363) explained coaches are not 'advice givers', and a directive approach to coaching is offering advice or direction that may not serve the client (see also de Haan, Culpin and Curd, 2011; Ellinger, Hamlin and Beattie, 2008). A coach's role is to guide the client to learn and change through their own initiation. Non-directive coaching is 'pulling' clients to help them help themselves, rather than 'pushing' clients towards a coach's solution (Thomson, 2009).

Non-directive questioning allows the client to choose how to engage in the coaching process, allowing for a more powerful outcome (Dolot, 2018). This allows the client to analyse their own situation and uncover valuable information buried within themselves (Clutterbuck, 2018). In *The Inner Game of Work,* Gallwey (2000: 210) wrote that '… coaching is not so much about telling the client what you know as it is about helping him to discover what he already knows or can find out for himself'. A non-directive question is broad, open and thought-provoking, and obliges the client to think (Franklin, 2019). Moreover, adopting non-directive questioning allows the coach to create a neutral and objective space, free of judgement and advice for the client to explore. Franklin (2019: 76) proposed that 'the less specific the question the better' as 'we don't want to tie clients into choosing'. In this space powerful questions emerge, and solutions are found.

Coaching demonstration

Being directive is only valuable in the context with the session structure to 'manage the conversation in the interest of the client' (Thomson, 2009). Nonetheless, the 'magic' is in non-directive questioning. The following extract from a coaching session illustrates how a coach can facilitate a non-directive approach to coaching:

1 **Coach:** Last session you've been working on the topic related to your interactions with the team and business.
    Client: Yes.

2 **Coach:** Is this what you would like to continue with or is there something else?
    Client: Yes. I would love to continue this topic, because there are significant shifts there already. I mean things I've come up with last time; me seeing what kind of activity is present in the office. That image that I have created during our last session. The image that was full of life… and now it's present in this office. I was there yesterday and everything was buzzing there. I came in yesterday for just a couple of minutes, everything was very active. So, thank you for that session. I would like to continue because I need the next step here.

3 **Coach:** What makes this next step important to you?
    Client: [sigh] Well, I understand that if I stop now, everything can go the other way. So, I need movement and it will be either forward or backwards [laughing]. Um… and that is why I want [to move] forward!

4 **Coach:** And may I mirror back something to you now?
    Client: Sure.

5 **Coach:** Something had changed in your tone when you said 'I need movement'.
    Client: Aha. You know, I've had this little insight! Because I've realized that everything is moving. And… um… considering that everything is moving, if I am not going forward, then it would go somewhere – to the left, to the side or backwards. If I am not moving in the desired direction or if I don't have a desired direction, then it appears that I am moving who knows where – to the side or backwards.

6 Coach: Ah! And in what direction would you like this movement to happen?
Client: I've thought about what I'd like to bring to the session. You know, it may seem a simple request at a first glance... um..., actually it's not at all. I want to create an atmosphere in the office so it would be appealing, so that people would want to come there and first of all [pause] um... employees, clients... um... I am now looking at it as a wide space. An office that is located in the centre of the city, the city that I love the most and this square, it's mine, you know, it gives me so much energy, strength... um... and I am looking at all of this as a whole. To create a space where I would want to come... um... [pause] And if I would want to come there, then the whole world would want to come there [laughing]. And everything will be great. And money would want to come, and... um... luck and business prosperity would want to come and people would want to come.

7 Coach: I am now noticing that you've exhaled, so... [pause]
Client: Yes.

8 Coach: What has appeared now here in this desire?
Client: [sigh] You know there is this warmth inside me... this warmth is spreading as if it's about me, who I want to be. I am sitting and enjoying myself now and I am enjoying this space. And I am enjoying myself in this space... and this space is around me. Listen, it's so interesting. Turns out that this space is mine, so it's me! Damn, this is such an insight! Look, turns out this space is following me, because, well, I am creating it. An office is important here, so that... it's important for the office to be the way that I want to go there. So, it's needed for me to want to come in here, not for others. Because if I am coming here, then the space is coming with me and even when I am leaving, some... some part of it stays for some time anyway, I mean this physical space is filled in and then people feel good there even if I am not present for some time. Well, yes!

9 Coach: You are the space!
Client: I am someone who is creating it... I am creating it, yes.

10 Coach: 'I am who is creating the space' and 'Me as a space', do I hear you correctly?
Client: Yes. I am who is creating the space. This would be more precise. Well, not even created, it's there. I mean, I am and the space is around me. Clearly I've done a lot to create it, well, because this is the way I am now. And it's there simply because I am the way I am. When I am walking around, my hair is there – because it is there, it has grown. Same with the space. It grew around me [both laughing].

11 Coach: How would you understand that this space has grown in the office, and on this square, and for your clients, and for your employees?
Client: [pause]... um, I will literally feel that they want to come there.

12 Coach: May I mirror back one thing to you?
Client: Sure

13 Coach: You've said that the most important thing is that YOU want to come there, to this space…
Client: Yes

14 Coach: …and now you are talking about THEM wanting to come there. How do these two relate to each other?
Client: Look… um… they relate beautifully. For them, it is if they are excited to come there. [Pause] For me, there are several criteria there… First is how often do I come there? Second is how often I come even if I don't have any specific tasks, like meetings or if my employees asked me to look at something. So, if I don't have a reason to come to the office that makes me come there, I simply get up, dress up and go there because I want to. Because I am comfortable there. And third is… um… how comfortable I am there. I mean, I am sitting there working. How effective I am, how cool it is to work there for me, how pleasant it is, how many tasks I can do lightly in one day. This is it.

Practical implications

Powerful questions

The main goal of a coach is to ask the 'right' questions without bringing their point of view or solution to the client. For a question to be most powerful it needs to be non-directive. An open-ended question is generated through the active listening and dedicated presence of the coach. Developing powerful open-ended questions reflects the coach's committed listening, which opens up a discussion within the client: all happening in a safe space created by the efforts of the coach. A powerful question creates favourable conditions for the client to think, invent, and spot patterns or obstacles that are holding them back. If formulated right, a powerful question will yield introspection, clarity and curiosity, and lead to acknowledgment, acceptance and empowerment.

Embrace the silence

Coaches, especially the ones who are jumpstarting their coaching career, sometimes feel uncomfortable after asking a question to the client. This discomfort is usually caused by the silence, the moment of emptiness that emerges within the client right after the powerful question has been raised. When this happens, don't panic! It is completely normal, praiseworthy even, that your question makes the client think. This is when the question you ask triggers reflection, and while you might think that nothing is happening, usually the opposite is the case. It is in this silence, where EVERYTHING happens. This is what coaching is about, everything else is a preparation for this very moment. The most fruitful outcomes are achieved when the client and the coach are silent. Don't be afraid of silence.

Powerful questions are not trainable

It is true that preparation may be key to success, but training for powerful non-directive questions cannot be practised per se. You cannot train yourself to ask a powerful question because anything that has ever been created, trained, prepared or thought about in advance does not have the same power and value as the question that comes to your mind in the space during the coaching session. Pre-planted questions do not lead to the insight and solutions that the client needs, which is why this competency cannot be trained, only *in vivo* of the session may a coach reflect on questions asked and their effectiveness. Taking a moment after a coaching session to ask, 'What went well?' and 'What would I like to have done differently?' are easy yet powerful tools to adapt to one's coaching practice. Similar to having ingredients to cook but no recipe, a solid foundation and understanding of basic skills, and knowing which ingredients best match will guide the coaching session. Indeed, being spontaneous, present and curious truly matters when asking the question.

WHAT CAN BE TRAINED

To hone the skills of asking the right questions, and to enable a successful coaching session we can sharpen and develop our listening skills, presence and create a safe space.

Listening skill: Deep and committed listening can be developed so the right questions can emerge in space. Sitting in silence and listening to the sounds close by and afar will allow us to hone into listening skills. Listening to the nuances in a conversation and mirroring back what you have heard can also help grow our listening skills. When the coach uses the deep listening technique, it not only promotes safety and builds trust between both parties, it also demonstrates empathy for others. If you have excellent listening skills, you can hear what the client actually has to say. You will also hear those crucial moments of silence, changes in tone and energy shifts that the client is going through – which is why listening is so important (see questions 4, 5, 7 and 12 in the coaching case extract above).

Presence: To be present means to possess the ability to be fully conscious both with yourself and with the client, at the same time, during a coaching session. Paying close attention to the client is presence. Here the coach is free of opinions, biases and assumptions, and listens to the client: what they want to deliver through their words. When you are truly present, you listen to comprehend and, if done right, you get the chance to ask those questions that have a true power inside them (see questions 4, 5, 7 and 12 in the coaching case extract above). Presence may take place on three levels of listening:

1 **Internal listening** is the consequence of lack of presence. Here the coach is talking to the client while simultaneously having a dialogue with themselves. Internally listening to yourself – here you listen to what the person says, but the two voices in your head belong to you and you! Just recall those moments when you read a book and forgot everything by the time you reach the next page.

2 **Focused listening** is being fully focused on what the client is saying, your mind is silent, with no interference from your own thoughts. This takes place when you talk to a client and actually hear what they say. An authentic conversation is happening between you and the person you are talking to.

3 **Listening when present** is when you are entirely focused on the client, but this time you hear more than just words. This is when you notice their energy shifts, body language, speech inflections, changes in tone, pauses and more. It is here where powerful non-directive questions emerge (see questions 13 and 14 in the coaching case extract above). Engaging in this third level of listening, you are fully absorbed by the client and what they have to say. There is no room for your opinions, assumptions or ideas: you hold an empty space for the client to reflect and find the solution in the emptiness, in the empty space you create and hold for them.

To practise presence a coach may consider meditation to train their brain to hold an empty space. Sitting in silence observing an object, such as a rose, for 30 minutes for example, without developing any judgement and evaluation, is challenging, and will grow the brain muscle to be present in the non-judgemental now.

BUILDING A SAFE SPACE

A safe space enables the trust for a long-lasting and fruitful coaching relationship. In this space the coach builds rapport through being a committed listener, hearing the client's emotions and words, and what the client is going through during the session. Adopting non-directive questioning allows the coach to create this neutral and objective space, free of judgement and advice for the client to explore. Practising deep non-judgemental listening skills and presence with the client and their journey will allow the coach to create a safe space for the client to explore what it is they want. The coach may consider envisioning their mind as an empty object, such as an empty vase, or look at a blank sheet of paper prior to the coaching session.

Final words

Non-directive questioning is a foundational coaching skill for a coach to adopt to enable their client to embark on a meaningful journey to reach a powerful outcome. At the client's side, the coach is curious and present, allowing for powerful questions to emerge in the coaching session. A coach is invited to grow their awareness through practising true presence and deep listening skills for powerful non-directive questions to emerge in a safe coaching space.

References

Clutterbuck, D (2018) Coaching and mentoring as conversations about context, Clutterbuck Coaching and Mentoring International, https://davidclutterbuckpartnership.com/coaching-and-mentoring-as-conversations-about-context/ (archived at https://perma.cc/UA6H-TTFZ)

de Haan, E, Culpin, V and Curd, J (2011) Executive coaching in practice: What determines helpfulness for clients of coaching? *Personnel Review*, 40 (1), 24–44, doi.org/10.1108/00483481111095500 (archived at https://perma.cc/4CXU-VXEB)

Dolot, A (2018) Non-directive communication techniques in a coaching process, *International Journal of Contemporary Management*, 17 (3), 77–100

Ellinger, A D, Hamlin, R and Beattie, R (2008) Behavioural indicators of ineffective managerial coaching: A cross-national study, *Journal of European Industrial Training*, 32 (4), 240–57

Franklin, M (2019) *The HeART of Laser-Focused Coaching: A revolutionary approach to masterful coaching*, Thomas Noble Books, Wilmington, DE

Gallwey, W T (2000) *The Inner Game of Work*, Random House, Toronto

Grant, A M and Stober, D (2006) Toward a contextual approach to coaching models, in *Evidence Based Coaching Handbook*, eds D Stober and A M Grant (pp 355–66), Wiley, New York, NY

Thomson, B (2009) *Don't Just Do Something, Sit There: An introduction to non-directive coaching*, Chandos Publishing, Oxford

10

Clarity from heart–brain connection to self-discovery

MIRJAM BLANK

ABSTRACT

The energy and life force of qi influence our presence and how we create a safe space for our clients. Projection of unexpected thoughts and emotions onto our own behaviour or the awareness of the client can disrupt the interaction, erode trust and raise feelings of insecurity. Being aware of these experiences and regularly reflecting on their origins and meaning help balance the close connection between the consciousness and heart – the often-overlooked systems of neurocardiology.

'I don't believe you', 'Late, again. Hmph', 'Was my move wrong? Will she return to the next session?' Disturbing thoughts or emotions, emerging judgements, or assumptions are felt by, conveyed and transmitted to your clients, creating either psychological safety or an unsafe space. What you may be experiencing in your coaching are the phenomena of projection and qi fields. These become more understandable when you know the science and the concepts of ancient disciplines and philosophy behind the powerful intrinsic parts and abilities of a human being. Increasingly, modern science starts to reveal the close connection between the human nervous and cardiovascular systems, or the brain and heart. In this chapter we elaborate on how you can become aware of these processes to enhance your confidence and skills, become a better coach, and how you can ensure that when these effects arise, you can direct them in your coaching to benefit yourself and your clients.

The nature of qi

We are not an island or an isolated existence. Life is part of the whole of which we are all a part. No matter what you look at, everything is connected with each other, and therefore influences each other. Qi is the most basic building material in the universe. Qi is mostly known as energy or life force, but it is actually more than just energy: it's a fully integrated form of material, energy and information, interacting with each other all the time. The concept of qi is one cornerstone of traditional Chinese culture with traditional Chinese medicine and qigong as examples of practices based on the law of qi (Tze, 2014; 34–6; 168–9).

Qi contains information and its specific qualities. The field formed by this qi and the information it contains are what is referred to as the qi field. Everything and every living being has its own qi field and its unique information. None of these qi fields are separate, they are inclusive of one another, they affect each other, and are all connected. Much of this happens automatically, without us giving it any conscious thought or being aware of it. Human beings are constantly projecting their thoughts and feelings to objects and beings around them, and even those that are further away. Every thought or emotion influences our own qi fields, the qi fields around us, and those of others (Tze, 2014: 168; HeartMath Institute, 2010). Maybe you can relate and have spent time at a place where you sensed a strange feeling, felt uncomfortable, something was troubling, or you wanted to leave right away, without really knowing why. The (negative) information of the qi field could very well be the reason. This phenomenon in traditional Chinese culture is called feng shui (Tze, 2014: 170). It also shows in another phenomenon which is known as countertransference. Transference and countertransference are forms of projection whereby the client or coach unconsciously transfers inner thoughts, beliefs or feelings onto the other person, usually based on unrelated past experiences (Bacon and Voss, 2012). In fact, it is impossible to prevent projection from happening in daily interactions. Invariably, we bring to every relationship a set of our own world views, judgements, perceptions, values, experiences, assumptions, emotions, needs and thoughts from all our previous relationships and filter everything through these lenses, and project them onto others. It's mostly driven or motivated unconsciously and can be triggered by traits, behaviours, emotions or patterns of these of a person we are interacting with that reminds us of a person, an experience, or feelings from the past (Bacon and Voss, 2012). This occurrence is not negative per se, but it is something to be aware of, as some of these lenses we look through might not be beneficial or healthy. Our own fears, doubts, emotional reactions, limiting beliefs or biases can slip silently and oftentimes undetected into a coaching session.

Another major unconscious driver can also be our own (unmet) needs or desires. Projecting your need of wanting to be liked and hence fearing rejection could manifest in you tainting your judgement of taking the action needed to create awareness in a session with your client. In other words, you may fear that when they feel uncomfortable, they would not like you or your coaching any more, and would leave you. This exemplifies that being able to identify and understand projection allows you to adhere to ethical contexts and codes, practise within boundaries, create psychological safety, and act in the best interest of your clients.

Coaching and your (personal) growth are inherently connected and both need to be cultivated and nourished constantly to be a great coach. Continuous self-discovery allows you to have more clarity in your thoughts, emotions, (unmet) needs and behaviour, when you feel disturbed or feel a shift in your energy. It enables you to recognize it in the moment, allows you to release it, instead of being unconsciously steered by thoughts, emotions and unfulfilled needs. When you can notice a disturbing reaction, you can choose to breathe the disturbance out, and any tension your body might be holding, to return to being present with your client. It requires constant practice and developing an observer's mind with high levels of self-awareness, and at the same time having the understanding that these automatic reactions are part of human instinct. This may sound easier said than done, and is a skill that needs to be built incrementally.

Coaching is not just a technique or skill coming from the brain or consciousness. Every person's qi field and the information it contains can be infinitely powerful when the consciousness and heart state is in the right place (Tze, 2014). Thoughts and emotions have consequences. They define our narratives, they steer how we feel and think, affect our state, our body and qi as well as what we do. Our consciousness and heart are both an integral part of human life. It takes the integration and unification of qi, body, consciousness and heart to create psychological safety, to be present and to receive with the whole being, as well as to create deep long-lasting transformation.

The heart is not just a physical or anatomical organ. It is a sensory organ of great intelligence, a sophisticated information encoding and processing centre that enables it to learn, remember and make independent functional decisions. It has its own intrinsic nervous system, decision-making powers, and connections to the brain, composed of a complex network of neurons and neurotransmitters (Armour, 2003; McCraty, 2005). When we are in a calm, caring, empathetic state, it can not only be felt by our clients, influence their state in beneficial ways, but can also facilitate transformation this way. This interaction can actually be measured (Guarneri, 2019: 113).

The heart and brain both generate electromagnetic fields, and the heart generates the largest electromagnetic field in the body. Its electromagnetic field is 5,000 times larger than that generated by the brain, and contains information or coding that is felt by every cell in the body, acting as a global internal synchronizing signal throughout and outside the body. These heart signals can reach higher brain centres, ultimately affecting our emotions, choices and perceptions.

Findings in neurocardiology on the brain–heart connection contemplate that emotional experiences are a product of the brain, body, more so the heart, all acting harmoniously in concert (McCraty, 2005). When we experience emotions such as anger, frustration or fear, the heart rhythms become more chaotic and disturbed leading to less synchronization in the interplay of the parasympathetic nervous system (rest and digest function) and the sympathetic nervous system (fight, flight, freeze response).

In contrast, when we feel uplifting emotions, such as love and respect for our clients, the heart rhythms show a high order, coherence and harmony, reflecting a greater synchronization between both branches of the autonomic nervous system, leading to an increased parasympathetic activity (McCraty, 2005). This internal unification becomes, in essence, presence, which is characterized as a neurophysiological state of trust and safety. When we feel safe with our whole being, the human instinctual need to defend and protect ourselves decreases, contributing to the conditions for growth and change to take place (Gellar and Porges, 2014; Reynolds, 2020: 149).

Applying qi in coaching

In the following section, I illustrate a technique I apply for myself and with my clients by engaging my heart and consciousness to help me surface deep hidden messages, and to see what I've been otherwise projecting. For this engagement to be effective, as a coach you must build a solid foundation to understand the roles and functions of your heart and consciousness, and to work on your own state and unhealthy patterns. This fundament facilitates the deeper engagement of heart and consciousness with your clients.

I am practising and building my observer's mind in every interaction, meaning I view everything that happens without judgement of the *shoulds*, *needs* or *musts*, such as 'I should've known better', I must not feel like this' or 'I need to get this right', hence maintaining a novice mindset of 'I know nothing', which is like seeing something for the very first time ever. Yet, I am also aware to notice these *shoulds* when they arise, because they give great insight on the expectations that I have formed, and on unhealthy patterns, thoughts and emotions.

Having the presence of an open heart with curiosity and to embrace with courage is essential when I observe what has emerged:

1 **Recognizing** – after I feel disturbed or am taken over by unpleasant thoughts and emotions.

2 **Watching** – every thought I have and how I feel, what I say or do after that.

3 **Embracing** – everything, the positive and the negative, the 'I like' and 'I don't like'.

4 **Acknowledging** – when I feel uncomfortable, disturbed and identify a quality such as 'this is negative'.

5 **Accepting** – for what it is, it has become reality.

Let me share an example to illustrate the arousal and effects of these thoughts: 'I don't believe you'. This thought had suddenly emerged in one of my coaching sessions. It seemingly came from nowhere and disturbed my state, causing me to lose my focus and presence with my client. Irritation followed the thought, and tension rose inside me. I noticed how I tried to ignore the thought and still attempted to be present for my client. However, the thought was quite pervasive and did not abate and move on.

I observed the changes within myself, the shift in qi, and how the thought changed how I judged what my client was saying. Then I embraced the thought and said 'Hello, what is this about?' I acknowledged its presence and only then I was able to release it and turn back to be fully present with my client again.

Similarly, 'You don't believe me' turned up when I was coached. Again, I noticed a shift in qi before the thought emerged. At first, it was like a subtle change in feelings; a break in the synchronicity between my coach and me. It became disturbing and jarring. A wave of irritation swept over me, only this time the emotion was much stronger, and boiling anger came with it. The emotion amplified the thought. 'You don't believe me,' I said out loud and accused my coach that she was not listening and not believing me. Although I sensed the power of the emotions and the disturbance it created inside, I nevertheless felt how the safe space with my coach crumbled into a thousand pieces. Hurt unfurling inside of my body, tainting me to believe I was being judged and not cared about by her. When we enquired further, I could only relate it to a past experience I had with a family member where I felt that person did not believe me. For days after our session, I noticed that hurt was present above all, continuing to disturb my state, accompanied by a strong urge to withdraw, to avoid my coach and to quit any future sessions.

The power of projection and the change in the qi field was what we had experienced. In both examples one might think the thought was part of the narrative of the situation. That I was indeed not believing what my client said to me, that my coach was really not believing what I said. Still, in both cases, the thought emerged seemingly from nowhere and yet influenced the present situation, disrupted the safe space, tainted my judgement and made me question our coaching relationship. A word, a gesture or a shift in qi had activated the thought and its accompanying emotions. But what was this, and the tendency to avoid my coach, really about? Was it just an experience with a family member from the past, or was there an even deeper message hidden for me, waiting to be uncovered?

To gain deeper clarity you must reflect objectively and soundly with an open attitude to what happened, and from multiple angles. For this I set aside time to meditate, to go inwards, and unify my consciousness and heart so that they support me in gaining more clarity. As we have already contemplated in this chapter, our consciousness, body and qi form a unity for all physiological, emotional and mental processes (Maciocia, 2015: 107). The heart is considered a source of our emotions, wisdom, insight and cognition. Within our body, the heart and consciousness communicate together in neurological, biochemical, biophysical and energetical ways (Alshami, 2019).

An essential part for the engagement of these intelligences to be effective is the preparation of adjusting the body to be in a comfortable position, going inward and connecting with your inner self. I am building a qi field for my practice with the intention of connecting my mind and heart:

Sitting comfortably and relaxing my body;

Closing my eyes and feeling inwards;

Connecting with my heart;

Feeling my heart, the power within;

My heart is a wonderful source of wisdom and knowledge;

Becoming silent inside.

Then I am ready to guide myself by using questions and allowing for each question the time that I deem right for my practice (I use a timer for the practice). To demonstrate this, I have created questions below. There are no fixed questions, these can vary from person to person. You can create your own questions according to your unique needs. Keep in mind that the answers are deeply hidden in your subconscious, and that they will emerge. Sometimes it takes time, like peeling off the layers of an onion, and often you will not receive the answers in one sitting. The key is in determination, practice, patience and not getting attached to a specific outcome. These are questions that will help you retrieve the hidden information in your qi:

1 What is the identified thought, emotion, behaviour you have discovered?
2 How do they show up?
3 Where do they come from, whether they are coming from the past, present; are beneficial or not?
4 What is it that you'd rather not want to feel, think or re-experience?
5 What is it that you need?
6 What are the negative effects?
7 What ways of thinking, mindset, attitudes and behaviour can you find to transform them?

Then I prepare myself to end the meditation. I feel inside, I feel my heart and allow myself to feel and see everything that has emerged for me. When I am ready, I open my eyes.

Final words

When you have truly reached the point of clarity with seeing what is driving you, or why you are doing, thinking or feeling a certain way, only then is it possible to initiate true change and transformation. When we project things onto others, what we think or feel are often messengers from deep within. Listen to the messengers.

In my case, the strong emotional reaction I had experienced and was projecting towards my coach allowed me to gain deeper realizations on already existing self-discoveries about the people-pleasing mechanisms that I had developed since my childhood. As a child I had learnt that, when I said yes to requests, or agreed with others' views, beliefs and values, I would receive acceptance from them. If, however, I received a no, or said no to a request, or disagreed with someone's view, belief or value, I perceived rejection. The strategies I came up with benefited me in meeting my need to be accepted, and at the same time protected me from harm such as feelings of rejection and hurt. However, they did not address where this fear originated from. They created a belief that I was doing the right thing when I said, 'I believe you', conveying a (somewhat false and fleeting) sense of feeling good. Furthermore, doubting my own beliefs and values helped me to feel safe believing in other's beliefs and values, fulfilling everyone else's needs first and neglecting my own. This false sense of security kept up the pretence that I was fulfilling my needs, protecting myself from harm, when in reality I was not fulfilling my needs, but harming myself: doubting, rejecting and hurting myself.

Being a coach is inevitably being bound to yourself. It is like taking care of a garden and the requirements of maintenance: watering, levelling the area, digging stones out of the soil, removing weeds. Deliberately listen to your heart–brain connection. Noticing any changes in thoughts, feelings, sensations or behaviour tells you that you may be projecting. Coaches who understand the phenomena of projection and focus on self-discovery can develop great insights into their own development, keep up to the quality and standards of ethical practice in the coaching profession, enhance their confidence in their skills, and create more growth for their clients' self-discovery journeys.

References

Alshami, A M (2019) Pain: Is it all in the brain or the heart? *Current Pain and Headache Reports*, 23 (12), 88, doi.org/10.1007/s11916-019-0827-4 (archived at https://perma.cc/EBT6-LYDT)

Armour, J A (2003) *Neurocardiology: Anatomical and functional principles*, Publication No. 03-011, HeartMath Research Center, Institute of HeartMath, Boulder Creek, CA

Bacon, T R and Voss, L (2012) *Adaptive coaching: The art and practice of a client-centered approach to performance improvement*, 2nd edn, Nicholas Brealey International, London

Gellar, S M and Porges, S W (2014) Therapeutic presence: Neuropsychological mechanisms mediating feeling safe in therapeutic relationships, *Journal of Psychotherapy Integration*, 24 (3), 178–92, doi.org/10.1037/a0037511 (archived at https://perma.cc/DDM2-TPLG)

Guarneri, M (2019) *The heart speaks: A cardiologist reveals the secret language of healing*, Atria Books, New York

HeartMath Institute (2010) The energetic heart is unfolding, Science of the Heart, 22 July, www.heartmath.org/articles-of-the-heart/science-of-the-heart/the-energetic-heart-is-unfolding/ (archived at https://perma.cc/HQK6-GRP6)

Maciocia, G (2015) *The Foundations of Chinese Medicine: A comprehensive text*, 3rd edn, Elsevier, New York

McCraty, R (2005) The energetic heart: Bioelectromagnetic interactions within and between people, in *Clinical applications of bioelectromagnetic medicine*, eds P J Rosch and M S Markov, pp 511–32, Marcel Dekker, New York

Reynolds, M (2020) *Coach the person, not the problem: A guide to using reflective inquiry*, Berrett-Koehler, Oakland, CA

Tze, Y (2014) *Wellbeing begins with you: Use your inner resources to heal your body and your life*, Yuan Tze Centre, Wellington, New Zealand

11

Seeking transformation versus focusing on solutions

NARINA HOVHANNISYAN
ISABEL RECHBERG

ABSTRACT

For a coaching session to carry true meaning, a client identifies and accomplishes their goal. To assist the client on that quest the coach may adopt a solution-focused or a transformation-focused approach. A solution-focused approach to coaching embraces strategies on how to reach the client's goal. A transformational approach allows the client to rise above their assumptions, to imagine their true potential. This may lead to a paradigm shift and deep spontaneous learning; here the client leaves the session changed. In order to adopt a transformational coaching approach, we propose to direct questions towards the client's values, identity, vision and mission, and explore the client's future from their future.

Introduction

Arguably the most significant motivation that brings a client to a coaching session is seeking change and development in their lives. The GROW approach to coaching coins Goal–Reality–Options–Will as the building blocks that can enable clients to reach their desired outcome. In a coaching partnership the coach facilitates the client to 'articulate in their own words: the goal that they want to achieve [and] the limiting assumptions that is holding them back from doing what they want and need to do' (Thomson, 2009: 41). To assist in identifying and accomplishing clients' goals the coach may adopt a solution-focused or a transformation-focused approach, both of which are discussed in this chapter.

Grant (2006: 153) stated that if 'coaching is essentially about helping individuals regulate and direct their interpersonal and intrapersonal resources to better attain their goals', then 'coaching is a goal-oriented, solution-focused process' (p 156). The solution-focused approach to coaching is a 'method of helping clients to reframe their challenges as practical problems and help them discover the required internal and external resources' to overcome the challenge (Ives, 2008: 106). According to Nancy Kline (1999: 39), 'usually the brain that contains the problem also contains the solution', which allows the coach to facilitate the client to seek the ideas and actions that are in line with their value to obtain their goal. Staying solution-focused allows the coach to be there with the client on their journey to reach their desired outcome.

For a coaching session to carry true meaning the focus is on the goal the client would like to reach. Eric Butterworth, however, found that 'you see things, not as they are, but as you are'. For this reason, it is important to consider seeking transformation for the client. Gray (2006) explained that it is transformational coaching that has the potentiality to enact powerful change in clients, as this approach may enable clients to look at their experiences free of bias. Mezirow (1994: 222) coined transformative learning as 'the social process of construing and appropriating a new or revised interpretation of the meaning of one's experience as a guide to action'. In other words, enabling a process of 'reaching a kind of renewed, deeper awareness, a reconfiguring and reintegrating world view' (Tosey and Mathison, 2003: 1). In transformational coaching the coach acts as the 'empathetic provocateur' (Cranton, 1992: 17), fostering critical self-reflection in the client to then take meaningful actions that may lay beyond their original assumptions. Adopting a transformation approach to coaching will raise a client's awareness and insight beyond their assumptions.

Case example

To better understand the difference between solution-focused and transformational coaching, consider the following example. A client wants to change their profession and a solution-focused approach will help them transfer from one job to another more easily and effortlessly. At the same time, if the same topic is being discussed within a transformational session, the client will be able to fundamentally reimagine their career potential, followed by awareness and harmony mobilizing the client to act, change and develop. Adopting a transformational coaching approach allows your clients to recognize their true abilities, driving forces and aspirations, obstacles and anxieties, and beliefs about themselves, their mind and body. Through this better self-awareness, clients will be able to examine how these factors affect their life, actions and world view. Here, clients will find the courage to set their own standards for pleasure, fulfilment and prosperity. We illustrate solution and transformational coaching techniques in the case extract that follows:

1   **Coach:** Can we [turn on] 'recording in progress'?
    Client: Yes. Sure.

2   **Coach:** Thank you. And you've started talking about this topic...
    Client: Yes. The topic that interests me is related to creating strategies that would allow me to be more effective in relationships with other people and in relationship with myself. Yeah. To notice that my inner... I am noticing that I judge myself a lot. I would like to become more [pause] wholesome and to accept some statuses of mine, my ranks, perhaps, maybe there is something else. I would like to explore my personal effectiveness in this broad spectrum. [Pause]

3   **Coach:** Aha. [Pause] Would you allow me to mirror back what I've heard?
    Client: Yes, yes, sure. [Pause]

4   **Coach:** Look, I've heard about you wanting to create inner strategies, about being more effective in relationships with other people and with yourself. You've also said that perhaps you are judging yourself and you would like to become more wholesome...
    Client: Yes.

5   **Coach:** ... to accept your statuses, ranks, and perhaps there is something else there. To explore your personal effectiveness in a broad spectrum?
    Client: Aha.

6   **Coach:** And when you've heard all of this mirroring back from me [smile], where does your energy shift?
    Client: Yes, towards personal effectiveness. I am really interested in understanding what it is for me. I've been thinking about it for a long time. I think that this is some level of personal effectiveness for me.

7   **Coach:** Aha. And when you would understand it, what would become possible then?
    Client: I am thinking that it's about a more wholesome, more joyful way of living a life. When there is a possibility to act in... to be more effective, lively, I don't know, more athletic. I see the impact on sports and on my creativity, and on my development and on my professional life. On everything. I think it would be really great.

8   **Coach:** Aha. And why did this question of personal effectiveness now become so relevant?

Client: I've got this image. An image of a person who is passing between two wings. One wing is this inner critic who is constantly judging me, and another wing is like this diamond that I am polishing. So, it's this metaphor of either two wings, or a traveller who is passing between the two wings. And I would like to understand how to get through interaction with all of this – at the same time using power, a power of some inner critical processes. Judging ones. Because I have this feeling… I am managing teams from time to time and some stones are thrown at me, but then I hear gratitude from the same teams. And of course, it hurts me on one hand, but on the other hand it motivates me. I understand that this is also some sort of inner process of mine. And I would like to understand what the middle ground would be. How do I walk without falling into excessive height and not being hurt by these sharp stones?

9   Coach: Aha. I am hearing as if this story, or rather these stories about interacting with teams might also be something important. Is this so?
Client: Yes! Yes! Well, of course this is inner… an external process that is reflected… most likely it's my inner process that is being reflected externally, that is why I would like for my inner process to be more… measured maybe, so that there would be a move forward. So that I won't get stuck in one state or another. In this situation. To get it to a minimum.

10   Coach: Aha. Would you allow me another question in order to define the direction – you've described this person between two wings, where one wing is a critic, and another is a diamond that you are polishing. And this person is walking on this middle path – not too high but also so they won't get high enough and at the same time not get hurt – who is that?
Client: Um… it's an image of this traveller who is walking with a cane between all of these processes. And there is… it's quite a calm, very simple person. He is just walking on this… with his inner power maybe. Yes. He has some inner wisdom. He is holding inner wisdom. Like, perhaps he understands. He quickly gets back to himself after mistakes, and he quickly returns to himself from a strategic vision. He is very authentic.

11   Coach: In what direction is it important for him to go? [Pause]
Client: It's important for him to go… it's a good question. [Pause] He is walking in the direction of light. Perhaps this would be right. It's interesting that these two constants, it's like they are standing around him. And he continues his path.

12   Coach: Which constants?
Client: Well, this 'right bank, left bank', and he is walking – as if he is walking on this riverbed. As if these are two cliffs. One is dark and another one is light. Yeah. One has rocks falling from it, another one sends accolades. And he is walking and… from time to time he drifts to one side or the other, but he is trying to walk straight down this road. This is how it… yeah. So that… I am

now noticing that he is drifting to either side from time to time. This is why his path becomes like this. I would like for this path to be straight, of course.

13 Coach: What for – and then, what would be a good result of our session today?
Client: Well. [Pause] I would like to stop all of this… fall… constantly falling to the left or to the right. I want to have a straightforward full action. So that I would be able to move straight in my direction, with awareness of myself in general, awareness of my processes and my path. In this aware, harmonious, and simple way. So, I like this. The most [important] thing for me would be – how do I execute this strategy on this path into my life? Perhaps how can this straight path be transferred in life? Like, in what way?

14 Coach: Aha. And how would you be able to understand that you've reached your goal by the end of the session?
Client: I definitely have three clear steps that… using which I would continue my path. Somewhat… well, perhaps it's going to be one to three steps, this would be good. There would be some actions. To change this whole picture. Because I think that there is a way that would allow me to bring more harmony to this whole system. Yeah. And I am thinking that this way would have one, two, three simple actions that would allow to change everything. [Pause]

15 Coach: One to three clear steps, actions that would allow to change this system, this picture. And what is already visible to you in this system, in this picture when you are looking at it now? [Pause]
Client: Well, I see that at least there is movement. This is good already. I understand that this right and left bank is not going anywhere. I see this person who is moving. Actually, he is moving okay. There is support. I mean, everything is actually working, like, I don't know, somehow, I mean, I have movement. Yeah. I understand that it's like this person doesn't acknowledge his power, the power of his movement. Perhaps I am not noticing?! He doesn't fully acknowledge it and that is why he is drifting.

16 Coach: What would you like to do with all this?
Client: Ummm… good question by the way. [Pause] I would like for him to continue walking towards his power and to follow it. Interestingly I am now noticing that this power, this path is a path of power. Cool. Like, he is walking on [this path]. This is where there is energy that he is walking for. A path of power, a path of power.

17 Coach: This is really beautiful. And while he is walking, how does he realize that this is a path of power?
Client: This is the problem – he doesn't realize that this is a path of power. Haha. I am just beginning to realize it. Yeah. And how is he walking now, realizing that this is a path of power? This is also a good question. I'll try to catch it now. If [I

will] be walking realizing that this is a path of power… then there will be much more calmness, harmony, this acceptance and depth. [Pause] Yes! I think that there is more passion for life even. And some simplicity. Like, he is accepting this life, accepting all the gifts that he is given, he is accepting everything that is happening to him. He is very calm.

18   **Coach:** What have you now said 'yes' to, what have you accepted?
Client: Ummm. [Pause] Well, it's like I am accepting this inner silence, this depth and serenity that accompany my acceptance of feeling, my emotions, my responses, my right to the path, my right to life, right to enjoy this life, right to joy… Suddenly I have a wind blowing here, it's so beautiful – the leaves are shining, so cool… right to freedom. I am seeing how… including the right to make a mistake. So, I understand that these rights are starting to be accepted. It's like there is an assembly of some sort.

19   **Coach:** How does it impact that straightforward full action?
Client: Ummm. [Pause] I become more flowy, it's like I am trusting this world even more and I am looking at how the world trusts me back. So, there is this trust coming. There is trust in the path. I am trusting this energy that I am walking for and that is guiding me, [I am trusting] this power. I am trusting this flow. I am saying 'yes, I agree'.

Following the coaching case example that draws on both solution-focused as well as transformational questions to help the client reach their goal, we turn to practical implications to facilitate transformational coaching.

Practical implications enabling transformational coaching

Transformational questions

It is the coach's responsibility to start the session from the right angle. The beginning of the session sets the tone for the session to be a success. Asking the right question will allow the client to dive deeper into the topic, which will make it easier for them to achieve the desired goal. Questions such as 'What is your topic?', 'What is your desire around that topic?', 'How would you know you have achieved it?', 'How is this important for you?' and 'What else would become possible when you achieve it?' are powerful questions that can generate transformation in a client (see questions 6, 7, 15, 17 and 18 in the coaching case extract above).

Exploration of the future from the future

This so-called exploration of the future from the future, as coined by Hovhannisyan here, assumes the position as if the client already has what they want, sees what they want, feels how they want it to be and who they want to become. Such perspective assists the client to explore what they want in their life. Through questions that generate the future, the client is feeling empowered to move to the state where they have already achieved their goal and where they can look for the indicators of those achievements (see questions 7, 15 and 17 and the client's response in the coaching case extract above). It is critical to realize that throughout this stage of the exploration process, the client is given complete freedom to think, believe and envision things on their own.

Seeking for energy shifts

Solutions are always born from the state of the unknown, indeed there would be no solution if you already knew the answer in advance. Coaches seek for clients to experience an energy shift during their sessions and might thus wonder how long to stay in the exploration state, what words to listen for, and how many questions they should ask before moving forward. Don't wait for words, phrases, opinions or content – the most valuable is to notice the energy shift. When the shift happens the client starts feeling what they want, as if they have already achieved the goal, and you will notice an energy shift in them. Pay attention to this change of energy – changes in the client's body language, tone, pace, the lighting up of their face, smile, bright eyes, a sigh, an 'aha' among others (see, e.g., the client's response under questions 18 and 19 in the coaching case extract above). After you have witnessed the energy shift, it is time to ask your client, 'What do you expect from the session so that it helps you achieve what you truly want?' It is important to 'bring the client back' to the here and now so they express what they want to get out of the session, what they expect to achieve, and why they are here in the first place (see question 18 in the coaching case extract above).

Transformation through values, identity, vision and mission

The outcome of a solution-focused coaching session is an action plan: strategies and actions that the client needs to enforce and complete to reach the goal set forth by the client (see questions 13, 14, 16 and 19 in the coaching case extract above). On the other hand, in a transformational session, the change occurs during the session and in the moment. The change is possible as a transformational session helps the client explore themselves from the inside out, by exploring their values, purpose, mission and vision, expectations, and presumptions. In a transformational session the client's self-awareness and self-perception changes (see, e.g., the client's response under questions 10, 18, and 19 in the coaching case extract above). In sessions where the client has imagined their future and potential the learning is so deep, the client is leaving the session already changed.

Final words

In summary, a solution-focused session embraces strategies on how to reach the client's goal. In a transformational session clients recognize their being, their value, purpose and mission, generating instant change. With the change occurring on the level of being and not the level of doing (see, e.g., Dilts' logical levels (2003) for detail), the paradigm shifts to deep spontaneous learning and transformation.

References

Cranton, P A (1992) *Working with Adult Learners*, Wall & Emerson, Inc, Toronto

Dilts, R (2003) *From Coach to Awakener*, Meta Publications, Capitola, CA

Grant, A M (2006) An integrative goal-focused approach to executive coaching, in *Evidence Based Coaching Handbook: Putting best practices to work for your clients*, eds D Stober and A M Grant (pp 153–92), Wiley, New York, NY

Gray, D E (2006) Executive coaching: Towards a dynamic alliance of psychotherapy and transformative learning processes, *Management Learning*, 37 (4), 475–97

Ives, Y (2008) What is 'coaching'? An exploration of conflicting paradigms, *International Journal of Evidence Based Coaching and Mentoring*, 6 (2), 100–13

Kline, N (1999) *Time to Think: Listening to ignite the human mind*, Cassell Illustrated, London

Mezirow, J (1994) Understanding transformation theory, *Adult Education Quarterly*, 44 (4), 222–32

Thomson, B (2009) *Don't Just Do Something, Sit There: An introduction to non-directive coaching*, Chandos Publishing, Oxford

Tosey, P and Mathison, J (2003) Mapping transformative learning: A neuro-linguistic programming perspective, in *Proceedings of Living Sprit: New Dimensions in Work and Learning*, University of Surrey, July 2003

PART THREE

Approaches

12

Holistic transformation

CHRISTINE GUIRGUIS

ABSTRACT

Using a holistic approach, coaches help clients get in touch and connect their body, mind and soul to serve in the healing process of emotional and physical pain. By acknowledging the connectivity, clients gain awareness of what is getting in the way of their success.

Introduction

The journey of a holistic transformation begins with the understanding that in order to fully heal, we must recognize that the body, mind and soul are one entity. These parts are interconnected and by focusing on the person as a whole it will benefit their overall health.

Trying to heal by focusing on just one aspect is like putting a Band-Aid on a deep wound, it is only a temporary solution. That wound will open up again and manifest itself in different ways.

By gaining a better understanding of what physical health, mental health and spiritual health mean, how they are connected, and how we as coaches can use this methodology, we help our clients heal and live their lives fully.

Body – physical health

Those who think they have not the time for bodily exercise will sooner or later have to find time for illness.

EDWARD STANLEY

What does physical health mean?

When looking at physical health you need to consider the condition your body is in. It is so important to recognize that your body is the physical vehicle you use to navigate through life. As long as everything is functioning well, it is easy to pay little attention and take your body for granted. Therefore, understanding which areas need focus and care will give you a step in the right direction to evaluate and consider what you want to do in order to optimize your physical health.

For the purpose of this chapter, I have narrowed physical health to three important factors, namely fitness, nutrition and self-care.

PHYSICAL AWARENESS

Exercise is undoubtedly one of the most talked about ways of getting healthier that can help improve many areas of your health. For one, it helps manage your weight, which decreases the chances of chronic disease (Semeco, 2023). Being fit also means the 'ability to execute daily activities with optimal performance, endurance, and strength with the management of disease, fatigue, and stress and reduced sedentary behavior' (Campbell, De Jesus and Prapavessis, 2013). So, it is not only about exercise, but also about listening to your body and its needs, so that you can function at an optimal level; recognizing when something is not up to par and giving yourself time to heal while building yourself back up at the right pace. People often struggle with fitness because it takes time, time that they may not have. In the best circumstances, the body works for you effortlessly, but when a person is sick, injured, or in pain, you must help them recognize it is time to take conscious actions in care of their body. First, one needs to be able to recognize when there is discomfort somewhere in their body. Mindful breathing is a great way to help with this process of discovery.

As the coach, you can ask your client to close their eyes and take a deep breath; this helps them bring their focus inward. You can guide your client to notice if there is any tingling, throbbing, rumbling, aching, heaviness, by asking the simple question, 'what do you feel in or around your body?'

NUTRITION

What you eat is just as important as how you eat it and why you eat it. Research has linked mindless or distracted eating with anxiety, overeating and weight gain (Stanszus, Frank and Geiger, 2019). Distinguishing emotional versus physical hunger cues makes a difference on how people relate to their food. The relationship a person has with their food can impact their overall health.

An effective holistic coach helps clients recognize why they eat, before improving on what they eat. The problem these days is that there is so much information on what to eat, what is healthy and what is not, some of which is likely to clash with what you have been accustomed to eating and culturally view as healthy. These disparities lead to confusion and can make a person feel guilty about the food choices they are making or avoid or restrict foods that are deemed 'bad' for them. This type of overthinking creates stress and anxiety when eating in social settings due to the social pressures of what others will think of their food choices (Davidson, 2020).

A great approach is to combine mindful eating with nutritional knowledge. Mindful eating means paying attention to the process and savouring the experience you are having while eating. It is important to build a positive relationship with food by enjoying all foods in moderation and honouring your body's hunger cues by eating when you are hungry and stopping when you are full. Research supports that this approach can lead to elevated psychological well-being, healthy body image and, most importantly, reduce the risk of chronic diseases (Warren, Smith and Ashwell, 2017).

To help your clients take the step towards becoming more mindful in their eating habits, you can ask them to keep a food journal (Table 12.1). They can track what they eat, when they eat and how they are feeling at the time. It allows them to see patterns and helps their coach assess their habits and identify the disempowering beliefs that may be holding them back from making the changes they want.

SELF-CARE

Self-care means making sure to take the time to do things that help improve your overall well-being. That requires you to check in with yourself and pay attention to what your body needs. For example, paying attention to how tired you might feel. Knowing when it is time to take a break and recharge. The way to recharge is unique for everyone since our needs differ from one another at any point of time in our lives. For the purpose of this chapter, I focus on one aspect that is not only critical but often overlooked as a method of self-care – sleep. Sleep is not only beneficial but necessary to recharge. Even so, many of us do not get adequate sleep every night. The

TABLE 12.1 Food journal

What you ate	Time	Mood	How hungry were you on a scale of 1–5? *1 – not hungry at all 5 – starving*	Did you enjoy your meal?	How did it taste?	How long did you eat for?	How do you feel about your food choice?

lack of sleep can lead to many health problems, some of which include hypertension, diabetes, obesity, depression and increased risk of cardiovascular conditions such as heart attack and stroke (Colten and Altevogt, 2006). Getting sufficient sleep helps improve concentration and productivity as well, which supports a healthy immune system and regulates emotions (Leech, 2022). It is important to view sleep as a form of self-care to help make it a priority in your life.

As coaches, we often hear our clients talk about feeling anxious or moody. Recognizing the direct connection between sleep and these emotional states helps the coach ask the right questions to discover more about how well your client is sleeping and if they are getting the right amount of sleep.

The amount of sleep one needs varies from one person to another. Cleveland Clinic (2021) suggests that the best way to know what the right amount of sleep is for a person is to take a sleep vacation. You can do that by committing to a sleeping time every night and allow yourself to wake up naturally. At first you might sleep longer because you are making up for lost sleep if you have been sleep deprived. After a week or two you will start waking up naturally at the same time every day and at that point you will be able to calculate how many hours you need. They also remind us to consider, when planning your bed and wake time, that you need to complete five to six 90-minute sleep cycles to feel recharged when you wake up. Disturbing a sleep cycle will make you feel groggy and sleepy when your alarm goes off.

A great way to help your client recognize patterns and see if they are not getting enough sleep is by keeping a sleep diary (Table 12.2).

How physical health is connected to your mental health

Science supports the body–mind connection. How you treat your body has a major impact on your mind (Semeco, 2023).

Exercise is literally able to make the brain grow. The hippocampus, a part of the brain that is important for memory and learning, gets larger in size when a person exercises regularly (Semeco, 2023). Not only that, but it has been proven to enhance your mood and reduce feelings of anxiety, depression and stress (Ensari, Sandroff

TABLE 12.2 Sleep diary

Bedtime
Time taken to fall asleep
Night interruptions (yes/no – how long?)
Wake time
Mood upon waking
Naps

and Motl, 2016). What is interesting is that it does not matter how intense your workout is, exercise benefits your mood (Semeco, 2023).

Nutrition plays a role in the health of the gut. Harvard Health Publishing (2021, para 2) states that, 'A person's stomach or intestinal distress can be the cause *or* the product of anxiety, stress, or depression. That's because the brain and the gastrointestinal (GI) system are intimately connected.'

Also, listening to your body and its needs, such as when you are feeling tired, and respecting that by sleeping will help strengthen your memory and goes through a process of elimination by getting rid of memories collected throughout the day that are not needed. It is also the time when your body can get rid of the toxins that have been accumulated in the brain during the day (Walton, 2016).

Mind – mental health

Mental wellness relates to how people think, feel and behave. When your state of mind is healthy, you are able to cope with the daily stresses of life and recognize your potential by becoming aware of your own abilities.

What does mental health mean?

When looking at mental health, understanding the psychological and emotional condition a person is in can be evaluated by how connected they are to their emotional states, their acquiring of new knowledge and how self-aware they are.

- **Emotions:** Connecting to our emotions implies that we are aware and know how to manage them. A coach can help their client to create this awareness by giving them a list of emotions to look at and choose which emotion best represents what they are feeling at the time of their trigger. We do not often realize that we lack the vocabulary to articulate how we feel. When clients can verbalize what they feel, they can understand and acknowledge what they feel. Only then will they be ready to look into why they feel this way and how it can be managed.
- **Knowledge:** Making space in one's life for growth and learning new things is key to feeling self-confident and gaining self-esteem. After formal education it is important to continue seeking ways to learn new knowledge.
- **Self-awareness:** Attaining self-awareness is the ability to understand the self and how one's actions, thoughts, emotions and character align with internal standards, including purpose, values and principles.

According to Verghese (2008, para. 4), 'Mental health has two dimensions – absence of mental illness and presence of a well-adjusted personality that contributes effectively to the life of the community.' Studies have shown that personality traits can be changed when people learn to understand themselves and others better through different types of change interventions. One such intervention was an 18-hour course given to undergraduates, where their increase in emotional competency that led to positive personality changes seemed to be long lasting (Nelis et al, 2011). Initially, this type of change needs to be a conscious effort that can be attained by gaining clarity through awareness before becoming ingrained. See Chapter 3 for tools to help your clients gain awareness.

How your mind connects to your body

Your mind is powerful, but when it is unwell you can actually manifest symptoms physically. For example, if you are feeling stressed, you can start to feel aches, pains, upset stomach including diarrhorea, constipation and nausea (Marks, 2021). Dr Carla Manley, a clinical psychologist, says that when this happens it's our body's way of telling us that we need to pay attention to something in our lives that might not be good for us. By learning to pay attention to our bodies and tune into our mental state, we can recognize psychosomatic symptoms that can tell us what we might need more, or less, of in our lives in order to feel happy and fulfilled (Ferguson, 2020).

If you are in a constant state of stress your body is filled with the stress hormones adrenaline and cortisol. These hormones increase heart rate and blood pressure and suppress the digestive and immune systems (Ferguson, 2020). Over time, these elevated levels lead to symptoms of physiological distress. For example, if one is suffering from a disempowering belief such as low self-worth, they may feel that they are being judged or rejected when the belief is triggered. As a result, fear creeps up and stress hormones release, preparing them to deal with the 'danger' ahead. Often misguided, the danger is not real, or exaggerated. So, having the self-awareness of what is really happening can help manage the emotions and fears, and regulate the physical stress reaction that happens every time fear is triggered – avoiding an acute reaction or stopping the stress response before it becomes chronic.

Soul – spiritual health

This is an area of your life you work on when you are ready to look inward and connect with something larger than yourself, as this practice helps us understand the connectivity between ourselves and everything/everyone around us. It is necessary to give attention and thought to this area of the self in order to allow the completion of uniting body, mind and soul.

What does spirituality mean?

Spirituality is deeply personal and unique to every person, which people draw on to find purpose, meaning and connectedness. Verghese (2008, para 2) describes it well:

> Spirituality is a globally acknowledged concept. It involves belief and obedience to an all-powerful force usually called God, who controls the universe and the destiny of man. It involves the ways in which people fulfill what they hold to be the purpose of their lives, a search for the meaning of life and a sense of connectedness to the universe. The universality of spirituality extends across creed and culture. At the same time, spirituality is very much personal and unique to each person. It is a sacred realm of human experience. Spirituality produces in man qualities such as love, honesty, patience, tolerance, compassion, a sense of detachment, faith, and hope.

More useful than trying to formulate a universally 'correct' definition, looking at the most common attributes helps us understand how we can get in touch with what we need to enhance our spiritual health. According to Martsolf and Mickley (1998: 294–5), the five attributes are as follows:

1 **Meaning** The search for the meaning of life, discovering one's purpose in life, making sense of life's unpredictability and turn of events.
2 **Value** Often described as ultimate values – the fundamental beliefs and standards that a person regards as important, which have to do with the truth, worth of a thought, beauty and object or behaviour.
3 **Transcendence** To recognize and appreciate a dimension beyond the self, by gaining a deeper understanding of the self and its unlimited potential as an integral part of everything.
4 **Connecting** To embrace a connection with all things – God/Higher Power, the self, others, the environment and the cosmos.
5 **Becoming** An 'unfolding of life that demands reflection and experience; includes a sense of who one is and how one knows among other things'.

A person starts their spiritual journey by bringing attention to these attributes. Exploration and daily practice are the cornerstones to one's spiritual health.

How your spiritual health is connected to your mental and physical health

The most widely used method of experiencing transcendence is meditation. Meditation is a practice used to help people draw themselves inward and focus on the present moment. Generally, it takes place in a seated position with the eyes closed and can vary in terms of time, anywhere between two minutes and multiple hours. While there are many forms of meditation, the most common form is focusing your breath and/or chanting mantras (chanting a word or phrase) with the intention to let go of any thoughts that arise and bring the attention back to the present moment.

There has been an overwhelming amount of research on meditation practices that supports the mind–body–soul connection. Scientific technology such as brain imaging – electroencephalography (EEG), can now detect what is happening to the brain by seeing relaxation-related changes such as theta and alpha brain-wave frequencies in real time. Theta is when the brain wave increases while being awake but is internally focused, such as when daydreaming, and alpha is the frequency of brain wave when it is relaxed, yet alert. Both states are linked to an increased learning ability and an enhancement in the overall well-being of the self (Howard, 2022). Once a person adopts meditation as a regular part of life, it can be beneficial for the brain's health over the long term (Hardt, 2007).

Meditation also has effects on the physical body. Schneider and his colleagues (2012) conducted a study with men and women who had coronary heart disease. After five years the group that had integrated meditation as a daily practice showed a 48 per cent risk reduction in deaths, heart attacks and strokes, as well as a significant drop in blood pressure, and a significant reduction in psychosocial stress factors. Another study showed that having a daily mindful meditation practice has a positive effect on the brain and the immune function (Davidson et al, 2003). These findings demonstrate that even brief meditation sessions over relatively short periods have a measurable positive impact on multiple aspects of most people's well-being.

Connecting the mind, body and soul through coaching

Using the method of visualization is a great way to reach the body, mind and soul. Bringing awareness to the physical body, tapping into subconscious thoughts – mind, and allowing the presence of a powerful source usually referred to as God, energy and, in this case, light – soul, allows new discoveries within the self, release of built-up emotions and deep healing to take place. The method described below requires a coach to have presence and connectivity to their own spirituality.

CASE STUDY

Sofie was a client of mine who discovered her disempowering belief was that she was not worthy. Through many sessions together, the pattern of unworthiness was undoubtedly evident as every situation that caused a disturbance to her life led to that conclusion. Her question to me was, now what?

The next step was gaining clarity on where this belief was rooted and how to find forgiveness towards the moment that started this disempowering belief to form.

Through a visualization method, I took her through a process of discovery. What shows up can be surprising and although, as the coach, you may find yourself questioning your client's memories, it is important to trust their process. What comes up will lead them to where they need to go regardless of whether it makes sense to you or not.

The process

Coach: Close your eyes and take a deep breath.

(Take the breath with the client so that they can hear the slowed-down rhythm of breath that you want them to follow.)

I want you to envision yourself in a place that gives you extreme comfort. Whether that is at the beach with the waves gently coming in and the sun shining on your skin or sitting in a field with a light breeze blowing your way... *(let the client sit in this moment for a minute).*

Now I'm going to ask you questions and I want you to reply with the first answer that comes to your mind.

How old were you when you first started to believe that you were not worthy?

Sofie: Zero

Coach: Who is with you in that moment, is it your mother, your father, or someone else?

Sofie: My mother.

Coach: Can you tell me what's happening with your mother?

Sofie: I'm in her womb, I can hear her talking, she is telling a friend she's not sure she's happy with her pregnancy. She doesn't want me. [Starts crying]

Coach: Where do you feel this in the present moment, in or around your body?

Sofie: *(She pointed to her abdomen)* [Sofie has been suffering from stomach and intestinal pain for many years].

Coach: Can you describe what it feels like?

Sofie: It feels heavy.

Coach: If it had a shape what would it be?

Sofie: A circle.

Coach: Can you describe what this circle looks like, does it have a colour, is it soft or rough, sticky, gooey...

Sofie: It's black, hard, heavy, cold like a stone but has sharp edges coming out.

Coach: I want you to envision the strongest, most brilliant light coming from above, and I want you to take this light and infuse it into this black, heavy, cold, stone-like circle. I want you to keep putting light in, till you cannot see anything left of this circle. All you should be left with is pure light. I'll have my eyes closed with you, whenever you are ready open your eyes and let me know that you have opened them. [I keep my eyes closed to stay present and not shift the energy of the room to anything distracting]

[Five minutes later]

Sofie: I've opened my eyes. [Tears streaming down her face]

Coach: How do you feel now?

Sofie: Better, the heaviness is gone. I feel light, I feel good.

Coach: What do you think about what just happened?

Sofie: I understand now, but I'm angry at her. Why did she have me if she didn't want me?

Coach: You think that's true?

Sofie: I don't know, but it makes sense.

Once she gained clarity, there were still unresolved emotions about her discovery to explore. The process of forgiveness was essential to move forward. But first, she needed to learn what forgiveness meant. For many people forgiveness means to forget. The truth is, we do not forget. However, how we feel when we remember is what lets us know if we have truly forgiven. When one wants to forgive, they need to let go of the anger and find compassion for the one that wronged them, or for themselves.

When we hold on to not forgiving someone, the only person that gets hurt is ourselves.

The truth is, when you build a wall to protect yourself from that person, you are not only leaving that one person out. No one gets in. Which will create suffering for the self and perhaps for the people we love the most.

Because Sofie and I have worked together for a long time, she already understood the concept of forgiveness; to let go of anger and find compassion and was open to continuing the process. It is so important that the client is willing and ready for this process.

Coach: How would you feel about doing another visualization on forgiveness?

Sofie: Okay.

Coach: Please close your eyes and take a deep breath. I want you to go back to the place you felt deep comfort. The sun shining on your skin with a light breeze gently stroking your skin. Take a deep breath. [Guiding the breath by breathing with her]

I want you to envision yourself standing holding a crystal ball.

Look into the crystal ball, it's the moment you described earlier, of you in your mother's womb and she's talking to her friend about not wanting to have another baby, not wanting to have you.

Can you see it?

Sofie: Yes.

Coach: I want you to bring your attention to the most brilliant light coming from above. It's so powerful and so bright, direct it towards the crystal ball.

Infuse the crystal ball with the light. Keep bringing light into it until there's nothing left except a ball of light in your hands.

When you are done, open your eyes and let me know that you've opened them. I'll have my eyes closed with you.

[Five minutes later]

Sofie: I've opened my eyes.

Coach: Would you like to share what happened?

Sofie: I kept filling the ball, so much that it was too much to carry, and I dropped it. The light carried me, and I felt myself floating. I wanted to share this magnificent feeling, so I gave light to my mother, my grandfather, I even gave light to you. My mother was in a bad situation, she was scared. It wasn't about me. It was about her. She didn't know any better.

This realization allowed Sofie to find compassion for her mother and that permitted her to let go of the anger she was carrying.

Through this visualization method that brought the mind, body and soul into the process of self-discovery, Sofie now has an increased sense of self-worth and self-esteem. This has benefited her in many aspects of her life. She's been able to excel in her work life, as well as build healthy relationships with the people she cares most about.

Conclusion

By paying attention to the three areas of the self – body, mind, soul – the coach can recognize where there is neglect in their client's life. Once the process of nurturing the area in need takes place, the process of self-discovery slowly starts to unfold. What has been holding a person back in the first place becomes visible. By understanding that the body, mind and soul are one symbiotic entity and using the visualization method, one can find deep healing. The process of recognizing what your physical body needs and where your mind wanders, while adding the connection of the soul – the existence of something larger than us, allows us to live a more connected and fulfilling life with ourselves, others and everything around us.

References

Campbell, N, De Jesus, S and Prapavessis, H (2013) Physical fitness, in *Encyclopedia of Behavioral Medicine*, eds M D Gellman and J R Turner, pp 1486–9, Springer, New York, doi.org/10.1007/978-1-4419-1005-9_1167 (archived at https://perma.cc/XH7U-Y6S6)

Cleveland Clinic (2021) How much sleep do I need? Plan your sleep cycles to feel well rested, 25 February, health.clevelandclinic.org/how-much-sleep-do-i-need (archived at https://perma.cc/Q5AG-HW9R)

Colten, H R and Altevogt, B M (eds) (2006) *Sleep Disorders and Sleep Deprivation: An unmet public health problem*, The National Academies Press, Washington, DC

Davidson, K (2020) How can I improve my relationship with food? Healthline, 3 December, www.healthline.com/nutrition/fixing-a-bad-relationship-with-food (archived at https://perma.cc/T6GT-KBPZ)

Davidson, R J, Kabat-Zinn, J, Schumacher, J, Rosenkranz, M, Muller, D, Santorelli, S F, Urbanowski, F, Harrington, A, Bonus, K and Sheridan, J F (2003) Alterations in brain and immune function produced by mindfulness meditation, *Psychosomatic Medicine*, 65 (4), 564–70, doi.org/10.1097/01.psy.0000077505.67574.e3 (archived at https://perma.cc/YU8X-3EH4)

Ensari, I, Sandroff, B M and Motl, R W (2016) Effects of single bouts of walking exercise and yoga on acute mood symptoms in people with multiple sclerosis, *International Journal of MS Care*, 18(1), 1–8, doi.org/10.7224/1537-2073.2014-104

Ferguson, S (2020) Yes, mental illness can cause physical symptoms – here's why, *Healthline*, 30 June, www.healthline.com/health/mental-health/mental-illness-can-cause-physical-symptoms (archived at https://perma.cc/99UC-E7G3)

Hardt, J (2007) *The Art of Smart Thinking*, Biocybernaut Press, Sedona, AZ

Harvard Health Publishing (2021) The gut-brain connection, 19 April, www.health.harvard.edu/diseases-and-conditions/the-gut-brain-connection (archived at https://perma.cc/JSX5-7YN8)

Howard, A (2022) How does meditation affect your brain waves? *PsychCentral*, 18 April, psychcentral.com/health/meditation-brain-waves (archived at https://perma.cc/9UB5-WXNV)

Leech, J (2022) 10 Reasons to get more sleep, *Healthline*, 6 January, www.healthline.com/nutrition/10-reasons-why-good-sleep-is-important#7.-Supports-a-healthy-immune-system (archived at https://perma.cc/MF96-QAUH)

Marks, H (2021) Stress symptoms, *WebMD*, 19 August, www.webmd.com/balance/stress-management/stress-symptoms-effects_of-stress-on-the-body (archived at https://perma.cc/47UB-SUF9)

Martsolf, D and Mickley, J (1998) The concept of spirituality in nursing theories: Differing world-views and extent of focus, *Journal of Advanced Nursing*, 27 (2), 294–303, doi.org/10.1046/j.1365-2648.1998.00519.x (archived at https://perma.cc/2DBF-QSUE)

Nelis, D, Kotsou, I, Quoidbach, J, Hansenne, M, Weytens, F, Dupuis, P and Mikolajczak, M (2011) Increasing emotional competence improves psychological and physical well-being, social relationships, and employability, *Emotion*, 11 (2), 354–66, doi.org/10.1037/a0021554 (archived at https://perma.cc/66NE-V7GX)

Schneider, R H, Grim, C E, Rainforth, M V, Kotchen, T, Nidich, S I, Gaylord-King, C, Salerno, J W, Kotchen, J M and Alexander, C N (2012) Stress reduction in the secondary prevention of cardiovascular disease: Randomized controlled trial of transcendental meditation and health education in Blacks, *Circulation: Cardiovascular Quality and Outcomes*, 5 (6), 750–8, doi.org/10.1161/CIRCOUTCOMES.112.967406 (archived at https://perma.cc/7AJM-XKXV)

Semeco, A (2023) The top 10 benefits of regular exercise, *Healthline*, 9 February, www.healthline.com/nutrition/10-benefits-of-exercise (archived at https://perma.cc/7HSP-QRFS)

Stanszus, L S, Frank, P and Geiger, S M (2019) Healthy eating and sustainable nutrition through mindfulness? Mixed method results of a controlled intervention study, *Appetite*, 141, 104325, doi.org/10.1016/j.appet.2019.104325 (archived at https://perma.cc/E6FN-VV7A)

Verghese, A (2008) Spirituality and mental health, *Indian Journal of Psychiatry*, 50 (4), 233–7, doi.org/10.4103/0019-5545.44742 (archived at https://perma.cc/HNT9-KHTU)

Walton, A G (2016) 7 Ways sleep affects the brain (and what happens if it doesn't get enough), *Forbes*, 9 December, www.forbes.com/sites/alicegwalton/2016/12/09/7-ways-sleep-affects-the-brain-and-what-happens-if-it-doesnt-get-enough (archived at https://perma.cc/4DHM-RQYN)

Warren, J M, Smith, N and Ashwell, M (2017) A structured literature review on the role of mindfulness, mindful eating and intuitive eating in changing eating behaviours: Effectiveness and associated potential mechanisms, *Nutrition Research Reviews*, 30 (2), 272–83, doi.org/10.1017/S0954422417000154 (archived at https://perma.cc/5A2K-VLKB)

13

Neuroscience-based coaching

JOAN SWART

ABSTRACT

Exponential advances in the study of neuroscience continue to increase our understanding of the mechanisms of many psychological conditions and experiences. Scientists and helping professionals progressively view human well-being and performance as the outcomes of a balanced neuropsychological functioning that includes healthy brain–body connections and balanced natural hormones. Based on this new, evidence-based knowledge, coaches can apply simple steps to improve their clients' lives sustainably.

Introduction

Our knowledge and understanding of neuroscience have increased tremendously over the past decade and continue to do so. On the back of rapid advances in technology such as computing speed, data processing and storage capacity, measurement sensitivity and *in vivo* observations, we can apply newly discovered information to many areas of human functioning and well-being. We have a better appreciation of how change occurs, how it can be set in motion, and change becomes part of our everyday lives to propel us to our real potential.

As we see repeatedly in this book and other resources, coaching is a process guided by a professional to help clients initiate and sustain change that is aligned with their goals and values. The brain's structures and brain–body connection are incredibly powerful to enable surviving and thriving. The brain is a connection machine! Constantly connecting inner experiences, e.g., thoughts, feelings, beliefs and memories, with the external environment through behaviour and biological processes facilitates constant feedback.

No two brains are wired the same. Each brain sees the world according to its own wiring. The brain hardwires everything it can as a precaution to speed up automatic reactions when needed. While it is difficult to deconstruct existing wiring, we can create new wiring by encouraging the development of different neural pathways that affect our habits, thoughts and well-being.

As neurobiology and neuropsychology are vastly complex and integrated systems, this chapter limits the scope to an overview of aligning, co-regulating and rewiring brain–body connections and utilizing just two natural hormones that play a role in our daily performance and relationships – cortisol and oxytocin.

Aligning, co-regulating and rewiring brain–body connections

The mind–body or brain–body connection is the link between a person's thoughts, feelings, beliefs, behaviour, physical sensations, and mental and physical health that is in constant interaction with their environment. As we participate in interpersonal exchanges and impact events around us, those experiences feed back to our brain–body systems to reinforce or counteract existing processes. This 'master system' encompasses everything we believe, do and experience. As a coach, we have a powerful impact on our client's systems, not only through the guidance we provide, but also our interaction with their nervous system.

Co-regulating the autonomic nervous system

The autonomic nervous system (ANS) regulates involuntary physiological processes such as the heart rate, breathing, digestion and sexual arousal that developed through evolution to support the survival of our species. It is made up of three divisions, namely the sympathetic, parasympathetic and enteric nervous systems (Waxenbaum, Reddy and Varacallo, 2021). The sympathetic nervous system (SNS) manages the fight-flight-freeze responses of elevated readiness and attention or shutdown. The parasympathetic nervous system (PNS) looks after the rest-and-digest processes that restart and recover optimal or normal functioning. The primary role of the enteric nervous system (ENS) is to enable muscles to contract, relax, digest and absorb nutrients, and regulate blood flow to fulfil these functions. In other words, the SNS kicks in to ready our defences when under threat, while the PNS and ENS manage our ongoing energy and recovery and automatic functions, respectively, which can only work optimally when the SNS is not triggered. For instance, the SNS takes over many resources when we believe we are in danger, which hampers the normal functioning that our PNS and ENS constantly manage.

According to polyvagal perspectives, social functions developed and strengthened over time to regulate and support a healthy nervous system, that is, reactions that are appropriate responses to real threats (Porges, 2021). In other words, sociality moderates the activation of the nervous system that supports mobilization (or immobilization) otherwise. Such a fight-flight-freeze response can become habitual or untimely when experiencing chronic or acute stressors, shut down the brain's thought and reasoning processes, heighten anxiety and fear-based emotions, and prompt instinctive action or shutdown (play possum). It heightens distrust and prevents stable moods that are a constructive basis for relationships and change.

Therefore, an insightful coach inherently recognizes the client's nervous system state and syncs it with their own to guide the client back to their 'safe' space, the rest-and-digest condition, away from fight-or-flight (mobilization), and freeze/shutdown (immobilization). In this safe space, the PNS and ENS are fully resourced while the SNS is in a resting state. What can we do to smooth yet simplify this process? The theory quickly becomes very complex and comprehensive, but here are a few simple ideas to try with your client:

- **Observe** your client carefully – their energy, pace, expressions, movements, posture in congruence with their words.

- **Explore** Attune your state of mind and feeling to their expressed nervous system responses. Strengthen your social engagement by synchronizing your face–heart system with your client's. Be present and attentive to your client's state of mind and adjust your pace, tone, energy and posture to theirs, but slightly dialled down if needed.

- **Focus** on sending signals of safety: send signals of safety continuously by showing compassion and empathy through a kind voice, words and gestures. Remind them that they are safe, protected and in control.

- **Focus** on your observations: acknowledge what you observe in your client and ask for clarification if needed.

- **Consistency** Effective co-regulation starts with learning to be self-aware and self-regulate.

- **Movement**
  o Use your distance and movement deliberately to reflect the client's perception of safety. Facing a client head-on in close proximity can be threatening to them, as can sudden or erratic movements. You may want to give the client a choice of seating arrangements when starting an in-person meeting, or, when online, observe the gaze and distance from the screen that seem to make the client most comfortable.
  o Try subtle and controlled movements such as tapping with your client to have them come out of an immobilization state. Ask them what movement they want to make spontaneously. Get feedback of their experience.

o   Encourage mobilization (movement) as a voluntary behaviour instead of an instinctive (defensive) reaction. Ask the client what movement they instinctively feel the need to make, encourage them to demonstrate, do it with them if possible, and observe and ask for feedback on their experience. For instance, did the movement change how they are feeling?

When co-regulating the nervous system, the primary objective is to bring the client to a position of safety where they can make informed decisions based on logic and reasoning instead of survival. Trust and socialization then form the platform from which to move forward. Always remember that 'talking helps but is not enough'. Engage your client in other ways too, such as movement, and 'synchronous and reciprocal interaction' is a strong neural exercise that strengthens the safety systems. This simply means to subtly copy your client's behaviour (synchronicity) and reacting appropriately (with presence, interest and non-judgement) to their words and behaviour (reciprocal).

Aligning the prefrontal cortex, limbic system and hypothalamus

We have talked about the fight-flight-freeze (PNS), rest-and-digest (SNS) and autonomic (ENS) states of the human nervous system in the previous section, and how to move up the ladder to the state of social safety through co-regulation. Aligning the prefrontal cortex, limbic system and hypothalamus activities of the brain is somewhat similar.

The prefrontal cortex is responsible for reasoning, problem solving, logical decision making, comprehension, personality control and personality expression. Optimal activation requires felt stability and safety. The limbic system houses emotional life and supports behavioural responses, emotional motivation, long-term memory formation and fear conditioning. The hypothalamus is the body's smart control and coordinating centre, regulating metabolic processes and activities of the autonomic nervous system. By synthesizing, releasing, stimulating or inhibiting the secretion of natural hormones, the hypothalamus also controls body temperature, hunger, thirst, sleep, fatigue, circadian rhythms and attachment behaviours. Importantly, it also reacts to distress signals by activating automatic motivational states that drive instinctive behaviour. Although scientists have made a three-way separation between the instinctive-emotional-thoughtful mind to help understand the different functions and processes better, the interplay and overlap between these systems are much more complex (Levine, 2017). Nevertheless, it is helpful for coaches to be aware that these three main centres exist and that an imbalance or overactivation of the reactive and instinctive part can reduce or block the prefrontal cortex from an optimal role.

For example, a client who is intensely emotionally reactive may find it difficult to formulate or believe logical thoughts and prevent emotions from driving their behaviour. Also, someone who is triggered by fear may instinctively shut down or withdraw without deliberate awareness or understanding. For a client to function effectively and be in the best position to pursue their goals, make sound decisions and implement change, they must be in a safe and stable space where their instinctive-emotional-thoughtful mind is in harmony.

Keeping in mind that it may be a slow and deliberate process to create awareness and balance all parts, here are a few easy ideas that a coach can use to help their client achieve a balanced state:

- **Observe** the 'whole' client, including inconsistencies in their words, body language and other behaviour.

- **Explore** and acknowledge the client's state of mind and difficulties they feel when sitting in front of you. Ask for confirmation and clarity about what you have observed. Acknowledge and normalize their inner experiences. For instance, 'You may believe that it was your fault, that you failed yourself. But what do you think could have happened if you didn't act in that way?'

- **Focus** on their *felt* experience, and whether that is interfering with their thinking and reasoning. Use effective questioning (see Chapters 9 and 35) to explore and understand the deeper beliefs(s) underlying an issue, including the attached emotions. If there appears to be a discord, slowly (and safely) integrate the two through careful reflection. In other words, if they do not believe alternative helpful thoughts on an emotional level, they will not truly change.

- **Move** at the pace of the client and do not hesitate to take a step back when needed.

- **Constantly** check the effect(s) the process has on you, as the coach, and consider your competency to safely guide the client.

Remembering the concepts of the instinctive-emotional-thoughtful mind will help you understand when your client seems to be stuck and unable to access their ability to logically reason and formulate and implement alternative thinking. Quite possibly, they need to move out of their instinctive and emotionally reactive mindsets first, before being able to regulate their moods and behaviour and change their thinking to complete the process.

Neuroplasticity: rewiring the brain

Neuroplasticity refers to the ability of the brain to change in terms of the strength of connections, activity of receptors, new neurons, density of white/grey matter and compensating for injury. In the context of coaching, it is important to note that the brain can physically change through 'self-directed neuroplasticity' (Bosman, 2021). So, what is this, how does it work and what does it mean in coaching?

In his book, *The Mind and the Brain*, US psychiatrist and world expert in the field of neuroplasticity and its applications Dr Jeffrey M Schwartz explains that 'The power of willful activity to shape the brain remains the working principle not only of early brain development, but also of brain function as an ongoing, living process' (Schwartz and Begley, 2002: 130). According to Hebbian learning, neurons that fire together, wire together (Shamay-Tsoory, 2021). When using neurons and brain areas, the activity raises the local energy and blood flow, which increases strength and recovery. It also encourages the same pathways to be used in the future. In other words, the repetition of thoughts and actions form and reinforce a neural network that can change the structure and functioning of the brain, however subtly, thereby establishing new habits, changes and abilities. The neurons or nerve cells in the brain compensate and readjust their potential in response to new situations or changing demands from the environment.

In coaching, you can utilize the principles of neuroplasticity by exploring with your client one or more habits that are holding them back, and helping them understand the triggers, blocks and negative effects. Clarifying the benefits of changing a habit generates the motivation to invest effort in repeating the desired behaviour or thoughts. With your client, identify small parts and actions steps by using the ADE method to add, delete, edit habits that block progress. Helping them to implement and master one step at a time makes it easier to stick to the process and repeat it to maximize the neuroplasticity effect. The process is best initiated when stress is managed to allow for longer-lasting and wider-ranging effects on the brain. To aid and reinforce the change process, clients can also apply positive self-talk, affirmations and visualizations to imprint enabling messages, which, over time, lead to positive beliefs as a basis for new behaviour and habits.

Balancing natural hormones

Scientists have identified more than 70 natural protein and steroid hormones in the human body. With functions involved in almost all biological processes, including reproduction, energy production, body growth, metabolism, and development of the brain and nervous system, hormones are also integral in regulating thoughts, emotions and behaviour by increasing the likelihood of specific inclinations (Nelson and Kriegsfeld, 2017). Hormones are the messengers that coordinate a person's physiology and behaviour with the ultimate goal of ensuring survival of the individual and species. For instance, when faced with an acute threat, the sympathetic nervous system activates and releases the fight-flight-freeze hormones adrenaline and noradrenaline. A chain reaction of arousal, including increases in heart rate, blood pressure and breathing rate prepares the body for action. At the same time, a host of other hormones determine your inclination in how you view the situation, your level of aggression, decision making, risk taking, motivational drive and perspective, among others.

In our day-to-day stress responses and connections with others, two hormones, cortisol and oxytocin, play an important role in our mental wellness and interpersonal relationships. Scientists found a mutual regulation between these substances that can offset the negative effects of stress and better balance our defence and attraction/care inclinations (Li, Hassett and Seng, 2019).

Regulating cortisol

High levels of stress, especially if prolonged or repetitive, are linked to distress and a lower quality of life. Cortisol is the natural hormone that plays a vital role in maintaining health and safety but must be managed in a fairly narrow range to be advantageous. Levels that are below optimal can present as chronic fatigue, while the opposite manifests as a cluster of risk factors that include high blood pressure, obesity, cardiovascular disease and type 2 diabetes. A prolonged elevation of cortisol is also associated with psychological distress, including depression (Nandam et al, 2019), anxiety (Lenze et al, 2011) and anger and hostility (Leggett et al, 2015). Lasting above-median cortisol levels can also be a biomarker of trauma exposure and reflect a higher risk of post-traumatic stress disorder (PTSD) occurrence (Inslicht et al, 2006).

Fortunately, regulating cortisol levels within healthy bounds can be fairly simple, depending on the motivation of a person to develop and sustain healthy habits. Guidance of a coach often makes a significant difference in a client's efforts, progress and resilience. First, a client who understands the role and effects of cortisol has a better awareness of the importance of managing stress to improve their daily lives (Brann, 2022). A coach can help increase this knowledge and explore the occurrence and impact of stress on a client to prioritize and select changes that are unique to the person's situation and lifestyle. The main areas of impact are the following.

- **Self-care and relaxation** A person cannot drink from an empty cup, and neither can you coach effectively without sufficient personal resources, including energy, presence and balance. Make sure to schedule self-care and relaxation time into your days and explore the same with your clients. Whether it is a hobby, travel, spending time with family and friends, or something else that rejuvenates you, monitor what works and build a habit (see Chapter 4).

- **Nutrition and hydration** The most helpful set-up is for a client to set and follow basic nutritional targets that are aligned with their weight and health goals, physical activity and other values. There are good, free apps available to guide this process. At an elemental level, look at monitoring the macro nutrients consumed daily – protein, carbohydrates, and fats, sugar and water intake. Eat 'clean' (know the ingredients of what you eat and avoid processed food), limit your sugar intake, and drink enough water (the NHS (2021) recommends 6–8 cups of fluids per day).

- **Mindfulness** Guru Jon Kabat-Zinn (1994: 24) defines mindfulness as 'awareness that arises through paying attention, on purpose, in the present moment, non-judgmentally'. As such, mindfulness is an attitude or deliberate attentional state that enhances acceptance and brings about various positive psychological effects (Keng, Smoski and Robins, 2011). These include an experience of well-being, emotional modulation and behaviour regulation that are all linked to preventing spikes of cortisol release (Turakitwanakan, Mekseepralard and Busarakumtragul, 2013). Brief and simple breathing and visualization exercises are a good way to start, as well as practising 'everyday mindfulness', or immersing yourself in common activities such as eating and walking in nature while paying attention to all five senses (see Chapters 15 and 25).

- **Recovery** Many studies have shown a significant bidirectional association between sleep quality and stress (cortisol) (Hirotsu, Tufik and Andersen, 2015). Definitely explore with your client their sleep habits and make changes or seek medical advice if problematic.

- **Recognize and manage triggers** Responding to triggers is often an automatic reaction meant to protect us from harm. Help your client identify those events and circumstances that repeatedly cause them stress. Probe deeper with them to find alternative ways to avoid or otherwise deal with these triggers.

- **Balance your work and personal life** Balancing work and personal life aims to create variety and create room for recovery and rejuvenation to prevent chronic and acute stress and burnout (see Chapter 24). Explore a client's routine, their stress cycle and roots of elevated stress. Sometimes stress is inevitable, but by limiting high-stress time and making sure that it is alternated with rest and recovery, lasting effects can be avoided.

- **Live according to your values** Any conflict between your personal life (actions) and values will likely cause stress. Discuss with your client their priorities using the Wheel of Life tool (see Chapter 20) or a semi-structured enquiry (questions covering different life areas). Identify their most important values (individual beliefs that motivate people to act) linked to one or more of these life areas. Look for ways to help them better align their values, priorities and actions.

- **Social interaction, touch and intimacy** Research has proved what we all instinctively understand: healthy social interaction, touch and intimacy help to lower and recover from stress (Ditzen et al, 2019). Listen to what your client shares about their relationships, whether their parents, partner, children, friends or even pets. How healthy and active is their contact with others? What is the scope to make positive changes?

These are a few simple ideas to investigate and implement with a client, depending on their particular needs and sources of stress. Everyone has a different stress profile and tolerance, and deals with it differently, so aim to find the routines and habits that work best for each individual client. Lowering habitual cortisol will almost certainly make a positive impact relatively quickly that will be noticeable in their overall health, well-being and functioning.

Harnessing oxytocin

Oxytocin is the natural hormone that is produced in the hypothalamus, a part deep in the centre of the brain, and released into the bloodstream with its main function being to form a bond between mother and child, generate sexual excitement and fall in love. Also known as the 'love hormone', oxytocin plays an enabling role in social bonding with a moderating effect on stress regulation, social anxiety and mental health (Olff et al, 2013).

The body's capacity and inclination to produce and release oxytocin stems from childhood experiences, especially related to attachment to a primary caregiver, which are perceived as secure or insecure. When subjected to chronic insecurity, including neglect, abuse and instability, children develop a default style that is either anxious-insecure, avoidant-insecure or disorganized-insecure. Their oxytocin release becomes dysregulated or resistant, and they have problems with bonding, trusting and interacting with other people, which mostly persist into adulthood.

So, oxytocin is involved in building trust and social bonding. Levels are suppressed when seeing threats and fear. On the flip side, feelings of care, safety, trust and belonging trigger the release of oxytocin. Trust makes interaction safer and more effective, as the body and mind are more receptive to new ideas, cooperation and exploring mutual benefits. Instead of being consumed by defensive reactions, our brain is freed up to engage in planning, decision making and creativity. When conditions of trust occur, the activity of the amygdala, the brain's processing centre of fear-related emotions, is reduced with the release of oxytocin.

So, how is oxytocin relevant to coaching? The answer is very simple. As coaches, we would like to create the conditions that will favour optimal levels of oxytocin in our clients:

- We set a calming environment and relationship based on trust, ethical principles and consistency.
- We observe and explore the client's natural inclination to trust the coach or anyone else, and how, when and which defensive mechanisms they habitually employ in interpersonal interactions.

- We convey unconditional acceptance and empathy, which does not mean that we agree with everything the client is saying or doing, but just that we acknowledge where they are now, their experiences, and that they genuinely want to do the best they can.
- We recognize the impact we and our coaching have on them, and the commitment to work to align their nervous system and cognitive, emotional and instinctive centres of their brain, so that they feel trust and a lesser need to engage in defensive behaviour.

With ongoing and deliberate practices to engage and integrate all their experiences, clients will gradually become more accustomed to developing a lived sense of trust on all levels. Oxytocin will then play a more consistent role in their lives and interactions with others.

Conclusion

Just a few years ago, few people considered the potential of applying neuroscience principles in coaching. Today, the pool of knowledge has increased so much and proliferated across different speciality fields, providing coaches with a more nuanced way to connect with their clients. We now consider more deeply the possibility that clients may have blocks and imbalances that prevent them from reasoning, making logical decisions, changing their thinking and connecting constructively with others.

They may be in a state of fight-or-flight (mobilization), withdrawal or shutdown (immobilization), intense emotions or instinctive reactions that rule their behaviour at the time and make engaging their prefrontal cortex difficult. An effective coach takes SMALL steps with their client, OBSERVE their reactions, constantly ASK for feedback, and RECOGNIZE their position and progress – SOAR. Using neuroscience, a coach can help their clients SOAR.

References

Bosman, M (2021) Self-directed neuroplasticity: Change your life by changing your focus, Strategic Leadership Institute, 18 August, www.stratleader.net/sli-blog/self-directed-neuroplasticity (archived at https://perma.cc/KT23-CQCQ)

Brann, A (2022) Neuroscience for Coaches: How coaches and managers can use the latest insights to benefit clients and teams, 3rd edn, Kogan Page, London

Ditzen, B, Germann, J, Meuwly, N, Bradbury, T N, Bodenmann, G and Heinrichs, M (2019) Intimacy as related to cortisol reactivity and recovery in couples undergoing psychosocial stress, Psychosomatic Medicine, 81, 16–25, doi.org/10.1097/PSY.0000000000000633 (archived at https://perma.cc/EJ3F-ALB7)

Hirotsu, C, Tufik, S and Andersen, M L (2015) Interactions between sleep, stress, and metabolism: From physiological to pathological conditions, *Sleep Science*, 8 (3), 143–52, doi.org/10.1016/j.slsci.2015.09.002 (archived at https://perma.cc/5NES-2NJ5)

Inslicht, S S, Marmar, C R, Neylan, T C, Metzler, T J, Hart, S L, Otte, C, McCaslin, S E, Larkin, G L, Hyman, K B and Baum, A (2006) Increased cortisol in women with intimate partner violence-related posttraumatic stress disorder, *Annals of the New York Academy of Sciences*, 1071 (1), 428–9, doi.org/10.1196/annals.1364.035 (archived at https://perma.cc/453Q-HUQM)

Kabat-Zinn, J (1994) *Wherever You Go There You Are: Mindfulness meditation in everyday life*, Hyperion, New York

Keng, S-L, Smoski, M J and Robins, C J (2011) Effects of mindfulness on psychological health: A review of empirical studies, *Clinical Psychology Review*, 31 (6), 1041–56, doi.org/10.1016/j.cpr.2011.04.006 (archived at https://perma.cc/YV2P-C2H9)

Leggett, A, Zarit, S H, Kim, K, Almeida, D M and Klein, L C (2015) Depressive mood, anger, and daily cortisol of caregivers on high- and low-stress days, *The Journals of Gerontology: Series B*, 70 (6), 820–9, doi.org/10.1093/geronb/gbu070 (archived at https://perma.cc/RZ9X-BZBL)

Lenze, E J, Mantella, R C, Shi, P, Goate, A M, Nowotny, P, Butters, M A, Andreescu, C, Thompson, P A and Rollman, B L (2011) Elevated cortisol in older adults with generalized anxiety disorder is reduced by treatment: A placebo-controlled evaluation of escitalopram, *The American Journal of Geriatric Psychiatry*, 19 (5), 482–90, doi.org/10.1097/JGP.0b013e3181ec806c (archived at https://perma.cc/F9QB-BXWB)

Levine, D S (2017) Modeling the instinctive-emotional-thoughtful mind, *Cognitive Systems Research*, 45, 82–94, doi.org/10.1016/j.cogsys.2017.05.002 (archived at https://perma.cc/X5HK-9K6H)

Li, Y, Hassett, A L and Seng, J S (2019) Exploring the mutual regulation between oxytocin and cortisol as a marker of resilience, *Archives of Psychiatric Nursing*, 33 (2), 164–73, doi.org/10.1016/j.apnu.2018.11.008 (archived at https://perma.cc/X39X-WXAH)

Nandam, L S, Brazel, M, Zhou, M and Jhaveri, D J (2019) Cortisol and major depressive disorder – translating findings from humans to animal models and back, *Frontiers in Psychiatry*, 10, 974, doi.org/10.3389/fpsyt.2019.00974 (archived at https://perma.cc/366M-RP8E)

Nelson, R J and Kriegsfeld, L J (2017) Hormones and behavior: Basic concepts, in *An Introduction to Behavioral Endocrinology*, 5th edn, pp 435–54, Sinauer Associates, Sunderland, MA

NHS (2021) Water, drinks and your health, National Health Service, www.nhs.uk/live-well/eat-well/food-guidelines-and-food-labels/water-drinks-nutrition/ (archived at https://perma.cc/M5K2-DQXZ)

Olff, M, Frijling, J L, Kubzansky, L D, Bradley, B, Ellenbogen, M A, Cardoso, C, Bartz, J A, Yee, J R and van Zuiden, M (2013) The role of oxytocin in social bonding, stress regulation and mental health: An update on the moderating effects of context and interindividual differences, *Psychoneuroendocrinology*, 38 (9), 1883–94, doi.org/10.1016/j.psyneuen.2013.06.019 (archived at https://perma.cc/Y2DK-JJ9C)

Porges, S W (2021) Polyvagal theory: A biobehavioral journey to sociality, *Comprehensive Psychoneuroendocrinology*, 7, 100069, doi.org/10.1016/j.cpnec.2021.100069 (archived at https://perma.cc/HAQ4-KAMB)

Schwartz, J M and Begley, S (2002) *The Mind and The Brain: Neuroplasticity and the power of mental force*, ReganBooks, New York

Shamay-Tsoory, S G (2021) Brains that fire together, wire together: Interbrain plasticity underlies learning in social interactions, *The Neuroscientist*, 28 (6), 543–51, doi.org/10.1177/1073858421996682 (archived at https://perma.cc/SW6N-K7S4)

Turakitwanakan, W, Mekseepralard, C and Busarakumtragul, P (2013) Effects of mindfulness meditation on serum cortisol of medical students, *Journal of the Medical Association of Thailand*, 96 (Suppl 1), S90–5

Waxenbaum, J A, Reddy, V and Varacallo, M (2021) *Anatomy, autonomic nervous system*, StatPearls Publishing, Treasure Island, FL, www.ncbi.nlm.nih.gov/books/NBK539845 (archived at https://perma.cc/BA4Q-NNJ3)

14

Masculine/feminine energy aspects in coaching

KASSANDRA PARKER

ABSTRACT

We all have the same amount of time in our days, and as coaches we know how important energy management is. But do we think about that energy? Are you aware that you hold four distinct energies within your body? These are healthy feminine, healthy masculine, and shadow feminine and shadow masculine energies. Are your clients aware of these internal energies? Have you discovered how to recognize those energies showing up within you and how to shift them to work for you? This chapter helps you understand what masculine/feminine energy is, how it affects us, and gives you the tools to notice an imbalance so that you can guide your clients towards a healthy balance.

Introduction

Imagine being able to tap into energies to help you with your life, health, connection to the self, and the overall sense of yourself in the world. This chapter is about helping your clients learn to recognize and harness their masculine/feminine energies. We all too often live in a way that is disconnected from our passions, our nature, our values and our energy, causing us to feel misaligned in our careers, love, relation to others, relation to self, spirituality, fitness and other areas. It is important to appreciate that our inner masculine/feminine energy has the ability to impact all of these areas and how we can help initiate change. Your clients benefit and become empowered through your questions, presence and practices that show an embodiment of the understanding of masculine/feminine energy. To best utilize the knowledge of masculine/feminine energies and optimize its effects through coaching, I define the concept, how to incorporate it into your session, and how it benefits the client.

What is masculine/feminine energy?

Caro (2019, para 2) reminds us that masculine and feminine energies are present in every human brain.

> There are functions of the brain that can be associated with masculine energy: rationality, logic, linear thinking and understanding. There are also functions of the brain associated with feminine energy: feelings of nurturing, caring, compassion, love and emotional qualities. Masculine/feminine energy is not about gender.

Whether female, male or non-binary, each person contains a mixture of masculine and feminine energy. And we can shift these energies within ourselves to help feel more aligned and balanced. When looking at the ancient Chinese philosophy of yin and yang, it is taught that the yang energy is masculine and is characterized by strength and power; whereas the yin energy is feminine, characterized by nurturing and gentleness. Chinese medicine holds that it is in the balance of the yang and yin, opposite energies, that each person connects to their life force (Li, 2018). The masculine and feminine energies play a large part in what balances every person. A misbalance causes misalignment, leading to the feeling that something is lacking in one's life. The typical qualities and expressions of the four energies are indicated in Figure 14.1.

Helping your client to look at these four energies – healthy feminine, shadow feminine, healthy masculine and shadow masculine – within themselves, and understanding how awareness of these energies in misbalance can bring light to their limitations, will allow for a life with fewer barriers and more abundance.

FIGURE 14.1 The four quadrants of feminine and masculine energies

Healthy feminine	Healthy masculine
Open	Directive
Inspired by love/heart-oriented	Driven by purpose/goal- or mind-oriented
Creative	Structured
Energy of creation/life/birth	Energy of stillness
Always changing/spontaneous/fluid (like the ocean)	Constant/solid/unwavering (like a mountain)
Intuitive	Present
Nurturing	Leader
Receiver	Giver
Soft/sensual	Strong/focused
Emotional	Rational
Patient and empathic	Confident and competitive
Loves to be seen, acknowledged	Loves to see, admire
Shadow (or unhealthy) feminine	**Shadow (or unhealthy) masculine**
Needy	Controlling (different than directive/purposeful)
Whiny	Aggressive
Jealous	Sometimes physically abusive
Emotionally manipulative	Dominated by ego
Deceitful, purposely misleading	Misogynistic, homophobic
Exploitative dependence	Sexual violence
Helplessness, compliance	Avoidance of emotions, callousness
Victim role	Persecutor role

Discovering a harmonious balance

It is not about balancing the masculine and feminine energies to be equal in each person. Most people actually have an ideal balance that is more feminine or more masculine. Rather it is first about helping your client recognize when their energies are not in a healthy pattern, as well as when they are out of their ideal masculine/feminine balance. Then it is about helping them to find a harmonious balance between the healthy feminine and the heathy masculine that works for each area of their life, keeping in mind that the ideal balance may differ from one area of their life to another. A female client may be at their ideal balance heavily in their feminine mode in their relationship, but closer to equal feminine/masculine energy in their career for example. So, 'learning to move fluidly between our two [energies] can improve our lives, relationships and careers in many ways' (Marianetti, 2016).

Being aware of masculine/feminine energy is important when we first start helping our clients produce a harmonious relationship with the self. When we work with clients towards their goals, helping them set steps, and achieving those steps, we are utilizing their masculine energy of goal-directness. This tends to be very common, as our society values masculine energy as it can lead to producing measurable external goals that can enhance our lives. However, for the client who is struggling to connect with their feminine energy, more masculine exercises, such as setting external goals, can actually push this client further into an energy imbalance, as they continue to overuse/reinforce the one side, often at the expense of the other.

Giving your client exercises that encourage them to value the internal heart-centred work to promote self-love, connecting to their heart and validating emotions of their inner child, can allow your client to shift towards a more feminine energy. To honour their inner child's deep emotions opens a doorway to reconnect to their heart and the vulnerable emotions that they have been covering up, leading to creating an unhealthy balance of energy (Garza, 2017). A powerful exercise to acknowledge the inner child is having your client put a picture of themselves from a pivotal age in their home to look at, daily affirming that child's emotions and sending them love.

It is also important when helping a client to reconnect with their feminine energy to bring in exercises that allow for more opportunity for creation, flow and receiving, as these are practices that bring about more feminine energy. Some examples of exercises for this are creating art, dance and breath work.

CASE STUDY 1
Recognizing and increasing feminine energy

This reminds me of a client, Katra*, whom I coached for nearly two years. She came to me for career reasons, as a few years before she had quit her high-paying job of working long hours and doing very structured number-focused (masculine energy-focused) work. She had benefited from the masculine energy in her that had helped her to climb the ladder in business, achieve her goals, make a lot of money and support her family. However, she had feelings of resentment and fear when reflecting on this part of her past and she did not know why at first.

Working together with a strong focus on the client's own self-reflection and empowerment, which was mostly accomplished through thoughtful questions and exercises, it became clear that Katra was too much embedded in her masculine energy. The questions and exercises were around expanding the client's perception of certain events and how, in this case, she would have benefited from being more attached to her feminine energy. I will expand on this more as we move on.

In our sessions I focused on three things: her body language, the words she said and the words she did not say (what a client repeatedly avoids can also be very telling). Katra, like many of us, was raised to value goals that others could see, that others could validate. She was also indirectly taught that emotions would slow down her success (basically to fear vulnerability). As we worked together, and I continued to introduce more feminine, heart-centred perspectives and thought processes, Katra started to notice how she was avoiding this feminine energy within herself and how it was leading to her feeling of disconnect and imbalance. I offered questions such as 'when did you start valuing logical thinking more than emotional feeling?' I continually encouraged her to come back to her feelings. Katra was heavily invested in her masculine energy, valuing the external goals over the internal, more emotional, ones. As we worked together, Katra began seeing a pattern of validating the masculine energy in herself and in others, while simultaneously devaluing the feminine energy. Her increased awareness of her imbalance and how it was negatively affecting her life was a very important first step to take ownership of her energy and create a desire for the shift towards a healthier balance.

I teach my clients pieces of masculine/feminine energy balance when it is relevant to their individual growth, and then, almost always, they ask for more as they start to see the benefit of this knowledge. Katra, as with all of my clients, noticed when her energy was leaning more towards masculine or feminine and she started to ask when she was unsure. Exposure to masculine/feminine energy in this way during coaching allows the sessions to remain client-centred with you focusing on coaching (not teaching) the individual client, while also empowering them through knowledge, when and how they ask for it, that applies directly to them.

With a shift in her mindset to value and welcome more feminine energy, Katra was open to incorporating exercises that encouraged her to embody more feminine energy, such as free dance and creating art, both of which she used to love. She went on to be a dance teacher and opened her own studio. She saw the shift in her energy as she connected deeper with her emotions. She expressed enjoying the benefit of embodying this soft feminine energy by incorporating dance, something that encouraged free self-expression. Katra expressed feeling more harmony, leading to greater energy, feeling more confident and having less difficulty in relationships, including with herself.

CASE STUDY 2
Re-establishing masculine energy

Our society has an increasing number of men who are finding their feminine energy and connecting with it deeper, which is incredible, but many men are losing touch with their healthy masculine energy (Deida, 1997). I have seen many male clients who are closed off to parts of their core masculine energy, showing up deeply connected with their feminine energy but devaluing, or even afraid of, their masculine energy. This can be recognized through a combination of the man highly valuing emotions while also avoiding taking initiative with leading in one or more aspects of their lives.

I coached a man, Braxton, who came to me about a year and half ago, expressing a loss of direction, focus and purpose; he said his energy was always depleted. Braxton had grown up in a home where he had witnessed shadow masculine energy in other men, some even causing harm to women. Braxton learnt to fear these energies, and ultimately disconnected from his own masculine energy, the shadow and the healthy. Braxton spoke about his deep emotional connection to his wife, which he was very proud of, but he alluded to their marriage lacking intimacy and he didn't know how to initiate this without damaging the emotional intimacy. Braxton also spoke about his lack of confidence, and his body language was very soft and slouched over. It was clear that Braxton highly valued emotions and was fearful of being perceived as dangerous to anyone, especially women. This hindered him making decisions in his marriage and his career, as he did not want to appear to be in control. Through daily journalling and our sessions, Braxton started to become aware that he was blocking out his healthy masculine energy and that this was having a negative impact on his life.

Braxton started taking the initiative at work by having clear boundaries around his start and finish times, as well as saying no to clients when they were being unreasonable. He also started to lead in his marriage. For instance, taking a salsa dance class together allowed Braxton to practise leading while also increasing the intimacy between him and his wife. Although many dance forms are more feminine oriented, salsa encourages a man to lead in his masculine state by separating and juxtaposing masculine and feminine energy and expression (Sekyiamah, 2008). Braxton began to embody his healthy masculine energy and he went from feeling depleted of energy every day to sleeping better, feeling energized, confident and more connected to himself and his wife.

Physical manifestation of masculine and feminine energies

This masculine/feminine energy balance can also affect us profoundly in our physical body. When our energies are out of balance and we are using the shadows of them to cover up or cope with fear, we can feel the stress and can actually suffer in our physical body.

When listening to your clients and forming questions to better understand them, it may help to pay attention to the types of physical symptoms they are experiencing as well as what side of their body they are experiencing them on. Our left side is feminine, and our right side is masculine; knowing the side of the body your client experiences symptoms in can tell you which energy they have too much of (Englezos, 2008).

One of the most extreme imbalances of energies I have seen was Samantha, whom I have been coaching for over two years so far. Samantha was always in her head, and similarly to Katra, was heavily into her masculine energy. Samantha was also experiencing physical pain and medical issues, such as sleep insomnia, severe stress, inflammation in one side of her body, and heaviness in her leg and foot that prevented her from getting enough exercise, and she was overweight. Severe stress can take the form of many physical ailments, such as inflammation, insomnia and even autoimmune diseases (Reinberg, 2018).

Interestingly, most of Samantha's pains were on the right side of her body. Having a knowledge of masculine and feminine energy, we worked together to increase Samantha's feminine energy through journalling and meditation to increase her self-awareness and accountability, and through embodiment and mindset practices, such as dance, ocean swims, breath work and vision boarding and visualization, allowing her to build a balance in her energies. With the new feeling of balance, within a year all Samantha's symptoms went away.

Practical steps to balance masculine and feminine energies

I use the following steps to encourage and empower my clients to shift to a healthier balance of feminine/masculine energy.

Increasing self-awareness of an imbalance and fostering the desire for optimal balance

Self-awareness can be best established through questions during your sessions that help your client to see that they have a misbalance of energy. Daily practice, such as journalling, also contributes to deepening their level of self-awareness.

A good question for them to reflect on is, 'How am I showing up to the session, at work, or home?' Have them reflect on if they are task-oriented and/or emotionally driven. Are they connected to their thoughts? Or more to their heart? Other questions that are effective to provide further insight into a potential misbalance are:

- How does your energy affect your work?
- How would your finances/career goals flourish from being able to manage your time and goals in a more precise manner?
- How would you benefit from being able to have space and energy for creativity and spontaneity due to this schedule?

Creating balance

Ask questions and offer exercises to help your client develop a more optimal balance of feminine/masculine energy. Encourage balance through consciously focusing on the energy that is suboptimal to provide more harmony in their life. Ask:

- How would your relationship with yourself differ if you had a clear understanding of your own optimal energy balance?
- How would your relationships with friends, family, kids and romantic partners benefit from you having a clear idea of your own optimal energy balance?
- When would it be beneficial to tap into your masculine energy and create a container where you work from a place of structure and organization?
- When would it be beneficial to tap into your feminine energy and allow more flow, intuition and receiving?
- How can you tap into a more feminine or a more masculine energy when you desire? For example, when taking your wife on a date, can you tap into a leadership role and plan out the whole date to allow your wife to let go and relax, knowing you have the lead. Or when you are triggered by a discussion and find yourself feeling tight/restricted around your chest/heart, would you benefit from asking yourself 'how can I open in this?' And allow yourself to curiously hear the other side instead of shutting down.

Table 14.1 helps you to assign different exercises to help clients move more into their masculine or feminine energy. The chart moves from mild/subtle exercises that may be more comfortable for clients just starting to work on their energy balance to more in-depth/complicated/potentially challenging exercises for clients diving deeper into their energy balancing.

TABLE 14.1 Exercises to increase masculine/feminine balance given different client behaviours

Client behaviours	Exercises to increase balance
Client says they're feeling stuck in their head and are overthinking	**Free dance** – to help clients connect with their free movement and creative flow. This exercise can just be free dancing in their living room
	Connects deeper with the feminine energy
The client is very rational, goal oriented. They may even present as rigid in their body language	**Art/creativity** – your client is possibly lacking connection to their feminine energy and is heavily invested in their masculine energy
	This practice will allow your client to connect deeper with their feminine energy, while confirming if your instincts are correct
The client is scattered or lacks structure. They have difficulty with solid plans. They may even state that they are lacking purpose	**Practise setting goals** – a solid morning and evening routine to hug the day and add some structure
	This client is heavily in their feminine energy and this will allow your client to connect with their masculine energy
Client really values external goals, but seems to devalue internal/emotional goals	**Practise shifting perspective** – enjoy or be curious about the process rather than focus on the end result
	This trust in the process and release of control can lead to a deeper connection with our feminine energy
They feel a constriction/tightness in part of their body (e.g. constricted chest)	**Touch** part of your body that you feel and send it love and breath in softness (e.g. hand on heart)
	This will lead to more connection with their feminine energy
Client is not feeling sensually connected to their partner	**Join a couples' dance class** where the client can practise leading their partner or being led by their partner. This person is seeking polarity in their partnership. Without polarity, the sensual connection can diminish
	Leading is a masculine practice, being led is a feminine practice

Back full circle to self-awareness and acceptance

It is important for your client to know they can, and will at times, come back to the beginning of this process as they may fumble, or discover new areas of their lives to balance. As they continue to deepen in their optimal energy balance, clients grow in a more empowered way as long as they recognize, reflect, reassess and rebalance their energy states. This work can continue to be done as your clients feel and discover new areas of their lives that feel out of balance or would benefit from a shifting balance as they grow and become more self-aware. This is a good opportunity for your client to reflect on their growth and write what they are grateful for, as this will strengthen their empowerment and desire to continue to improve their feminine/masculine energy balance.

Conclusions

Clients see a coach to help them improve their lives. Incorporating feminine/masculine energy practices into your coaching practice makes you a more rounded and effective coach. It helps you to recognize when your client's energy orientation is out of balance, and together you can work towards achieving a more optimal balance for your client. Just remember that each client is different, and this practice of helping your client find their optimal masculine/feminine energy balance requires you, as the coach, to keep your client feeling empowered every step of the way, so that they can continue to grow in the way that is right for their unique energy balance. Taking care to keep sessions centred around your client's individual needs, using your client's words, body language and progress as direction and celebration of discovery of their optimal energy balance will keep the client empowered. If you choose to use these practices in your coaching, you will be able to help your clients achieve their goals, both internal and external, with more ease and connection, leading to a healthier balance that will help them in their lives now and beyond.

*Names used in this chapter have been changed.

References

Caro, C (2019) Mastering the duality of feminine and masculine energies in the workplace, *Forbes*, 25 April, www.forbes.com/sites/forbescoachescouncil/2019/04/25/mastering-the-duality-of-feminine-and-masculine-energies-in-the-workplace (archived at https://perma.cc/BTM2-Q7WM)

Deida, D (1997) *The Way of the Superior Man*, Sounds True, Boulder, CO

Englezos, S (2008) Feminine and masculine energy, Aligned Nature, alignednature.com/feminine-and-masculine-energies (archived at https://perma.cc/4LCF-4C7L)

Garza, M (2017) How to connect to the healing power of the feminine, ChangeYourEnergy, 5 May, www.changeyourenergy.com/blog/1913/20170508-how-to-connect-to-the-healing-power-of-the-feminine (archived at https://perma.cc/83FN-EE6L)

Li, P P (2018) The epistemology of yin-yang balancing as the root of Chinese cultural traditions: The indigenous features and geocentric implications, in *The Psychological and Cultural Foundations of East Asian Cognition: Contradiction, change, and holism*, eds J Spencer-Rodgers and K Peng, pp 35–80, Oxford University Press, New York

Marianetti, O (2016) A. A. A. – balancing masculine and feminine energy, *Psychology Matters Asia*, 27 May, www.psychologymatters.asia/article/337/aaa--balancing-masculine-and-feminine-energy.html (archived at https://perma.cc/5WVR-T9PG)

Reinberg, S (2018) Severe stress may send immune system into overdrive, *Medical Xpress*, 19 June, https://medicalxpress.com/news/2018-06-severe-stress-immune-overdrive.html (archived at https://perma.cc/RZ4B-UG6Y)

Sekyiamah, N (2008) Challenging female & male relationships? Try Salsa! African Women's Development Fund, 22 August, awdf.org/challenging-female-male-relationships-try-salsa/ (archived at https://perma.cc/EB9U-MSAM)

15

Mindfulness and psychological flexibility in emotion-based coaching

JANA SIEDENHANS

ABSTRACT

Why is dealing with emotions in coaching essential when it is about long-term changes for clients? Which techniques can help me to approach this demanding topic so that I do not find my clients 'overwhelmed' by their emotions?

Background

This chapter introduces why dealing with emotions in coaching is necessary for sustainable behavioural changes. You learn techniques for helping your clients to calm down when emotionally activated, gain a deeper understanding of how to direct their attention purposefully towards their emotions. This practice already helps your clients to respond to 'what is' in the present moment instead of reacting instinctively. It will further show you how increased psychological flexibility calms your clients' habitual defences and opens a conscious choice of behaviour.

During your coaching your clients can stepwise learn using these techniques themselves: consciously observing their experience of the situation in a non-judgemental way, rather than letting their thoughts and feelings overwhelm them. This is a major part of every ethically strong and professional basis in the coach–client relationship: challenging your clients for their self-empowered personal development in a trusted space without harming them.

A review of the theory

The principles and concepts of schema therapy provide a foundation that coaches can use to improve their understanding of how they can effectively work with the emotional and behavioural transformation of clients (van Genderen, Rijkeboer and Arntz, 2012). By combining theories and techniques from multiple psychotherapy modalities like cognitive behavioural therapy, schema therapy addresses a client's core emotional needs for learning ways to meet their needs adaptively by exploring their experiences from childhood. Foundation and methods of schema therapy can be adapted into coaching for changes of behaviour, rooted in emotional reactivity. Especially dialogic techniques, visualizations, as well as the concept of limited re-parenting show remarkable impact as tools in schema coaching (Migge, 2013).

In the emotion-based coaching approach, a technique called affect labelling, or 'putting feelings into words', is additionally effective. Studies proved the impact of affect labelling in managing negative emotional experiences and to examine the underlying mechanisms (Lieberman et al, 2007). Further studies even underline that affect labelling additionally may not even feel like a regulatory process as it occurs. They suggest that one important component of affect labelling could be observing our emotions, requiring a degree of self-reflection. Being aware of and observing our own emotional experiences is a primary feature of dispositional mindfulness (Torre and Lieberman, 2018). Thus, affect labelling supports implicit emotion regulation while simultaneously creating a mindful attitude in a coaching client.

Mindfulness, as part of psychological flexibility, is the basis for self-knowing and intrapersonal self-control, the level of which determines whether we react impulsively or respond consciously. The conscious use of other mindfulness techniques in addition to affect labelling can lead to important insights into unhealthy emotional behaviour from a healthy, emotionally regulated distance (Newman, 2014).

Discussion

'Between stimulus and response there is a space. In that space lies our freedom and our power to choose our response. In our response lies our growth and our happiness' (Pattakos and Dundon, 2017: x). The quote by Stephen Covey attributing the principles of Viktor Frankl is not new to most of you. Let's look a little deeper into the 'space' he described. For the crucial question for coaches is, 'How can our clients enter this space in a way that they can see and make use of the freedom it contains?'

As coaches, we often start working with our clients by focusing on the mind. It is indeed relieving for clients to understand the 'why' behind their current disadvantageous behaviour. Self-knowing is an important aspect of our emotional intelligence. It forms the basis for our intrapersonal self-control (Newman, 2014).

Self-control, also known as impulse control, is crucial for the transformation of behavioural patterns. It is decisive for whether we rush into the space between stimulus and response and, driven by subconscious patterns, take the exit with the reactive flight forward, or whether we enter in clarity, and allow ourselves time to perceive what we recognize before consciously choosing the exit that leads to a mature response towards an emotionally challenging event.

The expression 'impulse control' shows that we may learn to control an impulse in order to decide in favour of better behaviour during emotionally triggering moments. It is generally accepted that the experience of emotional events produces a measurable autonomic signal, an impulse (Torre and Lieberman, 2018). This impulse guiding us straight through the exit to flight-forward behaviour is based on emotions and body perceptions, triggered by beliefs and memories in our minds (van Genderen, Rijkeboer and Arntz, 2012).

Modern schema therapy puts the interfering connection of thoughts, emotions and behaviours into a strikingly relatable concept, which is also supportive for coaches. The schema model gives it a clear context, especially relatable for coaches and clients (Figure 15.1).

Neither schema nor behaviour herein have to be dysfunctional. As coaching focuses on behavioural transformation though, going forward in this chapter I use the term 'schema space', defining it as: the space between stimulus and response in which the interaction of belief and memories (as dysfunctional thoughts), emotions and physical sensations lead to a high level of measurable autonomical signals, expressing difficult emotional stages that cause unwanted behaviour on the client's side'.

Thoughts and emotions are closely linked and often run together in unconscious behavioural patterns (Kellogg, 2012). Therefore, we cannot avoid getting in touch with the emotional parts of our client's behaviour patterns. Oftentimes, the emotional level rises naturally in coaching. When feelings show up unexpectedly, clients can easily over-identify with their intensity.

The better we support them in entering the schema space to explore the interdependencies calmly and from a healthy distance, the greater their opportunity for increasing self-knowing and self-control (Newman, 2014). But how can feelings be targeted without activating their intensity?

FIGURE 15.1 Schema model in detail

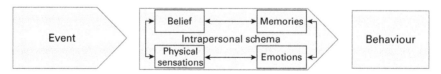

SOURCE Based on Roediger (2012)

In schema coaching, mindfulness practices, such as the conscious inclusion of sensory perceptions, are used for this purpose (Migge, 2013). Affect labelling also has remarkable effects on decreasing the physical sensations of our emotional experiences (Torre and Lieberman, 2018).

CASE STUDY
Schema coaching

To illustrate the principles of using mindfulness in coaching to enhance psychological flexibility, the following is a conversation in an online coaching session with my client S, who is female, in her 30s, and the head of sales in a medium-sized European company.

S shares a recent event: she leads a project establishing a new sales channel. In her last meeting with her project managers and the steering committee, it turned out that several important deadlines were no longer feasible without her being informed in advance. S was later called into a management meeting, where expectations of drastic improvement in reliability and speed of the project were set.

S's tension is expressed in her body language, choice of words and tone of voice.

Coach (C): It seems that the situation upsets you to a great extent.

S: I'm furious! I am only stopping myself from exploding and using maximum pressure to get everything back on track. I know that I have no chance of doing it alone. But I also can't find any way to talk to the team in any reasonable way.

C: Let's try something: Let's close the eyes and focus on the breath around the nostrils.

S: [Closes her eyes, and quickly breaks off]

S: Sorry, but this is so not working for me.

C: That's okay. What about keeping your eyes open and sitting on your chair, putting your feet flat on the floor.

S: [Strained] I'm wearing pumps.

C: Just take them off and put your feet on the floor. Ready?

S: [Continuing tensely] Yes.

C: Okay, now please look around and tell me five things you can see in your office.

S: [Listing quickly] My desk, my laptop, the door, the window and the chair across from my desk.

C: Can you now name four things that you can touch with your hands or otherwise?

S: [Sighs, continues, enumeration gradually slowing down] I can touch the tabletop, I feel the floor under my feet, the material of my chair, the keyboard from the laptop under my fingers.

C: What three sounds can you hear?

S: [Raises eyebrows, sighs, waits a moment] The fan from the laptop. [She concentrates] I hear people mumbling in the hallway. Also, there's the traffic noise from the street.

C: And what are two smells that you perceive?

S: Two?

C: Yep. Take your time to discover two smells you detect in your office.

S: I can smell the coffee but that's it.

C: What else?

S: That's all that's coming.

C: That's fine. Then name one more thing you can taste.

S: That's easy. [S takes a sip of coffee smiling a little wryly at the camera]

C: [Nods] Hmm, will you do me another favour?

S: Depends. [S looks a bit strained but continues to slightly smile]

C: Take another sip of coffee, close your eyes, and track to where you feel the warmth of coffee when you swallow it.

S: [Takes a sip and closes eyes] It's warm all the way down to the stomach – somewhere below the chest.

C: Keep your eyes closed now and imagine that you exhale through your feet.

S: How do you exhale through your feet?

C: Just imagine it.

S: [Keeps her eyes closed and breathes]

C: Can you feel the connection between your feet and the floor?

S: Yes.

C: How do you feel?

S: Calmer. But also [pause] sad.

S: [Voice becomes brittle]

C: Where do you feel the sadness in your body?

S: [Silent for a moment] Close to the heart.

C: What colour is the sadness?

S: Purple.

C: How does it feel?

S: Tenacious – like a viscous mass.

C: A purple, viscous mass near your heart, then.

S: Yes

C: Observe the tenacious, viscous feeling for a moment. Just observe from a distance. [Pause]

C: What happens now?

S: It's getting lighter.

C: Can you get closer?

S: Yes.

C: What's happening now?

S: It's still getting lighter; colour is more like pink.

C: Ask it why it's sad. What comes when you ask?

S: You have let me down.

C: Who is 'you'?

S: My team. [Few tears]

C: Ask it what it needs now.

S: To be able to trust.

C: Who?

S: My team. I want to work with people who care about me, too.

[Again, some tears come to S]

C: Can you slowly open your eyes?

S: [Opens her eyes, dries her tears, sobs]

C: How are you?

S: Better but also [pause] surprised.

C: What is surprising you?

S: That I'm not angry, but [pause] hurt.

C: What do we do with the message for your team: 'you want to be able to trust'?

S: Translate, I guess.

C: How?

S: I say what went wrong from my point of view and also that I really felt let down. And how this needs to go differently for me.

C: How likely are you to 'explode' during the discussion?

S: Unlikely the anger is gone. Could be more like tears coming. But also, the sadness kind of doesn't feel as intense now [pause] – more like disappointment.

As shown in the session extract, the first step was going through a breathing exercise with the client. Breathing is directly linked to our nervous system regulation, influencing the activity of the amygdala, a region in the brain associated with emotion generation (Lieberman et al, 2007).

As the client was too caught up in her emotions, the 5-4-3 method was used to shift her focus away from ruminating about her negative experience. Among other mindfulness techniques, it can be used to incorporate physical sensory perceptions into coaching for shifting a client's focus from one system to another (Migge, 2013), here from the mind- and emotion-driven memory system to the external system of her current presence. In addition to re-shifting the focus, distraction in general yields reduced amygdala activity (Torre and Lieberman, 2018). This was practised by letting the client focus on the sensation of the coffee in her oesophagus.

In a further step, physical sensory perception and breathing technique were combined in the imagination of exhaling through the feet, which supported both the conscious awareness of physical senses in connection with the external system and a repetitive calm breath pattern for the nervous system regulation.

After directing her attention, the technique of affect labelling was used to further reduce the intensity of stress. It leads to decreased emotion-generative activity in the amygdala and reduces emotion-related behavioural effects (Lieberman et al, 2007). Affect labelling shows immediate effects, as well as positive longer-term effects without reductions in affect-related emotional signals (Lieberman et al, 2007), which makes it especially valuable for the coaching process. As the intent to regulate one's emotions is not required for it to be effective (Lieberman et al, 2007), the application in coaching is particularly advantageous.

Next, it seemed appropriate to start exploring the schema space from a detached perspective. Relating to Victor Frankl's words: entering the schema space with more impulse control for exploring a healthy response activity.

The client's affect labelling insight of 'being sad' offered the opportunity of using an additional mindfulness technique: for further emotional and cognitive defusion, the schema space was explored from an observational position using body sensations and visualization aspects to keep the client detached from the predominant painful cognitions (Migge, 2013).

Visualizations in coaching are further discussed in Chapter 19 and are therefore not discussed in more detail here. Noticing body sensations and visualization led to a judgement-free exploration in a state of mindfulness and steps into acceptance in the present.

The short dialogue between client and the visualized sadness constitutes a dialogic technique. It supports her in entering dysfunctional thoughts in the schema space while staying grounded in the present (Roediger, 2012).

Next to a dysfunctional basic belief about 'being betrayed', the client identified a frustrated need for trust, which further on can be nurtured by limited reparenting, to enhance the client's impulse control in the related situation (Migge, 2013). Additional moments of affect labelling led to further emotional reassurance for her. Consequently, she could define first responsive, mature action steps. Table 15.1 gives an overview of the sequence and techniques used.

TABLE 15.1 Sequence and mindfulness techniques used in the session extract

Technique	Goal	Concrete application	Outcome	Specifics to be aware of
5-4-3-2-1 Grounding technique	Calming an over-reactive mind, which manifests as intense stress or mild anxiety, by focusing on what is immediately accessible with the five senses	Asking the client to focus on things to: • see • touch • hear • smell • taste in their direct surroundings	• Positive change in mood • Shifting focus from memories to the present • Reduction of stress-related emotional reactivity	Don't expect a perfect result. You may still need to manage your client's trigger, but this is one way to reduce the impact. Give the technique time to work, and if the client is receptive, repeat it a second time
Distraction	Reducing the activity of the amygdala, which causes stress	Letting the client focus on the feeling when sipping the coffee	• Curiosity and positive surprise at new emotional perceptions	Distraction is effective as a short-term intervention. For a substantial change in mood and a grounding effect, additional measures may be needed
Physical sensory perception + breathing technique	Regulation of the nervous system and change of focus from emotions to physical sensations to reduce stress and increase body awareness	Guided breathing pattern, including awareness of the feet	• Decrease of fight or flight mode	Depending on the client's current emotional state, the closed-eye breathing technique may be too big a change for the client to make in one step, especially if anxiety is involved

(continued)

TABLE 15.1 (Continued)

Technique	Goal	Concrete application	Outcome	Specifics to be aware of
Affect labelling	Sustained decline in amygdala function and corresponding behavioural effects for greater clarity and reflectivity	Asking the client how they feel after a sequence of grounding	• Increasing (self)-reflection capability, identifiying the underlying emotion of sadness	Directly asking for feelings and needs to have an appropriate context, and readiness of the client to engage with affect labelling. Alternatively, mirroring an identified emotion as coach can effect as affect labelling, too
Body sensation + visualization	Gaining information about the underlying emotion of sadness	Allocating the feeling in the client's body and visualizing its shape, as well as colour	• Judgement-free exploration of the central emotion of sadness from a dissociated observer perspective	Visualization techniques should be applied when the client is in a state of emotional processing, with low activity of the amygdala
Dialogue technique	Exploring dysfunctional core beliefs from a detached perceptual position	Guiding the client into a dialogue with the identified emotion of sadness	• Identification of a dysfunctional core belief and a frustrated need for trust	Dialogue technique is an advanced coaching tool, not to be applied with real clients without specific training

Conclusion and recommendations

In emotion-based coaching, mindfulness techniques are effective tools to enhance our clients' psychological flexibility: their ability to feel and think with openness and to voluntarily explore the experience of the current moment (Newman, 2014). Clients learn to withdraw from the triggering interference of feelings, thoughts and behaviours and to instead observe their experience non-judgementally, grounded in the present.

This form of openness helps you to overcome the inner protective mechanisms of your clients (Roediger, 2012). They can enter the schema space as an observing visitor, not as an overidentified resident. Herein lies your chance to ignite holistic self-awareness about beliefs, experiences, feelings and sensations for your clients. You grow their options for alternative behaviours within the schema space, and support them in increasing emotional control, as interrelationships and alternative actions become conscious.

Though based on elements of schema therapy, applying the concept of the schema model in practice does not necessarily enable coaches to support recovery from emotional or other psychological disorders such as anxiety without extended competency development.

Also, at the current state of research the limitations of affect labelling as emotion regulation are not yet fully answered (Torre and Lieberman, 2018). Both their successful effects go along with conscious and cautious application by the coach. They are additional tools for us to get overall 'healthy' people to shift their behaviour from reaction to response by detachment.

Detaching from the identification with our thoughts and feelings is the essence of mindfulness. With mindfulness techniques you help clients to dig free from the avalanche of thoughts they were buried under. Additionally, they can bring some light into the quaking of their agitated mind from an observational perspective. As observers they learn to identify what the brain is concocting into artificial worries. With this psychological flexibility they learn to choose supportive behaviours more consciously as a response.

References

Kellogg, S (2012) On speaking one's mind: Using chairwork dialogues in schema therapy, in *The Wiley-Blackwell Handbook of Schema Therapy: Theory, research, and practice*, eds M van Vreeswijk, J Broersen and M Nadort, pp 197–208, Wiley-Blackwell, New York

Lieberman, M D, Eisenberger, N I, Crockett, M J, Tom, S M, Pfeifer, J H and Way, B M (2007) Putting feelings into words, *Psychological Science*, 18 (5), 421–8, doi.org/10.1111/j.1467-9280.2007.01916.x (archived at https://perma.cc/95GE-YNGT)

Migge, B (2013) *Schema-Coaching: Einführung und praxis, grundlagen, methoden, fallbeispiele*, Beltz Verlag, Weinhein

Newman, M (2014) *Emotional Capitalists: The ultimate guide to developing emotional intelligence for leaders*, RocheMartin, London

Pattakos, A and Dundon, E (2017) *Prisoners of Our Thoughts*, 3rd edn, Berrett-Koehler, Oakland, CA

Roediger, E (2012) Why are mindfulness and acceptance central elements for therapeutic change in schema therapy too? An integrative perspective, in *The Wiley-Blackwell Handbook of Schema Therapy: Theory, research, and practice*, eds M van Vreeswijk, J Broersen and M Nadort, pp 239–48, Wiley-Blackwell, New York

Torre, J B and Lieberman, M D (2018) Putting feelings into words: Affect labeling as implicit emotion regulation, *Emotion Review*, 10 (2), 116–24, doi.org/10.1177/1754073917742706 (archived at https://perma.cc/Z2E5-LEHP)

van Genderen, H, Rijkeboer, M and Arntz, A (2012) Theoretical model: Schemas, coping styles, and modes, in *The Wiley-Blackwell Handbook of Schema Therapy: Theory, research, and practice*, eds M van Vreeswijk, J Broersen and M Nadort, pp 27–40, Wiley-Blackwell, New York

PART FOUR

Techniques and tools

16

Embodiment

ANNA ALLGÄUER

ABSTRACT

A challenge that coaching practitioners often face in their practice is the lack of ability to recognize and understand the physical presentation of mental information, and change bodily reaction patterns and underlying beliefs accordingly. In this chapter, embodiment is introduced as a concept to overcome this mind–body barrier and help coaching clients implement their thoughts into actions by working with the body.

Introduction

As coaches, we are all familiar with the fact that the brain – more specifically, the head-brain system – and the mental capacity of our clients can only process information to a certain point, which often does not easily transit into long-lasting action-taking. In other words, as coaches we support our clients to get from 'point A' (where they are now) to 'point B' (where they want to be) by helping them to find out what holds them back and what limiting beliefs they hold on to. We then work to change those underlying patterns into new actions that can lead them to find ways and tools to get to point B, or at least move in that direction.

The challenge that coaching practitioners often face is that newly gained information is cognitively understood by the client but not enacted on. Up to this point it is fairly easy to guide the client to discover new knowledge and insights by asking the right questions, but when it comes to action-taking and actually changing old patterns, we often witness that our client fails to implement the new actions and behaviours in their life that are needed. Old patterns pop up again and again, and they remain the ones ruling the behaviours of the client subconsciously while they seemingly cannot find a way to change their ways.

> This is where I often see coaching fail; when we as practitioners cannot find a way to get our clients to really FEEL the changes they want to make in their body and therefore get their bodies to act and behave in different ways.

So, in this chapter we explore how embodiment can be used as a powerful concept to overcome this mind–body barrier and how we can help our clients to transition new thoughts into new, lasting, bodily behaviour.

Understanding the definition and roots of embodiment allows us to get a better look into the current theory and research in the field of embodiment. Gaining knowledge of the three brains; head-brain, gut-brain and heart-brain, we discover the importance of paying attention to our body and how to relearn to listen to what it is trying to tell us (Gorman, 2019; Soosalu, Henwood and Deo, 2019). Through a case study, I display how embodiment can be used in coaching and give practical recommendations that coaches are encouraged to offer in their sessions, to use knowledge of embodiment as a tool with their clients to reconnect the body to the brain and therefore achieve better results in the overall coaching process and desired outcomes.

The theory of embodiment

Before we look closely at the application of embodiment in coaching, let's first take a moment to dig deeper into the current state of research in the field of embodiment.

Until two decades ago, in social and human sciences the human being was mostly seen as a centre of intelligence, as a thinking, feeling, data-processing being with moods and feelings (Cantieni et al, 2017). In social psychology and other fields, psychologists understood that all the above processes happen in a body (Bargh et al, 2012), but still, the body was often missing in the related descriptions and applications (Cantieni et al, 2017). However, recently scientists started to ask an essential question: how is it possible that we believed that our brain acts as our 'chief executive officer' and is able to function in total disconnection from everything that happens below the throat (Cantieni et al, 2017)?

Only in the 1990s did the study of embodiment develop into an independent field of research and theoretical approach (Bargh et al, 2012). Across the literature, especially when looking into the research of embodiment in different languages (in this case English and German), we find slightly different definitions of the word embodiment. Let's look at two that represent the most common approach to describe embodiment in the current literature:

1 In the first view of embodiment the mind is always related to the whole body, and body and mind are again related to the whole environment surrounding the body.

Also, the relationship between body and mind is reciprocal, referring specifically to a 'circular causality' and 'bidirectionality' (Cantieni, et al, 2017; Storch and Tschacher, 2017). In other words, the mind influences the body, and vice versa.

2 According to Maja Storch and her colleagues at the University of Zurich, embodiment means that the mind consists not (only) of information processing but is embodied. As such, a reciprocal relationship exists between processes of the body and the mind (also called 'bidirectionality'), meaning that our thoughts, feelings, actions or decisions are linked to movement in the body, our posture and physiology (Storch, Tschacher and Weber, 2018).

Now that we have a clearer understanding of the term embodiment and its origin, we can dig a little deeper into the field of embodiment to see its effect on human functioning and value in coaching. As shown above, research in recent years indicates that 'consciousness emerges from the brain and body acting together' (Soosalu, Henwood and Deo, 2019: 10). Studies also show that there are actually at least three 'brains' in our body, and that this knowledge can be very powerful when working with clients in the helping professions, including therapy and coaching (Henwood, Manea and Soosalu, 2018a). For example, in 1999 Dr Michael D Gershon published his findings about neurogastroenterology and his rediscovery of the 'second brain in the bowel', wherein he describes how the gut has working nerve cells that build their own 'brain' and can work without directions from the head-brain (Soosalu, Henwood and Deo, 2019). A few years later, in 2003, the Institute of HeartMath published their findings about the cardiac nervous system, postulating that 'the heart possesses its own *little brain*, capable of complex computational analysis on its own' (Armour, 2003: 15). Grant Soosalu and his colleagues concurred, describing how our gut and heart are involved as individual brains in the process of decision making (Soosalu, Henwood and Deo, 2019). They specify that each of the three brains has individual tasks and sends individual signals, with primary functions as follows:

- 'Head-brain': thinking, making meaning and cognitive perception
- 'Heart-brain' (affective brain): emotions, emotional processing, values and relational affect
- 'Gut-brain' (intuitive brain): core identity, self-preservation and mobilization

Maybe at this point you are asking yourself: Which are the parameters that scientists use to define those three organs as individual brains? Marvin Oka, author and expert for behavioural modelling, answers this question as follows:

They have their own intrinsic nervous systems. They've got neurons. They've got the whole range of [capabilities] in order to do complex adaptive processes. They can take on information, process it, store it, change, and adapt. Basically, if it can learn, it's a brain (Oka, 2016, para 6).

Therefore, intuition (= gut-brain) and emotion/affect (= heart-brain) are two different processing centres that interact with cognition (= head-brain) in the process of decision making (Soosalu, Henwood and Deo, 2019).

For example, embodiment expert from the Arizona State University, Arthur Glenberg (2010) shows through a variety of examples how psychological processes influence bodily processes (and vice versa) and reviews different approaches to embodiment.

In one experiment, participants were told to either hold a pen with only their teeth (forcing the muscles to do the same movement as when we are smiling) or hold a pen with only their lips (forcing the muscles to do the same movement as when frowning). The experiment showed that the participants 'smiling' understood sentences faster that described events that make people happy, while the participants 'frowning' were faster in understanding the sentences that described events that can make people sad. The authors concluded that 'Apparently, having the body in a matching emotional state facilitates comprehension of sentences describing emotionally congruent events' (Glenberg, 2010: 590). The findings illustrate the parallelism between the head-brain and heart-brain to influence emotions and linguistic processing bilaterally.

Furthermore, in a study by Williams and Bargh, cited by Glenberg (2010), participants were asked to hold a cup of warm or iced coffee in their hands for a few moments, showing how body states can strongly influence social behaviour and social judgements. Similarly, Glenberg's research found that emotions are 'strongly embodied', it's not just something our head-brain thinks about, but we feel (and manifest) emotions in the body, which then lead to action and cognitive reactions. Other studies also elaborated how the process of learning and understanding of abstract things such as numbers, letters or words require a cognitive process as well as 'grounding the term in bodily experiences' (Glenberg, 2010: 594), and finally Glenberg also commented on how short the time of research in the field of embodiment has been, but how surprisingly fast progress has been at the same time, which could be a sign towards the importance of embodiment for psychology and many other fields.

Even though research in the field of embodiment has only sped up in the last 20–30 years, there are already quite a few studies and case studies linking coaching and embodiment, including developing coaching tools based on the concept of the three brains, and embodiment applied to coaching practices. A coaching method worth noting is mBIT (multiple brain integration techniques), which is a coaching model based on neuroscience that addresses and works with the three brains in the body. First developed by behavioural change specialists Grant Soosalu and Marvin Oka, the tools and techniques of mBIT were applied in complementary therapy for stress management and resilience with promising results (Henwood, Manea and Soosalu, 2018b) and later adapted to coaching (Henwood, Manea, and Soosalu,

2018a). The mBIT approach helps clients to re-connect with their bodily wisdom and to use their three brains actively in their daily lives. The approach is based on changing the physiology of the body by changing its actions and responses, thereby changing the habitual behaviour of the client over time (Henwood, Manea, Soosalu, 2018b).

Extended from the principles of NLP (neuro-linguistic programming), cognitive linguistics and behavioural modelling, mBIT is also used successfully in leadership training (Henwood and Soosalu, 2014). The developers describe mBIT as a navigational map that applies techniques such as dream interpretation, neurolinguistics and rhythmic breathing, guided imagery meditation and biofeedback to align and integrate the three brains (Soosalu and Oka, 2012).

Another coaching model described in literature that contains embodiment approaches to make coaching more effective is the Zurich Resource Model (ZRM) (Storch, Tschacher and Weber, 2018). ZRM is a self-management tool that utilizes a combination of assessments, coaching, video learning and interactive self-help techniques to integrate the conscious (head) with the unconscious (heart and gut) to achieve harmony. Benita Cantieni argues that every professional working in the field of therapy, counselling or human research should look at the inclusive human body, including the interaction of body, soul, spirit, mind and emotions to discover the power and resilience of the whole system (Cantieni, Hüther, Storch and Tschacher, 2017).

Discussion

For psychologists, therapists, counsellors and coaches the key considerations are the thoughts, feelings and behaviour of their clients – both observed and expressed – and how they are influenced by the presence of other persons (Bargh et al, 2012). In my personal coaching practice, I use embodiment in many different forms to get clients to really feel in their body what they are telling me (such as decisions they have made, things they have discovered, etc). In the following case study of a client, I want to paint a picture of how to use embodiment in coaching, but before I do so, a word about embodiment techniques in general. There are many tools and techniques that involve embodiment, which depend on how they are used. Although a much deeper exploration is outside the scope of this chapter, the works by Benita Cantieni and her colleagues (2017), Maja Storch (Storch and Tschacher, 2017; Storch, Tschacher and Weber, 2018), Michaela Boehm (2018), Peter Levine (1997), Bessel Van Der Kolk (2015), and Henwood and colleagues (Henwood, Manea and Soosalu, 2018a), are good sources to find more information about embodiment techniques and tools for your coaching practice as well as profound information about trauma and related patterns that could arise when working with embodiment.

The most important thing when it comes to working with coaching clients and embodiment tools is actually very simple:

> Our conclusion from this experiment for coaching and training is as follows: when the personal embodiment is developed, there are no guidelines! An embodiment that is imposed on a person according to someone else's norms can not only be ineffective, but... it can even have a harmful effect (Storch, Tschacher and Weber, 2018).

So, my number one rule when working with coaching clients and embodiment is the following: let their body find the way! Nevertheless, a caveat – always be observant for signs that the client may experience potentially harmful distress, and practise within the bounds of your competence to the benefit of the client, and what you have contracted for (see Chapter 2).

CASE STUDY

Marie (name changed) is in her late twenties and comes to coaching because she wishes to learn how to take decisions for her life. She has a job that she really likes, but there's also a feeling within her that tells her that 'there's more', but she cannot really say what that is. That is why she has developed the idea to go travelling for a year to experience something totally different, but she is not sure if and when she should do so and if it is worth the consequences of losing the position in the current job she really likes and going against the wishes of her parents to have a secure income, among others.

I introduce Marie to the concept of the three brains and I ask her if she can distinguish between the three brains and when each one is talking to her. First, she says yes, but after some thought, she admits that she thinks that her head-brain is always talking instead of the other two brains and overriding them – and therefore taking decisions for them. I explain to her the following exercise to learn how to distinguish between and listen to her three brains.

Embodiment exercise

I tell my client, 'Stand up, close your eyes, and allow your body to move if it wants to move. Take your hands and start to tap with your fingers over your head, try to feel your skull. Try to connect with the head-brain that lies under the skull. Ask your head-brain: How are you today? What are you thinking today? Your head-brain will answer you in words. Just listen to the words that come up, don't judge, just listen, and if you want, you can move your body to those words in every way that feels good in that moment.

'Then, go with your hands a bit deeper and start tapping over your sternum. We're now connecting with the heart-brain. Try to feel the bones under your hands and try to connect with the heart that lies under the bones. Ask your heart: How are you feeling today? Your heart-brain will answer in sensations and feelings, like warm, cold, the feeling of tightness or width, and the sudden arising of emotions and feelings. Pay attention: Are you hearing words that explain what's happening? Then, you're listening to your head-brain once again. If this happens, don't be hard on yourself or your head, it's just trying to do its job to protect you from potential harm (and it's doing it darned well, I'd say!). You could say something like: 'Thank you head-brain, I hear you, but now I want to connect a little with the other two brains' to your head-brain and then you could restart and try to only listen to sensations and emotions arising from your heart-brain, and if you want to, just move your body with whatever comes up in this second.

'After some minutes, once more go deeper with your hands and start tapping or stroking over your belly and gut area. Feel your hands on your clothing, the skin under your clothing and try to connect with your gut-brain. Ask your gut: What do you need right now? I always explain the gut-brain like the bottom of Maslow's Hierarchy of Needs, it will communicate with you in the way that it'll let you know if your most basic needs are met, if you feel safe or not, if you're hungry, need to go to the toilet or if you're maybe afraid of something. So again: if you're hearing words at this point, it's the head-brain talking to you. Try to connect with your gut-brain and see what it has to say to you, and again, if you'd like, move with whatever comes up.'

Impact of embodiment work

In our next coaching session three weeks later, Marie tells me that through this exercise she found out that it is her heart telling her to go travelling, her gut is motivated and has a lot of energy, but also experiences some fear around this plan, and her head-brain is sternly stopping her from the travelling plans, it tells her over and over again that it makes no logical sense to go travelling, leaving her safe job, making her parents feel insecure, and so forth. When I ask Marie whose voice is speaking in her head, she thinks for quite a while, then she starts to smile and admits, 'I think it's my mum's voice talking to me!' When I ask her on behalf of which voice she wants to take her decision, she is quite clear: 'On behalf of my own! And two of my three brains know exactly what to do!'

And that's it, all of a sudden, a decision is taken that Marie has carried with her for several years without being able to get clarity around it. She smiles and all of a sudden wants to start planning the trip and quitting her job.

The last thing I ask her to do is tell me about the picture that comes up in her head when she thinks of how she feels right now. She says, 'I think of a captain of a ship sailing into the sunset.' I ask her if she could capture for me a 'captain position' with her body, and she shows me one. I mirror it to her (I copy her position) and ask her how that looks and feels like to her. She just smiles and says, 'really good and strong, and like a free bird.' I tell her to use this position whenever the voice of her mum is getting strong again in her head over the next months, specifically now as she prepares for her trip. Every time she does her 'captain position' it will help her to get back into her own body, out of her mum's thoughts, and reconnect her to her heart- and gut-brain.

Practical recommendations

So, to recap, embodiment is the manifestation of cognitions that reside in the head-brain in the body through the heart-brain and the gut-brain. If the three centres – head, heart and gut – experience misalignment or conflict, all three are affected by experiencing indecisiveness, fear, anxiety, physical distress and pain, among others. To put it in a nutshell:

1 Embodiment techniques seem to have the potential to have a big impact on desired coaching outcomes, as we invite our clients to not only think about change, but really feel it holistically in their bodies and BE the change where the head-, heart- and gut-brains are aligned and in harmony.

2 There is a vast variety of embodiment techniques and approaches out there, and it lies in your hands as a coach to get informed and trained to find the ways that are beneficial to you and your clients in a way that is safe, ethical and beneficial.

3 Never try to impose embodiment on to your clients. For example, do not tell them to 'do this or that position, move in this way', etc. Let them find their own unique way to get comfortable in and with their body, as shown in the case study. Let them choose if they want to move their body or not when connecting to the three brains. Let them choose their own metaphors, images or analogies (like the captain analogy) and ask them how their body would represent this picture, instead of showing them 'this is how a captain's position is done'.

4 Play around with the thought of the three brains in a narrative or metaphorical way and just have fun while exploring how you could assist your clients in finding ways to reconnect to their whole body, including the three 'brains'. By doing so you open a new world of possibilities for you and your clients and that is often all the impetus needed to get going.

Without learning and incorporating embodiment into your coaching practice, I believe you are missing an important opportunity to serve your clients better. When a client feels stuck or in distress, it is often because their head-brain, heart-brain and gut-brain are misaligned. In other words, towards the end of the coaching process they may believe everything is fine and they have changed their negative beliefs and thoughts, for instance. But if they do not 'feel' it in their bodies, the change will likely not be convincing and durable.

References

Armour, J A (2003) *Neurocardiology: Anatomical and functional principles*, Institute of HeartMath, Boulder Creek, CA

Bargh, J A, Meier, B P, Schnall, S and Schwarz, N (2012) Embodiment in social psychology, *Topics in Cognitive Science*, 4 (4), 705–16

Boehm, M (2018) *The Wild Woman's Way: Reconnect to your body's wisdom*, Atria/Enliven Books, New York

Cantieni, B, Hüther, G, Storch, M and Tschacher, W (2017) *Embodiment: Die Wechselwirkung von Körper und Psyche verstehen und nutzen*, German edn, Verlag Hans Huber, Hogrefe AG, Bern

Glenberg, A M (2010) Embodiment as a unifying perspective for psychology, *WIREs Cognitive Science*, 1 (4), 586–96, doi.org/10.1002/wcs.55 (archived at https://perma.cc/A8DN-BWE9)

Gorman, B (2019) Change leadership: Why your head, heart and gut are critical to listen to, *Forbes*, 4 March, www.forbes.com/sites/forbescoachescouncil/2019/03/04/change-leadership-why-your-head-heart-and-gut-are-critical-to-listen-to (archived at https://perma.cc/M7ZC-3MCR)

Henwood, S, Manea, A and Soosalu, G (2018a) mBIT as an experiential coaching and therapeutic approach, a series of case studies and scientific background, *Journal of Experiential Psychotherapy*, 21 (1), 24–33

Henwood, S, Manea, A and Soosalu, G (2018b) mBIT as an experiential coaching and therapeutic approach in stress management and resilience building – a series of case studies, *Journal of Experiential Psychotherapy*, 21 (4), 14–22

Henwood, S and Soosalu, G (2014) The three brains of leadership: Harnessing the wisdom within, conference paper, ILA 16th Global Leadership Summit, San Diego

Levine, P A (1997) *Waking the Tiger: Healing trauma*, North Atlantic Books, Berkeley, CA

Oka, M (2016) The three brains: Why your head, heart and gut sometimes conflict, Australian Spinal Research Foundation, 26 July, spinalresearch.com.au/three-brains-head-heart-gut-sometimes-conflict/ (archived at https://perma.cc/7KW8-DXXF)

Soosalu, G, Henwood, S and Deo, A (2019) Head, heart, and gut in decision making: Development of a multiple brain preference questionnaire, *SAGE Open*, 9 (1), 1–17, doi.org/10.1177/2158244019837439 (archived at https://perma.cc/X4XG-CUTS)

Soosalu, G and Oka, M (2012) *mBraining: Using your multiple brains to do cool stuff*, mBIT International, Victoria, Australia

Storch, M and Tschacher, W (2017) Grundlagen des Embodiment-Ansatzes in den Humanwissenschaften, *Motorik*, 3, 118–26, doi.org/10.2378/mot2017.art20d (archived at https://perma.cc/PH6S-D57X)

Storch, M, Tschacher, W and Weber, J (2018) Embodiment in coaching and training, *Supervision: Mensch, Arbeit, Organisation*, 3, 19–24.

Van Der Kolk, B (2015) *The Body Keeps the Score: Mind, brain and body in the transformation of trauma*, Penguin Books, New York

17

Identifying and challenging blind spots in coaching

FRIDA BRUHN

ABSTRACT

Blind spots are areas of people's thinking or behaviour that they cannot see. For many clients, these are roadblocks that prevent the awareness that is the basis of their growth and progress. Without identifying and shining a light on blind spots, one can find oneself repeating the same behaviour patterns in an endless loop and not understanding why. The key is in appreciating what blind spots are, how to spot them as the coach, and which methods and tools can be offered to help clients see clearly to make the changes that will allow them to reach their goals in life.

Introduction

A minimum prerequisite for change is awareness of an issue, its impact and triggers (an understanding of the root causes will help too). As the core undertaking of coaching is to help a client bring about change to achieve their desired outcome(s), a lack of awareness is a certain dead end. According to the American Psychological Association (APA), a blind spot is 'a lack of insight or awareness – often persistent – about a specific area of one's behavior or personality, typically because recognition of one's true feelings and motives would be painful' (APA, 2022, para 2). Therefore, blind spots that block goal achievement are one of the first barriers that a coach will work on with their client.

In coaching, we often speak about the awareness development process in terms of 'peeling the layers of the onion'. If this deep exploration feels uncomfortable for the client, or they seem defensive or detached, it is likely associated with a blind spot. Coaches not only need empathy, listening, questioning and other coaching skills, but also self-awareness to ensure that their own blind spots are uncovered so as not to interfere with the coach–client exchange.

Without the commitment to lifelong learning, self-discovery and development, a coach's blind spots could interfere with their practice. But, as we are all humans and conditioned beings, it is understandable (and perfectly normal) for us to have a subjective reality and assumptions about our clients, ourselves, others and the world. To help our clients best discover and manage their blind spots, coaches should therefore also tend to their own at the same time.

This chapter shows different forms of blind spots, what they are and how to spot them, as well as introduce tools and methods to challenge your clients' blind spots by raising their awareness and thereby enabling their ability to create meaningful changes in their lives.

Understanding blind spots

In a study about self-assessment, Ethan Zell and Zlatan Krizan (2014) analysed 22 meta studies. They discovered the large majority of more than 200,000 participants had severe problems with self-assessment. Most participants exaggerated their strengths and disregarded or underestimated their weaknesses. Such skewed perception means you can only see what you are ready to see. When recognizing your true qualities, circumstances, feelings or motives is painful you are more likely to ignore them, often subconsciously. The subconscious can also repress information as a defensive or coping mechanism after a traumatic event, due to cultural and other conditioning during childhood, or even persistent access to one-sided information. These effects are some of the underlying causes and dynamics of a blind spot. In fact, the variety of areas in which you find blind spots cover the full range of human perception capacity. Some of the most common blind spots that a coach is likely to come across present as cognitive biases.

Cognitive biases

Every human being is an assumption machine. Assumptions happen spontaeously based on biases to speed up thinking or fill in the blanks of the unknown. The human brain is naturally 'lazy' as it tries to conserve energy for other life functions that may be more needed at the time. Also, we have an inherent need to find meaning and coherence in everything we experience, so our minds tend to fill gaps, make up stories and take shortcuts where something is incomplete.

Our individual upbringing influences these processes and how we view experiences, leading to how people automatically connect dots to make sense of somebody, a topic, a situation or a problem. Collectively, these thinking patterns are called cognitive biases, which often lead to misinterpretation, irrationality and inaccurate judgements. Therefore, by subconsciously simplifying information and taking short-cuts, you can find yourself making quick and efficient decisions, which is useful when detecting a real (or perceived) threat and need a quick response for survival, or when faced with an overload of information. However, the thinking patterns and association become a habit that our brains engage in even when not in 'danger' mode.

Therefore, understanding the cognitive biases hiding in the subconscious can help unravel blind spots. The following activities help uncover thinking errors and other blind spots:

- **Awareness** Thinking and reflecting about your thoughts, feelings and behaviour, the impact, and origins, as well as engaging with other people and receiving their feedback, help uncover people's blind spots.

- **Consider current factors that may be influencing your decision** The past is the past. We do not live in it any more, but we could learn from it. The present is different. Utilize mindfully what is useful from the past, but appraise only current factors to make your decision, thereby discarding pointless biases.

- **Reflect on the past** The past is where your modes and habits of thinking originated. What made you feel unsafe in the past may not be part of your present life any more, but the sensitivity and associations have already been created.

- **Seek multiple perspectives** Blind spots are borne from your individual experience and how you viewed it at the time, which created coping mechanisms in terms of thinking and reactions. It is all based on a single perspective that may be out of place now or misguided then. Getting other perspectives help to find an objective 'truth', highlight the difference between then and now, and reappraise a situation from a less emotive viewpoint.

- **Look for disconfirming evidence** When you identify a bias, which is like an erroneous belief, challenge it by weighing evidence supporting its truth against evidence that proves its flaws. Thereby, you can find a more useful alternative way of thinking that bypasses the automatic responses of the subconscious and involve the thinking centre of the brain more directly.

By following these actions, your thinking may be slower but more appropriate to your real situation. With a clearer mind that is void of distracting biases, it is still useful to identify imminent threats and respond quickly, and you make fewer errors and misjudgements. For instance, if you were unlucky enough to meet a sabre-toothed tiger, it is good not to meditate in depth on your perception of it but get to safety quickly. On the other hand, a colleague criticizing you is not a sabre-tooth tiger, and a thoughtful response will be more constructive.

Identifying and eliminating cognitive biases and other blind spots are important for coaches too. Successful coaches develop a deeper awareness of their cognitive, perceptual, emotional and behavioural systems, and become aware of blind spots and their impact. Such awareness prevents making wrong assumptions about a client, projecting ill-conceived feelings onto a client, and, as a result, making decisions and taking actions that may not be the best.

To date, social scientists have come up with and named almost 200 different cognitive biases. Table 17.1 lists 12 of the most common ones found in the coaching space and looks at their relation to blind spots and what coaches could do to help their clients (and themselves) reveal and eliminate these.

TABLE 17.1 Common cognitive biases linked to blind spots

Bias name	Definition	How blind spot is connected to bias	How to help clients see their blind spots
Horn bias	Judging people based on one negative trait	Often a projection of one's own insecurities	Why do you think X did/acts that way? This opens the conversation to help the client see another perspective
Confirmation bias	The process of information in which one looks for, interprets and recalls things in a way that is aligned with their belief system	They will unintentionally ignore anything that is inconsistent with their beliefs, therefore not accurately recalling information the way it happened; instead they recall it in the way that they *believed* it happened	Ask for a different possibility, view, interpretation, perspective. Look at evidence for and against all views
Loss aversion	When one weighs losses more heavily then gains	The fear of failure and its attachments to what would happen if they were to fail	Do a SWOT analysis. Explore with the client what failure would mean in 5–10 years' time and what positive could come from it
Herd mentality	To conform with the actions of a larger group with the assumption that everyone knows what they are doing	Fitting in with social norms and allowing it to cloud their judgement, and actions	Gain clarity on values, character, principles. Ask if they feel what is happening is in alignment with them
Self-serving bias	When one takes credit for positive outcomes and blames external factors for negative outcomes	A limited mindset might attach results to self-worth	For negative outcomes, explore with the client what was in their control to do differently (circles of control). A person and their self-worth are not defined by their failures and what happens to them

(continued)

TABLE 17.1 (Continued)

Bias name	Definition	How blind spot is connected to bias	How to help clients see their blind spots
Overconfidence	Tendency to assess our skills, talents or intellect as greater than they actually are	Overestimate how fast they can do a task and underestimate how long it would take them	Do you feel that's realistic? Follow up with a breakdown of what such a task would require
Authority bias	Blindly following the beliefs, methods and strategies of a person with authority, without putting any thought into it	When one internalizes an obedient response in family, society, home, school or work environment	Gain clarity on values and what is important to them and compare it to the current situation
Expert bias	The coach thinks they know the situation, and therefore the client and solution	The coach is inclined to judge, give advice, suggest reasons and solutions, while not realizing their strong tendency	Every coach needs a coach (and a supervisor) to provide a reflective space to deeper understand their own value and position
Negativity bias	Tendency to focus on negative experience while minimizing positive ones	A person does not realize that they push their baseline level of happiness down, thereby overlooking positive opportunities and strengths	Ask client to list positive experiences and accomplishments. Focus on strengths that support their goals. Look at the positives in negative situations
Similarity trap	Thinking what we've gone through before or with another person, is happening again	A person does not understand why or notice that repeat responses always get them in a similar situation	Identify, question beliefs linked to unhelpful repeated behaviour. Formulate new beliefs
Status quo bias	Preference for staying with the current situation and opposing changes	A person has a strong reluctance, fear or aversion to change that they do not consciously acknowledge	See Chapter 29 on how to help clients overcome fears and step out of their comfort zone to fulfil their potential
Principle of humanity	Thinking that others are somehow better (or worse) than you	Every single person is exactly what you would be if you were them, lived in their shoes and had their experiences	Encourage empathy with your client. For them to see others as they wish to be seen, explore the interconnectedness of everything

These and other cognitive biases (or errors) are sometimes also referred to collectively as bias blind spots due to their effect of hiding or covering reality. As such, they are mostly subconscious phenomena related to self-preservation, not only of the physical self, but the ego as well. Clients stuck in these patterns of subjective (limiting) thinking such as confirmation bias ('I have to do everything as my colleague is lazy'), authority bias ('This is what the boss wanted so it must be right') and objectivity illusion ('I am objective, you are misinformed') – to name just a few out of hundreds of named cognitive biases – are less likely to stick to new habits, be motivated to change and achieve their goals than their peers with more awareness and an open mindset. These are all qualities and results that coaches generally pursue with their clients.

When you see blind spots for the first time, you might think that Pandora's box just opened before you. The width, depth, texture and volume of blind spots related to the impact they could play out in the life of clients within the client–coach relationship, us and others, are endless. As coaches, we serve our clients by creating spaces where dreams can unfold. Sudden insights can feel like magic. More expansive thinking, including unseen dots becoming visible and connecting with one another, could reveal what has been in your way all along. Extended awareness helps the client develop action steps for their desired change by unblocking unhelpful thinking patterns that used to be blind spots.

Discovering your blind spots in the learning process

Blind spots and the associated biases that represent them are natural mechanisms designed to keep us safe. Nevertheless, to function optimally in our social world, exposing and understanding our blind spots support self-mastery, which makes us more connected. Swiss psychiatrist and father of psychoanalytic theory Carl Jung said:

> There can never be absolute freedom from prejudice, for even the most objective and impartial investigator is liable to become the victim of some unconscious assumption upon entering a region where the darkness has never been illuminated and where he can recognize nothing (1954: 168).

In simpler terms, prejudice and assumptions are natural and typical human decision-making and behaviour qualities. However, these are blind spots as they reside in the subconscious, meant to protect us but often misguided. Only awareness and learning can illuminate the darkness of a blind spot to allow conscious consideration of its existence, meaning and impact.

In the 1970s, training guru Noel Burch developed a learning model that he called the 'Four Stages of Learning Any New Skill'. According to Burch, the skills and abilities needed to master a new skill are acquired in four stages. Figure 17.1 shows

FIGURE 17.1 The four stages of learning

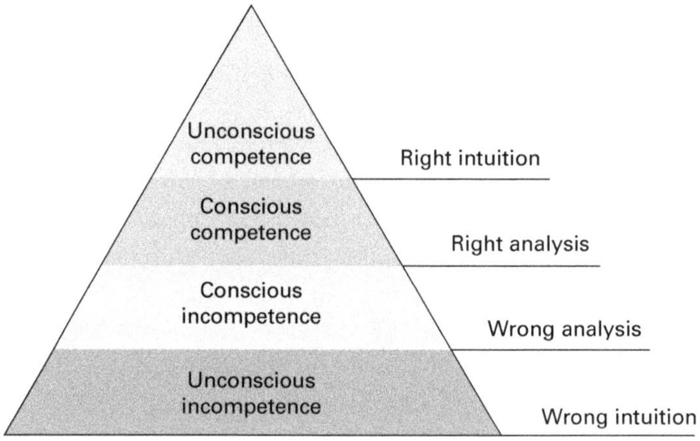

SOURCE Kavis (2015), image by I Kokcharov

these four stages of learning in progressive order, namely 1) unconscious incompetence, 2) conscious incompetence, 3) conscious competence, and 4) unconscious
competence (Kavis, 2015).

Unconscious incompetence

Typically, learning experiences start in the unconscious incompetence area. According
to Dunning and Kruger, the journey begins on what they called 'Mount Stupid'
(Swart, 2022a). Somebody who has just started learning a new skill and does not
know yet what they do not know is in this position. They are unconscious of their
incompetency. Not (yet) aware of what they do not see, they are free of worry, which
can lead to a state of high spirits, overconfidence, arrogance and complacency. If left
on their own, the newbie will likely make decisions and take uninformed and potentially harmful actions.

As a coach, you may find yourself in this position in areas where you are not
competent but do not give it a second thought and, therefore, coach outside your
ethical boundaries (see Chapter 2). To remedy the risk, participate in continuous
professional development (CPD), utilize supervision and peer support, and constantly
self-reflect to know and expand your competencies.

When your client is at this stage, progressive questions can help them gain a
deeper awareness of their strengths and competencies. They will find out about gaps
that need to be addressed. It will strengthen their curiosity and eagerness to learn
and develop. First, establish a client's level of knowledge and experience. Then, ask
questions such as 'Which risks do you associate with that decision?' 'Is there something you don't know or understand yet that can change your response?' 'If you were

to look at the issue from the other side, what would it look like?' These, and similar questions, will help to create an awareness of the client's knowledge limitations, obstacles and gaps.

Conscious incompetence

Now reality hits. A client's shortcoming comes into their view as insight. The more unconscious incompetencies were hidden, the bigger the surprise for the learner. Experiencing imposter syndrome is natural (see Chapter 22). The person feels like a fraud who has lived in a make-believe world and got ahead just because they managed to fool others into believing they know what they are doing. They are fearful of being exposed as incompetent, which also creates a compelling reason to learn. So, this is a great place to continue working on becoming aware and learning. Dunning–Kruger names this point in the learning process the 'Valley of Despair' (Swart, 2022a). With the increased anxiety, there is pressure on you and your client to quit, so you must work on commitment and motivation levels to get through the anxiety and continue learning. As a coach, remind yourself why knowledge and competence are essential for your practice and ability to serve your clients better. Set a schedule and build a routine of CPD activities and self-reflection.

With your clients, ask questions that reinforce their motivation to learn and the associated benefits of gaining knowledge and experience. Questions like 'How could this competency change your life?' and 'Which one small thing do you have to master or learn to continue developing this competency?' Also, help your client accept and manage anxiety around feeling like an imposter. Let them become aware of what might be holding them back when their heightened frustration and fear of failure kicks in. You can ask, 'Can you think of any positive aspects of your feelings of uncertainty?' and 'How do you think your fear of failure can help your progress?' Remember that recognizing imposter syndrome and that one is in a stage of conscious incompetence is not only a normal experience but can be productive as well, in providing the motivation and direction to increase knowledge.

Conscious competence

Up to this stage, competencies have grown slowly but consistently to the extent where the person can apply their knowledge effectively by putting thought behind it. Positive results and encouraging feedback from peers or authorities in the field of expertise support the effort to use one's well-earned knowledge effectively and continuously. Dunning and Kruger speak about the 'Slope of Enlightenment' when you can start to experience significant and even exponential growth on the learning curve.

This stage is probably associated with intense satisfaction and celebration of a well-done job. But do not become overconfident or complacent, as there is always much more to learn and experience! As a coach, do not neglect self-reflection and exploring other blind spots and unconscious incompetencies that you may want to address. Do not become complacent, and remember that learning is not a unipolar and one-dimensional exercise. You will likely find yourself in different learning stages in multiple areas of your profession. For example, you may have done career coaching up to now and have become very proficient but want to add trauma coaching to your repertoire, an area you're not experienced in. While maintaining and updating your knowledge in the career coaching area, you will now go through the same learning stages from the beginning in the trauma field.

When overconfidence or complacency comes up with your clients, question the potential consequences of such attitudes to create an awareness of the need for responsibility and continuous learning. Ask, 'What is next for you?' 'What new can you learn or practise to continue your progress?' There is always room for growth and improvement. Help your client stay conscious of where they are, what they know (and don't know). Knowledge is not static but grows all the time in the direction where it is needed in the world. Also, when your client is in the stage of conscious competence, they may want to consider teaching others to grow into the same position.

Unconscious competence

Practitioners may eventually arrive over time to the point of unconscious competence, where their complex mastery has become unconscious. Here, the routine might feel enjoyable and risk free. Their practice and actions become second nature without much deliberate thought underlying it. Remember that it is easy for your mind on autopilot to miss a special circumstance or an unexpected consequence. In areas of importance (coaching a client always is!), do not be complacent but engage your higher thinking functions and make every question and action deliberate. If the joy fades, boredom, dissatisfaction and even a lack of purpose might appear again. According to the motto 'thrive or die', a new learning experience often rejuvenates a person and keeps their brain at the highest level of functioning.

So, using an understanding of the learning process to manage our relationship towards our and our clients' blind spots enables us to stay committed and find joy and fulfillment to diligently continue our craft towards mastery. We appreciate that we all are works in progress.

The Johari window as a coaching tool to create awareness

Signs of blind spots can be spotted when watching yourself and your clients. For example, your conversation includes (unexplained) negativity, vanity, arrogance, defensiveness, inattentiveness when listening and prejudices. Joseph Luft and

FIGURE 17.2 The Johari window diagram

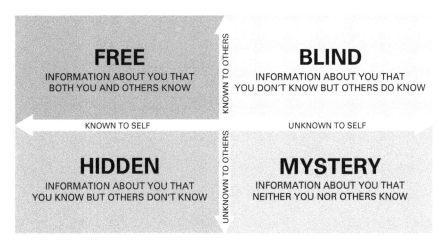

SOURCE Shutterstock

Harrington Ingham, both psychologists, developed the Johari window as a technique to help people explore their insight into their relationship with themselves and others (Swart, 2022b). The Johari window has four quadrants (Figure 17.2), indicating qualities:

1 Known to the self and others (open area)

2 Known to the self but not to others (hidden area)

3 Known to others but not the self (blind area)

4 Known to the self or others (mystery or unknown place)

Completing the Johari window stimulates the self-awareness and elimination of blind spots required to interact constructively with others and build better self-knowledge and confidence. Therefore, offered to clients, it is a simple but effective tool to explore and develop self-awareness.

Johari window exercise

1 The client uses the copy of the Johari window adjectives list (Table 17.2) to choose 12 adjectives that they believe best describe themselves.

2 The client asks 3–5 other people – partner, family member, colleague or friend – to choose eight adjectives that best describe them.

3 Of these, adjectives on the client's list are placed in the Open quadrant, while those not on the client's list go to the Blind quadrant.

TABLE 17.2 Johari window adjectives

Able	Critical	Impulsive	Nervous	Self-conscious
Accepting	Decisive	Independent	Observant	Self-contained
Adaptable	Demanding	Influential	Open	Sensible
Adventurous	Dependable	Ingenious	Organized	Sentimental
Aggressive	Dignified	Innovative	Patient	Shy
Assertive	Diplomatic	Inspirational	Powerful	Silly
Autocratic	Dominating	Intelligent	Private	Spiritual
Autonomous	Empathetic	Introverted	Proud	Spontaneous
Bold	Energetic	Intuitive	Quiet	Sympathetic
Brave	Even-tempered	Kind	Reflective	Systematic
Calm	Extroverted	Knowledgeable	Reliable	Talkative
Caring	Flexible	Listener	Relaxed	Tenacious
Cheerful	Friendly	Logical	Religious	Tense
Clever	Giving	Loving	Responsive	Thorough
Complex	Happy	Loyal	Risk-taker	Trustworthy
Compliant	Helpful	Mature	Searching	Warm
Confident	Humorous	Modest	Self-assertive	Wise
Courageous	Idealistic	Motivator	Self-aware	Witty

4 Any adjectives on the client's list that were not mentioned by observers are placed in the Hidden quadrant.

5 After completing the Johari window, the coach asks the client questions to help them reflect on their blind spots. 'What was surprising for you according to the perceptions of others?' 'Which adjectives in the hidden area would you be willing to share with others?' 'How can you do that?' 'Was there any description with which you could not relate?' 'If any, what are the adjectives that may be "in the closet", so to speak, that are currently unknown but may be significant in the future in the context of your goals?'

The Johari window process of coach–client exploration helps identify 1–2 blind spots to focus on and illuminate by building awareness through questioning and deeper exploration with the help of techniques like the GROW system (see Chapter 18). It can also highlight unknown areas to develop and utilize, and give the confidence and understanding to own and open up hidden areas. Each area potentially forms the basis of creating a specific action plan to eliminate blind spots.

Conclusion

As a coach, make it your commitment to shine light in the proverbial darkness. Shine a light on your and your clients' worlds. Spread freedom by starting to heal shadows within yourself. It will benefit your clients, co-workers, people, community, culture and everyone else around you. Never compromise on guidance or inspiration. Find your style. Do not count ups and downs. Obstacles will not stop you when walking in trust, honesty and a knowledge of who you are.

Think of the unconscious competence quadrant – this is your direction towards mastery. It will not always be easy. There will be hard times and setbacks. However, understanding and illuminating your blind spots (and those of your clients) is a solid foundation for improved progress and satisfaction.

References

APA (2022) Blind spot, *APA Dictionary of Psychology*, American Psychological Association, dictionary.apa.org/blind-spots (archived at https://perma.cc/Q79K-DU53)

Jung, C G (1954) *The Collected Works: The practice of psychotherapy, volume 16*, 2nd edn, Routledge, London

Kavis, M (2015) The four stages of cloud competence, *Forbes*, 21 October, www.forbes.com/sites/mikekavis/2015/10/21/the-four-stages-of-cloud-competence (archived at https://perma.cc/3D49-7YZN).

Swart, J (2022a) When you think you know more (or less) than anyone else – the Dunning–Kruger effect and imposter syndrome, *Global Scientific Journals*, 10 (10), 1382–95, eoi. citefactor.org/10.11216/gsj.2022.10.77783 (archived at https://perma.cc/PJ27-XYT4)

Swart, J (2022b) The Johari window as a coaching tool, *ResearchGate*, doi.org/10.13140/RG.2.2.31350.27203 (archived at https://perma.cc/5WBV-9FW2)

Zell, E and Krizan, Z (2014) Do people have insight into their abilities? A metasynthesis, *Perspectives on Psychological Science*, 9 (2), 111–25, doi.org/10.1177/1745691613518075 (archived at https://perma.cc/XPZ9-ZVU9)

18

Coaching tools and techniques

LOUISE SOCKETT

ABSTRACT

Edgar Dale explained in his 'Cone of Experience' that we internalize about 20–50 per cent of what we see and hear (1969). However, an effective coaching process requires a deeper learning experience for the benefit of both the coach and clients. The purpose of this chapter is to present coaching tools and techniques that could provide coaches with deeper experiential learning options with which to extract internalized information from clients to help raise their awareness and insight.

Introduction

Clients do not seek coaching solutions 'done to them'. They seek coaching to find solutions 'done with them'. The role of the coach in a 'done with them' session is to guide, support and encourage the client to achieve a specific goal. However, a coach needs the right tools and techniques to address the right situation. The question is, what could be substantiated as the 'right tools' for the 'right situation'?

The listening, risk taking, goal setting, GROW framework, and making decisions tools and techniques in this chapter were identified through a lean survey as the core of what is causing clients' frustration, lack of self-worth and unravelled confidence. By implementing and using these tools, a coach can empower a client to overcome short-comings such as listening skills and risk taking, applying the GROW framework, goal setting and decision making. Even though the chosen learning experiences can be seen as basic and taken for granted, clients perceive the development of these skills as essential.

Learning by doing motivates clients to turn their aspirations and ideas into action. Learning by doing focuses on (Clutterbuck and Megginson, 2005; Driver, 2011; Hawkins, 2011):

- Healthy relationships instead of toxic ones
- Strengths rather than weaknesses
- What works, rather than what does not work
- Success and how to achieve it, instead of stumbling blocks and how to avoid it
- Goal and desired outcomes instead of unsolvable problems
- Personal development, resilience and a growth mindset rather than poor coping and negativity

This viewpoint creates a canvas of opportunities for clients to regain their balance and harmony in life. Having balance implies that all parts of their life – mental steadiness, emotional stability, habit of calm behaviour and judgement – form a harmonious whole (Martens-Schmid, 2007; Mumford, 2007). Being off-balance suggests the opposite. Feelings of overwhelm, neglect and lack of control can send a client over the tipping point. Balance implies control of yourself and your goals, your decision making and ability to take calculated risks (Coach U, Inc, 2005). We want to help our clients take steps towards regaining that balance in their lives. In addition, balance provides flexibility, allowing clients to choose what to let go of, and how they want to express their needs in a coaching session (Jones and Gorell, 2018).

Tool #1: Listening

Listening is an everyday activity but multifaceted and complex. Even if we listen, people do not always hear what others have to say (Jarvis, Lane and Fillery-Travis, 2006). HOW we listen has a major impact on the quality of our relations with others. WHY we listen provides some evidence of who we are and the impact we have on those around us (Franklin, 2019). Do we listen to better understand others, learn more, obtain information, or enjoy the exchange, connection, or something else? Tool #1 underscores the importance of helping clients to appreciate the significance and effects of active listening versus critical, judgemental or distracted listening.

The literature explains three types of listening (Martin, 2001; Richardson, 2004), for example:

- **Active listening** Active listening is often fuelled by both our verbal and subconscious awareness of the other person's nonverbal cues. Such listeners are not trying to evaluate the message or suggest their own opinion. For them it is important to make the speaker feel heard and validated by catching and understanding the entire message and verifying their understanding.

- **Critical listening** Hearing and understanding the client's message. This is typically what a coach will do to help a client with their dilemma. We still need to understand what the other person is saying, but we also have the responsibility to evaluate what is being said and how it is being said.
- **Judgemental listening** Making judgements while listening to the client creates a barrier and the speaker's message is not understood.

The following activity puts the theory into practice. The client may do a similar activity with two friends or colleagues at work and report back to the coach in the next session:

- **Person #1** is from Iceland. During the cold winters they wear jackets to stay warm.
- **Person #2** lives in the Sahara Desert where temperatures soar to exceptionally high levels. They are not familiar with wearing jackets.
- **Person #3** checks that all goes well.
- *Person #1* must explain to *person #2* how to put on a jacket.
- Both of them stand back-to-back, looking in opposite directions, about five feet apart.
- Both close their eyes, keep them closed, and stay in position.
- *Person #3*, the observer, must turn the jacket upside down before handing it to *person #2*.
- *Person #1* is ready to explain to *person #2* how to put the jacket on.
- *Person #3* rates the 'performance' of both participants on a scale from 1 to 10 (1 being poor and 10 being excellent).

The coach asks the following questions for group discussion and reflection:

- How difficult or easy was this activity? What made it hard or easy?
- What lesson related to 'listening' have you learnt? What will you do differently in future, based on this lesson?
- Provide feedback to your coach and discuss your success or commitment to improve your listening skills.

The biggest challenge with communication is not the message as such, but rather the ability to hear what has been said without making assumptions. At its simplest, communication is transferring a message from one person to the next. The message could be verbal, using voice, written or in print; visual, explaining how to put on a jacket; or non-verbal, using gestures, tone and pitch of voice. Even though the individual has prior knowledge of how to put on a jacket, they may not be able to translate the message into action. Miscommunication is often the result of not being able to see the other person and interpret both their voice and non-verbal gestures, as in this case.

Tool #2: Risk taking

US Navy Rear Admiral Hopper once said, 'A ship in port is safe; but that is not what ships are built for' (Galford and Maruca, 2006: 139). People are no different. Risk taking embraces the challenges in the world with the self-belief that you are able and capable of achieving success. Risk taking is an opportunity to learn new things and become more visible in society or at work. Failed risks are not always negative. It provides the opportunity to learn valuable lessons of what to change, why and how. What we need to overcome is the willingness to take a small risk and then, as our self-confidence and awareness increases, take a bigger risk.

Former Secretary of State Colin Powell had a particular approach when faced with making a quick decision. He called it the 40/70 rule. He strived not to make a decision with less than 40 per cent of the information needed, then ultimately make the decision when he had at most 70 per cent of the information (Els and Sockett, 2022). How much information do you need to make a decision? We never have all the information before we make decisions. Therefore, mitigating some of the risks to offset gaps in information is a good idea. Timely decision making has become a sought-after skill in the fast-paced world we live in.

DECISION-MAKING EXERCISE

The coach reads out the following story to the client (Hopson and Scally, 1985: 222). Every now and then, the coach must say 'PAUSE for 20 seconds and decide whether you want to act or not'. This helps the client get an opportunity to make a decision to act before the story ends.

You are on holiday walking along a lonely beach one evening. (PAUSE).

You come across a pile of neatly folded clothes but there was no one around, only a dog some distance away. (PAUSE).

You walk on and notice the waves washing over a surfboard. (PAUSE).

The dog is sniffing at the surfboard, barking, and whimpering and looking out at sea. (PAUSE).

The waves are now pounding onto the beach. Do you hear faint shouts above the noise? (PAUSE).

Out at sea, between the ebb and flow of the waves, you can see something floating. (PAUSE).

It looks like a bright yellow life jacket, but it's not clear. (PAUSE).

At the end of the beach is a coastguard's telephone and just a few feet away, is a sign that warns people about the danger of swimming in this area. (PAUSE).

The dog is now getting frantic and running backwards and forwards between the surfboard and the clothes. (PAUSE).

Once you are done with the activity, reflect on your 'PAUSE' decision:

- What did you decide and why?
- When did you decide? Was it early enough?
- Why do you think your decision was the best given the circumstances?

Now, reflect on why you avoided a decision:

- Why did you not decide?
- What else would you have needed to know before deciding?
- What type of hindrances or feelings prevented you from making a decision during the activity, for example sadness, discomfort, powerlessness or anything else?
- What in your mind could have been the reason(s) for it?

The coach helps the client understand that uncertainty can block action taking. The coach discusses feelings of uncertainty and powerlessness that the client may have experienced, which are the most common issues. What we do not know (uncertainty) and what we cannot control (powerlessness) creates the emotional condition of anxiety. Anxiety is at its peak when there are many unknowns. Coaches can guide their clients to ask themselves, 'What can I control?' 'What do I have power over right now and how can I release the things I cannot control?' (Conley, 2013). To focus too much on uncertainty leads to feelings of helplessness, a common experience of many clients in this case.

Tool #3: Goal setting

Paul Solomon, known as the American 'sleeping prophet', teacher and humanitarian, once said, '… you came into the world to accomplish something, and that the something you came to accomplish is not small or insignificant. That's not worthy of you. You came here to make a major contribution to life on this planet' (Shapiro, 2006: 705).

Setting and accomplishing goals cannot be 'small or insignificant'. You are here to make a meaningful difference. That includes everything you want to be and can be in life.

It aligns your focus and promotes a sense of self-mastery. Often attributed to Peter Drucker (2018) it has been said, 'If you can't measure it, you can't improve it'. If you don't measure, then how do you know how you are doing? How do you know whether your performance is significant? Or poorly? In the end, you can't manage what you don't measure and you can't improve upon something that you don't properly manage. Setting goals improves productivity, focus and the effective use of time.

Clearly defined goals and actions provide clients with the opportunity to live a life that is tailored to their beliefs and values. Goals give direction towards the things that they most want to achieve. They also mould our individual efforts and motivate us to develop the behaviours that will keep us on course and allow momentum. Without momentum, there is no progress or tangible success (Whitmore, 1992). In fact, without clarity and momentum procrastination kicks in.

The question is, where do we start and how do we set goals? Goal setting is a two-fold process: 1) identify the goal and 2) list the actions to be taken to achieve the goal:

- **Step 1: Start with the end in mind**
  Goal setting starts with identifying the 'topic' of the overarching goal so that the client can visualize what it is they anticipate. Before doing the activity, think about your end goal and what it is you want to achieve. Do you want to improve something? Design something? Save money? Let's say you want to save money for a new car. Now answer the following questions: Who (person) wants to do what (action), when (due date) and where (location), why (reason) and how (method/strategy)? However, not all these questions are relevant to every goal. Select the information that's providing direction, clarity and specificity. For example: '(Who?) I will (what?) save $8,000 (why?) to buy a brand-new car (when?) before 5 January 2024.' This your first attempt. In step 4 you will revisit your goal and add or change what's necessary.

- **Step 2: Minimum effort**
  This is where success starts. No goal is achievable without specific and well-defined actions planned ahead. What are the minimum effort or micro-commitments you must achieve to achieve your goal? If you can define and achieve the most basic part of your goal, you will slowly but surely gain momentum. Let's say your end goal is 'I will save $8,000 to buy a brand-new car on 5 January 2024'. The smallest action to take is to think about how and where you can save money. Make your list of possibilities, for example, 'Prepare your food at home instead of dining out several times per week'.

- **Step 3: Target goal**
  Your third step is to dive deeper. Now that you know how and where you can save money, determine the more significant and specific actions you need to take to generate savings. For example, to prepare your own food at home and save money, you need to 'Search google for economical and healthy recipes'. You are now taking action to refine what you will be doing to eat healthy food at home, so that you save more money to buy a car.

- **Step 4: Stretch goal**
  This is the big one! A stretch goal is an ambitious one. If you do not earn a big salary, then saving $8,000 before 5 January 2024, is an immense challenge. *Step 4* is where you evaluate whether your goal is a high-effort goal, set above normal standards to stretch you to attract opportunities, experience, rewards or simply

to buy your dream car. We all need stretch goals to unlock potential and growth, to test out limits and to apply new skills and talent. A stretch goal is the peak of the mountain and demands a commitment, energy and focus to get done.

Listing all the necessary actions and tracking your progress is quick and easy. Most clients who do not gain momentum are also not achieving their goals. Yet, to have a goal is only one part of achieving anything. Well-defined micro-actions and clear targets are what guide the client in how to achieve the goal. Using a sheet to list micro-commitments and target actions that lead to the stretch goal is helpful (see Table 18.1).

TABLE 18.1 From micro-commitment and targets to stretch goals

Initial goal: I will save $8,000 to buy a brand-new car on 5 January 2024	
No Micro-commitments	Target actions
1 Stay at home one weekend per month	List things to do during my stay-in weekend
2 Cut back on travelling	Travelling every second year
3 Open a savings bank account	Save $571 per month for 14 months
4 Quit smoking	Avoid the Smoker's Club at work
5 Save 10% of my income	Keep a record of every dollar earned
6 Explore the car market and prices	Keep a photo of my new car in my wallet
7 Prepare food at home instead of dining out	Search Google for heathy and economical food recipes
8 Work longer hours twice a week	Reschedule activities to create balance
Final goal: I will save $8,000 to buy a brand-new car on 5 January 2024, (how?) by cutting back on all my luxury spending	

The 'eight sunrays to goal achievement' exercise and visual aid is another way to list and track commitments and goals.

EXERCISE

Eight sunrays to goal achievement

There are many ways to set a goal. The following activity, shown in Figure 18.1, is designed to assist you in setting goals in a more visual and creative way:

- Draw a big circle in the middle of an A4 page. Then draw a smaller circle in the centre of the big circle.

- Write the first version of your *stretch goal*, the ultimate achievement, in the centre of the circle.

- Draw eight lines from the middle of the big circle to the outer edges of your page – like sunrays.

- Brainstorm several *minimum effort actions (Step 1)* before you select the most significant eight actions that will eventually lead you to achieve your *stretch goal* in the centre. Record the actions on the outer edge of your sunray – one action for every sunray.

- Brainstorm your eight *target actions* and write the chosen ones in the middle of your sunray lines. Target actions is a refinement and further elaboration of how to achieve the *micro-commitment* actions in *Step 1*. For example, if your minimum action is 'to quit smoking', then your target action may be 'to avoid the Smoker's Club at work'.

- Consider your initial stretch goal again to determine whether it is specific, measurable, achievable, realistic and timebound. You now have all the information needed to accomplish your *stretch goal*.

Once you have mastered the eight sunrays to goal achievement, you might want to try out SMART goals, a more comprehensive goal-setting technique (see Chapter 30).

FIGURE 18.1 Eight sunrays to goal achievement

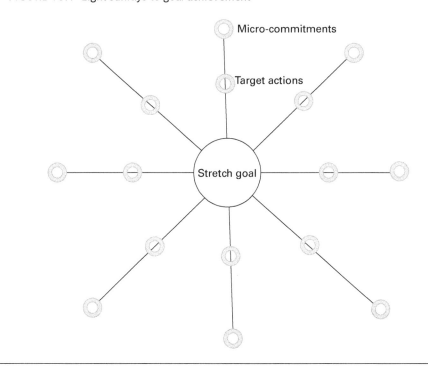

Tool #4: GROW framework

The evergreen GROW framework, designed by Sir John Whitmore and his colleagues, is still one of the most popular frameworks to guide a conversation with clients (Stoltzfus, 2008). In its purest form, this model uses the ask technique to help clients understand their situation. Questions, when formulated clearly, are the quickest path to appropriate solutions (Adams, 2022).

1 *Step 1* of the GROW framework allows clients to explore what they want from life or how to overcome specific problems and challenges. Finding clarity and meaningfulness help clients to envision their future and the steps they need to take to move forward and to set the goal that will take them there. Once they have a clear vision of their direction, they can set their *Goal*. Over time the client develops a personal connection to that goal.

2 In *Step 2* clients are faced with the *Reality* around them. It allows them to explore their motivational connection to the goal. Stocktaking is an important part of the framework to help clients to identify their strengths and areas for further development. What is blocking their progress? What could enhance their progress?

3 In *Step 3*, depending on where clients are in life, the coach will help them to either explore the available *Options* to achieve the goal, or to identify and work with the *Obstacles* blocking progress. It is a vital stage. One of the most popular questions at this stage is to ask the client, 'If you had no problems with people, money, time or skill, what would you find yourself doing?' It both identifies the options and creates awareness of what the current obstacles are.

4 In *Step 4*, the *Way forward*, the client gets the opportunity to create action plans. The client can use either Table 18.1 or Figure 18.1 to list the actions that lead to success in goal achievement. But the client needs to be willing and accountable to put in the time and energy to move towards their goal in a structured way.

Following the framework process provides a predictable outcome when it is aligned with the ability, needs, pace and commitment of the client – as long as it is not rushed through.

For most people the starting point is to set goals, to check the current reality, consider possible options and obstacles, and to encourage the individual to 'will' forward, as explained below (Bressler, Bressler and Bressler, 2010; Woolley and Fishbach, 2017). Questions to use during a coaching session cannot be predicted, but sound preparation can accelerate the process.

In conclusion, the solution focused GROW framework is a significant practice if facilitated by a trained professional. Effective coaches ask powerful questions to open the potential of the client and empower and encourage the individual to find the answers themselves. The client sets the goals, they determine the actions, and in the process, also what success looks like for them. The results speak for themselves when there is commitment, collaboration, dedication and the resilience to work with and not against the process. However, it is not without limitations. A client's lack of time and resources, low levels of skills, and resistance to the challenges of change, are some of the most common reasons for failure, but can be overcome by a skilled coach through motivation, reinforcement, adapting goals and approaches, and client development.

Tool #5: Making decisions

Living without making decisions is as inconceivable as living without breathing (Aguilar, 2021). We make up to 35,000 decisions every day, even if we are not aware or are barely aware of making most of them (Hoomans, 2015). Yet, we often spend a great deal of time thinking or even agonizing over less-important decisions. However, we cannot make progress in life without the sound ability to make decisions. Decision making is our gateway to our life's journey and the main propellant of self-empowerment and self-management through action.

Significant decisions require all our capabilities, which include both our intuition (feelings) and our reasoning (thinking) as explained in Figure 18.2. However, that does not guarantee the outcome we anticipated. Many situational factors can confound or overcomplicate our decision-making process and therefore also the outcome (Hawkins, 2011).

Decision-making approaches can be quite diverse. Much of how we make decisions has to do with two main approaches:

- **Rational approach** The first approach refers to the sequence of steps designed to *rationally* develop a desired solution. Drawing particularly on our experiences and attitudes, it does this by helping us to cut through the excessive information that can overload and delay decisions.

- **Intuitive approach** The second approach is more *intuitive,* instinctive, subjective and subconscious in nature. This implies that our decisions are based on judgements that are affected by a range of factors, including our experiences, values, attitudes and emotions.

In Figure 18.2, we explain both approaches to determine the preferred approach in making decisions.

Discover your preferred decision-making style using Table 18.3.

- Redraw the table on an A4 sheet of paper.

- Put together a list of 10 decisions you must make at work, at home, about friends, shopping, and more.

TABLE 18.2 GROW framework

GROW framework	Meaning	Questions
G = Goal	A *goal* is a target that you work towards with effort and determination	• What do you wish to work on? • What do you want the outcome to be after answering the set of questions (e.g. a first step/solution)? • What goal is related to this issue? • When are you going to achieve it? • How will you know that you have achieved your goal? • What are the benefits for you in achieving this goal? • Who else will benefit and in what way? • What will it be like for you to achieve your goal? • What will you see/hear/feel?
R = Reality/ context	*Reality* refers to the things in life that are commonly observed and verified to exist as real	• Where are you now in relation to this goal? • How much control do you have over it? • What is moving you towards your goal? • What is hindering you in reaching your goal?
O = Options/ obstacles	An *obstacle* is something that blocks your way so that movement or progress is prevented or made more difficult. An *option* is the opposite	• What different kinds of options do you have to achieve your goal? • What else could you do? • What are the principal advantages and disadvantages of each option? • Are there any new options that were not available before?
W = Will	*Will* refers to a strong desire or determination to do something	• Which options will you choose to act on? • When are you going to start each action? • How committed are you, on a scale of 1–10, to taking each of these actions? • If it is not a 10, what would make it a 10? • What will you commit to doing? (Note: It is also an option to do nothing and review at a later date.)

- First identify the approach, i.e., rational or intuitive, you want to follow for each of the 10 decisions.
- Then decide which decision-making style in Table 18.3 would best fit each of the 10 pending decisions on your list.
- Tick the box on the scale, from rational to intuitive, that applies to how you prefer to make decisions most of the time.
- What is your preferred approach to decision making? Explain.

FIGURE 18.2 The two-factor decision-making style

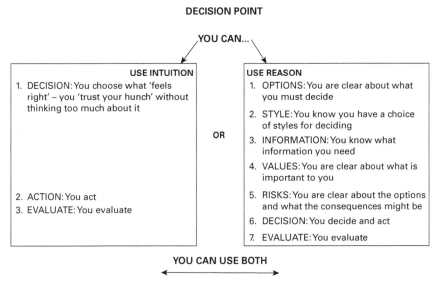

DECISION POINT

YOU CAN...

USE INTUITION	USE REASON
1. DECISION: You choose what 'feels right' – you 'trust your hunch' without thinking too much about it	1. OPTIONS: You are clear about what you must decide
	2. STYLE: You know you have a choice of styles for deciding
OR	3. INFORMATION: You know what information you need
	4. VALUES: You are clear about what is important to you
2. ACTION: You act	5. RISKS: You are clear about the options and what the consequences might be
3. EVALUATE: You evaluate	6. DECISION: You decide and act
	7. EVALUATE: You evaluate

YOU CAN USE BOTH

SOURCE Hopson and Scally (1985: 161)

Although there is no right or wrong answer, it is to your advantage to learn how to apply both approaches. Revisit the story about the individual we assumed to be somewhere in the ocean. Reflecting on the decision-making style you have applied in the story; would you change your decision-making approach based on what you now know?

Before you refine your decision-making style, let's elaborate on what the checklist explains.

- **Rational decisions** We choose rational decision making when we follow strict procedures utilizing our objective knowledge and logic. It is expected of you to identify the problem to solve, to gather facts, identifying outcomes and analysing them, consider relationships and make the decision.

- **Intuitive decision** We choose intuitive decisions when there is little to no information to guide your decision making, when you are pressured to make the decision right away, or when you are under time pressure. It could also include ambiguity and lack of clarity or data.

Reflect on each of the following questions and discuss the answers with your coach:

- What have you learnt about decision making from this activity?
- How do you know that your decision-making style is the most appropriate to follow for the decision you have made?

TABLE 18.3 Decision styles

	From rational to intuitive decision making					
Pending decision	Think it through	You just know	Go along with others	Feels right	Wait and see	Get on with it
Whether to find a new job or not				X		

SOURCE Adapted from Hopson and Scally (1985)

- Will you make decisions differently in future based on the insight(s) you have gained?
- How can you further improve your decision-making skills, whether simple or complex?

In conclusion, decision making is an art. There are so many reasons why your decision could be the wrong one for the situation you are in. It is therefore critical to learn, not only how to make decisions, but to also recognize your preferred style and why it serves you well or not. Added to it, timely and efficient decision making is an essential component of success – from the ground up. Practise, practise, practise.

Final thoughts

Coaching is like teaching someone to fish. There are specific techniques to follow if the fisherman wants to be successful. The techniques that save time and make coaching a pleasant experience are adaptable, clear, relevant and reusable (Williams and Menendez, 2015). Ample reading of coaching resources on various platforms are required before tools or techniques can be developed. These are not supposed to be overly structured or prescriptive, but it does give peace of mind that they are designed to inch the client forward (O'Connor and Lages, 2004; Passmore, 2006).

Personal development inspires individuals to leave their comfort zone, develop their strengths, improve their self-awareness and other-awareness, and boost their confidence. However, coaching people to follow the coaching process demands a coaching style that fits the experience, personality, values and skills of the coach and their clients AND is derived from science. Understanding when to use a certain type of coaching can improve efficiency in meeting goals. The same holds true when it comes to the tools coaches use to enhance the outcomes of a coaching session. The chosen tools in this chapter – listening, risk taking, goal setting, GROW framework and making decisions – are all interrelated and acknowledged as the most basic skills required in the workplace today.

With the trend to be more humanistic in dealing with employees and their problems, and the growing escalation of them quitting quietly, coaches are in high demand to support organizations in their quest to create a people-friendly culture. The right tools for the right person and situation can fast-track this vision.

References

Adams, M (2022) *Change Your Questions Change Your Life: 12 Powerful tools for leadership, coaching, and results*, 4th edn, Berrett-Koehler, Oakland, CA

Aguilar, E (2021) *The Art of Coaching Workbook: Tools to make every conversation count*, Jossey-Bass, Hoboken, NJ

Bressler, M, Bressler, L, and Bressler, M (2010) The role and relationship of hope, optimism and goal setting in academic success: A study of students enrolled in online accounting courses, *Academy of Educational Leadership Journal*, 14 (4), 37–51

Clutterbuck, D and Megginson, D (2005) *Making Coaching Work: Creating a coaching culture*, CIPD, London

Coach U, Inc (2005) *Coach U's Essential Coaching Tools: Your complete practice resource*, John Wiley, Hoboken, NJ

Conley, C (2013) *Emotional Equations: Simple steps for creating happiness + success in business + life*, Atria, New York

Dale, E (1969) *Audio-Visual Methods in Teaching*, 3rd edn, Dryden Press, New York, NY

Driver, M (2011) *Coaching Positively: Lessons for coaches from positive psychology*, Open University Press, Maidenhead

Drucker, J (2018) You are what you measure, *Forbes*, 4 December, www.forbes.com/sites/theyec/2018/12/04/you-are-what-you-measure/ (archived at https://perma.cc/SC4D-TY5S)

Els, L and Socket, L (2022) *Where is THERE? Finding THERE through your calling, vision, and goals*, Self-published

Franklin, M (2019) *The HeART of Laser-Focused Coaching: A revolutionary approach to masterful coaching*, Thomas Noble Books, Wilmington, DE

Galford, R M and Maruca, R F (2006) *Your Leadership Legacy*, Harvard Business School Press, Boston, MA

Hawkins, P (2011) *Leadership Team Coaching: Developing collective transformational leadership*, Kogan Page, Philadelphia, PA

Hoomans, J (2015) 35,000 Decisions: The great choices of strategic leaders, The Leading Edge, 20 March, https://go.roberts.edu/leadingedge/the-great-choices-of-strategic-leaders (archived at https://perma.cc/VU7E-84GL)

Hopson, B and Scally, M (1985) *Decision*, Leeds University, Leeds

Jarvis, J, Lane, D A and Fillery-Travis, A (2006) *The Case for Coaching: Making evidence-based decisions on coaching*, CIPD, London

Jones, G and Gorell, R (2018) *50 Top Tools for Coaching: A complete toolkit for developing and empowering people*, Kogan Page, New York

Martens-Schmid, K (2007) Die 'Ganze person' im coaching. – Ambivalenzen und optionen, *Organisationsberatung, Supervision, Coaching*, 14 (1), 17–29

Martin, C (2001) *The Life Coaching Handbook: Everything you need to be an effective life coach*, Crown House, Bethel, CT

Mumford, J (2007) *Life Coaching for Dummies*, John Wiley, Chichester

O'Connor, J and Lages, A (2004) *Coaching with NLP: A practical guide to get the best out of yourself and others*, Element, London

Passmore, J (ed) (2006) *Excellence in Coaching: The industry guide*, Kogan Page, London

Richardson, P (2004) *The Life Coach: Become the person you've always wanted to be*, Hamlyn, London

Shapiro, F R (2006) *The Yale Book of Quotations*, Yale University Press, New Haven, CT

Stoltzfus, T (2008) *Coaching Questions. A coach's guide to powerful asking skills*, Author, Virginia Beach, VA

Whitmore, J (1992) *Coaching for Performance*, Nicholas Brealey Publishing, London

Williams, P and Menendez, D S (2015) *Becoming a Professional Life Coach: Lessons from the Institute for Life Coaching*, 2nd edn, W W Norton & Company, New York

Woolley, K, and Fishbach, A (2017) Immediate rewards predict adherence to long-term goals, *Personality and Social Psychology Bulletin*, 43 (2), 151–62, doi.org/10.1177/0146167216676480 (archived at https://perma.cc/78RC-H8PK)

19

The eyes watch but the brain sees

*Visualization as a coaching tool for shifting
the client's present view*

JANA SIEDENHANS

ABSTRACT

Why is visualization one of the most powerful tools in coaching? What makes imagining
our goals a real matter of fact? How can different ways of imagery serve different
purposes and how to apply them?

Background

The idea of being the author of our life chapters is quite commonly known. But what if the idea of writing their story doesn't empower our clients? Though visualization techniques are well used as a complementary tool in areas such as professional sports or cancer care, we rarely talk about its application in coaching. This chapter is your start to gain the understanding, why and how mental imagery is for real. Based on facts from neuroscience, you learn why visualizing is one of our higher cognitive functions, which supports the transformation of the behavioural patterns hardwired in our brains (Kosslyn, Ganis and Thompson, 2001).

Review of theory

Visualization techniques enable us to work with the inner images from our clients' memories that strongly influence their lives – often unconsciously. They support the coaching process in finding out basic needs such as shelter, belonging or acknowledgement, which were not sufficiently satisfied during childhood. They hold the possibility for our clients to nourish these longings themselves. Most importantly: by rewriting inner stories through new visualizations, they help to positively change dysfunctional belief systems.

Thus, mental imagery emotionally accompanies the coaching client's path to new self-empowering behaviours (Migge, 2013). The positive emotional effects of such nourishment are noticeable, not only on a mental but also on a physical level: giving oneself a positive feeling with the corresponding mental images leads to a measurable positive reaction in our nervous system and the corresponding brain areas for emotion processing. These physical effects on the client when practising visualization can be similar in magnitude to when the client actually experiences the visualized situation (Kosslyn, Ganis and Thompson, 2001).

Corresponding studies also show that the perspective taking within visualization makes a difference on the effects. A distinction is made between the field perspective, for example revisiting a childhood memory through the eyes of the younger self, and the observer perspective, for example revisiting a childhood memory as an uninvolved, almost 'invisible' third party. In mental imagery from the observer perspective, individuals are more likely to undergo (self-)reflexive processes (Grol, Vingerhoets and De Raedt, 2017). More interpretation and evaluation are inherently implied, which can lead to enhanced emotional experiencing. As a result, the intensity of the emotional response in the nervous system and amygdala differs between the two perspectives (Grol, Vingerhoets and De Raedt, 2017).

This awareness is important to be watchful for and avoid possible re-traumatization, and ensure the most helpful insights and changes when visualization techniques are used in the context of relevant client experiences.

In addition, recent brain research findings on neuroplasticity demonstrate the ability of humans to learn and unlearn experiences, attitudes and behaviours well into adulthood. Neuroplasticity is the brain's ability to actually change its physical structure as a result of learning. In changing structure, studies show the brain makes very little distinction between a strongly imagined vision and the actual experience of the event, as long as the event is actively visualized and not exclusively a desired outcome.

Thus, with frequent repetition and sufficient time, visualization in coaching can be a mental support that even physically reshapes the client's brain while they, of course, also actively practise the transformation of behavioural change (Swart, 2019).

Therefore, visualization in coaching can help to create the alternative to maladaptive behaviour rooted in childhood experiences and beliefs: a positive story on the mental level that becomes a reality for the client in physical terms as well – as Gloria Steinem has said, 'It's never too late for a happy childhood' (2020: 45).

Visualization means using the power of your own imagination to see, feel and experience something in your mind without actually experiencing it. We can catch a glimpse of what is our preferred future but also find ways to retroactively change our perception of the past on deeply ingrained levels. The inner images we have developed from experiences influence tremendously how we actually live (Migge, 2013). Therefore, systematically imagining a different 'past' also impacts our future when it is about changing deeply ingrained basic beliefs about ourselves and our lives.

Though this might sound vague at a glance, it turns out to impact the transformation of behaviour in a powerful way. Our brains constantly form new connections via so-called neural pathways. Among other effects, this is how we learn, store and remember beliefs and habits (Swart, 2019). Luckily the pattern and strength of these connections constantly can and do change; we have the capability to both learn and unlearn things if we want to (Swart, 2019).

Furthermore, research shows that the same neural pathways are established in the brain when you visualize doing something or when you actually do it (Swart, 2019). In other words, if we practise an imagination over and over in our mind, our brain will begin to respond as though it was a real object in the world – with a little lower but still remarkably impactful intensity. Additionally, mental imagery of emotional events can activate the autonomic nervous system and amygdala in a similar way to perception of the same events (Kosslyn, Ganis and Thompson, 2001). This opens the chance to use visualizations for travelling back in time with our clients to change the future that previously appeared to be hardwired in their brain.

CASE STUDY

In illustration, I present a coaching session with Irene, a 40-year-old American. At the beginning of her new job as a department manager she sought coaching for support: she quickly gets stressed when a multitude of demands are placed on her, and her new employer is fast-paced and demanding. Additionally, she has a lot of new content to learn and is not yet 100 per cent productive for the company. The coaching process is about developing supportive responses towards the pressure she perceives in the overall situation. By asking about specifics of the situations within which the pressure comes up, we identify the root cause as internal instead of external. Drilling deeper into the basic assumptions behind the sensation of pressure, we identify a basic belief. We go back to a specific childhood memory, which is subconsciously connected to this basic belief and from there explore it on a visualized level by starting a so-called imagery re-scripting.

The client is therefore guided to revisit the memory. At a key point in the memory a re-scripting intervention takes place to create a new outcome and re-establish power over the narrative of the event. The aim is to connect to the client's unmet core needs resulting from the experience and to redefine and create new neural networks in the brain through repetition.

Coach (C): What's behind the pressure you feel?

Irene (I): The expectation to do everything right and quick, whatever I get as tasks. To understand quickly what's going on and how things are going without demanding other people's time to get there. Performance – instantly!

C: Who triggered this expectation?

I: Good question – I don't know. [Pause] With all the tasks that were put on my table in a very short time, it came naturally. I immediately panicked that I wouldn't be able to do everything.

C: What does 'it came naturally' mean? It sounds to me like it's coming from within, is that right?

I: Well nobody told me I had to deliver by certain dates. I just think that I have to make it all possible quickly, otherwise … [breaks off] So yes, somehow it comes more from within me.

C: Let's go back for a moment. You said that you had to make it all possible quickly, otherwise… I'm interested in the 'otherwise'. What happens if you don't make it all happen quickly?

I: I don't do my part.

C: What happens if you don't do your part?

[Pause]

I: I don't want to be a burden. If I don't add value [pause] then I'm superfluous after all.

C: Interesting belief: If I don't add value then I'm superfluous. Where does that come from?

[Pause]

I: My mother often told me that I was a troublesome child.

C: Do you have a specific example of that?

I: She told me that out of all her children, I am the one who causes the most trouble. That she wants me to have children like me, so I know how this is like. I guess that's kind of like being a burden.

C: What other images come to mind about that memory?

I: She said that to me in the laundry room. I can still see her standing in front of me.

C: How old are you at that moment?

I: Ten I think somehow.

C: How did the ten-year-old feel?

I: I don't know. I see the situation very clearly but I kind of don't feel anything. I know that I only kind of pretend as if I don't mind it. But I can't feel what I'm indeed feeling right now. Does that make sense?

C: It makes a lot of sense to me. I'd like to look at this memory with you from the outside. Do you feel like trying that out with me?

I: Okay.

C: Please close your eyes for this. Does that feel doable for you?

[**I** closes her eyes]

I: No problem.

C: Imagine you, 40-year-old Irene standing in the laundry room watching this memory you just described to me. Can you see where you are standing there in the laundry room? [*The memory is consciously entered from the observer perspective of the adult client to lower the possibility of emotional re-traumatization and engage in (self-)evaluative processing of (re-) called information. The client's observer perspective as an adult is repetitively pointed out through the process of the imagery re-scription for the same reasons.*]

I: I'm standing in the corner by the washer and dryer.

C: What else can you see?

I: I'm standing behind my mother, maybe two metres away. It's daytime, the light is shining through the windows on the left side of me into the basement room. It is bright. I recognize the light beige tiles. I know exactly where I am standing, I can see the room. I also see exactly where my mother and I, that is, the young me, are standing. But I don't really see them. I know they're there, but I don't really see them.

[*C is explicitly not trying to make the memory clearer as the consciousness of the client currently does not allow it to lead towards a possible re-traumatization.*]

C: You see quite a lot clearly in front of you, that's totally okay. Could you perceive anything else besides what you see?

I: Yes, I can hear my mother saying these sentences.

C: What sentences?

I: That I am the most trouble, that she wants me to have children who are like me.

C: Who do you, 40-year-old Irene, perceive right now? Your mother or your younger self?

I: My mother.

C: You, as the adult Irene, watching your mother, from the corner in the laundry room: can you describe what you are seeing there, as the adult woman?

I: My mother is overwhelmed. There's a lot of frustration that's being released at that moment.

C: With whom does the frustration have to do?

I: With herself, with her life, actually only very little with me.

C: Does your 10-year-old self know that?

[Pause]

I: I don't see her; she's covered by my mother's back (even though I don't really see that either – I just know she's there). But I know she doesn't understand.

C: What do you observe then, what is resonating with young Irene?

I: That she is troublesome. I don't want her to be troublesome any more.

C: Can you tell what she is feeling?

I: I can feel her pressure.

C: What kind of pressure?

I: Pressure from shame of being useless.

C: What happens when she is useless?

[I's voice becomes uncertain.]

I: Then she doesn't add value. She's not loved for that.

C: Irene – you as an adult watching this: how do you feel about young Irene?

I: I'm angry because she's experiencing this. I'm sorry this is happening.

C: What would you like to do now?

[I becomes teary.]

I: I want to squat down in front of her. Tell her that mom is not mad at her, but at herself. That, she's perfectly loveable.

C: Would you like to try telling her that?

[Pause]

I: She doesn't understand my words.

C: What would do good now?

I: A hug.

C: Can you give her that?

I: Yes.

C: What happens now?

[Pause]

I: She relaxes. The pressure is easing – she feels [pause] safe.

C: What would you like to say to her?

I: Thank you for being there, otherwise I wouldn't be here now.

C: How does young Irene react to that?

I: She smiles.

[I also smiles]

C: Is there anything you need before you return to your room from the laundry room?

I: No, I don't think so.

[I opens her eyes]

C: What are you thinking right now?

I: That this pressure is not 'my pressure' at all. It's little Irene who has the pressure – it comes from her shame. Feels kind of good to understand that it's not for real.

C: The pressure of young Irene you mean? Why does it sound familiar to you?

I: Well, it's just what I feel on the job when people give me tasks. Crazy.

C: Could you say you're back in the laundry room then?

[I smirks]

I: I never thought of it that way, but yeah, that totally sums it up. I then become young Irene in the laundry room again.

C: You were just in the laundry room as adult Irene with young Irene. What was different now?

I: I was me and the pressure belonged to young Irene. Does that make sense?

C: Absolutely. What does that change for you?

I: I think I no longer feel so at the mercy of the pressure.

Discussion

Migge (2013) reminds us that the imaginative focus on inner experiential processes that otherwise stay unaware, brings coaching clients into deep contact with unconsciously reigning belief and emotions. In the presented session, the client was able to distinguish between her stable adult self and insecure childlike parts of her personality that are activated by external triggers. Revisiting memories as imagery from an observer perspective, individuals are more likely to engage in (self-)evaluative processing (Grol, Vingerhoets and De Raedt, 2017). As such, the observer perspective here helped her to process the memory from a reflective state, assessing it from the point of view as the adult she now is instead of being drawn into the helpless identity of her younger self. Also, the activation of intense negative emotions about the memory was more likely prevented in this perspective.

The client gained the insight that the perceived pressure to perform often originated more within herself as rooted in a childhood belief rather than being externally put on her. Additionally, she experienced resources she as an adult possesses to cope with the subjectively arising pressure – in this case by imagining hugging her 10-year-old self.

She started nurturing frustrated basic needs from her childhood, causing a difficult emotional dynamic in her adult life, in the original situations they had been frustrated. This is also called limited reparenting.

It was the client's first step of switching the inner beliefs we have, with which we as humans organize our external reality, from victim to actor of her inner system (Migge, 2013). As such, she was able to access and get distance from a problematic childhood memory, yet simultaneously got closer to overcoming the resulting negative consequences of this memory in her current life.

In the course of our coaching, visualizations and metaphors play a significant role for the client to relive old experiences in new ways and shape new inner experiences leading to different responses on the outside. She developed actions to 'relax the pressure of young Irene in the laundry room'. Images such as 'being in the laundry room', 'young Irene' or 'adult Irene' became central elements of our coaching conversations. So did a specific childhood symbol for Irene as recall of a positive autobiographical memory: a small gaming console, which had been a special gift from her parents during her childhood. This concrete positive imagery strengthened the effects of positive memory recall in her emotion regulation when she faced stressful situations in her job again, as we established it as a positive metaphor.

On the one hand, she visualized herself playing on the gaming console with 'young Irene' in the laundry room. This visualization became her limited reparenting ritual to nurture the frustrated childhood needs of acknowledgement and safety. With time, she could switch the negative basic belief from having been a burden in her childhood to having been as much of a gift as her siblings.

Though the transformation of the belief was connected to an object, the emotional identification was strong, as thinking about past events in terms of the experiences evoked by features is related to a field perspective of people re-experiencing or re-scripting an event through their own eyes, as mentioned by Grol, Vingerhoets and De Raedt (2017). The field perspective imagery is associated with more positive feelings afterwards than observer perspective.

Additionally, she practised installing practices of self-care in her new job reinforced by evidence that she became aware of being valued as an employee in her company. We also called the activities 'gaming consoles', which involved consciously practising focusing on positive feedback she got, as well as practising to call for support, and reinforcing experiences that this behaviour did not have negative impact for her.

With these activities we refocused the client's childhood memories towards positive ones and shifted her focus to positive experiential values in the present. Over time this led to sustainable transformation of her belief system, perception and behaviour. As a result, her feeling of overwhelm and pressure decreased significantly. The practice of visualization was a relevant part of this shift. It also supported the development of new neural pathways in the client's brain for unlearning old and learning new beliefs and behaviour sustainably.

Final thoughts

As we have seen, the positive effects of visualization have been scientifically proven. To me, its application in coaching stays an intuitive rather than a cognitive decision. The basic prerequisite is an established basis of trust.

As coach, it needs the capability to start cautiously and confidently by exploring the unknown inner imagery with the client. Take small steps and be curious about what shows up. Use the observer's perspective to begin with, for decreasing the possibility of re-traumatization. Always stay connected with your client by asking attentive questions. It makes them aware of being in safe company. Stay attentive to reactions that might feel too intense. In concern – gently guide your client back into the presence of your common session. Always get feedback from the client afterwards about their experience and takeaway.

Research additionally shows that for lasting changes in behaviour or attitude, sufficient time must be given to strengthen the development of neural pathways and synapses in our brain (Swart, 2019). Therefore, repetitive work with visualizations over time is needed to shift beliefs and behaviour. At a certain point this can feel frustrating as there might be periods of little or no progress, so-called learning plateaus. It's important to know that those are normal, especially in transformations involving routine practice and habit formation. We can support clients through these periods by pointing out the progress so far, discussing the phenomena of a learning plateau, and excite their motivation again with exploring the benefits of a goal to reach. The outcome is well worth it.

Remember though, inner pictures are a powerful coaching support, but they are not ultimate truths. They are pictures, hints and opportunities. What they offer is material for you and your client to work with on the transformations your client is looking for (Migge, 2013).

Although it may be tempting to explore the fascinating inner world of our clients, visualization is not an end in itself. Its meaning lies in figuring out how the information we discover can be used to achieve the change a client is seeking.

So, let's always keep in mind to identify the goal our clients set out for and make imagery work as a powerful tool to reach it.

References

Grol, M, Vingerhoets, G, and De Raedt, R (2017) Mental imagery of positive and neutral memories: A fMRI study comparing field perspective imagery to observer perspective imagery, *Brain and Cognition*, 111, 13–24, doi.org/10.1016/j.bandc.2016.09.014 (archived at https://perma.cc/BVG7-VJTH)

Kosslyn, S M, Ganis, G and Thompson, W L (2001) Neural foundations of imagery, *Nature Reviews, Neuroscience*, 2 (9), 635–42, doi.org/10.1038/35090055 (archived at https://perma.cc/JT2X-NJFS)

Migge, B (2013) *Schema-coaching: Einführung und Praxis, grundlagen, methoden, fallbeispiele*, Beltz Verlag, Weinheim

Steinem, G (2020) *Revolution from Within: A book of self-esteem*, Back Bay Books, New York

Swart, T (2019) *The Source: The secrets of the universe, the science of the brain*, HarperCollins, New York

20

The Wheel of Life

CHRIS HAWKINS

ABSTRACT

The Wheel of Life is a resource loosely based on the ancient Tibetan Wheel of Life, useful in coaching to explore the broad range of a client's life areas in a systematic and semi-structured way. The outcome serves to identify priorities, raise awareness of any imbalances that cause distress or block goal achievement, and sets the foundation for the development of an action plan to rebalance life priorities and align actions with values.

Introduction

As with any tool or project, you need the correct tool. You do not use a hammer when a screwdriver is required and vice versa. You can try tools that are not common for the job or project, but you may not get the desired results. Takeaway is to have the right tool for the job or project. My passion for this chapter was not truly realized until I started to collect materials and began creating my own Wheel of Life (Figure 20.1) and guidelines.

As with most coaches we are told early on of the many 'tools' available for coaching. One of the most popular seems to be the Wheel of Life and becomes the main ingredient in the 'client welcome packet' with most new coaches, which we require all new clients to complete as part of their onboarding process. I too had it as part of my 'to do' list as I felt that I had to show the client that we were going to be 'doing' something. This is part of 'coach doing' versus 'coach being', which is a transition that many coaches make, but some do not (see Chapter 27).

In looking at the Wheel of Life as a 'tool', I feel that we are already going into 'fix-it' mode vice allowing a relationship to be formed between the client and the

FIGURE 20.1 The Wheel of Life template

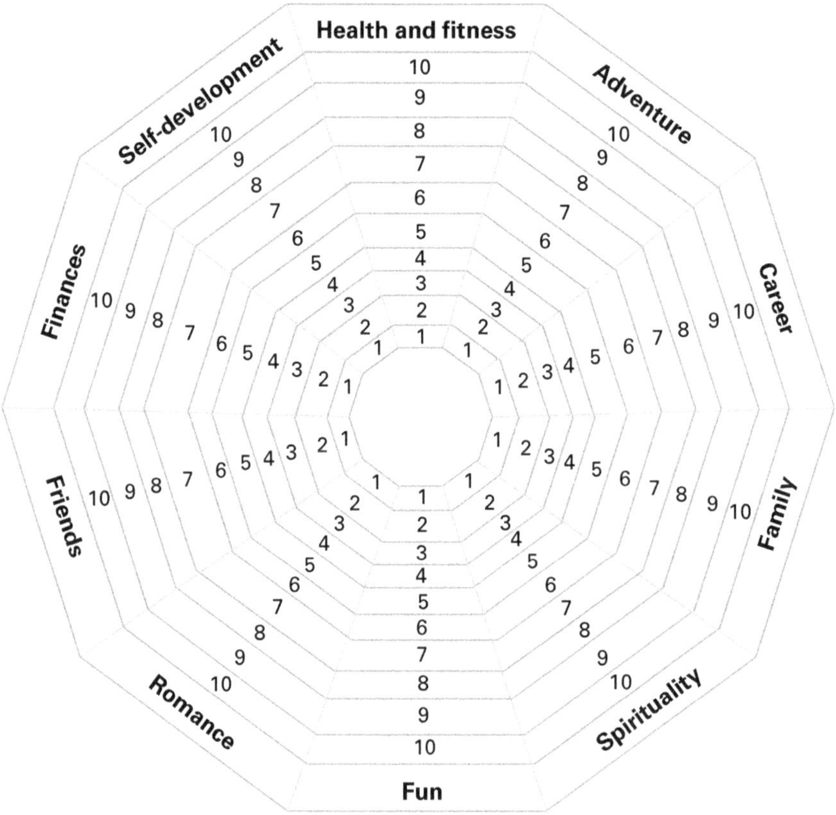

coach. Rather than the use of the word 'tool', I propose that the Wheel of Life is a 'resource' as it supports the search for the obstacles, root causes, priorities and more that the client is hoping to discover.

Yes, the Wheel of Life is a simple visual representation of how the client feels about areas in their life as defined by the version of the Wheel of Life that you use. One does not have to look very far to find many different versions or categories used on the Wheel of Life. From personal experience, I have even seen sublayer versions of the Wheel of Life that would allow for a deeper dive into each of the areas on the main Wheel of Life.

Origin of the Wheel of Life

In researching the Wheel of Life, I was not able to find an official claim to the person or persons that created it. Most unofficial sources noted it as being Paul J Meyer and he created it in the 1960s. He founded the Success Motivation® Institute in 1960. Paul J Meyer was a thought leader and coaching industry pioneer.

Some have noted that the wheel that Meyer created was based on the Tibetan Wheel of Life. I encourage readers and coaches to look into the Tibetan Wheel of Life as it derives a focus on a much different level. It is not only the question that you may or may not use the Tibetan Wheel of Life in your coaching practice but rather to know of other sources that may benefit you in a coaching conversation or personal reflections.

Wheel of Life categories and the focus of each

According to Byrne (2005: 123), 'The Wheel of Life, a familiar concept in many religious and spiritual cultures, represents the constant movement and change in life and comprises a wheel/circle divided into eight segments into which the individual places the top eight top priorities currently in force in their life'. As you look at the many versions of the Wheel of Life, there are many 'descriptors' for the categories. For example, an area that might be on the Wheel of Life is finances. Use your imagination for examples of the things that the client may consider in each category. Keep the explanations both genuine and simple. The goal is to help the client focus on areas based on how they feel about the category. If your client decides that they want to change the categories, be open to it as the tool is as much for them as it is for the coaching relationship.

Conducting the Wheel of Life

The first step in the Wheel of Life exercise is to select a life area and carefully consider the value and priority in a person's life, using a series of questions that go broader (to ensure that every angle and aspect of a category is covered) or deeper (to narrow the scope of their priority). Having a client selecting the order of categories to discuss could give the coach additional information about the pain points of the client and their priorities.

Then, the client assigns two numbers on a scale of 1–10 (with 1 no significance and 10 a non-negotiable high priority) to the life area under discussion. The first number represents their idea of the status of their time and attention spent on that area at that time. The second number indicates the priority the client ideally wants to attach to the same life area in the future (ideally 6–12 months forward), which, if different, likely means changes in time and attention.

The difference in the numbers represents a gap that indicates the priority for change needed in that area. The numeric values only provide a basic starting point for further exploration with the client and, together, the coach and client clarify their priorities, starting with 1–2 areas. The narrower scope allows for a deeper discussion of these areas to identify underlying concerns, considerations, support and action steps for change in the desired direction.

Applying the introspection needed to consider questions in each area to complete the Wheel of Life, clients also raise their level of awareness and understanding of the balance and need for changes in their life areas. As such, using the Wheel of Life, we can guide our clients to find where the imbalances lie in their lives at present and start to plan what they are going to do to address them (Byrne, 2005).

When the Wheel of life is most beneficial

When working with a client, they may come to you and not know where to start or what areas to even consider but know that they want to improve or find peace in their life. This is a GREAT time to use the Wheel of Life. It will reduce the pressure on you as a coach to try to find areas to explore and make it equally easy on the client as they will have areas for consideration. Granted, the client may experience an 'aha' moment and bring other areas for exploration. Consider the Wheel of Life as a way to get the creative juices flowing.

Shortfalls with the Wheel of Life and coaches using it

A shortfall that I have seen is that some coaches force this resource on clients as a must-do item, even when the client tells the coach the area they want to work on in their life. Sure, this well-rounded resource is great for discovering things under the surface BUT forcing this resource at the wrong time will take the client off track and might impact the coaching relationship.

Another issue that I see is coaches completing the Wheel of Life for the client. Let clients do their Wheel of Life, either on their own as a first round and basis for further discussion, or in conversation with their coach. This way they are more engaged, they know their own life and situation best, plus they have a feeling of ownership. If you do it for the client, how much are you really having them engaged in the process or just simply asking them questions and making assumptions?

Another potential drawback is when forcing the client to complete all aspects of the Wheel of Life. If a client is doing the Wheel of Life and has an 'aha' moment, pause the Wheel of Life and check-in. There is no requirement to do the entire Wheel of Life at once, or even at all. Again, it is used as a resource to explore possible areas for change.

Should you finish the entire Wheel of Life, do not force the client to select the lowest numbers as a starting point. Sometimes, the client is lacking confidence (which, by the way, might just be the entire struggle they have and, as a result, they are throwing spaghetti at the wall and hoping something sticks). Let the client pick a starting area. They may have all 5s but one 8. For confidence building and a bit of fear, they may go for the 8 area and work on that and then should the confidence kick in, they go after the other areas. This is all part of avoiding target fixation. Just because you see a low number does not mean that you go after that area. Step back and let the client not only pick the area of interest but where to start. Again, we are not trying to FIX anything, just simply using the resource to expand the mind to areas of possibility.

There are many terms that coaches use to describe what they use as part of their process in coaching, which include coaching tool kit, bag of tricks, etc. The most important thing to consider is if the resource you are using is relevant to the coaching session. If the client knows what they want to explore, there is no need to do the Wheel of Life.

Introducing the Wheel of Life to your client and checking its effectiveness

The best way to introduce this resource is to simply ask for permission. It can be introduced at an appropriate time with something like 'I might have a resource that can help with that. Would you like to try it?' If they say yes, then you say the name of the resource. Rather than lead in with 'Here is the Wheel of Life and you need to do it', you might learn that the client has had a bad experience with a previous coach that was a 'you-will-or-I-will not' coach, as I call them.

If you are using the Wheel of Life, you want to check-in to see how effective it is in the process from time to time, usually once in a goal-setting cycle. It might be working great or actually making the client feel as though the coaching process is too rigid.

Closing thoughts

The biggest takeaway is to impress upon readers and coaches that the Wheel of Life is just one of many resources in your coaching toolkit and must never be a requirement or you are going against what coaching is by taking control of the coaching vice allowing the client to drive the train.

Some coaches use the Wheel of Life as a two-part process in that they have the client complete it at the beginning of the coaching relationship and at the end of the coaching relationship. This might be a way to 'show' that something (or many things) changed. I believe that the results speak for themselves and that you do not have to prove anything as a show of worth. If you coach the client and not the problem, you will help the client in more ways than one and they will walk away from the coaching relationship not only a changed person but, most important, know why.

As I close this chapter, I want to go back to the words 'tool and resource' that I opened this chapter with. It really does not matter what you call the Wheel of Life, be it a tool or resource.

My aim is to allow you to look outside the box of what the Wheel of Life is, where it came from, along with the how and why, so that you instinctively know when and when not to use it in order to achieve a greater level of success in your coaching relationships. May you have a transition from a coach 'doing' to coach 'being' as all we really need to do is 'be' a coach vice doing coaching.

I leave you with a final thought: in my research for this chapter, I found limited resources but many different versions of the Wheel of Life that a coach can use. If you want, create your own Wheel of Life (much like I did) with the various areas that you feel your ideal clients may find of greatest relevance, taking your specific niche and areas of competence into consideration.

Reference

Byrne, U (2005) Wheel of Life: Effective steps for stress management, *Business Information Review*, 22 (2), 123–30, doi.org/10.1177/0266382105054770 (archived at https://perma.cc/5GBE-TYV7)

PART FIVE

Transforming theory into practice

Application and implementation

21

Transitioning from theory to practice

JOAN SWART

ABSTRACT

Without practice, theory is wasteful. Without theory, practice is irresponsible. Research is the prerequisite fibre that weaves theory and practice together in a stronger fabric. In this chapter, I explore the importance of theory and research to inform an effective and ethical practice, how the research process works to transition from theory to practice, and the status of research and evidence-based practice in coaching.

Introduction

Theory and practice are intricately linked. However, where experience, training and knowledge lack, this is not always the case. There are many thought-provoking quotations about this interplay. Kant's 'theory without practice is empty; practice without theory is blind' is perhaps the best known. Marx's version stated that theory without practice is sterile, meaning that it is unused, unlived, untouched and untested. My favorite analogy is by Langeveld, 'theory without practices is for geniuses, practice without theory is for fools and rogues, but for the majority of educators, the intimate and unbreakable union of both is necessary' (Morrison and Van der Werf, 2012: 399). I can probably spend a lifetime debating the wayward influence of fools and rogues but, for now, I suffice by saying that practice without evidence is unethical, unpredictable, wasteful and has a high probability of being harmful.

As a relatively young speciality practice among the helping professions, coaching has catching up to do alongside its 'older' siblings – psychotherapy and counselling. Although a lot is said about distinguishing coaching from other helping roles, including therapy and mentoring (see Chapters 1 and 2), there are many reasons why the roles are increasingly blurred. Coaching does not (and should not) stand on its own but borrows valuable knowledge from many branches of social sciences that describe and model human behaviour from different lived experiences, perspectives and contexts.

As such, sharing knowledge between different disciplines is indispensable. While still recognizing their own boundaries of competence and ethical responsibilities, coaches benefit from increasing their knowledge and training in related fields, especially psychology and social sciences. This way, they become familiar with theories about human cognitive, emotive, neurobiological and behavioural processes that are also important in the coaching relationship and process. Coaches can also formulate new ideas or adapt theories to propose for research, thereby ensuring that practices are suitable for coaching. Networks, platforms, interest groups and industry bodies play a valuable role in this process. So, the holy grail of evidence-based practice is theory but why is it important, how is it used and where does it come from?

Why is theory important?

'Philosophy and theory are perpetually linked; philosophy influences how one sees the world, theory shapes how one intentionally interacts with that world' (Himes and Schulenberg, 2013, para 8). Theory is a set of ideas or organized principles in explanation of observed or conceptualized phenomenon. So, theory, as an explanation of why something is happening and how it plays out in a certain situation or context, is an essential consideration when making coaching decisions by recognizing signs that can fit into an existing theory.

However, when making decisions to inform coaching methods and plans, how many coaches consider theory in their practice? In a study of college educators, Jaeger and her research team found that most use previous experience, common sense,

FIGURE 21.1 The value of evidence-based practice

precedents and peer advice while less than 10 per cent draw on theory to make decisions that impact their students (Jaeger et al, 2013). It appears most coaches turn to what they are familiar with and have easy access to rather than assimilating new theory as a basis for their practice. In other research, of 2,200 psychotherapists surveyed, most identified as having an eclectic orientation or more than one theoretical orientation (Cook et al, 2010). These two studies, and others (e.g., Martin, Garske and Davis, 2000; Prochaska and Norcross, 1983), showed that individual therapy was the most popular modality and relationship-oriented techniques (e.g., showing warmth, acceptance, empathy and understanding) were most frequently applied. Cook et al (2010) also pointed out that the least frequently endorsed techniques such as neurofeedback and hypnotherapy seem to require specialization or certification beyond what is provided in standard training or education. This means logically that coaches are much less likely to use theory when they do not have formal training in an area. Competence – as a requirement of ethical practice – is linked to their ability to understand and apply the relevant theory, which is only gained in further study.

As most certification training programmes cover theory at a basic level that is often modular in terms of selected tools, techniques and skills, coherent approaches are lacking that will give the coach a discretionary ability to select the most appropriate overall approach for the client presentation and situation. Examples are psychodynamic, cognitive, behavioural, polyvagal and emotion-focused theories, to name a few. These theories may be traditionally applied in psychotherapy but are increasingly recognized as equally valuable in coaching if used by a competent coach within the bounds of coaching ethics. Two other 'systems' that consider different theories together are integrative and eclectic therapy or coaching. Rather than implying that the professional chooses approaches or techniques haphazardly according to their intuition or familiarity without a basis in theory, they are well-grounded in several theories, thereby able to match the client's needs with the theory and associated evidence-based methodology that are likely to produce the best outcome.

Therefore, 'Theory is used to describe, explain, predict, influence outcomes, assess practice, and generate new knowledge and research' (Jones and Ames, 2010: 151). The process from philosophical thought and theory to practice through research is illustrated in Figure 21.2.

Theory is the basis upon which methodology that guides practice is formulated. The process is dynamic, with research not only informed by theory but feedback from practice too. Different outcomes, populations, contexts and situations continuously feed into theory and experiments to create an ongoing adaptation to best practice guidelines. It is part of a coach's professional responsibility to stay abreast with these developments in their area to ensure that they provide an effective and responsible service.

FIGURE 21.2 From philosophy to theory and practice

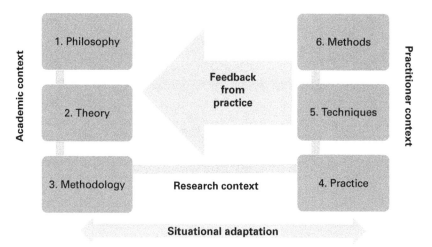

How is theory used?

The primary objective of research is to develop, inform and test theory but, more than this, apply theory to practice and investigate the validity and reliability of the application. Reliability refers to the consistency of the method, i.e., whether the results can be reproduced under the same circumstances. Validity is the accuracy of a method, i.e., whether the results are what they set out to be. Although science is a living concept that is constantly shifting and adapting to new ideas and information, the process of developing scientific theories, often from observations or thought experiments, must be rigorous and based on sound procedures, and overseen by an objective community of peers. The benefits of using such a scientifically supported and well-researched methodology extracted from theory are the following.

- **Predictability** If a researcher or practitioner applies the method accurately in the same (or very similar) circumstances, they achieve the expected outcome (within an acceptable degree of variability determined by research).

- **Replicability** If a researcher or practitioner (or different researchers, practitioners) repeats the method in the same (or very similar) circumstances, they achieve the same outcome (within the range of predictability).

- **Specificity** If applied correctly, the method is focused, effective and efficient in delivering the expected outcome – in other words, it addresses what it is supposed to.

- **Normalization** The process of organizing research data to determine the 'normal' (average) outcome for a specific population group (such as differentiated by age, gender, race, location, setting and other subject characteristics) and qualify what a level of variability means. For example, research shows that a coach applying a specific method can (normally) expect a certain level of change in a specific time with a known variability in time or level (given a client with a certain set of characteristics).

- **Consistency** A well-researched method yields consistent results over time within established parameters.

- **Peer review** An evidence-based method is peer-reviewed in the relevant scientific community, which means that the majority of experts agree that it adheres to the standards of good practice, scientific principles and sound theory.

- **Testability** The hypothesis (or hypotheses) or theory on which a method is based can be tested in an experiment to provide a well-grounded answer (Samens, 2017).

These measures give the practitioner confidence that, if they apply the methodology correctly, they know that it works how it is intended to, what the expected outcome is, and are in the best position of professional coverage if their practice is questioned, especially if they are not a years-long expert with extensive training and education.

Where does theory come from?

Research to transition theory into an evidence-based practice follows a relatively typical process that often starts with an observation or thought (Figure 21.3):

1 **Observations and thought experiments** The human brain developed with the intense need to understand our experience and create meaning of it. Unanswered questions about our observations of reactions to events, patterns, trends and causal effects motivate exploration to create this understanding that we crave. These 'observations' do not have to be literal but can also be 'what-if' and other cognitive musings. Philosophy is a field of study that often feeds the development of science (Figure 21.2). As such, 'thought experiments' – inductive or deductive arguments as part of an 'imaginary investigation' (Brendel, 2004: 91) or simulation of possible situations – are instruments of scientific enquiry that help provide insights about the world (Brown and Fehige, 2019).

2 **Questions** Observations and thought experiments are the cauldron of questions. Driven by our need to understand and for the meaning of what is happening to us (or, indeed. what might happen to us), we formulate questions to guide and provide the scope and boundaries for further investigation.

3 **Hypothesis** A hypothesis is a proposed answer for the question to explain the observation or thought experiment. As educated guesses or untested deductions,

FIGURE 21.3 The research process

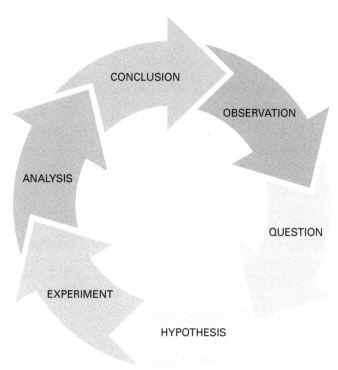

hypotheses suggest an outcome based on preliminary observation, thought, or an extrapolation of a similar problem. A working hypothesis is the steering wheel that drives the engine of an experiment. As such, it is the guide to inform problems that are in the formative phase from which to build a theory that can drive actions.

4 **Experiment** The experiment is a scientific procedure that is designed according to established principles and methodologies to prove (or disprove) the hypothesis. For example, with a working hypothesis of 'brief individual coaching improves performance', a researcher might design an experiment using a quantitative approach that assesses clients after six coaching sessions with a well-being questionnaire and survey to make a before-and-after comparison. A quantitative approach collects and analyses numerical data to draw conclusions while qualitative research collects, organizes and analyses non-numerical data such as text, video, audio and images from interviews, diary accounts, focus groups and case studies. A combination, called mixed methods approach, can also be used. The choice depends on whether the hypothesis is best suited by a statistical analysis (of numbers) or analysing explanations or experiences to support understanding (Lowhorn, 2007).

5 **Analysis** The data collected in the experiment is organized, processed and analysed depending on the research design and hypothesis. Techniques and applications vary in complexity from simple Excel spreadsheets to software such as SPSS, SAS, STATA and R. The choice depends on the researcher's familiarity with the application and programming, size of the data set, cost sensitivity and research design. As the most concerns often arise from the research design and data analysis, a thorough peer-review process is required, which may need access to raw data.

6 **Conclusion** The researcher makes a conclusion based on the data, accepting or rejecting all or some of the hypotheses. In theoretical research – also often called fundamental research, the conclusion increases understanding by developing a new theory or scrutinizing an existing theory (De Gooyert and Größler, 2019). Applied research, on the other hand, is aimed at practical applications of existing theory, in social sciences 'deliberately intended to bring about social change' (Babbie, 2013: 18).

Other important considerations in the research process are ethical conduct, for instance, keeping data secure and private, and ensuring the safety, well-being and autonomy of human subjects. As both the driver of theory and the link between the transition from theory to practice, research is the stimulus of scientific progress that cannot be neglected, cut corners, or be avoided if we want humankind and the world to continue evolving.

The status of research in coaching

Viewing coaching as an expression of applied psychology, a deliberate practice to enhance learning leading to insight and change, the increased professionalization accompanied by formal training, certification, accreditation and regulatory bodies requires continued rigorous development (Passmore and Evans-Krimme, 2021). The coaching industry is still emerging and relatively immature as it lacks self-sustained growth, diversification, and widespread use to a certain extent. It remains a small industry worldwide with many independent practitioners, albeit with a small but gradually growing number of provider platforms and groups (Passmore and Evans-Krimme, 2021).

Lacking formalization and regulation, science was also slow to penetrate coach practices and understanding. Increased access to research through Open Access journals (*International Journal of Evidence Based Coaching and Mentoring*, *PLOS*, *Frontiers in Psychology*), the emergence of research platforms (e.g., ResearchGate, Academia), library websites (e.g., Sci-Hub, Science Open), and search tools (e.g., Google Scholar, Microsoft Academic) are all contributing to a surge of knowledge in coaching.

Multidisciplinary knowledge sharing and research have a vital role to play in coaching as it 'borrows' ideas, theories and applications from fields in or alongside human behaviour, such as psychology, neuroscience, anthropology, sociology, economics, linguistics and philosophy. Such information triggers new questions that are converted into hypotheses and researched to test and validate or formulate new theories and practices unique to coaching populations, settings and contexts. These new insights make coaching – as a methodology and industry – more effective, efficient, reliable and credible. At the same time, coaching diversifies to new applications where it can potentially support overburdened services such as mental health, education, corrections, immigration and family support.

The indications are clear that coaching has tremendous potential to support positive change in a strained world, if, among other structural and regulatory aspects, the industry can grow its foundations of knowledge based on proven scientific principles to ensure safe and responsible practices that benefit clients. The process is only emerging and there is a long but exciting road ahead.

CASE STUDY

A simple study of character strengths among coaching students and prospects

The case sample presented is a very simple study showing that a researcher does not have to have expensive resources, vast experience in complicated statistical analyses, or work at an academic institution. Anyone with an interest in moving a topic further by informing theory and practice through answering a question in a systematic and well-considered way can contribute to the pool of knowledge. My study, using simple spreadsheet-based calculations and the survey results of 2,400 coaching students and prospects, ranked the VIA character strengths endorsed by the respondents, and compared it to published population studies (Swart, 2022).

As part of the positive psychology movement, Martin Seligman and Christopher Peterson introduced the concept of character strengths in 2004 that led to a framework with which to pursue positive performance and satisfaction by developing strengths that support individual goal achievement (Peterson and Seligman, 2004). They divided the 24 character strengths into six categories.

1 **Wisdom and knowledge** – creativity, curiosity, judgement, love of learning, and perspective

2 **Courage** – bravery, persistence, integrity and zest

3 **Humanity** – love, kindness and social intelligence

4 **Justice** – teamwork, fairness and leadership

5 **Temperance** – forgiveness, humility, prudence and self-regulation

6 **Transcendence** – appreciation of beauty and excellence, gratitude, hope, humour and spirituality

A straightforward count in my study found that participants most endorsed kindness, honesty, fairness, appreciation of beauty and excellence, and gratitude (in ranked order) with self-regulation, bravery, judgement, perseverance and humility in the bottom spots (in ascending order). In coaching, judgement is linked to critical thinking and avoiding unsubstantiated conclusions and biases that are essential in building trust and exploring potential and opportunities. Perseverance enables a coach to work with a client who is stuck or relapses by patiently accepting where they are and looking for creative alternatives. I believe that humility, together with curiosity, is a core strength of an effective coach as it helps them to stay present, accept that they are not the expert, strive to learn, and be genuinely interested in the client. Self-regulation is an equally important skill in coaching, indicating a person's ability to manage their impulses and emotions, which are valuable in interpersonal interaction.

As the study showed that these skills rated in the bottom five among a sample of student coaches, coach trainers, supervisors and coaches may consider exploring these further and adding development measures to strengthen lagging areas. This simple study is an illustration of how *theory* (character strength framework and test) can be used to explore a *question* (which character strengths that are relevant to effective coaching may need development?) and provide results that are valuable in *practice*.

Final thoughts

Passion bears ideas, which are organized into theory. When standing alone, theory is merely a casual interest. Theory needs to be acted upon to add value and effect change. The transition from theory to practice is made through research that must also be accessible to practitioners, both in availability and understandability. As coaches, we owe it to our clients (and ourselves) to stay abreast of the science of coaching by reading, training, participating in ideas exchange, and sharing feedback and knowledge. Applied research is the propellant that will help coaching take off as a life-changing industry.

References

Babbie, E (2013) *The Practice of Social Research*, 14th edn, Cengage Learning, Boston, MA

Brendel, E (2004) Intuition pumps and the proper use of thought experiments, *Dialectica*, 58 (1), 89–108

Brown, J R and Fehige, Y (2019) Thought experiments, *Stanford Encyclopedia of Philosophy*, plato.stanford.edu/entries/thought-experiment (archived at https://perma.cc/P56H-GM7E)

Cook, J M, Biyanova, T, Elhai, J, Schnurr, P P and Coyne, J C (2010) What do psychotherapists really do in practice? An internet study of over 2,000 participants, *Psychotherapy*, 47 (2), 260–7, doi.org/10.1037/a0019788 (archived at https://perma.cc/CN9P-GV42)

De Gooyert, V and Größler, A (2019) On the differences between theoretical and applied system dynamics modeling, *System Dynamics Review*, 34 (4), 575–83, doi.org/10.1002/sdr.1617 (archived at https://perma.cc/2K26-45V4)

Himes, H, and Schulenberg, J (2013) Theoretical reflections: Theory and philosophy should always inform practice, *Academic Advising Today*, 36 (3), nacada.ksu.edu/Resources/Academic-Advising-Today/View-Articles/Theoretical-Reflections-Theory-and-Philosophy-Should-Always-Inform-Practice.aspx (archived at https://perma.cc/CPJ8-2EGX)

Jaeger, A J, Dunstan, S, Thornton, C, Rockenbach, A B, Gayles, J G and Haley, K J (2013) Put theory into practice, *About Campus: Enriching the Student Learning Experience*, 17(6), 11–15, doi.org/10.1002/abc.21100 (archived at https://perma.cc/6PBU-S29W)

Jones S R and Ames E S (2010) The nature and uses of theory, in *Student Services: A handbook for the profession*, eds J H Schuh, S R Jones and S R Harper, pp 149–67, Jossey-Bass, San Francisco, CA

Lowhorn, G L (2007) Qualitative and quantitative research: How to choose the best design, presented at Academic Business World International Conference, Nashville, Tennessee, May, papers.ssrn.com/sol3/papers.cfm?abstract_id=2235986 (archived at https://perma.cc/S9HC-2CDQ)

Martin, D J, Garske, J P and Davis, M K (2000) Relation of the therapeutic alliance with outcome and other variables: A meta-analytic review, *Journal of Consulting and Clinical Psychology*, 68, 438–50, doi.org/10.1037/0022-006X.68.3.438 (archived at https://perma.cc/K2FM-HZ58)

Morrison, K and Van der Werf, G (2012) Editorial, *Educational Research and Evaluation*, 18 (5), 399–401, doi.org/10.1080/13803611.2012.695513 (archived at https://perma.cc/XMT6-A9SH)

Passmore, J and Evans-Krimme, R (2021) The future of coaching: A conceptual framework for the coaching sector from personal craft to scientific process and the implications for practice and research, *Frontiers in Psychology*, 12 (715228), 1–8, doi.org/10.3389/fpsyg.2021.715228 (archived at https://perma.cc/BP6Y-2GP4)

Peterson, C, and Seligman, M E P (2004) *Character Strengths and Virtues: A handbook and classification*, Oxford University Press, New York

Prochaska, J O and Norcross, J C (1983) Contemporary psychotherapists: A national survey of characteristics, practices, orientations, and attitudes, *Psychotherapy: Theory, Research & Practice*, 20, 161–73, doi.org/10.1037/h0088487 (archived at https://perma.cc/K2TC-7ZDH)

Samens, J M (2017) Testability, in *The SAGE Encyclopedia of Communication Research Methods*, ed M Allen, pp 1751–3, Sage, Thousand Oaks, CA

Swart, J (2022) What do the character strengths of coaching students tell us? *ResearchGate*, doi.org/10.13140/RG.2.2.36448.97285 (archived at https://perma.cc/V6J8-89P9); www.researchgate.net/profile/Joan-Swart (archived at https://perma.cc/7H5A-UZPR)

22

Imposter syndrome

CHRISTOPHER MITRA

ABSTRACT

The impact of imposter syndrome remains underrecognized and unmanaged. Imposter syndrome describes the severe feelings of self-doubt and insecurity typically underlined by childhood conditioning and beliefs. Associated with underperformance, dissatisfaction and feelings of anxiety and depression, many coaches are likely to encounter a client with these struggles and can use relatively simple strategies to help manage imposter syndrome.

Introduction

Out of all the struggles that I had in my life, there are only two that I have been unable to overcome. The first is a never-ending desire to consume chocolate.

The second (and more troublesome) issue is a strong, unshakeable belief that I'm a phoney. That I have neither the skillset nor intelligence to support my claim that I am a talented coach.

This struggle did not appear when I became a coach; it has been with me all my life. It was with me during my 18-year IT career and followed me for 10 years as I became an entrepreneur with a tech company. Only when I became a coach did I discover the label of this negative mindset as 'imposter syndrome' (IS).

You might be hard-pressed to find a coach who has not encountered a client touting imposter syndrome as an issue in their life. It can be masked as a lack of confidence, self-doubt, and even increased anxiety in social situations. The purpose of this chapter is to give you a background on imposter syndrome and how you might see it manifest in clients. Then I discuss some of the ways you can work with a client to help rewrite their imposter syndrome code.

The theory of imposter syndrome

The term imposter syndrome was coined by clinical psychologists Pauline Clance and Suzanne Imes of Georgia State University during a 1978 study on the experience of intellectual phoniness among 150 high-achieving women. These women had earned PhDs, received praise and recognition for their work, and were considered professionals in their field, yet internally, they self-identified as fakes. The belief was so strong that they credited any success to luck or a mistake in a selection process but could not say it was due to their skill and talent. According to Clance and Imes (1978), one woman, a PhD laureate, heavily lettered with academic accomplishment, went so far as to believe she was not qualified to teach a remedial college class.

Originally called imposter phenomenon, imposter syndrome, as it's now usually called, is commonly understood as a false and sometimes crippling belief that one's successes are the product of luck or fraud rather than skill. Although you will never receive an official diagnosis of imposter syndrome, medical professionals admit that it is an intense form of self-doubt often coupled with anxiety and depression. Clance and Imes (1978: 241) emphasized that a critical element is a fear that 'eventually some significant person will discover that they are indeed intellectual impostors'. In a client with IS, you will find that they do not accept compliments well and may not celebrate their success. Also, if they receive negative feedback, it can be devastating and will linger in their memory as evidence of their inadequacy.

The Clance and Imes study found that the women could not self-recognize the phenomenon. The subjects reported general anxiety, lack of confidence, depression and frustration. On deeper analysis, they found that imposter syndrome originates from two factors. The first is sex-role stereotypes, where women are taught to explain failure due to lack of ability, and success as a temporary, external cause like luck.

The second factor involves family history, where the subjects, at a young age, were categorized as either intellectually inferior or superior. When the subjects were either overpraised or criticized, the long-term effect resulted in self-doubt in both cases. It is easy to see the correlation between IS and someone who is criticized as a child. Yet, when someone is viewed as gifted or perfect by parents and then inevitably encounters difficulty in life, they start to distrust their parents' perceptions and then begin to doubt themselves.

The result of either factor is that the participants developed a self-image of being phoney. With the women in the Clance/Imes study, this self-image was reinforced by (mostly) outdated societal views of women and their potential.

At this point, we should probably address the elephant in the room: can imposter syndrome affect males if the original study had all female subjects? The answer back in 1978 was yes, but to a lesser degree than females. The authors do not address why men suffer at a more secondary level (Clance and Imes, 1978).

Luckily, there has been much more research on imposter syndrome since the 1978 original study, which has added more science around that anecdotal supposition. A 2019 research article looked at 62 studies on the phenomenon involving over 14,000 participants and found that imposter syndrome was common among both men and women and across all age groups, with some marked increase in ethnic minority groups (Badawy et al, 2018).

Now that we know that imposter syndrome transcends gender and ethnic classes, discussing how this issue may appear in your coaching sessions is helpful to support your effective practice. While IS may be more prevalent to appear in a client in the workplace setting, it can also occur in students, stay-at-home parents and even the unemployed.

At a basic level, IS is all about doubt in ourselves and our skills and abilities. A sense of belonging and competency is paramount for living a whole and content life, and IS hinders that process. The top three areas of the triangle that represents Maslow's Hierarchy of Needs, deal with our need to feel that we are part of a group and be confident in our skills and knowledge (Maslow, 1954). A client with IS will continue to tread water in the bottom two levels of Maslow's triangle, the base human physiological and safety needs, until they deal with it.

The term 'dealing with it' is fundamental to working with clients with IS. A client's feelings of self-doubt were not created by a single event but rather through a lifetime of negative programming. That self-programming has now become the standard internal voice that the client hears. There is not a single exercise or 'life hack' that will remove these negative beliefs. Maria Gray (2022: 9) states in her article, 'Befriending the imposter', 'The notion of overcoming a syndrome, however, immediately creates a sense of pressure to take action and find the "culprit". In my view, this can often deepen the client's sense of being somehow inadequate'.

In addition to having a very personal experience with IS, I have worked with many clients who present IS as an obstacle in their life. Some of them know the term 'imposter syndrome' and the topic enough to recognize its effects. Others are more general in their descriptions and use the words 'lack of confidence', 'don't feel like I belong' or 'I just feel useless'. One interesting trait I have witnessed is the display of one of two types of body language when clients talk about these experiences. One group shows a dropping of the shoulders, speak in a slower, more monotone voice, and has a dejected facial expression. The other group talks with a smile and somewhat nervous laughter at the subject, almost as if they feel it is ridiculous to admit they have this problem given their credentials. Just as there is not an official IS diagnosis, this physical 'tell' that I usually observe is not based on science and cannot be used to draw any definitive conclusion without further exploration. Ineffective or low-power body language can adversely affect performance, but it is not seen in all IS subjects, and not all the time (Cuddy et al, 2015).

CASE STUDY

My client, Mark, was a 54-year-old C-level executive with an impressive résumé and two university degrees. He was likeable, with a great sense of humour and unique talent of being fully present in any conversation. Combine that with his lovely family, volunteer work and financial achievements, and Mark would appear to anyone as a confident, driven professional.

Mark first approached me to talk about concerns he had with his focus at work. He had no shortage of tasks that he needed to complete but often found himself unable to tackle any of the work. Mark would often resort to filling his schedule with easy chores or shutting his door and playing solitaire on his computer. He would ignore the work, get frustrated that he disregarded it and then find an excuse to overlook it even longer. This created a circular and growing feeling of frustration that was compounded with the knowledge that he helped found the company that he now seemed to be avoiding.

In my initial session with Mark, one of my first questions was to ask him WHY he thought that he was avoiding the assignments in front of him. He responded jokingly, 'Because I don't want to do them.' My immediate response of 'Why don't you want to do them?' was enough to get him to think deeper. His updated answer was, 'I'm not sure how to do them, and I really don't want to mess up. It's easier to leave them.'

Mark had not obtained his position by starting at the bottom and working his way up to the top. Nor had he upgraded his position through a series of career moves. He was a C-level executive because he helped create the company. At the root, Mark did not feel like he deserved the title. His networking lunches with other local CXOs were an awkward affair where he did not feel he had the right to contribute.

Further conversation showed that Mark had grown up with a father who demanded high academic achievement from his children. When that was not met, the father responded with anger or 'the silent treatment'. With his slight learning disability, Mark could never reach the bar set and always felt incapable. Despite a lifetime of success, he always seemed to be chasing the approval he never got. Mark self-identified as having imposter syndrome and was one who laughed at the irony of having this feeling despite his achievements.

I worked with Mark semi-consistently for over a year. Our sessions were not limited to dealing with imposter syndrome but focused on varied topics, including succession planning, entrepreneurship, goal setting and personal branding. We spent time at the cornerstone of every call talking about accomplishments and identifying opportunities. This consistent, positive focus slowly helped Mark ease up on his mental ownership of IS and become less demanding and critical of himself.

Dealing with imposter syndrome in coaching

Not everyone with IS has the same story as Mark, yet there is benefit to having the client identify the genesis of the issue. As a coach, we know that achieving any goal (in this case, reducing IS as a roadblock) requires knowing where the finish line is and from where we started.

Clients with IS often suffer a sense of isolation by believing that they struggle alone while their peers seem to excel effortlessly. A 1993 study by Langford and Clance on the imposter phenomenon talks about the benefits of chatting with the client about the general concept of IS and its widespread occurrence in the general population. This not only allows the client to put a name to their held limiting beliefs but also to detach from the issues by knowing that they are not alone (Langford and Clance, 1993).

The same study also suggests that there may be benefits to having clients talk about the imposter experiences in a group setting. Similarly, they get to acknowledge that others with similar accomplishments are in the same boat. Removing that sense of isolation is beneficial to our experience of belonging. Still, the study does warn that some individuals may not be open to discussing such a deeply personal issue with others out of fear of criticism. Completely understandable, given that critical feedback in the past may have been a culprit in their development of IS. With the Langford and Clance study stating both a positive and negative outcome from group coaching, I suggest that a coach ask the client their preference. Do not force a client into a group discussion if they are apprehensive.

I stated earlier in this article that IS is primarily an issue of self-doubt. As a coach, if we are going to help our client, that is where we need to focus, but before we talk about how we approach the client, we should spend a moment preparing ourselves. We must be present during our sessions and understand the power of empathy. Also, when dealing with an IS client, we need to be vigilant in our responses. Your client has had a lifetime of negative programming. We may add to those negative beliefs and damage our relationship with the client if we disregard, downplay or refute any of their comments. While this does not mean you must agree with everything the client says, just acknowledge and understand it.

Rewriting the client's code

In my pre-coaching life, I was a computer geek, so when I look at a client with imposter syndrome, I immediately compare it to lousy programming code. There is an acronym in the software industry called GIGO or Garbage In, Garbage Out. Suppose my client has developed self-doubt through a lifetime of negative feedback (the garbage in). In that case, they will undoubtedly display that through their thoughts and actions (garbage out). The only way to fix wrong code is to overwrite it with good code that gives us the desired outputs. I use three simple yet powerful techniques when working with my clients:

- Journalling

- Affirmations
- Meditation with visualization

Journalling

First, I work with each client to start a journalling habit of defining their strengths, positive traits and successes to date. Your client may protest that they have very few of these in their life, but their 'garbage code' stops them from seeing them as anything more than completed tasks. Guide them to dig deep and discover them. Some questions you may want to ask are:

- Tell me about your most outstanding achievement. How did it make you feel?
- Describe to me a time when you overcame an obstacle in your life and how it changed your life.
- What are your best personality traits, and how have they served you?
- What would your close family and friends say that you are good at?

Positive affirmations

Next, I have the client build a list of positive affirmations they can use daily to overwrite limiting beliefs. Positive affirmations are so powerful because they are based on the self-affirmation theory that describes how we can maintain our sense of self-integrity by telling ourselves (or affirming) what we believe in positive ways (Steele, 1988). There is no limit to the number of studies showing the benefits of affirmations to challenging negative or unhelpful thoughts (Critcher and Dunning, 2015; Sherman et al, 2009).

I emphasize to my clients that an affirmation practice is best done when a quiet, dedicated focus can be given to the words. It is almost akin to a mini meditation session where the client says the words and feels the emotions that go with them. Your client should create their own affirmations using their language, nuance and tone, so it's more natural. The statements should be short (one or two sentences), written in the first person, and have positive wording. Urge your client to recite their affirmations a minimum of two times daily, but there is no upper limit. Some examples of positive affirmations are:

- I believe in myself and my skills and trust my capabilities.
- I am successful and have earned my accomplishments.
- I am confident and capable of what I do.

Visualization

Finally, I want the client to incorporate visualization to remove their limiting beliefs. Visualization can help clients feel more in control and more confident by having them mentally rehearse a situation in a positive light. What I love about this tool is that it is used by many high achievers and Olympic athletes and has been studied in depth. According to the International Coaching Academy's neuroscience and visualization research paper, 'if you exercise an idea over and over [in your mind], your brain will begin to respond as though the idea was a real object in the world' (Batchu, 2013: 2).

Have the client define a past situation where they experienced imposter syndrome. Then have them visualize that experience, but instead of self-doubt, they see themselves with high confidence and self-esteem. This upgraded memory should be positive and uplifting with an outstanding conclusion. For example, suppose your client stays reclusive in department meetings because they feel that their comments will show a lack of skill. In that case, you could get them to visualize a forum where they sit and interact confidently at the table. Have the client see themselves adding their comments and ideas into the discussion and have them experience the rest of the team positively acknowledging and appreciating the input. They could even visualize their boss coming up to them after the meeting and saying something like 'You did an outstanding job in the meeting today'.

Remember these are NOT 'one and done' exercises. Remind the client that a daily, dedicated habit is the most effective way to facilitate the change they want. Your client may be unable to see their way through navigating to a new mindset, so take your rightful place as their partner and help guide them.

Final thoughts

Imposter syndrome is something that I still encounter to this day. Like my affinity for chocolate, it can be suppressed but never eliminated. It makes itself known when I am feeling anxious, down, or in a large group and feel isolated. That harmful code still gives some wrong outputs, but for the most part, my system runs smoothly with only the occasional need for a software patch. Similarly, by helping your client become aware of these feelings, recognize them as the 'faulty programming' of imposter syndrome, and rebuild their belief with the help of journalling, affirmations and visualization, their systems can run much smoother too!

References

Badawy, R, Gazdag, B, Bentley, J and Brouer, R (2018) Are all impostors created equal? Exploring gender differences in the impostor phenomenon-performance link, *Personality and Individual Differences*, 131, 156–63, doi.org/10.1016/j.paid.2018.04.044 (archived at https://perma.cc/8Z7V-ZJ4Q)

Batchu, B K (2013) Neuro-science behind visualization, *International Coach Academy*, 3 December, coachcampus.com/coach-portfolios/research-papers/bala-kishore-batchu-neuro-science-behind-visualization (archived at https://perma.cc/UW5S-VF4U)

Clance, P R and Imes, S A (1978) The imposter phenomenon in high achieving women: Dynamics and therapeutic intervention, *Psychotherapy: Theory, Research and Practice*, 15 (3), 241–7, doi.org/10.1037/h0086006 (archived at https://perma.cc/9JNS-M53U)

Critcher, C R and Dunning, D (2015) Self-affirmations provide a broader perspective on self-threat, *Personality and Social Psychology Bulletin*, 41 (1), 3–18, doi.org/10.1177/0146167214554956 (archived at https://perma.cc/SDU8-5X8R)

Cuddy, A J C, Wilmuth, C A, Yap, A J and Carney, D R (2015) Preparatory power posing affects nonverbal presence and job interview outcomes, *Journal of Applied Psychology*, 100 (4), 1286–95, doi.org/10.1037/a0038543 (archived at https://perma.cc/CDP7-X6U9)

Gray, M (2022) Befriending the imposter, *Coaching Today*, 43, 9–11

Langford, J and Clance, P (1993) The imposter phenomenon: Recent research findings regarding dynamics, personality and family patterns and their implications for treatment, *Psychotherapy: Theory, Research, Practice, Training*, 30 (3), 495–501, doi.org/10.1037/0033-3204.30.3.495 (archived at https://perma.cc/7RVF-CGWL)

Maslow, A H (1954) *Motivation and Personality*, Harper and Row, New York

Sherman, D K, Cohen, G L, Nelson, L D, Nussbaum, A D, Bunyan, D P and Garcia, J (2009) Affirmed yet unaware: Exploring the role of awareness in the process of self-affirmation, *Journal of Personality and Social Psychology*, 97 (5), 745–64, doi.org/10.1037/a0015451 (archived at https://perma.cc/7SWB-PJ63)

Steele, C M (1988) The psychology of self-affirmation: Sustaining the integrity of the self, *Advances in Experimental Social Psychology*, 21 (2), 261–302, doi.org/10.1016/S0065-2601(08)60229-4 (archived at https://perma.cc/3HJV-6HSD)

23

Ikigai

NATALIA PIVOVAROVA

ABSTRACT

A plethora of research shows that knowing one's life purpose is linked to improved physical and psychological well-being. The question we attempt to answer here is how one can attain this knowledge. In this chapter, we review a universal framework of ikigai, an ancient Japanese way of exploring life purpose, which provides a structured process to help clients to establish better goals and priorities that lead to better decision making and behaviours focused on the pursuit of purpose.

Background

Ikigai, a Japanese concept, can be translated as 'a reason for living'. In fact, the true meaning of the word 'ikigai' in Japanese is difficult to express, and one can find varying definitions (Hasegawa et al, 2003). Japanese psychologists and professors explain that ikigai gives individuals a sense of a life worth living (Nakanishi, 1999). Some other popular definitions include 'meaning of life' and 'purpose in life'. For the purposes of this chapter, I will use the concepts of meaning and purpose interchangeably.

Research on purpose reveals a wide variety of benefits that a meaningful life provides, including higher levels of happiness, life satisfaction and general well-being, reduced risk for anxiety, and greater physical health. Most psychologists state that people are not born with a sense of purpose, but it must be found, created or learnt (Hasegawa et al, 2003). However, a lot of people struggle to identify their purpose in life, and some people never attain the goal of finding their 'ikigai', unless they are guided throughout the process, for example, via a positive psychology intervention (Schippers and Ziegler, 2019). Positive psychology is a scientific field established from studies over the past two decades, which resulted in multiple exercises, activities, techniques and interventions that can be used for coaching, to achieve more satisfaction and well-being in professional and personal life by identifying and focusing on strengths and potential rather than weaknesses and dysfunctions.

This chapter intends to help you understand the power of ikigai, explore the framework of ikigai as a tool that can enable you as a coach to facilitate the search for purpose process and mitigate the psychological distress that often accompanies it. For beginner coaches who might still be in the process of building confidence to conduct structured coaching sessions, the ikigai framework would be an excellent stepping stone to advance their skills in promoting their clients' positive outcomes. For experienced coaches, the review of the framework would be equally beneficial to expand their understanding and application of the concept in their practice. In general, the ikigai framework can be used in coaching to address the following issues: lack of motivation to act, finding reasons for change, commitment, resilience, general well-being, sense of hope, growth mindset, decision making, goals and priorities setting.

Theory and literature review

With the rise of positive psychology, the meaning of life has become a major research topic. Martin Seligman, who is widely credited as the father of positive psychology, described it as the field of study 'about valued subjective experiences: well-being, contentment, and satisfaction (in the past); hope and optimism (for the future); and flow and happiness (in the present)' (Csikszentmihalyi, 2014: 280). Scientists study these concepts to help individuals thrive and live their lives to the fullest. Later, Seligman included meaning in his five-component model of well-being summarized by an acronym PERMA, for positive emotion, engagement, relationship, meaning and accomplishment (Csikszentmihalyi, 2014).

Decades before the establishment of positive psychology, Viktor Frankl (1985: 150), an Austrian psychiatrist and holocaust survivor, concluded that 'challenging the meaning of life is the truest expression of the state of being human'. He used his experience in a concentration camp, and finding personal meaning that helped him survive, to establish a new school of existential therapy called logotherapy. At its core logotherapy is an intervention focusing on the future and building resilience and endurance to find meaning in periods of hardship. Paul Wong, a Canadian clinical psychologist and professor at Trent University, explained the basic assumptions of logotherapy and how to apply a meaning-seeking model to facilitate meaning research and intervention in the 21st century. He summarized one of the important contributions of Frankl's work as the need for a radical shift from self-focus to meaning-focus that will bring an individual to self-actualization (Wong, 2014).

Research on meaning in the last ten years linked purpose in life with better health (mental and physical) and health behaviours (Sone et al, 2008). Although the exact biological and neurological links between purpose and better health remain unclear for the moment, recent findings suggests that people who report to have purpose in life are more proactive in taking care of their health (Sone, et al, 2008). Some studies also showed that people with a purpose in life are less likely to experience conflict when making health-related decisions (Kim, Strecher and Ryff, 2014). It is not a stretch to conclude that having a purpose raises the energy levels, resilience, hope and other qualities associated with positivity. At the same time, experiences of negativity abate, including unhealthy stress, depression, lethargy and unfocused aggression that often disrupt healthy cognitive functioning such as decision making, planning, and prosocial behaviour.

Furthermore, research demonstrated that meaning in life is connected to increases in longevity (Hill and Turiano, 2014: 1482). The authors reported that 'having a purpose in life is an indicator of healthy aging for several reasons including its potential for reducing mortality risk'. Moreover, these findings are not culture specific, as research has shown similar benefits in a Japanese study with respect to a sense of ikigai, or a 'life worth living' (Sone et al, 2008: 709). These outcomes may be explained best by considering the importance of self-motivated and self-determined goals established with the drive and passion that come from having a purpose (McKnight and Kashdan, 2009; Schippers and Ziegler, 2019). Finally, having a purpose in life may in turn be related to forming and sustaining organized goal structures and goal pursuit, and provide centrality in a person's identity. Therefore, as attested by burgeoning scientific studies, my review concludes that identifying and enhancing meaning and purpose in life brings numerous benefits in an individual's life, and the ikigai concept can be used in coaching to facilitate this process.

Most people, however, find it difficult to identify their purpose in life, and some people never manage to find their 'ikigai' (Park, Park and Peterson, 2010). Research on the 'search for purpose' indicates that most people almost always encounter anxiety during their search for purpose, regardless of their age (Rainey, 2014). Purpose anxiety encompasses 'the negative emotions experienced in direct relation to the search for purpose – experienced either while struggling to find or struggling to enact one's purpose in life' (p 60). Based on the research conducted on the search for meaning, Professor Schippers concluded that 'even if people search for meaning, they may not find it, unless they are prompted to do so in an evidence-based manner, e.g., via a positive psychology intervention' (Schippers and Ziegler, 2019: 2).

This statement is relevant to the ikigai and coaching for two reasons. First, the search for purpose is challenging without support and guidance, and an effective coaching process provides the structure needed to maintain progress. Also, anxiety is almost inevitable in any personal exploration and change, but an observant coach guides the process at a pace and comfort level that suits their client. The coach emphasizes the idea that a life purpose is usually not lofty and earth-changing but serves each person in their own life according to their personal values. For instance, being a plumber, teacher, farmer or parent provides value to others that support their lives. It enables purpose to disseminate and spread in a society where everyone matters. Rather than finding that one BIG thing, clients are encouraged to apply their values in everything they care for, thereby finding purpose in many aspects of their lives.

Using the ikigai in practice most closely resembles the principles of two coaching approaches to maximize these benefits. Positive psychology can provide coaching with a bounded scope of practice, with interventions and measurements that work (Seligman, 2011). With a primary focus on strengths and potential, the positive psychology system is empowering and sets the client up to develop the character strengths and values aligned with their passion and purpose. The existential coaching approach can be used to identify and understand existential values, assumptions and beliefs that are at the core of a person's purpose, a process that is also intrinsically aligned with and enabled by the ikigai framework (Spinelli and Horner, 2019).

Applying the ikigai framework in coaching

If you search for ikigai as a tool for finding meaning in life, you most probably will find two models, and most users swear by one or the other. The original Japanese version has a more existential perspective, while the adapted 'Western version' is more geared towards balancing your life in terms of being able to combine your passion and profession.

Model 1: Western ikigai – the Purpose Venn diagram

In the West the concept of ikigai is often associated with the Purpose Venn diagram (Figure 23.1) that is based on four components one needs to complete in order to find their ikigai: what you love, what you are good at, what the world needs, and what you can be paid for.

This popular Venn diagram is often used as a framework aimed at evaluating one's career and a way to balance it with life purpose in the narrower meaning of a profession and earning a living. For instance, this is a great tool to start with when a client wants to address career transformation. But, based on my coaching practice, I have found that the Purpose Venn diagram can also be used effectively as a stepping stone for further exploration of clients' existential questions. For instance, a client may be struggling with creating their life vision. They may be wondering how to include various areas of life in it and expecting to get clarity and direction from the coaching process. Using the ikigai in a structured way with a client ensures that they

FIGURE 23.1 The Purpose Venn diagram

get a better overall perspective and explore all areas impacting their lives, even those that they may have overlooked, thereby enhancing their clarity and direction.

HOW TO USE THE PURPOSE VENN DIAGRAM IN YOUR COACHING PRACTICE

These are the steps that I use to guide a client through the Purpose Venn diagram to help them find their answers. Firstly, start a coaching conversation by exploring and writing down everything your client loves doing, including their quirks, passions, hobbies, hidden talents and secret obsessions. It may help to use the following questions and scoring each item on a three-point scale where 1 = being of little interest and 3 = keeping the client's attention and curiosity. The following questions are from my personal 'question bank' that I find useful in the ikigai process:

- What activates joy within you?
- What activities make you lose track of time?
- What day-to-day tasks do you enjoy?
- What do you do in your free time?

As a second step, a coach suggests exploring what the client is good at by scoring the skills level of each item mentioned in the first step. The clients' self-awareness of their competencies and strengths would affect the coaching innovation leading to decisions and actions because it increases self-confidence, provides a sense of ownership, and creates momentum to use intrinsic motivation to act according to their strengths. The book *Now, Discover Your Strengths* by Gallup highlights the importance of strengths and its contribution to success in one's life (Buckingham and Clifton, 2001). The book provides access to the Clifton StrengthsFinder 2.0 assessment, which is valuable for clients to complete to discover what they naturally do best and how to develop these talents into strengths.

To deepen the reflection on what a client is good at, a coach may use the following questions (from my 'question bank' again):

- What are you recognized for?
- What are you able to do naturally, quickly, or with joy that other people aren't able to?
- What do people thank you for doing for them?
- What do people ask you to help with most often?

As a third step, a coach moves the conversation to explore what the world needs, using the following questions, also from my 'question bank':

- What issue or challenge would you like to help solve?
- What greater cause do you strongly believe in?
- What will move society forward?
- If you could make any positive impact in the world what would that be?

Here, I suggest looking at the United Nations (UN) Global Goals list as a guiding post to find one's mission (United Nations Department of Economic and Social Affairs, 2015). These items are aimed at sustainable development of humankind by improving health and education, reducing inequality, and spurring economic growth. Currently, the 17 sustainable development goals (SDGs) to transform our world are:

- GOAL 1: No Poverty
- GOAL 2: Zero Hunger
- GOAL 3: Good Health and Well-being
- GOAL 4: Quality Education
- GOAL 5: Gender Equality
- GOAL 6: Clean Water and Sanitation
- GOAL 7: Affordable and Clean Energy

- GOAL 8: Decent Work and Economic Growth
- GOAL 9: Industry, Innovation, and Infrastructure
- GOAL 10: Reduced Inequality
- GOAL 11: Sustainable Cities and Communities
- GOAL 12: Responsible Consumption and Production
- GOAL 13: Climate Action
- GOAL 14: Life Below Water
- GOAL 15: Life on Land
- GOAL 16: Peace and Justice Strong Institutions
- GOAL 17: Partnerships to achieve the Goal

A coach can also explore with their clients the concept of wicked problems. These are social or cultural issues that are very difficult or impossible to solve as they are typically highly interconnected, we lack an understanding of their occurrence, there is contradictory information, or solutions have collateral damage (Kolko, 2012). Progress requires new boundaries of thinking, creativity, empathy, abductive reasoning, and rapid and robust prototyping and implementation. Examples are global climate change, natural disasters, healthcare, epidemics and pandemics, organized crime, nuclear weapons, homelessness and social injustice.

In the fourth step a coach guides their client to assess the likelihood of getting paid if the previously listed items were offered as a product or service. A coach may facilitate this step by asking the following questions:

- Where does such a service or product already exist?
- What problem are you solving for potential clients/customers?
- What could be your specific selling point (specific difference that your product or service could make in your customers' lives)?

A client may be struggling to answer these questions without finding out more information on the subject. A coach's role is to help the client to come up with strategies for self-directed learning (it may include self-guided reading, self-planned learning, self-education). For example, when I used this diagram before becoming a coach, I didn't know that people would pay for my skills of asking questions and listening. It required some research to find out that coaching is a viable profession.

So, have the client list everything they enjoy doing, however informal or quirky it may seem (see Table 23.1 as an example). Ask them to score every activity on a three-point scale for the aspects of interest level, skill level, needed in the world, and whether people will pay for it. Add the scores in each line to get a total.

TABLE 23.1 Ikigai spreadsheet example

Passions, hobbies, quirks	Interest level	Skill level	Useful/needed in the world	Would people pay?	TOTAL
Dancing	2	1	2	2	7
Listening to friends	1	2	3	2	8
Photography	3	1	3	3	10
Watching anime	3	3	1	1	8
...					

Once you have the total scores, the aim of further reflection is to facilitate the identification of gaps and development of a growth mindset. They may not necessarily choose the highest-scoring activity as their priority, but it is a good start to a fruitful discussion.

Clients often decide to hire a coach after a failed attempt to figure it out on their own. They may come to a coach frustrated and believing that they do not have valuable skills, or that what they can do, no one needs or would pay for. So, they lack a growth mindset where they believe that they can develop strengths and talents over time to meet their passion and purpose, or even have any at all. And, they may also have a poor sense of how to formulate their purpose and align the different parts of the ikigai diagram. These are areas where an effective coach can facilitate the process.

As such, the coach's role in using this framework is to explain the concepts and broaden clients' view to encourage flexibility, thoughtfulness and creativity, as well as to co-create the direction and motivation for the client. The semi-structured ikigai is a good starting point, in conjunction with coaching skills such as questioning, listening, showing empathy, acceptance and acknowledgment, and providing a safe space where the client can be open and grow without fear of failure.

Model 2: Japanese version – self-actualization model

English-language experts who researched ikigai in collaboration with Japanese psychologists confirm that the original concept of ikigai from Japan is designed to facilitate a deeper self-reflection that leads to self-actualization (Kemp, 2022). Work, although an important part of one's ikigai, is not the only focus. Ikigai includes *all* aspect of one's life.

There is no diagram, chart, or framework that the Japanese use to understand or find their ikigai. They learn and understand its multifaceted meaning as they experience life. Kemp, an ikigai expert, attempted to represent what ikigai means to Japanese practitioners in the diagram presented in Figure 23.2.

FIGURE 23.2 The Japanese ikigai system

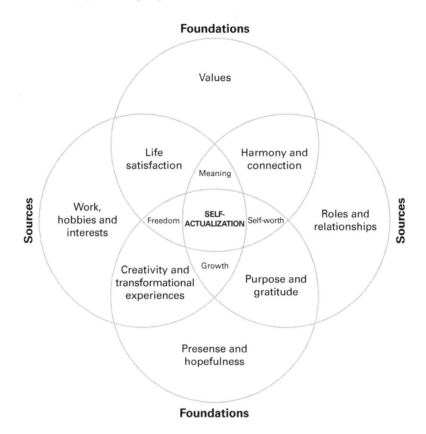

SOURCE Adapted from Lakshmanan (2021)

HOW TO USE THE JAPANESE IKIGAI SYSTEM IN YOUR COACHING PRACTICE

In the original Japanese version, there are two foundations of ikigai: one's values and one's hopefulness. The review of ikigai starts with values. Only when one lives in alignment with their values can they live an authentic life because your values determine what you pursue and accomplish (Whitener, 2021). It is important to identify whether the expression of values ensures the feeling of 'life worth living' for that individual. There are numerous ways to explore one's values. In my practice, I typically start with the tools provided by the VIA Institute on Character (VIA Institute on Character, nda). The basic assessment, the VIA survey, is a self-assessment questionnaire that takes 15 minutes to complete and identifies a client's most- and lesser-used character strengths, with which to explore further and align with their purpose and goals (VIA Institute on Character, ndb).

Another foundational component of ikigai is hopefulness, where you recognize things that you look forward to and believe that your life is going towards a brighter future. In this sense, a coach can explore the client's goals and aspirations for their ideal future to build a sense of hopefulness, which is an important part of drive and motivation.

The sources of ikigai – or a sense of purpose – provide feelings that enhance one's life and create a life worth living (Kemp, 2022). A coach can explore hobbies, interests, work, relationships and roles as the source of a client's ikigai. Take for example a client of mine. Through reviewing multiple sources of ikigai they were able to expand their perspective on life purpose and reduce the pressure by mitigating their purpose anxiety. In particular, they were able to let go of the attachment to the outcome and timeline constraints for finding their purpose that they had put on themselves. They also realized that, to them, it matters more how they are doing things (through fulfilling multiple sources of their ikigai) rather than what they are doing (perceived obligation to follow a certain path). This insight empowered them to make a career decision following their intuition and heart with more ease. In this way, looking at multiple sources of ikigai became a measurement of self-actualization in their daily living while pursuing bigger goals.

As illustrated in Figure 23.2, when the sources of ikigai (work, hobbies and interests; roles and relationships) overlap with the foundations of ikigai (values; presence and hopefulness), one experiences the feelings of ikigai that can be grouped as 1) life satisfaction, 2) creativity and transformational experiences, 3) purpose and gratitude, and 4) harmony and connection. These multiple expressions of ikigai in a client's daily life can then enable the change in their life in four core areas: meaning, self-worth, freedom and growth. So, by applying the Japanese ikigai system diagram systematically, from the outside in, starting by identifying and prioritizing the sources (work, hobbies and interests; roles and relationships), followed by exploring the foundations (values; presence and hopefulness), the core feeling and expressions of the client's unique ikigai can be defined.

THE IKIGAI-9 ASSESSMENT TOOL

The Ikigai-9 is a psychometric tool originally developed and published by Japanese researchers Tadanori Imai, Hisao Osada and Yoshitsugu Nishimura in 2012. In 2019, this construct was translated into English and validated in the UK (Fido, Kotera and Asano, 2019). The Ikigai-9 consists of nine statements evaluating one's reason for being, through measurements of emotions towards one's life, attitudes towards one's future and the acknowledgement of one's existence. The following are the Ikigai-9 statements:

1 I believe that I have some impact on someone

2 My life is mentally rich and fulfilled

3 I am interested in many things

4 I feel that I am contributing to someone or to society

5 I would like to develop myself

6 I often feel that I am happy

7 I think that my existence is needed by something or someone

8 I would like to learn something new or start something

9 I have room in my mind

Participants are asked to rate whether each statement applies to them on a five-point scale (1 = does not apply to me, 5 = applies to me a lot). After adding up the totals, one can assess how close they come to experiencing a sense of ikigai. However, in the coaching process, the most value of this assessment may be in the qualitative analysis and reflection of the individual items. After completion of the questionnaire, a coach may suggest focusing on items that scored the lowest and those that scored higher in the context of the client's priorities, so that they can be more focused on those aspects that contribute to a higher sense of ikigai. As such, the Ikigai-9 is a useful tool to facilitate the self-reflection process that helps to identify the gaps and create concrete steps to move forward in life.

Conclusion and recommendations

The choice of which framework to work through with a client would depend on the client's goal for coaching and reasons they decided to engage with a coach. This goal does not need to be concrete, but can be, at least initially, more of an abstract vision (Price, 2020). Part of the coach's role is to meet clients where they are. For example, my practice showed that some clients found more meaning with less anxiety by utilizing the Japanese ikigai system versus feeling stuck in trying to find their purpose using the Purpose Venn diagram. The latter addresses more concrete aspects based on work and career factors and is less esoteric than the Japanese ikigai. However, both ikigai frameworks can help clients find personal meaning in life and work, and foster motivation and the journey towards the inner self (Fido, Kotera and Asano, 2019). Moreover, the research on ikigai in existential executive leadership coaching showed that it can also help to build an organizational culture of common visions, and alignment of individual and organizational values and approaches. Model 1 provides guidelines to find fulfilment in one's career and leads towards efficient goal setting. Through Model 2 a person is empowered to discover meaning in daily living towards facilitating growth, improving self-worth, developing freedom and fulfilling their purpose in life. Both models require deep reflection and I suggest conducting the process with a client over several sessions. Further, following the Japanese philosophy of ikigai, we understand that it is a dynamic concept and I recommend reviewing it periodically, such as once a year.

References

Buckingham, M and Clifton D (2001) *Now, Discover Your Strengths*, Free Press, New York

Csikszentmihalyi, M (2014) Positive psychology: An introduction, in *Flow and the Foundations of Positive Psychology*, pp xv-xxiv, Springer, Dordrecht

Fido, D, Kotera, Y and Asano, K (2019) English translation and validation of the Ikigai-9 in a UK sample, *International Journal of Mental Health and Addiction*, 18, 1352–9, doi.org/10.1007/s11469-019-00150-w (archived at https://perma.cc/4YFC-8UPU)

Frankl, V E (1985) *Man's Search For Meaning*, Simon & Schuster, New York

Hasegawa, A, Fujiwara, Y, Hoshi, T and Shinkai, S (2003) Regional differences in ikigai (reason(s) for living) in elderly people: relationship between ikigai and family structure, physiological situation and functional capacity, *Nihon Ronen Igakkai Zasshi*, 40 (4) 390–6, doi.org/10.3143/geriatrics.40.390 (archived at https://perma.cc/8SNU-Y6DT)

Hill, P L and Turiano, N A (2014) Purpose in life as a predictor of mortality across adulthood, *Psychological Science*, 25 (7), 1482–6, doi.org/10.1177/0956797614531799 (archived at https://perma.cc/PB8Y-BDGC)

Imai, T, Osada, H and Nishimura, Y (2012) The reliability and validity of a new scale for measuring the concept of ikigai (Ikigai-9), *Japanese Journal of Public Health*, 59 (7), 433–40

Kemp, N (2022) *IKIGAI-KAN: Feel a life worth living*, Intertype Publish and Print, Melbourne

Kim, E S, Strecher, V J and Ryff, C D (2014) Purpose in life and use of preventive health care services, *PNAS*, 111 (46), 16331–6, doi.org/10.1073/pnas.1414826111

Kolko, J (2012) *Wicked Problems: Problems worth solving*, AC4D, Austin, TX

Lakshmanan, S (2021) A path to discover our ikigai, American College of Cardiology, 19 January, www.acc.org/Membership/Sections-and-Councils/Fellows-in-Training-Section/Section-Updates/2021/01/19/00/15/2021-A-Path-to-Discover-Our-Ikigai (archived at https://perma.cc/5FKN-W9BN)

McKnight, P E and Kashdan, T B (2009) Purpose in life as a system that creates and sustains health and well-being: An integrative, testable theory, *Review of General Psychology*, 13, 242–51

Nakanishi, N (1999) Ikigai in older Japanese people, *Age and Ageing*, 28 (3), 323–4, doi.org/10.1093/ageing/28.3.323 (archived at https://perma.cc/VSM3-RCVB)

Park, N, Park, M and Peterson, C (2010) When is the search for meaning related to life satisfaction? *Applied Psychology: Health and Well-Being*, 2 (1), 1–13

Price, R E (2020) Goal-setting in coaching, in *The Coaches' Handbook: The complete practitioner guide for professional coaches*, ed J Passmore, pp 79–91, Routledge, New York

Rainey, L (2014) The search for purpose in life: An exploration of purpose, the search process, and purpose anxiety, Master of Applied Positive Psychology (MAPP) Capstone, University of Pennsylvania

Schippers, M C and Ziegler, N (2019) Life crafting as a way to find purpose and meaning in life, *Frontiers in Psychology*, 10 (2778), doi.org/10.3389/fpsyg.2019.02778 (archived at https://perma.cc/UXE3-QWE5)

Seligman, M E P (2011) *Flourish: A visionary new understanding of happiness and well-being*, Free Press, New York

Sone, T, Nakaya, N, Ohmori, K, Shimazu, T, Higashiguchi, M, Kakizaki, M, Kikuchi, N, Kuriyama, S and Tsuji, I (2008) Sense of life worth living (Ikigai) and mortality in Japan: Ohsaki study, *Psychosomatic Medicine*, 70, 709–15, doi.org/10.1097/PSY.0b013e31817e7e64 (archived at https://perma.cc/BR4R-B68A)

Spinelli, E and Horner, C (2019) An existential approach to coaching psychology, in *Handbook of Coaching Psychology: A guide for practitioners*, 2nd edn, eds S Palmer and A Whybrow, pp 169–79, Routledge, New York

United Nations Department of Economic and Social Affairs (2015) #Envision2030: 17 goals to transform the world for persons with disabilities, www.un.org/development/desa/disabilities/envision2030.html (archived at https://perma.cc/7MQ4-G3CC)

VIA Institute on Character (nda) Character strength survey and character reports, www.viacharacter.org/ (archived at https://perma.cc/VWY3-BWMQ)

VIA Institute on Character (ndb) VIA Character strength survey, www.viacharacter.org/survey/pro/RSH3C5/account/register (archived at https://perma.cc/VWY3-BWMQ)

Whitener, S (2021) How to live in alignment with your true values, *Forbes*, 5 October, www.forbes.com/sites/forbescoachescouncil/2021/10/05/how-to-live-in-alignment-with-your-true-values (archived at https://perma.cc/B7V2-X36V)

Wong, P T (2014) Viktor Frankl's meaning-seeking model and positive psychology, in *Meaning in Positive and Existential Psychology*, eds A Batthyany and P Russo-Netzer, pp 149–84, Springer, New York

24

Preventing burnout by attaining a healthy work and personal life balance

NEELA PIRWITZ

ABSTRACT

Burnout is the most common work-related syndrome linked to chronic stress, causing emotional exhaustion, a loss of performance and satisfaction, and feelings of hopelessness and bitterness. The condition is costly on a personal and organizational level and has been increasing in recent years. Yet, if we can cultivate awareness, intervention can be straightforward, such as activity monitoring and energy management.

Introduction

Work and personal life balance has an underlying goal, which is to fit our work into our lives, rather than trying to fit our lives into our work. The focus of this chapter is to explore burnout prevention by first gaining awareness on what burnouts are, looking into *how* to prevent burnouts through a work–personal life balance, by monitoring activities evaluating their impact on your energy balance, and balancing activities to optimize energy. Through efficiency, planning and routine we, as coaches, can help ourselves and our clients to take the steps necessary to prevent burnout.

Understanding burnout

Burnout is one of the most common work-related syndromes (Amsterdam UMC, 2020) incited by the current way of corporate and societal structure (Mayo Clinic Staff, 2021). Often, burnout is the result of ineffective attempts to regulate chronic work-related stress or ignoring it altogether. There is a discrepancy between the energy an affected person puts into work, and the results they attain. The result is a 'feeling of emotional exhaustion, depersonalization and diminished personal accomplishment at work' (Montero-Marín et al, 2009: 1). According to the WHO, burnout is characterized by 'feelings of energy depletion or exhaustion, increased mental distance to one's job and reduced professional efficacy' (Borysenko, 2019: 1). Even though this definition implies that burnout can only affect people working a job, burnout can occur in anyone who is exposed to chronic stress (Abramson, 2022).

Since the pandemic, burnout rates have been at an all-time high. This is not only true for health care workers, first responders or educators, but for everyone (Abramson, 2022). The burnout rate climbed from 32 per cent for women and 28 per cent for men in 2020 to a staggering 42 per cent and 35 per cent respectively in 2021 (McKinsey & Company, 2021).

The health implications of burnout are significant, and include the following:

- Heart disease and the consequences thereof, like not being able to return to work, having to follow a long and difficult road to recovery, both mentally and physically (Toker et al, 2012).
- Strokes, caused by long working hours (Pega et al, 2021).

Therefore, it is essential that we can recognize the symptoms of burnout in ourselves, and in others. Smith, Segal and Robinson (2022) divide the symptoms of burnout into three different categories:

Physical symptoms of burnout

- Feeling tired and drained, more often than not
- Getting ill frequently
- Regular headaches and muscle pain
- Change in appetite
- Change in sleeping habits

Emotional symptoms of burnout

- Feeling of failure and self-doubt
- Sense of helplessness, being trapped or defeated
- Detachment

- Low motivation
- Increases of cynicism and negativity
- Lowered satisfaction and a reduced sense of accomplishment

Behavioural symptoms of burnout

- Retracting from responsibilities
- Self-isolation
- Procrastination
- Coping through drugs, alcohol or food
- Letting out frustrations on others
- Skipping work partially or altogether

It is clear that the impact of burnout is very concerning. In 2016, an estimated 745,000 people died due to strokes and ischemic heart disease as a consequence of long working hours (55 or more hours per week). This number mirrors an increase of 29 per cent since 2000 (WHO, 2021), and provides us with a clear indication that the treatment of burnout is not enough. **We need active prevention.**

The role of coaches in recognizing burnout

The first step towards achieving balance and preventing burnout is to recognize the warning signs of burnout (Smith, Segal and Robinson, 2022). Different clients may show different signs of burnout. According to Bourg Carter (2013), the following signs can be used as indicators of burnout:

Signs of physical and emotional exhaustion

- **Chronic fatigue** The client might feel constantly tired, drained or dreading what lies ahead.
- **Insomnia** The client might have difficulties falling or staying asleep on a regular basis.
- **Forgetfulness and impaired concentration and attention** The client experiences a lack of focus to the extent of not being able to work at all.
- **Physical symptoms** These include (but are not limited to) short breath, chest pain, dizziness or headaches.
- **Weakened immune system** The client might get sick more than usual.
- **Loss of appetite** The client may skip meals and/or lose a significant amount of weight.

- **Anxiety** The client might experience worry building up to a point where it interferes with working productively or generates issues in the client's personal life.

- **Depression** The client may experience feelings of hopelessness, guilt or worthlessness, and have lost an interest in social interaction and other activities they used to enjoy.

- **Anger** The client might be unusually aggressive and experience emotional outbursts.

Signs of cynicism and detachment

- **Loss of joy** The experience may be limited to the work environment or extend to other areas of life.

- **Pessimism** The client might experience general pessimism, which can develop into trust issues with those close to them, indecisiveness, withdrawal, apathy or avoidance.

- **Isolation** The client may experience resistance to interacting with others or avoid them altogether.

- **Detachment** client might experience a feeling of disconnectedness that may result in them skipping their responsibilities.

Signs of ineffectiveness or lack of accomplishment

- **Feelings of apathy and hopelessness** The client might feel that nothing has value.

- **Increased irritability** The client may feel frustrated or irritated, which interferes with their productivity and relationships.

- **Lack of productivity or poor performance** The client may notice a lack of concentration and drive that can lead to an increase in incomplete or delayed projects.

Addressing burnout and achieving work–personal life balance

Listed below are three exercises that can help us as coaches, and our clients, to recognize whether our client is at high risk of burnout, and how to reprioritize certain aspects of their lives to find balance and take charge.

1 The activity log gives an insight into the activity load a client is experiencing on an average day and the energy associated with each activity. This helps us estimate whether the client has too much on their plate, or if the problem lies in the execution, timing or combination of the activities, rather than in the volume.

2   The priority-setting exercise allows us to guide our clients through the process of reprioritizing different aspects of their lives and to take the first step in reestablishing balance in their lives.

3   The third exercise centres on energy management. By scrutinizing the energy outcomes of every activity and considering their priorities, a coach can help their client rebuild their day to optimize energy.

Activity tracking

Monitoring one's daily activities with a time audit is a handy exercise to understand where a client is right now. Such a time audit allows us to find out how much time we use for which activity each day and how much of our time is unaccounted for. To conduct a time audit, we need to think about our average day. Every day has 24 hours. In the example presented in Table 24.1, the client accounted for 148 hours, or 21 hours per day averaged over seven days. This means they have three hours each day that are not listed. We then help the client figure out how they may use this time consciously to do something they love that can add to their well-being, which will in turn allow them to feel an increased sense of balance in their daily life. By doing this exercise, most people will realize that they do not actually need more hours in the day. They just need to use the time they have more consciously and more actively. The chart below will give you a good understanding of how this can be accomplished using the hourly log template.

But that is not all! By having the client rate their perceived energy gain/loss for every activity, we can factor in the non-negotiables (duties, responsibilities, etc.) while rearranging the other activities to optimize energy.

Reviewing the results together, the coach asks the client to reflect on the results and how they feel about what they are seeing. Explore which changes can be made without compromising their responsibilities and performance, for example, including adding activities that they feel will benefit their well-being.

Priority setting

Additionally, it is helpful for us to help our clients define how they want their life to look. Here are some questions you can ask to help your client gain insight:

- How do you want to feel?
- What are your personal boundaries?
- Your non-negotiables?
- How can you get there?

A good way of approaching this is to have our clients write down their ideas in whichever way they come to them. We might give them five minutes to write down everything that is important to them and everything that they want to incorporate into their daily life or ask them to do it at home. Then we explore what is keeping them from doing these things now. Once they write everything down, we help them to organize their thoughts by establishing categories of boundaries, non-negotiables and wishes for the future. Then, we help the client rank these by importance and to prioritize them. Finally, we explore how to implement these priorities, build a sustainable strategy, and how to manage potential stumbling blocks.

Using the priorities template in Table 24.2, the client can build the structure they need and zoom in to look at what is really important to them. In this way we as the coach can help the client to gain a feeling of control over their life, allowing them to take important steps towards balance and burnout prevention.

Energy management

Preventing and recovering from burnout is much more about optimal energy management than doing occasional exercise, meditation or friendly chat. It is about learning to balance and manage energy effectively on a daily basis that is sustainable and aligned with our flow and values. We achieve 'flow' when we are immersed in, energized through, and feel joy and satisfaction from an activity. Although it is not necessarily good in an absolute sense (e.g., when unchecked, it can contribute to burnout), when balanced with other activities to attend to responsibilities or create a break, flow is invigorating if timed well. This simply means that too much of a good thing is not always good.

Every day, use the list of your activities to attach an energy rating to each (Table 24.3). Use any scale that suits you. The example uses a scale of -1 (complete depletion of energy) to 10 (feeling completely refreshed and recharged, ready to go!).

Use the energy ratings in the activity log (Table 24.3) to eliminate activities that diminish energy and schedule more of those that generate energy, while prioritizing flow items, priorities, boundaries and wishes identified in the priorities exercise (Table 24.2). A person can also distinguish energy according to the physical, emotional and cognitive impact to help create a balance on an even more detailed level.

For example, a client finds that a one-hour meeting is cognitively uplifting but a two-hour meeting is cognitively depleting. As a result, where possible, they limit their meetings to one hour. They find that working at their charity is emotionally satisfying if limited to one day per week, otherwise they experience emotional distress. Similarly, three exercise sessions per week contribute to the energy levels but they struggle to recover and feel fatigued when exercising more times a week. Also, look

TABLE 24.1 24-Hour activity log template

Activity description	Time (min)							Weekly totals		Note/takeaway From time study
	Mo	Tu	We	Th	Fr	Sa	Su	Minutes	Hours	
Work	480	480	480	480	480	0	0	2400	40	
Commute	45	45	45	45	45	45	45	315	5.25	
Entertainment – at home	0	0	0	0	0	120	60	180	3	
Entertainment – outside the home	0	0	60	0	0	0	0	60	1	
Exercise	0	60	60	0	60	60	0	240	4	
Family and friends	0	60	0	0	0	0	60	120	2	
Study (class)	0	0	0	0	0	0	0	0	0	
Study (homework)	0	0	0	0	0	0	0	0	0	
Internet and social media	60	60	60	60	60	60	60	420	7	
TV	120	120	120	120	120	120	120	840	14	
Meals and eating	60	60	60	60	60	60	60	420	7	
Personal care	45	45	45	45	45	45	45	315	5.25	
Recreation	30	30	30	30	30	30	30	210	3.5	
Sleep	480	480	480	480	480	480	480	3360	56	
Travel								0	0	
Total	1320	1440	1440	1320	1380	1020	960	8880	148	

TABLE 24.2 Priorities template

What I want to incorporate	Obstacles to incorporate
1.	
2.	
3.	
Top three boundaries I want to incorporate	
1.	
2.	
3.	
Top three non-negotiables I want to incorporate	
1.	
2.	
3.	
Top three wishes for the future I want to incorporate	
1.	
2.	
3.	

at the negative items that cannot be avoided. Are there better ways of doing those in terms of energy demands? Look at every activity and ask:

- What is the energy impact?
- What is the priority level?
- What changes can I make in method, timing, duration, etc to make it more energy efficient?
- How can I reorganize or reschedule my days to optimize energy while keeping my priorities?

By considering these factors, a coach can help their client reconfigure their day without compromising priorities but creating a better energy balance that protects them from burnout.

TABLE 24.3 Daily energy ratings for activities

Activity description	Energy ratings (−10 to 10)							Average for the week	Note/takeaway from energy rating
	Mo	Tu	We	Th	Fr	Sa	Su		
Work	−6	−3	−6	−3	−6	0	0	−3.4	How can I make work more positive?
Commute	−5	−5	−5	−5	−5	−5	−5	−5.0	Is there another option?
Entertainment – at home	5	4	5	4	5	4	5	4.6	
Entertainment – outside the home	4	0	4	0	4	0	4	2.3	
Exercise	5	0	5	0	5	0	5	2.9	
Family and friends	−2	2	−2	2	−2	2	−2	−0.3	Why are there negatives?
Study (class)	−4	−4	−4	−4	−4	−4	−4	−4.0	Why is this so negative?
Study (homework)	−5	−5	−5	−5	−5	−5	−5	−5.0	Look at different ways, schedules, etc
Internet and social media	−8	−7	−8	−7	−8	−7	−8	−7.6	Cut back on social media
TV	2	3	2	3	2	3	2	2.4	
Meals and eating	5	4	5	4	5	4	5	4.6	
Personal care	3	3	3	3	3	3	3	3.0	
Recreation	2	3	2	3	2	3	2	2.4	Is there more positive recreation to do?
Sleep	−5	−2	−5	−2	−5	−2	−5	−3.7	Look at ways to improve sleep
Travel	0	0	0	0	0	0	0	0.0	What would travel contribute?
Daily average	−0.6	−0.5	−0.6	−0.5	−0.6	−0.3	−0.2	−0.5	Aim to make this positive!

Building burnout prevention habits

Lastly, we need to help our clients to build resilience to stress. To do this, we need to encourage them to take care of their physical and emotional health. According to Smith, Segal and Robinson (2022), these efforts might include:

- Our clients rely on their support system of family and friends, or actively being more social in the workplace while limiting the energy they give to negative people.
- Reevaluating their priorities, such as reserving time to recharge, and learning to say 'no'.
- Trying to find value in their work, by focusing on how their job can be helpful to others or by finding at least one aspect they enjoy about their workday.
- Prioritizing physical exercise and quality rest.
- Boosting our mood and energy levels by following a healthy diet, such as limiting food and beverages that can negatively impact our client's mood and mental state (e.g., caffeine, alcohol, processed foods).

Further, it is helpful to create a clear plan of action that will allow us to follow a routine to achieve our goals. The structure of such a plan is dependent on the needs, preferences and lifestyle of the individual. For instance, some people are comfortable working on multiple aspects at once, others will want to focus on one step at a time, adding another aspect only once they are comfortable with the step they have already implemented. Generally, the plan should include different burnout-preventing habits, like, for example, physical exercise such as strength training or aerobics (Dyrbye, Satele and Shanafelt, 2017), meditation (Green and Kinchen, 2021) or yoga (Alexander et al, 2015), the individual wishes to incorporate into their lives.

Final thoughts

Overall, achieving balance contributes to the prevention of burnout. It is not so much about balancing work and personal life activities than optimizing energy. Energy deficiency leads to proneness to stress that precedes burnout. By helping clients to monitor and prioritize their activities, and assign energy scores to each, they gain clarity into how to best achieve balance for them. Reorganizing and reshaping daily schedules to protect energy levels while still adhering to priorities and setting boundaries is the most effective countermeasure against burnout.

References

Abramson, A (2022) Burnout and stress are everywhere, *Monitor on Psychology*, 53 (1), 72, www.apa.org/monitor/2022/01/special-burnout-stress (archived at https://perma. cc/2LSE-KBAQ)

Alexander, G, Rollins, K, Walker, D, Wong, L and Pennings, J (2015) Yoga for self-care and burnout prevention among nurses, *Workplace Health & Safety*, 63 (10), 462–70, doi. org/10.1177/2165079915596102 (archived at https://perma.cc/4G8Z-SFZ9)

Amsterdam UMC (2020) Beroepsziekten in cijfers, 14 September, www.beroepsziekten.nl/ content/beroepsziekten-cijfers-2020 (archived at https://perma.cc/75WU-RUM3)

Borysenko, K (2019) Burnout is now an officially diagnosable condition: Here's what you need to know about it, *Forbes*, 29 May, www.forbes.com/sites/karlynborysenko/ 2019/05/29/burnout-is-now-an-officially-diagnosable-condition-heres-what-you-need-to-know-about-it (archived at https://perma.cc/FH8A-PJXH)

Bourg Carter, S (2013) The tell-tale signs of burnout… Do you have them? *Psychology Today*, 26 November, www.psychologytoday.com/gb/blog/high-octane-women/201311/ the-tell-tale-signs-of-burnout-do-you-have-them (archived at https://perma.cc/754V-KMSL)

Dyrbye, L, Satele, D and Shanafelt, T (2017) Healthy exercise habits are associated with lower risk of burnout and higher quality of life among U.S. medical students, *Academic Medicine*, 92 (7), 1006–11, doi.org/10.1097/ACM.0000000000001540 (archived at https://perma.cc/7VRK-SL3L)

Green, A and Kinchen, E (2021) The effects of mindfulness meditation on stress and burnout in nurses, *Journal of Holistic Nursing*, 39 (4), 356–68, doi.org/10.1177/ 08980101211015818 (archived at https://perma.cc/6948-7M6C)

Mayo Clinic Staff (2021) Job burnout: How to spot it and take action, Mayo Clinic, 5 June, www.mayoclinic.org/healthy-lifestyle/adult-health/in-depth/burnout/art-20046642 (archived at https://perma.cc/WP5N-KE44)

McKinsey & Company (2021) Women in the Workplace, wiw-report.s3.amazonaws.com/ Women_in_the_Workplace_2021.pdf (archived at https://perma.cc/G45A-UE76)

Montero-Marín, J, Garcia-Campayo, J, Mera, D M and López del Hoyo, Y (2009) A new definition of burnout syndrome based on Farber's proposal, *Journal of Occupational Medicine and Toxicology*, 4 (31), doi.org/10.1186/1745-6673-4-31 (archived at https:// perma.cc/6Z9Q-4WM5)

Pega, F, Náfrádi, B, Momen, N, Ujita, Y, Streicher, K, Prüss-Üstün, A, Descatha, A, Driscoll, T, Fischer, F, Godderis, L, Kiiver, H, Li, J, Magnusson Hanson, L, Rugulies, R, Sørensen, K and Woodruff, T (2021) Global, regional, and national burdens of ischemic heart disease and stroke attributable to exposure to long working hours for 194 countries, 2000–2016: A systematic analysis from the WHO/ILO joint estimates of the work-related burden of disease and injury, *Environment International*, 154, 106595, www. doi.org/10.1016/j.envint. 2021.106595 (archived at https://perma.cc/BP8Z-YXZS)

Smith, M, Segal, J and Robinson, L (2022) Burnout prevention and treatment, Help Guide, www.helpguide.org/articles/stress/burnout-prevention-and-recovery.htm (archived at https://perma.cc/NGW6-FMNV)

Toker, S, Melamed, S, Berliner, S, Zeltser, D and Shapira, I (2012) Burnout and risk of coronary heart disease: A prospective study of 8838 employees, *Psychosomatic Medicine*, 74 (8), 840–7, doi.org/10.1097/PSY.0b013e31826c3174 (archived at https://perma.cc/W3M4-FL26)

WHO (2021) Long working hours increasing deaths from heart disease and stroke: WHO, ILO, World Health Organization, 17 May, www.who.int/news/item/17-05-2021-long-working-hours-increasing-deaths-from-heart-disease-and-stroke-who-ilo (archived at https://perma.cc/Y36X-NFRW)

25

Combining coaching
and mindfulness

MARTIJN VAN EIJK

ABSTRACT

Mindfulness is an awareness of the present moment with acceptance and non-judgement that is linked to objectivity, clarity, empathy and lower stress, which benefit coaching clients. I present a practical guideline of how coaches can use mindfulness in coaching sessions. The chapter covers pieces of fundamental knowledge, practical building blocks, and provides the coach with different techniques and know-how on how and when to apply mindfulness with clients.

Introduction

Mindfulness practices for coaches is an incredibly valuable tool when it comes to creating clients' self-awareness, and breaking their reactive and returning thinking and behavioural patterns. Through understanding what mindfulness is, how it can be used in coaching, gaining knowledge on the seven pillars of mindfulness and discovering how to overcome the limitations that can be presented with mindfulness, which this chapter endeavours to showcase, coaches can serve their clients more effectively.

Applying skills to become aware of the separate sensations of thinking, physical feelings, emotions and behavioural tendencies will support the development of the client's mind and self (Kabat-Zinn, 2013)

You can only apply mindfulness techniques for clients if you, as a coach, apply them to yourself (Brandsma, 2017). In the process, you will need to learn to be in and act from the moment.

Mindfulness is an experience-driven practice and is built around a few basic core principles and methodologies. In mindfulness you will always combine the following principles: education, enquiry and practice (experience).

Mindfulness is a continuous process that moves with the waves of life and therefore encompasses goal setting and result expectations that can be different from other coaching techniques. When applying the skills of mindfulness, we focus on developing the client by cultivating awareness and understanding their patterns rather than achieving a certain result.

The definition of mindfulness

The definition of mindfulness is 'awareness that arises through paying attention, on purpose, in the present moment, non-judgmentally' (Kabat-Zinn, 2013: 4).

Life is made up from a series of events. Events that have already happened (the past), events that are happening right now (the present) and events that might happen (the future). When practising mindfulness, a person focuses on the present. As humans we tend to get stuck, with the cognitive part of our brain, in thoughts about past events or in future events that are unknown or might not happen. We keep analysing and adapting with a keen sense of survival. The problem of getting stuck in the past or future is that we are not present in the current moment and always try to anticipate or remember what is not here (any more).

By practising the techniques of mindfulness, you are invited to allow yourself to experience every current moment wholeheartedly. As a coach we provide our clients with the tools to do this in a systematic way (Kabat-Zinn, 2013). Mindfulness is simple, yet not easy. When practising mindfulness, our clients learn to be aware of the reactivity of the mind and how to actively tune back into each moment with the intention to stay aware and awake. You could say they are practising being. This is practising mindfulness (Kabat-Zinn, 2013).

Learning how to stop 'doing' and switch to 'being'; learning to observe what is happening in your mind from moment to moment, how you can look at your thoughts and how you can let go of them without getting caught in them or fuelled by them. Learning how you can create space for new ways of looking at old problems, and recognizing the way they are connected; these are just a few lessons you can learn from mindfulness (Kabat-Zinn, 2013). The more frequently and systematically you practise mindfulness, the more powerful it is and the more benefit you get from it.

Benefits of mindfulness

Limiting beliefs, unsurfaced emotions or negative thought patterns that we create during our early lives have a significant impact on how we look at ourselves and the world around us today. They become the core of how we perceive everything in this world and what our place is in it. These patterns will also bring positive emotions like happiness, joy and contentment. Other patterns will carry sadness, loneliness, and even feelings of desperation and hopelessness.

It happens often that our thoughts become entire stories. Humans have an innate need to construct meaning and, therefore, tend to make assumptions, fill in gaps, or even generate memories and nuances to construct stories we tell ourselves about the world, about others, about our past and the future. However, when we look at and explore our entire thinking process and our emotional lives with mindfulness, we will find that most of our thoughts are incorrect or at most partially true (Kabat-Zinn, 2013). This can cause tremendous problems for us because these beliefs and behavioural patterns can 'capture' us for many years. We become blind to how our mind creates this 'reality', we start to ignore the 'noise', and we close ourselves off to new experiences and opportunities.

Automated responses of the mind are also called the 'autopilot' mode. With mindfulness we invite our client to explore, stay curious and observe in the moment. We explore our body, mind and self, and dissect every piece of each experience as we experience them. Not to change it, just to get to know it and to understand our response and sentiment towards it. We take away the weight we used to put into thoughts and feelings by neutral observation, and we start to normalize, accept and listen to our experiences.

The more often we practise this orientation, we learn the temporary nature of our experiences. A person finds out how life is nothing but an ocean of waves that come and go. You learn that nothing is forever and there is no need to judge or react to all of your experiences; how to 'surf the waves' instead of trying to change them.

Mindfulness also teaches you about your values, boundaries and direction in life, because you will be able to feel and know what you want through the clarity you have gained. Through the guidance of the coach, the client can start to understand what works for them personally and choose to take constant action to incorporate it in their daily lives to reach peace of mind, have less stress, and live a healthier, more fulfilling life.

How to use mindfulness in coaching

The learning process in using mindfulness as a practice is very structured. The application of mindfulness in both training and coaching consists of three important working methods: practice, enquiry and education (Brandsma, 2017).

Practice

Awareness exercises and meditation create situations that will stimulate us to be more aware and present. During the practice of mindfulness, we invite our clients to do the opposite of their usual behaviour. We invite them 'to be' instead of *doing* something. When we are in our 'doing mode', we try to create something, change something or make a situation better. When we practise 'being', everything is already good as it is and there is no need to change anything. Everything that happens during the practice of 'being' is what we call 'the experience'. As mindfulness is an experience-driven technique, clients' experiences are crucial to learn how certain patterns work for them. By being in the present moment, they are able to zoom in to the reactivity of their mind and body, which allows the client to grow their awareness. You help a client transition from doing to being by using different mindfulness tools like meditations, body scans or breathing exercises.

In mindfulness we use meditation as one of the basic tools for cultivating awareness. The idea behind this practice is that you stop yourself from 'doing' and focus your awareness on the sensation in the current moment. This way, the client is forced to point their awareness inwards.

MEDITATION

The most effective way is to literally stop the body from moving by doing a body scan or a sitting meditation. Stopping the body from moving eliminates automated physical reactions and magnifies the urge of moving, solving and changing situations. By not moving we learn to focus on the activity of the mind. You could use a simple three-minute breathing exercise at the beginning of the session to help the client transition into a state of being, or when you notice that a client has difficulties with describing feelings and sensations, you could use body scan to help them to zoom in on sensations. Here is a brief explanation of the three exercises to quieten the body and mind to raise a mindful awareness:

- **Sitting meditation** A seated meditation is between 10 and 45 minutes, where you are invited to turn inwards and explore the senses. A sitting meditation generally starts by following the movement of breathing, then by exploring physical sensations, thoughts and sounds, and ending with open awareness/being with all senses.

- **Body scan** The body scan teaches you to be present by connecting with the body. During this meditation you explore every body part from head to toe by simply noticing physical sensations like temperature, weight, tingling, tension, movements, and so forth.

- **Three-minute breathing exercise** This is a short exercise to help focus and gain clarity by using an awareness funnel technique. It starts with a wide awareness of checking in with the entire body, followed by focused awareness on the movement of breathing only, ending with open awareness of body and environment.

These exercises allow the client to become aware of the role their thoughts play in their overall experiences. This is an amazing learning experience, as clients learn how thoughts are not the reality. They will learn to feel the actual sensation and feeling in that moment and eliminate the weight and importance of their thoughts.

EVERYDAY MINDFULNESS

It is also possible to apply meditation skills to normal daily activities like walking, eating or brushing teeth – often called everyday mindfulness. Instead of mindlessly brushing teeth, a client can focus on all their senses and the reactivity of the mind during the activity. This makes it easy for the client to practise mindfulness during the daily routine. Practising mindfulness during daily routines is a very powerful practice as these actions are usually fully automated by our brain, and so is the reaction of our mind. During automated actions we easily tend to get carried away in thoughts. Focusing awareness on the experience/sensations include the following:

- Physical sensations in the body – temperature, tingling, pressure, etc
- Activity in the mind – pace, quantity, content and reactivity of thoughts
- Emotions – fluctuation of emotions, intensity, the temporary nature of them

The intention is to observe and become familiar with the variety of sensations and how they are connected to your current behaviour.

For example, while brushing our teeth one could observe that thoughts spiral into work problems and finding solutions for those problems. When this seems to be a pattern it can mean that a client spends a lot of time having unnecessary stress and negative thoughts, as that event is not pressing at the time. Mindfulness creates an opportunity to step away from non-current issues by disconnecting from these thoughts and being in the present.

By doing this repeatedly, you will break the automated loop of overthinking and instinctive emotional reaction. This helps us to be more present in situations where we feel overwhelmed, and one might experience release, relaxation and healing. Daily practices can be introduced as 'homework' from the first sessions going forward.

Enquiry

Enquiry can also be defined as 'questioning' or more informal 'debriefing'. During enquiry you facilitate a space where the client can explore their own experiences of the practice, their reactions, patterns, and the context of where they can see these patterns and the implications of them. During enquiry the client is invited to transcend known perspectives and create a new understanding of their reactions, thoughts and experiences. This is where your work as a coach is extremely valuable.

When clients start with mindfulness, they usually have a lot of questions and doubts. Thoughts like: 'Am I doing it correctly?' or 'I'm not feeling anything' can trouble a client. As the focus of mindfulness is on the process and not on a specific result, the first couple of times of practice might feel uncomfortable. Clients might fall asleep, have negative and judgemental thoughts, or feel like they are not achieving anything.

As a coach, it is your task to guide the clients' awareness repeatedly to their experience of the exercise or to the current moment and not to get caught in solving thoughts, storylines and discomfort. When you notice a client does get stuck in a story that is not related to the experience you are exploring, you could simply say: 'Well, it seems like there are a lot of thoughts, can you also tell me what you felt in your body at that moment?' By doing this, you help the client to get away from the story and get back into the moment.

The focus for you as a coach is to help them discover their experience by bringing the attention to the three pillars: the body, mind and emotions (Brandsma, 2017). You can also help the client to make connections between observations of the practice and the rest of their lives. When a certain physical reaction or response of the mind keeps coming up, you could ask if a client recognizes this from other situations. This can help to surface deeper patterns.

It is equally important for a coach to have a solid personal mindfulness practice. That means regular mindfulness practice, enquiry with peers or self-enquiry, and gaining knowledge by any source of preference. Without, it will be hard to make any valuable enquiry (Brandsma, 2017). You need to understand how different experiences arise and to be as present as you want your client to be. You also need to be aware of your own internal triggers and patterns while doing an enquiry with the client.

Education

Education shifts the attention from the context of the specific personal experience to the context of the general human experience (Brandsma, 2017). You cannot act on something you do not know and that is why education explains how things work in general, based on scientific evidence, which ties all work methods together. Something you have explained, then practised during an exercise and discussed during an enquiry, supplements the value of education.

The most valid, effective and durable resource is scientifically proven education. Think about books, research and facts. It can help your client to make sense of their issues and experiences and motivates them as it answers the beginners' questions of 'Why do I go through or do this?' Education can also be shared in stories, metaphors or poems. Sharing scientifically proven education with a client is like sharing information during any other coaching session. Based on the topic of the session, you can share educational information that will help develop the client.

Mindfulness and autopilot

Next to the working methods of mindfulness there are also a few areas of focus that make this intervention incredibly impactful. Humans are incredibly resilient creatures. We manage to survive based on our willpower, imagination and love for life. Our body plays a big part in this survival. Our brain, heart, muscles and nervous system form a state-of-the-art system that helps us adapt to different situations, and our brain plays a big part in our behaviour and health (Kabat-Zinn, 2013). One of the reasons that our brain is so useful in survival is that it can respond very quickly in potentially threatening situations. The brain triggers the entire body to act as soon as possible, and these processes are automated. In other words, you don't have to think about your actions when in a potentially dangerous situation. The amygdala and hypothalamus act as a command centre that bypasses slower thoughtful responses. In mindfulness we also call this the 'autopilot'.

The autopilot mode is a highly purposeful system, therefore some of the automated behaviours we show are helpful and necessary for our survival. Up to 55 per cent of our actions during a day are managed by this autopilot mode (Andrews-Hanna, 2012). Our brain can react quicker and more efficiently in autopilot mode than with our conscious mind when in danger. Without awareness our autopilot controls how we react to situations, people and relationships, as well as how we avoid and attract things.

There are moments when the autopilot becomes less helpful. Especially when it is applied to situations that are not life threatening, but when our body responds as if they are. This happens because our brain doesn't know the difference between a situation that is made up (thoughts) or something that is actually happening. The brain helps to keep us safe, so you can say it always has the best intentions. However, without becoming aware of the influence of your brain, it might control your life and you will continue to experience the same discomfort repeatedly. Stress can become a significant part of your daily life and it will be hard to break this pattern.

By practising mindfulness and using it in coaching we become aware of when the autopilot mode is switched on. We explore how it feels in your body, what happens in your mind, and what your behavioural tendencies might be as a result. This awareness is powerful because when you become aware of an automatic pattern, you have instantly created a moment of pause. A millisecond of not immediately responding to automated behaviour. This is an opportunity to choose a different route for yourself. Different reactions that will give you the opportunity to free yourself from being stuck in unhelpful behaviour and repeating thought patterns.

The seven basic attitudes of mindfulness

When building a solid mindfulness practice for both client and coach you have to learn more about the foundations of mindfulness. Cultivating awareness requires a certain level of effort and a supporting attitude. Effort is an intention and the energy you put into your practice. Effort requires making the time and space to practise and to dedicate yourself to your practice on a consistent basis. When you start developing your practice, it is helpful to regularly check-in with yourself so you can keep cultivating your awareness.

The following are the seven basic attitudes of mindfulness (Kabat-Zinn, 2013):

1 **Non-judgemental**
   Becoming aware of the judgemental inclination of the mind and taking a broader perspective by consciously taking a neutral standpoint towards your experiences and reminding yourself to only observe any experience that unfolds. That is, allow it to come and go naturally rather than trying to control, change or avoid it.

2 **Patience**
   The understanding and acceptance that things need their own time to unfold.

3 **Beginner's mind**
   To understand the richness of each current moment, we need to understand how we can endlessly start over again and how we can look at things as if we are seeing them for the very first time in our lives.

4 **Trust**
   The art of trusting your own intuition and power instead of looking for help and validation outside of yourself.

5 **Non-striving**
   Practise without a goal or to reach a certain result.

6 **Acceptance**
   See things as they are in the present with empathy, and embrace.

7 **Letting go**
   Practise not to attach and learn to let go of the experiences of the mind.

When starting meditation, the person who practises will encounter different experiences. Physical experiences, emotions and events of the mind, like thoughts and beliefs. Our thoughts are usually driven by the previously mentioned 'doing' mode. They are focused on driving you to do or preventing you from doing something. As mentioned in the autopilot section, thoughts can be judgemental and push you into certain patterns or get stuck in an unhelpful loop of negativity. Letting go is important to get rid of these pressures.

This is where the seven basic attitudes come into play. They are designed to always remind you of how you can stay in the current moment, and where and how you can improve the development of your awareness. For example, when you notice judgement about your physical sensations, you can remind yourself to simply observe the sensations from a neutral standpoint, which will allow the thoughts to subside naturally. When you feel that you are pushing yourself to become relaxed or to have a specific emotion, you can (gently) remind yourself to trust the process and not to strive for a specific result. By simply reminding yourself during practice, these attitudes help you to stay present in the current moment.

When I work with clients, I give them a small card with the seven attitudes of mindfulness on it so they can carry it with them. You can also ask the client to reflect on them after a work day or meditation, so they develop the ability to work these pillars. For example, if a client is very impatient, you could simply ask how they could create more trust in their process and focus less on striving.

CASE STUDY
Beliefs versus reality

My client Susanna is a perfect example of how mindfulness can help you to improve the quality of your life. Susanna is a communication professional in her 30s. Since she graduated from university, Susanna has been focusing on her career. She went through a fast-tracked development and had several promotions in a relatively short amount of time.

Recently she started noticing how her energy levels were dropping and she did not feel the same fulfilment from her work as she used to. Despite her several attempts to change the situation, she felt overwhelmed by thoughts that stressed her out and she started to feel burnt out. Like many, Susanna had many thoughts about how her professional life should look and she had very high expectations of herself. She designed her professional life based on these beliefs. Even though the life that she designed was perfectly in line with her beliefs, she did not feel well. Susanna wanted to know how she could find the balance and joy in her work again.

When I first met Susanna, we only spoke about her question. I did not introduce mindfulness to her in the first conversation. I asked her to do a simple recording of her thoughts, feelings and sensations in the body whenever she had a positive or negative experience at work. She logged these situations in a journal. During our next meeting we used her examples to dive into the exercise based on the enquiry techniques. The more she started to share, the more she also spoke about reasons why she thought certain things happened. I simply took her out of the stories and back to the experiences, questioning what happened in her thoughts, feelings and body at the time.

I asked her if she could reflect on what we discussed and if she noticed anything specific. She started to see that when she did something she was not good at, her thoughts started to spiral into the negative. She could immediately feel her energy and mood going down, and procrastinate and resist the work she had to do.

As soon as we defined that one clear pattern, I introduced her to the autopilot theory by sharing some education about it. After telling her about this principle and how to interrupt its occurrence, I invited her to come up with a way of practising being in the current moment more often. I gave the option to use a daily activity and she agreed on using her daily coffee drinking to be present by focusing on her experiences in the moment.

Susanna noticed how her autopilot was influencing her in different situations. She became more aware of when this mode triggered her to avoid or attract certain situations and feelings. Throughout the sessions, I did not give her additional meditation or practices. We stayed with the recordings, daily routines, enquiry and education.

We now had an opening to create a different strategy at those moments the autopilot was influencing Susanna the most. She learnt how old thoughts were triggering her now in new situations and how not to respond to them.

After only six sessions, Susanne said she felt she had gained more awareness of her thought patterns and how this was affecting her behaviour and decisions. She realized how old thoughts and beliefs, like 'I have to work five days to be successful' and 'I always need to be online as a manager', were keeping her from making change. She was afraid of failing. After she understood how these thoughts were not true, she was able to make several changes in the way she reacted to situations and executed her role. As a result she felt more balanced, and interested in learning more about awareness and mindfulness.

Limitations of mindfulness

There are no special requirements for people who would like to experience mindfulness. Mindfulness is very accessible, and there are plenty of training options for everyone to participate in. If you can read, write, listen and talk, want to practise with silence, explore and observe, you have everything you need to start.

Nevertheless, it seems that for some mindfulness is less helpful. There are some clear contraindications and therefore it is important to understand to what extent the client might benefit from mindfulness (Brandsma, 2017).

Although Thich Nhat Hanh said, 'Mindfulness is the most reliable source of peace and joy that exist, everybody can work with it' (Kabat Zinn, 2013: 17), it is prudent and ethical to verify if a client is interested, willing and able to follow the exercises. You can do this during the intake with your client. Investigate if the client is coachable and ask if they are open for mindfulness-based methods. Anxiety, depression, psychological crisis, starting therapy, addiction, autism, ADHD and trauma are all possible counterindications (Brandsma, 2017). As with every coaching client, it is up to the coach to verify whether the client is coachable within the range of our capabilities (see Chapter 37). During the introduction process for mindfulness coaching, it is important that the clients understand what the techniques and exercises mean and entail.

During mindfulness we essentially stop people from doing and, instead, we let them observe and feel. We invite them to investigate sensations they would normally avoid. Therefore, it is important to ask clients how they feel, what challenges they had, and how their experience measured up to their expectations (Brandsma, 2017).

Farias and Wikholm (2016) argued that the emergence of difficult emotional material from mindfulness practice may be a positive rather than an adverse circumstance. Even though mindfulness became my personal way of life, it's understandable that for some, the practice of mindfulness is not an easy journey. It can be triggering and painful, which can be discouraging and make some people not want to continue. Looking inward can amplify emotions we associate as negative. This can feel uncomfortable and scary for the client if they are used to suppressing and ignoring their emotions. This is why it is important to explain to clients that mindfulness is a process and that any uncomfortable feelings are likely temporary as part of the learning curve of acquiring a new skill. When clients are well informed, they are more motivated to keep practising, which can prevent them from having unhelpful outcomes or quitting prematurely.

Final thoughts

My personal experience of mindfulness is based on a sentence I use often: 'What you see, you cannot unsee.' In my opinion this applies to the practice of mindfulness, as it invites a person to feel and observe things they would normally ignore, or at least try to. For me, from the beginning, I felt like I had to continue practising arriving at a space of clarity and peace. Even though the journey was not always easy, it was worth it. Therefore, I think it is very important to verify – using education and enquiry – whether your client is likely to benefit from mindfulness practices and wants to take this direction.

References

Andrews-Hanna, J R (2012) The brain's default network and its adaptive role in internal mentation, *The Neuroscientist*, 18 (3), 251–70, doi.org/10.1177/1073858411403316 (archived at https://perma.cc/R75R-4MEJ)

Brandsma, R (2017) *The Mindfulness Teaching Guide: Essential skills and competencies for teaching mindfulness-based interventions*, New Harbinger, Oakland, CA

Farias, M and Wikholm, C (2016) Has the science of mindfulness lost its mind? *BJPsych Bulletin*, 40 (6), 329–32, doi.org/10.1192/pb.bp.116.053686 (archived at https://perma.cc/YW5Q-8GJZ)

Kabat-Zinn, J (2013) *Full Catastrophe Living: Using the wisdom of your mind and body to face stress, pain, and illness*, Bantam Books, New York

26

Establishing an effective coaching dialogue

LUCIAN LO

ABSTRACT

Elements of an effective coaching dialogue are the right mindset, a brilliant method and a heuristic model. This chapter explores a framework that unlocks the true power of coaching by delivering quality coaching sessions, enhanced coaching presence, elevated active listening, better coaching competencies overall, and allowing continuous growth as a coach through setting up and maintaining the coaching dialogue.

Introduction

My initial challenges in coaching included the tiniest things, such as conducting and holding a proper coaching conversation. Countless times, I caught myself springing into consulting or advising mode. I discovered later that questioning helps, asking questions steer me away from a tendency to consult and advise. After all, coaching is all about asking questions, right? I studied and prepared tons of 'powerful' questions, thinking it would lead to coaching dialogues with breakthroughs in thinking, or big 'aha' moments with my clients. I did just that, and ended up as a 'checklist' coach, checking through my extensive list of questions while compromising my presence. It turned out to be more frustrating than helpful (Reynolds, 2020).

Not only did I spend more time in my own head preparing for the next 'useful' question to ask, but I also did extremely little listening, there was no coaching presence. The conversation itself did not feel natural in any way, and my clients probably felt they were talking to a chatbot most of the time. Instead, coaching should be a spontaneous process between the coach and client that is as natural and human as possible, not a robot following scripts or algorithms. As such, my aim here is to explore the approaches in eliciting insights and bringing positive changes to the client through masterful dialogue, which I hope will help your coaching practice as much as it has helped mine.

What is coaching?

Coaching is not consulting, not advising, not teaching, not counselling, not problem solving, nor therapy. Since coaching is none of these, the aforementioned qualities naturally should not emerge in a coaching dialogue. Therefore, coaching dialogue does not contain elements of recommending, suggesting, instructing, commanding or giving orders. It is not a transfer of knowledge, it is about eliciting insights that transform the coachee's perspective and behaviour. What matters most are the positive changes a coach helps their coachee to make from their own insights, rather than leading change.

Theory and literature review

It is important to appreciate that effective coaching dialogue does not just happen automatically in a coaching session. There is groundwork involved. The preparation work begins pre-session, before any coaching dialogue takes place. First and foremost, we need to adopt the right coaching mindset to establish psychological safety in the subsequent coaching session atmosphere. Being present, curious and reflective are qualities of a coaching mindset that does not lead a client but empowers and encourages.

Pre-session

How many of us have experienced when the client has difficulty opening up, no matter what we say, ask, or do? This often happens because there is a lack of psychological safety. It is crucial to establish psychological safety as the foundation from which to develop a sound coach–client relationship. Psychological safety is often described as the belief that one can speak up or reveal information without the fear of being vilified, humiliated or shunned. With its absence, it is inconceivable to continue with an open conversation, let alone exploring deeper and uncovering the clients' needs and their challenges in achieving their desires and goals. The client should feel safe and comfortable being themselves in front of their coach (Reynolds, 2020).

Setting the space conducive to psychological safety requires a coach to establish a mindful coaching presence, remember the intention of partnership, in other words, being a thinking partner, and genuinely believing in coachee's potential (Reynolds, 2020). 'Thinking partner' is the best designation given to a coach that I have come across. It instantly places the coach into the most helpful position, and eliminates misconceptions of a coach's role, which is not telling clients what to do, solving problems on behalf of clients, or teaching based on personal experience. When a coach exudes coaching presence and serves as a thinking partner who has absolute belief in the client's potential, it creates a safe and judgement-free space for them to be more relaxed and willing to speak freely to fully participate with their coach.

During session

Having a coaching mindset continues seamlessly from the preparation phase to the session, where its objective is to establish a strong base for the important work to come. We need to carry over and maintain psychological safety throughout a coaching session. If we catch ourselves deviating from it, we need to align our mind to return back to the safe space soonest, so the coachee can continue to feel safe in having an honest, exploratory dialogue.

To maintain psychological safety, a coach exerts mindfulness and self-awareness, and is mindful of self-conduct while constantly reminding ourselves (as coaches) to show care, respect and attentiveness to clients. In the process, we are constantly aware and watchful, asking ourselves, 'Am I judgemental?', 'Have I stepped over the boundary?', 'Was I impatient?'

We have to be highly conscious of our own body language and facial expression, including micro-movements such as eye rolling, pursed lips, a smug grin, a frown, a yawn, and so forth. As well as subconscious verbal expressions such as a 'sigh', and the tone of voice used – it is all about how we say it, not what we say.

We also observe the same for the client. Whether they close up, do not seem willing to talk, use disengaging dialogue, put on their protective shield, or appear agitated with what the coach has just said, display uncomfortable body language, or say something like 'I'm not comfortable talking about that/discussing this', these verbal and non-verbal clues help move the conversation forward effectively.

When we notice a disengagement, disalignment or resistance from the client, we take measures to restore the harmony and flow of discussion by shifting back to emotions that re-establish trust; enhance our presence, step up listening, demonstrate care, calmness, curiosity, love, benevolence and patience. Most of the time, when the flow is disrupted, taking a step back, slowing the pace and reducing the intensity will restore the situation. Of course, there are times where we notice something amiss but are unable to identify the actual cause of why the safety bubble is punctured. In this case, we can always ask the client directly if everything is fine, if anything is wrong and whether they still feel safe and comfortable with the ongoing dialogue.

REFLECTIVE INQUIRY

Marcia Reynolds (2020) reminds us that questions seek answers, but inquiry provokes insight. Coaching is much more than asking good questions. We aspire to elicit insights. The action of reflective inquiry helps to attain that. Inquiry means requesting information about someone or something. Therefore, in the coaching context, reflective inquiry refers to when a coach asks something that orients the coachee to reflect in deep thought, see things in a new light, and possibly develop a new perspective (Deshpande, 2020). As such, effective coaching is a process of enquiries, where the intent is not to find solutions but provoke critical thinking about one's own thoughts (Reynolds, 2020).

Marcia Reynolds also said that questions and reflective statements combined or used in tandem make up reflective inquiry (2020). In other words, adding reflective statements to questions makes coaching feel more natural and effortless. My old habit of formulating breakthrough questions in the back of my head while the client was talking often distracted me and made my timing feel unnatural. In time, I learnt to eliminate overthinking and regurgitating, which allowed me to be more present and attentive in the moment.

Reflective techniques include recapping, summarizing, paraphrasing, labelling, drawing distinctions and using metaphors on clients' statements to redirect them back in a different way to optimize clarity and understanding:

- **Recapping** is restating and playing back the client's word or statement to them, for example, 'So, you're saying [client's words/statement]…'
- **Summarizing** means to sum up what the client has said. 'In summary [summarized statement]…, is that correct? Is that the issue you're currently facing?'
- **Paraphrasing** is to express the meaning of the speaker using different words, in a simpler and shorter form to make the original meaning clearer. For instance, the client may say, 'My boss brought in this young MBA graduate as our manager, who knows nothing about the real world out there…' The coach paraphrases, 'You don't think he is very experienced.'
- **Labelling** is to give a title to, or label, the client's statement or story. When a client tells a long story about the toxic, corrupted environment in their workplace, 'they're all dishonest, immoral, insincere, deceptive, don't honour their words, back-stabbing,' the coach asks, 'no integrity?' and the client confirms, 'yes, that's right.'
- **Drawing distinctions** is normally used when there is a conflict of desires. For example, a client wants to pursue a counselling path as she wants to help with the rising mental health issues in the population. At the same time, she still wishes to stay in her current position with the family business. The coach may say, 'I am hearing two things here…' After much exploration and deliberation, we come to know

that the real issue is that she did not know how to tell the elder uncle (Chairman of the company group) that she wanted to leave the family business.

- The **metaphor** is another form of paraphrasing. For instance, asking, 'it seems that you have a decision to make at this crossroad, what are the options?' or 'it looks like you're swimming against the tide?'

Reflecting on their own statements and words enables clients to think deeper in querying and examining their own thoughts, feelings and behaviours, and if they are in line with their core values deep down inside (Reynolds, 2020). Applying the practice of reflective inquiry frees a coach from always feeling the need to finding the perfect, best and right question to ask. The technique also helps clients discover new information and understanding that is necessary for breakthroughs in thinking.

The dialogic orientation quadrant

My previous 'checklist coaching' flaw, in scanning through a lengthy series of pre-prepared questions for that magical question to ask next, had always distracted me from listening fully to my clients. Discovering a simple heuristic tool named the dialogic orientation quadrant (DOQ) developed by Haesun Moon helped me orient myself more effectively to what they are sharing. Moon explains DOQ as a generative and divergent process in the dialogue within and between people for shared meaning making, which serves as a glue that interlocutors can build on (Moon, 2019). The word 'orientation' suggests that a coach's role is to orient clients' attention. A coach uses language as an intentional tool to support their clients to curate, not just narrate, better stories of their lifeworld (Moon, 2019: 2).

A graphical presentation of the DOQ model on two axes – time and valency – is presented in Figure 26.1. The quadrant contains a timeline of the narrative on the horizontal axis, where towards the right is the 'future' and left the 'past'; and a content (or valence) of the narrative on the vertical axis, where the positive content is at the top while the negative content is at the bottom.

The four quadrants are as follows (Moon, 2018):

Q1: Preferred future: this orientation is the positive thing/event to happen in the future, the desired positive outcome in the time to come.

Q2: Resourceful past: the positive thing/event that happened in the past, such as valuable experience and lessons that have become useful resources to utilize today or in a future context.

Q3: Troubled past: the negative thing/event that happened in the past, which is still causing emotional trauma.

Q4: Dreaded future: the negative thing/event that has not happened yet, which causes fear, resistance or anxiety.

FIGURE 26.1 Dialogic orientation quadrant

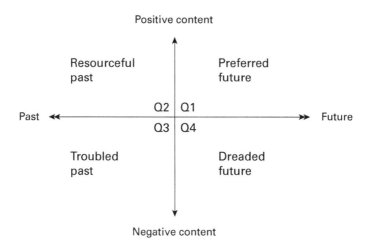

SOURCE Adapted from Moon (2018)

A coach can use the four quadrants of the DOQ in practice by orienting the client to one or more positions to explore what is coming up in their life at the moment. Thereby, through targeted dialogue, they have a better understanding of where they are and where they want to be.

Using the DOQ in practice

A coach can use the DOQ model intentionally and systematically in their reflective inquiry to achieve the following outcomes.

1 Spotting opportunities. By listening closely, coaches identify from clients' narratives where some of the opportunities lie.

2 Exploring potential response options. Once an opportunity is identified, coaches decide on their responses, which could be a simple nod as acknowledgement, a brief smile as encouragement, or a further reflective inquiry to delve deeper.

3 Gauging our coaching role and contribution. What has been the client's progress? What role did we play and where can we develop further to be even more effective?

4 Making coaching progress visible. By observing how the narratives of clients change throughout the session, or over time after several sessions. What and how has the coach influenced and contributed to the coachee's curation process? Has the position of the client shifted on the DOQ, how, and what were the most likely reasons? (Moon, 2019).

Perhaps the most useful aspect is that the DOQ method helps translate the ephemeral nature of a dialogue into a tangible form. It makes the interactional patterns of language use visible, and one can easily see how narratives are elicited, shaped and organized. The shifting of client narratives can be mapped on the DOQ as the coaching process progresses (Moon, 2019).

Discussion

When the 3Ms (mindset + method + model) are put together and implemented systematically, an effective coaching dialogue framework is established.

Reflective inquiry is the *what* to use in coaching dialogue; DOQ is *how* to use it; while the coaching mindset is the enabling attitude that must always be present and active. In essence, DOQ serves as a map to capture a narrator's content; it could fall in any spectrum according to the four quadrants. By looking at 'What is the story here?', 'Is it a past event or future story (timeline)?' and 'Is it of positive or negative nature (content)?', observing our stories and thoughts become more obvious and transparent. For instance, whether our inner experiences are trapped and held captive in the past, or are we free to explore tomorrow's possibilities? The language (words) used in our narratives are essentially our thoughts. In other words, narratives and thoughts are directly linked. Words are like bridges to the mind. This inherently manifests whether the narrator is pessimistic or optimistic about something or someone. A coach can then use this valuable information to work on the relevant quadrant to orient the conversation forward.

Adding DOQ in my coaching

I take notes during coaching sessions and incorporating DOQ into my note-taking has been invaluable. As a result, the conversation becomes vividly clear and I can see a lot

FIGURE 26.2 The 3M framework for an effective coaching dialogue

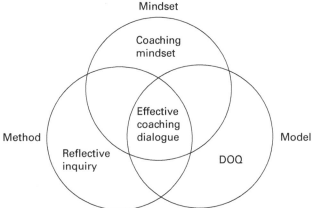

of conversation contents fall below the line (see Figure 26.3), which is not surprising, because human brains are hardwired to perceive negativism subconsciously (Rastegari and Shafer, 2017). Our job as a coach is to help rewire it to the positive half by reorienting the client, with the help of the DOQ framework and repeating the exploration until the shift and new orientation become the default pattern.

On a more holistic level, I use the DOQ model as part of the encompassing 3M framework (Figure 26.2) to make the process more seamless and practical.

1   For me, the coaching mindset is always operating and running in the background

2   I use reflective inquiry to stimulate insights

3   I use the DOQ diagram to locate where the narrative falls, where the thoughts are, and then rewire and shift them to above the line (refer to Figure 26.3)

4   More importantly, I use the 'DOQ concept' to eventually orient a client's attention to the preferred future (quadrant 1)

However, getting the client to shift towards identifying and acknowledging their preferred future also requires recognizing their strengths and potential, and bringing these into the realm of their desired outcome. I look at the process as assimilating two halves to create a powerful momentum towards a positive future.

Working with the two halves – above the line and below the line

Most effective coaching conversations explore future-focused timelines while identifying and developing client strengths and potentials (positive content) (Moon, 2020: 254). I

FIGURE 26.3   The two halves – above and below the line

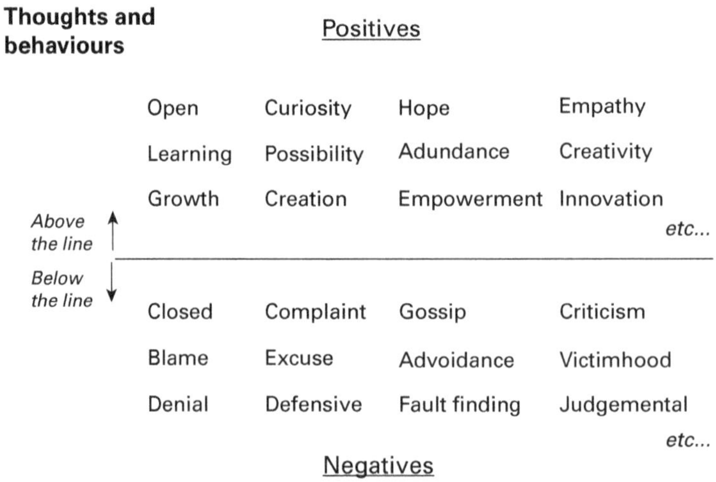

SOURCE   Based on the Conscious Leadership concept (Dethmer and Chapman, 2014)

first look at the client's position in the two halves, with the idea to shift them from their negative half to the positive half where relevant. It is important to realize that the negative contents are not 100 per cent bad but are merely watchful messages to warn us of pain and possible danger. Pain is helpful, says Positive Intelligence founder Shirzad Chamine, when he talks about the analogy of pain alerting us to a hot stove. 'The very important question is, how long would we like to keep our hand on the hot stove before we get the message?' (Beyer, 2018, para 8). Coaches can use this metaphor with their clients to help them notice the presence and meaning of negative messages and accept them as a natural part of life so that they can start moving to the positive half.

Part of the dialogic process is that coaches do their best to awaken the consciousness in clients, bringing them to better clarity and increased self-awareness, with the eventual objective of shifting them to the positive half above the line. So first, we, as coaches, observe and recognize the existence of the two halves within our client's story. We help build their awareness through reflective inquiry so that they understand and choose what they need to work on, to get to where they want to be. Many times, for them, it is a deliberate choice to move to 'above the line' or stay 'below the line', when the time is right for them – after developing awareness, understanding and acceptance.

EXERCISE

As a coach, fill in your own words and descriptions in the diagram (Figure 26.3) that resonate most with your values and niche. How would you implement 'above the line' in your coaching? Think of 2–3 questions that you can ask a client to help them appreciate the value of being above the line. For instance, 'Which word in the top or bottom half feels the most powerful to you?' Let's say the client chooses 'hope'. 'What is one difference having hope instead of despair will make to your daily life?' Encourage them to be specific and practical.

The four quadrants

Before sharing some question examples that worked well in my coaching conversations (Figure 26.4), just a reminder that the DOQ technique is very versatile and effective with various coaching approaches such as solution-focused, narrative coaching, cognitive coaching, neuro-linguistic programming (NLP), and others. Feel free to adapt or formulate questions based on your preferred model. While the intention is not to use the questions as a preset list that can interfere with the coach's presence and the flow of the dialogue, they help direct the exploration forward in a systematic, semi-structured reflective inquiry/DOQ process.

FIGURE 26.4 Examples of questions in the four quadrants

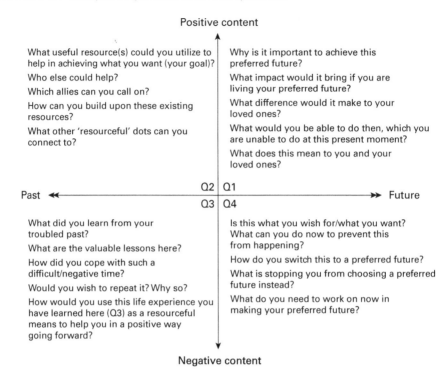

My overall approach when applying the dialogic orientation method is to shift clients from where they may be below the line to above the line in the positive half by creating awareness, and formulating and working on action plans together to support achieving their preferred future. In the following (shortened) version of a 60-minute session, I demonstrate the use of some reflective inquiry techniques and DOQ in practice to facilitate the client's shift to the Q1 quadrant.

CASE STUDY
Coaching dialogue example

The client, who is a small business owner, came into the session looking low in spirit. I greeted him, asking how it was going, and he replied saying he was a bit demotivated, and felt disheartened. I then clarified what the outcome was that he would like from our coaching session – he wanted to be driven and feel uplifted.

When I further enquired for more details, he went on with his story, and at one point he said, 'The dark gloomy cloud came all over my head again… just like before…' [*gloomy cloud (metaphor) just like before (Q3)*].

Me: Dark gloomy cloud? (recapping)

Coachee: Yes... this dark cloud always comes hovering over my head when I am in despair and down.

Me: Sounds like you're describing the emotion you're currently feeling about the current situation. (paraphrasing)

Coachee: That sounds correct.

Me: What does the cloud look like?

Coachee: It is this big thick dark, gloomy cloud in a bad storm.

Me: How did you last cope with this bad storm? [*Troubled past (Q3) – coach trying to elicit coachee's resourceful resources (Q2).*]

Coachee: [(in deep thought) and then responded]: The courage and confidence my wife gave me.

Me: Is that what you need now?

Coachee: I guess it is...

Me: What does courage and confidence do for you? (digging deeper...)

Coachee: They give me power. [Q2]

Me: It sounds like it's your source of power. (labelling)

Coachee: yes... you can say that.

Sensing something might still be missing, I continued with the following...

Me: After you've gained this power, is there anything else you need?

Coachee: I think I also need more positive energy to push this through.

Me: Where do you get that?

Coachee: ...from my teammates.

Me: What exactly do you need from your teammates (to push this through)?

Coachee: Collaboration, tighter teamwork and strong unbeatable synergy. [Q2]

Noticing from all the positive facial expression and body language that he is all pumped up, and sensing that there is a plan he had just devised in his head; I asked: 'Has the storm now passed?'

Coachee: Yes, the sun has come back up now, hahaha... (he laughed)

Me: What are we going to do now that the sun is back?

Coachee: First, I'll have a heart-to-heart talk with my beloved wife, and remind myself what is important to me (my family, my kids) and why I am doing this in the first place. And then I shall gather my teammates to put our heads together to pierce through this storm. This Covid lockdown WILL NOT stop us from forging ahead [Q1].

As a 'bonus', the coach analyses the session after it has ended, to continuously improve their application of the reflection inquiry, DOQ model and mindset.

1 First, as an analysis tool for watching playback of recorded sessions to evaluate and study, in particular reflecting on the following:

   a. Which reflective statements are suitable in which quadrants?

   b. Which questions work and do not work in conversation orientation, and how to work better?

   c. How to improve their reflective inquiry techniques (what, when and how else to use questions and reflection in which quadrant).

2 As a revision tool as a coach. What and where did something go right or wrong, and how to improve yourself for the next session.

3 As a performance tool in tracking the client's progress from session to session.

4 Occasionally, I use it for reflection (especially on my own judgement), and what type(s) of conversation content triggered my emotion and get drawn into coachee's world.

Closing thoughts

Having the right coaching mindset, using reflective inquiry, being attentive and present, being curious and deep listening to the client's narratives are important skills a coach could use to create a powerful coaching session. These skills can be learnt, practised and be applied in any coaching dialogue. They have made major improvements in my coaching sessions, and I hope you can benefit and enjoy the 3M and DOQ frameworks in your coaching practice too.

I would like to end this chapter with my own COACHING acronym pertaining to the all-important coach–client relationship and coaching dialogue.

C: **Collaboration** The **coach and coachee** collaborate in a partnership where they co-construct meaningful purpose, progress and possibility to pivot.

O: **Observation** The coach **observes** closely what coachees say and do; their words, including non-verbal communication such as body language and facial expression.

A: **Active/attentive listening** The coach learns to listen closer using the DOQ as a listening map and GPS.

C: **Curiosity** The coach stays curious all the time, and uses reflective inquiry based on curiosity.

H: **Hope** The coach instils hope and light in their coaching dialogue.

I: **Inspiration:** The coach inspires and motivates clients.

N: Navigate coachees to Q1 – plan for the preferred future. By asking questions to get awareness and acceptance of their current reality, the coach helps the client formulate and navigate to their preferred future.

G: Gratitude The coach recognizes and shows gratitude to everything in the past (Q3). The coach guides the client to be grateful for the people and situations that have taught them valuable lessons and experiences from where they can build today.

References

Beyer, R (2018) How to be resilient, *Stanford Magazine*, 12 July, stanfordmag.org/contents/how-to-be-resilient (archived at https://perma.cc/USY6-34SE)

Deshpande, H (2020) The power of reflective inquiry in coaching, International Coaching Federation, 23 November, coachingfederation.org/blog/power-of-reflective-inquiry (archived at https://perma.cc/FH9D-VGRP)

Dethmer, J and Chapman, D (2014) Locating yourself – a key to conscious leadership, Conscious Leadership Group, 15 November, conscious.is/video/locating-yourself-a-key-to-conscious-leadership (archived at https://perma.cc/9JP7-QMYN)

Moon, H (2018) Model #1: dialogic orientation quadrant (DOQ), Canadian Centre for Brief Coaching, 18 June, www.briefcoaching.ca/blog/dialogic-orientation-quadrant (archived at https://perma.cc/SM9H-CVZ7)

Moon, H (2019) Making progress visible for learners of solution-focused dialogue, SOLWorld: Solution Focused in Organizations, Budapest, Hungary, August

Moon, H (2020) Coaching: Using ordinary words in extraordinary ways, in *The SAGE Handbook of Social Constructionist Practice*, eds S McNamee, M M Gergen, C Camargo-Borges and E F Rasera, pp 246–57, Sage, Thousand Oaks, CA

Rastegari, I and Shafer, L (2017) A better way of thinking, *Usable Knowledge*, 20 November, www.gse.harvard.edu/news/uk/17/11/better-way-thinking (archived at https://perma.cc/Q5TF-SHN4)

Reynolds, M (2020) *Coach the Person, Not the Problem: A guide to using reflective inquiry*, Berrett-Koehler, Oakland, CA

27

Expanding modes of mind

From doing to being and becoming

BERNICE FABI

ABSTRACT

'To be or not to be?' is the famous line from Shakespeare's *Hamlet*. In this famous soliloquy, Hamlet laments over the pain and injustice of life. How Hamlet could have really benefited from having a life coach! Humour aside, the in-depth reflections we engage in as a result of our experiences and emotions are an introspective means that enable us to achieve more clarity and understanding of life. This chapter explores the different modes of mind and how you, as a coach, can transcend from occupational and transactional DOING to transformational BEING and inspire your clients to do the same in their lives and organizations. To clarify, coaching is not one or the other of doing or being, it is a combination of both modes that inspires a full life and true change that are balanced and intentional.

Introduction

I'd like to coin my own phrase, 'Be and do to become'. The International Coaching Federation (ICF) defines coaching as 'partnering with clients in a thought-provoking and creative process that inspires them to maximize their personal and professional potential.' In the simplest context, we may think of coaching as a 'doing' process linked to goal-directed actions. Coaching can be much more than that. How can you expand coaching in the balance of being and doing to help your clients become what they are truly capable of? In other words, how can coaching help a client reach their fullest potential in a complete human-centric way?

The theory behind the practice

A leading occupational researcher, Dr Ann Wilcock, presented a critical analysis of 'being', 'doing' and 'becoming' specifically related to the field of occupational therapy (1999). She defined occupation to include 'all the things that people do, the relationship of what they do with who they are as human beings and that through occupation they are in a constant state of becoming different' (Wilcock, 1999: 10). This is a perspective that life coaching benefits from significantly. First, let's take a deeper look at the terms 'doing', 'being', and 'becoming' respectively, to get some clarity on what they really mean and how they contribute to the full coaching experience.

Doing

Do you sometimes feel that you are caught up in the drive of 'doing'? Are you continually promoting goal setting, task-related activities and striving for outcomes? Perhaps you and your clients are controlled by to-do lists and checklists and success is based solely on achievement. Here's something to think about:

> The wish to live as intensely as possible has subjected humans to the same dilemma as the water flea, which lives 108 days at 8 degrees Centigrade, but only twenty-six days at 28 degrees, when its heartbeat is almost four times faster, though in either case its heart beats 15 million times in all (Zeldin, 1995: 352).

The heartbeat of Western society, particularly, is a fast-paced replica, squeezing more and more of these 'to-do' items into life. The term 'busyness' has become an aspirational status symbol for many (Bellezza, Paharia and Keinan, 2017). The outcome of life in the fast lane is stress, health risks, and counterproductivity in organizations and personal lives (Clarke, 2022). The role of the exemplary coach is to move organizations and clients in innovative ways beyond what our clients believe is possible and to make difficult and impossible things happen. Our role involves creating an atmosphere wherein our clients are introspective, as this is when the greatest possibilities are created. Organizations and individuals can only move away from 'doing' and a 'doing mindset' by disengaging from task- and goal-oriented activities in order to access their intuition and creativity. In order for this to happen, we and our clients must also move away from 'busyness' and towards mindfulness.

My intent is not to undermine the importance of goal setting and achievement. However, individuals with a driven-doing mindset can become so absorbed with their goals that they then add layers of anticipation, which increase anxiousness and agitation along with a 'should be', 'could be', 'would be' habitual pattern of thinking and living. The driven-doing mode is considered goal-oriented, wherein clients are motivated to reduce a gap between the way things are and how they want or need them to be (Segal, Williams and Teasdale, 2013). It is easy for our attention as coaches to become narrowly focused on the discrepancies of these two states and achieving a result instead of sustaining an ethical and effective coaching presence and process. Along with recognition of a driven-doing mode, herein lies an opportunity for you as a coach to help your clients uncover the hidden potential for improving their lives by helping them acknowledge their passion for life, their needs and their drive to contribute. This is really at the core of human existence and can only be discovered by scrutinizing one's life closely enough to know their innermost self (Ventegodt, Merrick and Andersen, 2003).

Being

Being is quite the opposite of doing, in that it focuses on thoughts and feelings of the present moment. The definition of 'being' is the most intangible of the three states and embedded in words such as essence, entity and existing (Wilcock, 1999: 237). Approaches to 'being' are varied and often debated. Let's take a closer look at each:

1 **'Being as essence' – who are we by our very nature as human beings?** This is a disputed concept, which, I believe, correlates best with a purely psychological-philosophical-spiritual dimension proposed by Hitch, Pepin and Stagnitti (2014). As such, being is seen as the emergence of and being faithful to the true self (Pickens, O'Reilly and Sharp, 2010; Steindl, Winding and Runge, 2008). It might be safest to say that 'essence of being' is also defined by each individual's own truth or moral compass.

2 **'Being as entity' – who do we understand ourselves to be?** (Del Fabro Smith et al, 2011). This perspective relates more specifically to who we are in terms of our personal self-discovery, thinking and self-reflection. In defining the essential role of each individual's personal abilities and capabilities, Wilcock (2006: 117) included untapped potential, aptitude, ability, talent, trait or power with the term 'capabilities', stating that these are the building blocks of occupational beings.

3 **'Being as existing' – how do we relate to the need for space and time to just be?** Wilcock (1999) alludes to 'being as existing' as a means of self-discovery, thinking and reflection that is also related to lived experiences. Living independently of occupational engagement, individuals also value time spent with emotions and co-existing in the same space as others. This view can also be expanded to include creativity and expression, as well as the need for space and time to just 'be'.

At a deeper level, 'being' is about identifying self-truth at a biological inner-based level to our essence (Maslow, 1968). It is what is unique about our individuality and what we bring to others as part of our relationships and in what we do in life. As such, being requires people to take time to look inward to discover who they are, what they think, and how they reflect and exist.

Furthermore, doing and being differ within the element of time experienced. In doing mode, it is typical for the mind to move between the present, past and future with a primary focus on outcome that becomes goal oriented. By contrast, the ability to experience the intimacy of the present moment, including all feelings and emotions, to the broadest extent and magnificence, is only possible in being mode.

It is fundamental to our role as a coach to recognize the differences between doing and being modes in ourselves and our clients, and to utilize both, in balance, for a full coaching experience that encompasses action and reflection. With that in mind, let's proceed to the mode of becoming, the dimension of change and development.

Becoming

Wilcock's perspective of becoming is 'to become, to grow, for something to come into being' (2006: 148). Becoming incorporates the concepts of human potential and growth, of transformation and self-actualization (Fidler, 1983). By enabling our clients to both do and be, we are helping them to transform or change their lives in a positive way by facilitating their potential in terms of talents and abilities not yet in full use. In this way, we are part of their process of becoming, which is an important task to realizing their fullest potential (Wilcock, 1999).

Self-actualization and transcendence play a vital role in the process of becoming. It's important to address each separately and together for clarity. The Hierarchy of Needs has been a widely accepted motivation framework, wherein psychologist Abraham Maslow theorized the concept that only unsatisfied needs influence human behaviour, and each need, once satisfied, is no longer a motivator. According to the original theory put forth, physiological needs are at the foundation, followed upward by safety, love, belonging, esteem and ultimately, self-actualization (Maslow, 1943). Self-actualization for human beings occurs when one reaches their full potential or ideal self. Examples may include realizing dreams, finding truth or achieving inner peace. As such, self-actualization really implies the need for personal growth and development throughout one's life.

Published by his family a year after Maslow's death, his later ideas were revealed in *The Farther Reaches of Human Nature* (Maslow, 1971). Most significant within this book is a definition and process that is beyond the self in self-actualization, encompassed in concepts such as selfless, devoted, working on a calling and 'being-values' (Maslow, 1971: 128). Herein, we are introduced to transcendence, which is becoming one with everything. According to Maslow, a person transcends when they achieve the highest level of human consciousness, and behave and relate as an end state rather than a means to the self, all other beings and the cosmos.

As such, the concept of transcendence refers to the human experience, significance, or existence beyond self, the ultimate level of being. This is further backed by Victor E Frankl in his book *Man's Search for Meaning*. 'The more one forgets himself – by giving himself to a cause to serve or another person to love – the more human he is and the more he actualizes himself' (Frankl, 2006: 110-11). In other words, self-actualization is a by-product of self-transcendence.

I have addressed the concepts of doing and being in the first part of this chapter and how they interrelate within the concept of becoming. Now, I continue by exploring ways to interrupt an automatic doing-mindset coaching pattern and identify ways to bring more awareness into our coaching. When we start to do this, we realize that we can and are creating opportunity and space for being. This is the first step toward becoming our best selves and assisting our clients in the same way on their journeys. Thus, our journey begins with being.

Key concepts worth exploring and practising

Although the following is not an inclusive list, these key concepts have been instrumental to enhancing both my personal life and coaching practice. The aspects of 1) presence and empathy, 2) a values-based practice, 3) self-acceptance, and their supporting practices and exercises have been a beneficial means of identifying all that I am (being), and growth and development (becoming) that are foundational to any coaching practice.

Developing presence and empathy

Being implies a deep connection with the full self, others and the world. To harness these connections, presence in the moment and an ability to appreciate all perspectives are needed through the context of empathy. Brain research identified three types of empathy: 1) cognitive empathy allows us to understand how the other person thinks and see their perspective; 2) emotional empathy allows us to feel what the other person is feeling; and 3) empathic concern or caring is compassion for others (Goleman and Davidson, 2017). In much the same way, presence and empathy are valuable in coaching to establish a safe and trusting space that enables the client and coach to be vulnerable, which promotes new possibilities and learning. Below are eight strategies that may be helpful to you and your clients to develop empathy and presence:

1 **Be insatiably curious** Develop a sincere and empathetic curiosity about those you meet and would like to meet. Ask open-ended and thought-provoking questions to your clients that invigorate the same curiosity and awareness in themselves and others. Practise these skills of curiosity with your family and friends to establish deep connections.

2 **Step out of your comfort zone** When was the last time you learnt something new or even challenged a personal fear? When we are present in the moment, as a new and challenging activity requires, we tend to forget our fear. This is also being.

3 **Ask for honest feedback** This includes friends, family and colleagues, regarding your active listening, relationship skills and body language. How others see us may not be the same way we see ourselves. Listen with an open heart to accept feedback with gratitude to be the best you can be.

4 **Be honest about your own biases** Challenge them. Be sincerely interested in others, without judgement. Learn from your differences and celebrate your similarities.

5 **Step into another's shoes** Seek out people to spend time with who you don't know or don't usually connect with. Get to know their situations, develop relationships and build your community. Get involved in shelters, kitchens, or youth or literacy programmes.

6 **Participate in tough conversations** These are not limited to but may include conversations to support or be supported in situations of grief, relationship issues, forgiveness or financial hardship. These conversations are often avoided and yet, support, mend and create closer relationships and foster forgiveness and acceptance.

7 **Join a shared cause** Create and work together on community projects, support groups, charitable causes or human rights movements.

8 **Expand your knowledge** There is great material available through all mediums, including books, research papers, podcasts and audiobooks. Autobiographies, biographies, history and memoirs are great options to broaden your perspective as well.

Presence and empathy have diverse benefits within any social interaction and coaching relationship, and are effective skills for handling challenging behaviours and thought patterns. Empathy enhances cooperation, understanding, empowerment and a supportive atmosphere. Mastering your own focus, personal reflection and worldly outlook enables your being as coach, and the same development in your clients. In order to minimize the doing mode and focus on any of these activities, immersion with a whole-body presence shifts the activity to a being perspective.

Maintaining a values-based practice

Coaching maturity is intertwined with coaching presence: you are unlikely to develop one without the other... They [coaches] work intuitively with their clients... They [coaches] are self-aware, understanding what is impacting and influencing them and their interventions and how they are impacting and influencing the client (Iliffe-Wood, 2014:16–17).

There is a need to look inside ourselves, to explore our own existence in life. Maturity as a coach requires a consistent practice of self-reflection. This is time spent contemplating your coaching conversations and practice, which includes the intent and management of your conversations, the outcome, and options available to you to reprioritize and re-centre in your practice. Journalling can also add another dimension to self-reflection. It is a foundation of my coaching practice and a means to reflect on my growth and development as a coach, which is also becoming.

Exercise (reflection)

Consider the time immediately following a coaching session as an opportunity to reflect on the session itself. Periodically, at minimum, review recorded sessions. Tune in to your perception of your own body language, any biases you may have felt, speech tone, feedback to the client, and pace and flow of the session. Ask yourself:

- Did you maintain an undistracted presence?
- Were you curious?
- Did you ask insightful and thought-provoking questions?
- Did you allow adequate silence for your client to immerse themselves and get to the adequate depth of their thoughts and emotions? In other words, did you enable them to BE as well?
- How did your presence affect how your client responded to you?

Although there is an aspect of doing in reflection, the activity largely requires an internal focus, which brings up thoughts and feelings. When we do this without expectation or being critical, but just acceptance for what is and what comes up, we are in a mode of being. When we ask ourselves how we can improve in our reflection or go back on past reflections, we are reaching into becoming mode.

Practising self-acceptance

There is a need to be self-aware and explore our own existence in life. This includes self-acceptance which is the state of complete acceptance of oneself. True self-acceptance is unconditional, free of any qualification. We can recognize our weaknesses or limitations, but this awareness in no way interferes with our ability to fully accept ourselves (Seltzer, 2008). Self-acceptance is uniquely rewarding as you are present with yourself and accepting of your truth or existence. From this you evolve to be all you can be, sometimes not to change, but to understand more fully. Unconditional self-acceptance also means awareness that you have made errors and have flaws, but they do not define who you are. The next time you look in the mirror acknowledge the great and worthy work in progress looking back at you. The following is an introduction of a mindful meditation practice, one of many aids for self-acceptance, but one that specifically enables the being mode.

Exercise (mindful meditation and mental fitness training)

'The greatest thing in the world is to know how to belong to oneself' (De Montaigne, 1993: 272). In our current fast-paced society, there has never before been a greater need to explore who we truly are. Although research is continually ongoing to gain understanding of the benefits and impact of meditation, it has been recognized as a practice that can help (Mead, 2019).

Mindful meditation, specifically, is a process of self-acceptance, which allows focus on your observation or sensations in the moment without judgement. This parallels the mode of being which is about 'accepting' and 'allowing' what is, without any urgency to change it (Segal, Williams and Teasdale, 2013: 72). Mindful meditation calms the mind by training it to focus on the present moment; therein it teaches you to slow down racing thoughts, release nervousness, agitation, anger or other strong emotions. The focus in meditation is not hard concentration, rather, it's comparable to the touch of a feather. Any interruption in a moment of practice simply presents a choice about what to do in that moment rather than frustration or the need to control.

Mindful meditation typically includes being present with the rhythm of your breath, fully experiencing your body sensations, or focusing on your five senses. You may choose a time in your day to be in stillness for several minutes or more. Mindfulness or the practice of mental fitness can also be incorporated into daily activities such as brushing your teeth, washing your hands, doing the dishes, exercising without music, listening to music, enjoying your morning coffee or driving to work. The opportunities are endless. Here are a couple of detailed examples: When you hug someone you love, practise full presence. Feel your feet on the ground and their breathing and heartbeat. Feel your own breathing as well, rather than being lost in your thoughts. Focus directly on your loved one when you talk to them. Softly observe the colours, their pupils and the sparkle in their eyes (Chamine, 2012: 108).

Mental fitness training as outlined in the book *Positive Intelligence* by Shirzad Chamine is backed by groundbreaking research in psychology and neuroscience (2012: 9). It involves shifting as much of your attention as you can to your body or one or more of your five senses, your breath or internal body sensations for at least ten seconds or three breaths, the equivalent of one PQ (Positive Quotient) rep. This is done 100 times throughout the day or the equivalent of 5-15 minutes of intense daily practice. The comparable of PQ reps for mental strength is repeatedly lifting a dumbbell for physical strength. In doing so, we stimulate the middle frontal cortex of the brain (MPFC), and the right part of the PQ brain (Chamine, 2012: 105, 110). Functions of the MPFC include 'observing yourself, pausing before action, soothing fear, staying centered in the middle of challenging situations and gut wisdom' (Chamine, 2012: 103). The right brain 'deals with the big picture, imagery, nonverbal language, and the detection of invisible things such as energy and mood. It helps with awareness of our physical sensations and emotions' (Chamine, 2012: 103).

Regardless of how we might incorporate meditation, a mindful practice or mental fitness training into our lives and/or suggest such a practice to our clients, note that it requires prioritization of time and focus to complete and in itself is a process of slowing down. While we can strictly focus on an elevated aspect of being, there is also a more practical capacity within reach of every one of us that can benefit and that is a life best defined as flourishing (Goleman and Davidson, 2017).

Summary

The BEING of a coach is a state that goes beyond any of the separate aspects of presence, empathy, a values-based practice or self-acceptance, and this list is certainly not exhaustive by any means. We require continual awareness and practice to change and grow in all dimensions as a coach. As you mature as a coach, you embody a concept of wholeness by strengthening and combining individual aspects that are more powerful than the individual components put together. In other words, you BECOME by balancing DOING and BEING.

Finally, I would like to expand on the practice of asking questions. In your personal reflections and your coaching practice, I encourage you to focus on the questions you ask, not the answers you receive. Ask yourself and your clients questions that inspire deep reflection, questions that require a full sense of presence and engagement. I recall the most profound question I was ever asked, and it continues to stick with me. The question was, 'What is the one question you don't want me to ask you?' I know my certification examiner was less concerned about my answer but rather the dimensions of reflection and being I had to grapple with before responding. Those are the questions we need to aim to ask as seasoned coaches. Slow your conversations down and allow the time for reflection. In doing so, you will enable the process of becoming and, as I tell my fellow coaches, appreciate 'everything you and your clients currently are and are capable of becoming'.

References

Bellezza, S, Paharia, N, and Keinan, A (2017) Conspicuous consumption of time: When busyness and lack of leisure time becomes a status symbol, *Journal of Consumer Research*, 44 (1), 118–38, doi.org/10.1093/jcr/ucw076 (archived at https://perma.cc/N7JK-6JWC)

Chamine, S (2012) *Positive Intelligence*, Greenleaf Book Group, Austin, TX

Clarke, J (2022) How constantly being busy affects your well-being, *Verywell Mind*, 23 May, www.verywellmind.com/how-the-glorification-of-busyness-impacts-our-well-being-4175360 (archived at https://perma.cc/LY3S-LGSD)

Del Fabro Smith, L, Suto, M, Chalmers, A and Backman, C L (2011) Belief in doing and knowledge in being mothers with arthritis, *OTJR: Occupation, Participation & Health*, 31 (1), 40–8, doi.org/10.3928/15394492-20100222-01 (archived at https://perma.cc/W68G-SBAS)

De Montaigne, M (1993) *Michel de Montaigne: The complete essays*, Penguin Classics, New York

Fidler, G (1983) Doing and becoming: The occupational therapy experience, in *Health Through Occupation: Theory and practice in occupational therapy*, ed G Kielhofner, pp 267–80, F A Davis Co, Philadelphia, PA

Frankl, V E (2006) *Man's Search for Meaning*, Beacon Press, Boston, MA

Goleman, D and Davidson, R J (2017) *Altered Traits: Science reveals how meditation changes your mind, brain, and body*, Avery, New York

Hitch, D, Pepin, G and Stagnitti, K (2014) In the footsteps of Wilcock, part one: The evolution of doing, being, becoming, and belonging, *Occupational Therapy in Health Care*, 28 (3), 231–46, doi.org/ 10.3109/07380577.2014.898114 (archived at https://perma.cc/HC4J-CRVD)

Iliffe-Wood, M (2014) *Coaching Presence: Building consciousness and awareness in coaching interventions*, Kogan Page, London

Maslow, A H (1943) A Theory of human motivation, *Psychological Review*, 50 (4), 370–96, doi.org/10.1037/h0054346 (archived at https://perma.cc/XB22-LLRX)

Maslow, A H (1968) *A Theory of Human Motivation*, Wilder Publications, Mansfield Centre, CT

Maslow, A H (1971) *The Farther Reaches of Human Nature*, Penguin Random House, New York

Mead, E (2019) The history and origin of meditation, PositivePsychology.com, 27 May, positivepsychology.com/history-of-meditation/ (archived at https://perma.cc/86U4-HK6X)

Pickens, N D, O'Reilly, K R and Sharp, K C (2010) Holding on to normalcy and overshadowed needs: Family caregiving at end of life, *Canadian Journal of Occupational Therapy*, 77 (4), 234–40, doi.org/ 10.2182/cjot.2010.77.4.5 (archived at https://perma.cc/5TXL-2XPB)

Segal, Z, Williams, J M G and Teasdale, J D (2013) *Mindfulness-Based Cognitive Therapy for Depression*, 2nd edn, The Guilford Press, New York

Seltzer, L (2008) The path to unconditional self-acceptance: How do you fully accept yourself when you don't know how? *Psychology Today*, 10 September, www.psychologytoday.com/gb/blog/evolution-the-self/200809/the-path-unconditional-self-acceptance (archived at https://perma.cc/7HBL-4WH2)

Steindl, C, Winding, K and Runge, U (2008) Occupation and participation in everyday life: Women's experiences of an Austrian refugee camp, *Journal of Occupational Science*, 15 (1), 36–42, www.doi.org/10.1080/14427591.2008.9686605 (archived at https://perma.cc/4RDY-94YU)

Ventegodt, J, Merrick, J and Andersen, N J (2003) Quality of life theory III: Maslow revisited, *The Scientific World Journal*, 13 (3), 1050–7, doi.org/10.1100/tsw.2003.84 (archived at https://perma.cc/67SC-7V8K)

Wilcock, A (1999) Reflections on doing, being and becoming, *Australian Occupational Therapy Journal*, 46 (1), 1–11, doi.org/10.1046/j.1440-1630.1999.00174.x (archived at https://perma.cc/S4ZN-E4XM)

Wilcock, A (2006) *An Occupational Perspective of Health*, 2nd edn, Slack, Inc. Thorofare, NJ

Zeldin, T (1995) *An Intimate History of Humanity*, HarperCollins, New York

28

The power of intention

Life coaching and the gap between intention and action

SHARON HOOPER

ABSTRACT

Intentions do not guarantee action. If they are devoid of passion or disconnected from values and beliefs, intentions reduce to wishful thinking. Yet, having passionate intent does not necessarily sustain the action needed to achieve success. Clarity and perseverance are equally important. I explain how a coach can facilitate the process leading from intentions to effective action.

Introduction

Much of what we do as life coaches is focusing on how to bridge the gap between a client's intention and action: in other words, how to make one's intention more powerful and, therefore, successful. Scholars in psychology, philosophy, behaviour science, physiology and neuroscience have attempted to develop a theory of intention and set of strategies to address this issue. As Wieber, Thürmer and Gollwitzer (2015: 2) noted, 'Indeed, research has observed a pervasive gap between people's intended and actual behavior. Examples of such intention–behavior gaps can be found in various domains including intentions to exercise more or to eat more healthily'. Wieber went on to conclude that, 'Behavioral and physiological findings on the intentional control of action suggest that a strong intention or goal commitment is not sufficient for goal attainment'.

Now, new research questions are being asked, such as, how do a person's bad habits limit the formation and execution of intentions? What are the keys to effective self-regulation? These are the kinds of questions that life coaches work with every day. We have found that, while the answers vary from individual to individual, addressing the gap between intention and action is crucial to a client's success.

Some scholars call for action control as a mix of conscious and unconscious processing, leading to new avenues of interdisciplinary research (Wieber, Thürmer and Gollwitzer, 2015: 1). These are insights that life coaches have perceptively known and addressed with their clients for a long time. While there remains much debate within and between disciplines about how to bridge this gap, authors generally agree that the question is tied to 1) intentions as goals and 2) self-regulation leading to action. Debates have concerned questions such as the following: What are intentions? What is the relation between intentions and other mental entities such as beliefs, desires, plans and commitments? What is the relationship between belief and action? Why do people fail to act on their intentions? However, there is no established theory of intention within any of these disciplines, let alone a theory that accounts for all the phenomena identified across all of the disciplines (Gollwitzer, 1999; Gollwitzer and Oettingen, 2011). Future studies would benefit from considering the practical knowledge of life coaches about the power of intention, and why and when it is not successful.

Reflexivity as a stimulus

Reflecting upon my 20 years of coaching, I see that many of the struggles I have observed with clients have paralleled my own struggles to achieve my desired goals. This reflexivity – using oneself as the research instrument – is inherent in the practice of life coaching. The following anecdote, written prior to becoming a life coach, is followed by several insights and techniques I have developed over the years to bridge the gap between intention and success to make intention more powerful for both coaches and clients.

On one perfectly normal California day, a friend said to me, 'I'd like you to go out and sell my environmental recordings'.

'What?!' I replied. 'I'm not a salesperson, and I don't have the slightest idea how to do this. Furthermore, I don't know why anyone would buy them.'

Richard had been travelling around California with his professional recording equipment, where he had recorded thunderstorms in the Big Sur mountains, crashing ocean waves in Carmel, and rippling brooks accompanied by singing birds. I thought the sounds were nice, but why would anyone purchase them as a recording?

About 30 days after his first request, and being fed up with my government job, I finally gave in to his incessant nagging and said I would give it a try, even though I didn't have the slightest idea what I was doing. And there were some big hiccups. I had always worked for someone else. Sure, I had an entrepreneurial spirit, but had never struck out on my own. All the self-doubts about success came crowding into my mind: 'I'm not smart enough, I'm not a salesperson, no one will listen to me, I can't be successful on my own, I have no experience doing this.'

One day, totally frustrated, I entered Richard's office in tears, threw up my hands, and said 'I don't know what to do!' His response was, 'Just make a list and do it.'

Honestly, I thought, 'What kind of list? What items go on the list? What is my intention, my goal? Why am I even doing this?'

Overcoming struggles can foster resilience, strength and determination

I struggled with how to proceed with this challenge and opportunity. As my mind began to race forward with possibilities, the doubts, insecurity and negative feedback came in, so I decided to go back to square one: spend more time reading a variety of self-help and sales books and articles to shore up my confidence and provide inspiration. Three especially helpful magazines were *Fast Company*, *Entrepreneur*, and *Inc*. A few books I included were *Awaken the Giant Within* by Tony Robbins, *Zen and The Art of Making a Living* by Laurence G. Boldt, *The E Myth* by Michael Gerber, *Everyday Sacred: A woman's journey home* by Sue Bender, *The Pursuit of WOW!* by Tom Peters and any books by Caroline Myss, Elinor Stutz and Byron Katie.

I began to notice a shift in my thinking from 'I can't' to a glimmer of 'What if?' *What if* I could make something big happen? *What if* I could pour my energy into an independent job like this? *What if* I didn't have to answer to anyone, as long as I was taking actions towards a goal?

My immediate intention was simply to stay positive and to take one step at a time.

When I began to outline the plan for marketing the recordings, I first had to get clear about why I made the choice to do this. Besides being bored with my current employment, why would I take a risk and jump into the unknown? What was drawing me to move forward with this plan? I identified three major themes:

1 I loved challenges.
2 This project would give me the opportunity to do whatever I wanted, really break through all the constraints that were imposed on me by other employers.
3 I would have the freedom to create however I wanted.

It was vital for me to incorporate what was most important in my daily life and to test my abilities to create something much bigger than myself. From past experience I knew that success meant that I had a reality-based intention, a strong goal, and the commitment and perseverance to carry through to the end result. Little did I know that my unsure beginnings would build a multi-million dollar recording label, headquartered on a remote and idyllic island in the Pacific Northwest.

First action steps to success

My first action step in the plan to market the recordings into the gift industry was to make a point-of-purchase display for the recordings. Then I drove to Santa Barbara, California, in order to locate what I thought would be appropriate stores to sell the product. Finding a popular street full of shops, I sat on a bench and watched the busiest stores. When I had narrowed my choices down to three, I entered a Hallmark store, carrying my display. Before I opened my mouth, a gentleman walked toward me, noticed the display and said, 'We don't sell music.' Gulp! I was frozen momentarily, but not about to give up. This was my first attempt, and I was going to make it work.

I began talking anyway, telling him he wouldn't be billed for 30 days and that if he didn't sell the CDs, we would be happy to issue a UPS call tag. I even suggested a place where he could place the display and play the recordings rather than his canned music.

Whatever I said worked and I went merrily on my way thinking, 'Hmmm... I'll use the same spiel everywhere I go.' That weekend I opened 11 accounts, returning home to Monterey and my government job.

Two weeks later, every account I had opened called and said, 'I can't believe these sold, but we're all out. Please send us another order.' This was the beginning of a full-fledged record label. From our humble beginnings of four environmental recordings, and while adding ten musical recording artists living in the United States and Europe, we eventually produced more than 90 CDs, some purely environmental and many blended with music. The success that I experienced planted a seed for a future career in life coaching. For if I could do it, anyone could!

Knowing what is most important to you

Looking back, *knowing* what was important to me was basic to my goal and gave me the freedom to create and to experience the dynamic results of my own success. I had been taught not to bring attention to myself, to do things for others, and not to expect a reward other than the gratitude of another person. For decades I had repeated the formula – until I was given this opportunity to make something happen on my own.

There is often a tension between our intention and what we are facing on a daily level. When I began my work for the record label, life had felt uncertain, and I thought that if I didn't take some educated risks, I would be stuck *wishing* forever. There were no guarantees then, and, for the most part, there are none now.

The power of intention is *knowing* that you are committed to bringing forth something big, new and wondrous. Every time we experience something, we make a choice. Why not choose each step in accordance with what brings us closer to our intended dream? When we are on a journey to fulfil a powerful dream, it's important to focus on the process, because each step of the process brings us closer to our intended purpose.

Stepping out of my comfort zone

My biggest discomfort in creating the record label was stepping outside my comfort zone, initiating conversations with unknown professionals in other fields, travelling to unfamiliar destinations, and generally entirely changing the role I had played for so long – and changing my habits from negative patterns to ones that exemplified who I really was.

Every day, every week, I made a commitment to do one more thing that was totally out of my comfort zone. This is where real growth happened for me. I expended my energies and observed a newness that kept moving me forward. The more comfortable I became jumping into an unknown world, the more desire I had to learn and want more. Real personal growth happens when we have the courage to move away from our comfort zone. Brave – and unfamiliar – steps forward create spaces to grow into instead of staying still.

How to achieve your intention with a clear plan of action

Intention can be really powerful when used with tangible action steps if our inherent values and beliefs support our intention. There has been much talk about values, but what does the term really mean? Our values help us to shape our lives and create intention.

When you are planning your life, creating the intention or helping your client do the same, think about: *What makes me smile inside, what do I need to feel fulfilled, what activities am I engaged in when I'm feeling true joy?* While creating an intention, take an inventory of emotions to make sure you are designing the best possible intention for the moment. A person's intention may change along the way, however, and when and if it does diverge into something different, you must know that you made a conscious decision to alter it. When you (or your client) are clear about what you want in life, you will not make decisions unconsciously. Refer to your (or your client's) written statements about what is true for you to guide you to make wise choices.

The following questions may help you (or your client) reach deep to a place of conscious awareness of what is important for you to live a happy, fulfilled life:

- When am I feeling true joy?

- Do I spend time with people who support me?
- Are there people or situations that drain my energy?
- In my perfect world, who and what is included?
- What are the strengths that help me navigate life successfully?

When we assure that our most important beliefs are incorporated into a purpose, then developing the action plan to create a strategy will come more easily.

Addressing false beliefs and other obstacles: the relationship between belief and action

When we are growing up, we observe and experience everything in our surroundings, including how people interact with us. Of course, we do not realize that we are already forming opinions about life from such a young age. However, child development specialists have shown that the first seven or eight years of our existence are the years that form our basic opinions about life. Dr Jack Shonkoff, a leading scholar on early child health and development, and the director of the Harvard Center on the Developing Child, states, 'Early childhood experiences from birth to age eight affect the development of the brain's architecture, which provides the foundation for all future learning, behavior, and health. A strong foundation helps children develop the skills they need to become well-functioning adults' (Shonkoff, 2007, para 2).

When you help your client understand the links that extend from these unconscious behaviours and how they relate to the present, they can find a new freedom to go forth and manifest their passionate intention, dreams and goals. They will need to make a choice to consciously change their thinking, create new patterns and habits. It is ultimately up to clients, but coaches can play a determinant role through guided exploration and reflection. Everyone makes choices every minute of the day, and you can help your client make those decisions that will help them continue on their intended path.

A clarifying exercise to use yourself and with your clients

When I begin coaching with someone, we create a vision mapping of what that person wants to achieve. It is a free-form process that helps to clarify the goal, an intention to make something happen, or simply a desire to live a more fulfilled life. There are endless variations, but the heart of each mapping needs a specific focus. This focus might shift and change through our discussions but having a place to start gives us a foundation for direction and conversation. After processing ideas on several sheets of easel paper, we are ready to co-create a beginning plan of action.

Exercise

Draw a circle, oval or any shape, in the middle of a piece of paper. Inside the shape, write exactly your intention or goal as though it's already happening, like getting up in the morning, excited about the day ahead because you've reached your current goal and every day is perfection. Then, add a specific date when you envision the finished plan taking place. *Don't worry about how to make this happen.* You will learn along the way. There are many people you can reach out to in order to strengthen and manifest your intention – coaches, counsellors, professional friends, someone you don't know and whom you admire. The most important part of your intention plan is believing that it will take place, and that you are committed to the timeline and end result. Do this exercise with your client or have them do a draft between sessions. This is an excellent foundation for any further exploration.

Here is an example of using an intention from my current life: I want to have my trilogy of books ready to send to agents on 1 September 2025. Committing to a timeline is extremely important so that I can stay on target, week by week and month by month. In other words, I need to design a plan and have the intention to reach my goal within my timeline.

As a life coach, and on my personal journey, I have learnt many things along the road of intention. Most importantly, I have learnt that we have finite hours each day to live what we believe, what we desire in life, and how to make those a reality. After working, sleeping, commuting and eating, we may have four or five hours a day (plus a weekend) to absorb ourselves in what's most important to us.

I suggest to my clients that they carry a small notebook with them for two weeks and jot down every time they feel joyful. Where were you? What were you doing? How do your happy times relate to your new intention? Read through the notes after a few days and capture the themes. Use the journal to organize the steps to build on this joy. In the process, my clients and I discuss:

- Observing the people in their life and taking notice of who supports them and who might drain their energy. Think about any changes you may want to make in this area.

- Becoming aware of habits that might be negative and can slow them down. Dr Bruce Lipton frequently states that our limiting beliefs can turn into negative habits (see https://www.brucelipton.com/resources). Ask clients to take an honest look at themselves and decide what unfavourable habits they might want to change. Remind them to be patient as they transform these. It can take about three months of committed effort to change one habit. While mostly deemed anecdotal, with the unsubstantiated popular idea that a new habit is formed in 21 days (Maltz, 1960), research indicates anywhere between two and three months

(Lally et al, 2010; Van der Weiden et al, 2020). In my experience, a new habit takes at least three months to become entrenched and sustainable.

- Noticing new opportunities along the way that will support their goal.

- Creating a calendar for one month and filling in all activities and/or work schedule. Determine how many hours a client is willing or able to devote to their intention on a daily and weekly basis. Decide which activities they may have to sacrifice or alter, in order to stay true to their intended goal.

- Celebrating and offering themselves rewards along this journey. Working non-stop, even if it is something we love, can become exhausting.

- Forming their own *advisory team*, consisting of supportive people from various occupations, with whom your client can talk each week – one person one week, and another the next week, for example. It can be challenging to keep momentum for months at a time, so share your intention with others. Integrate them where possible. For instance, a client can 'repay' their team by hosting a monthly luncheon or bartering for services. Be brave about sharing this journey with friends, family, peers and other supports. The more we talk about our intention, the firmer it becomes in our mind.

- Brainstorming, with your client or by themselves, on large pieces of paper, such as easel paper, so that you can be expansive, even when writing with markers. My plans to work on the record label started out with free thinking, jotting down whatever came to mind, which eventually became concise plans of action. It is amazing what can be observed when a person is not being held to straight lines in a notebook.

- Acknowledging and recognizing fear. Being afraid and anxious at any time during this period of expansion and intention is a natural part of the growth or change process. However, we do not need to let fear slow us down. We encourage our clients to act anyway, knowing that fear is present to teach a person about life and stand strong and courageously as they walk forward on their path. If a client feels overwhelmed or needs support, we show acceptance and support and explore reaching out to a loved one, a friend, colleague or professional to back them up – no one has to walk this journey alone.

- Reminding clients to believe in their abilities. Every person is the architect of their own life!

Starting with practical actions, such as simply acknowledging where you are right now, will take you to the next step, and the next. When clarity breaks through, your clients will begin making decisions for themselves that matter in a more heartful way and that are more aligned with their intention and goals.

Final words

Always ask, 'What are your heart and mind saying?', 'What are you doing by rote because you haven't dared to look deeper?'

Life's decisions are about choice. We can choose to explore our deeper nature in order to be more awake, or we can stay stuck in habitual patterns that deflect our true purpose in life, delaying the steps we need to take in manifesting our intention.

Thus, invite your clients to discover their places of energy and inspiration. To *do* something every day, every week. To keep positive energy swirling around them as much as possible. Successful results take place when people believe in themselves, persevere, and take the necessary steps to accomplish their targeted goals and dreams.

> **Passion + Intention + Clarity + Perseverance + Action = Resounding Success**

Therefore, always remember, intention is not enough to initiate and sustain directed action that leads to success, unless built on passion, steered with clarity and held together by perseverance. Helping your clients find their value-based intention and stepping up with determination and grit will start a lifelong pursuit of purpose.

References

Gollwitzer, P M (1999) Implementation intentions: Strong effects of simple plans, *American Psychologist*, 54 (7), 493–503, doi.org/10.1037/0003-066X.54.7.493 (archived at https://perma.cc/96RL-V7TE)

Gollwitzer, P M and Oettingen, G (2011) Planning promotes goal striving, in *Handbook of Self-Regulation: Research, theory, and applications*, 2nd edn, eds K D Vohs and R F Baumeister, pp 162–85, The Guilford Press, New York

Lally, P, van Jaarsveld, C H M, Potts, H W W and Wardle, J (2010) How are habits formed: Modelling habit formation in the real world, *European Journal of Social Psychology*, 40 (6), 998–1009, doi.org/10.1002/ejsp.674 (archived at https://perma.cc/GLZ4-V7NH)

Maltz, M (1960) *Psycho-cybernetics*, Prentice-Hall, Englewood Cliffs, NJ

Shonkoff, J (2007) Why early childhood matters, The North Carolina Department of Health and Human Services, www.ncdhhs.gov/about/department-initiatives/early-childhood/why-early-childhood-matters (archived at https://perma.cc/4U2B-KET7)

Van der Weiden, A, Benjamins, J, Gillebaart, M, Ybema, J F and De Ridder, D (2020) How to form good habits? A longitudinal field study on the role of self-control in habit formation, *Frontiers in Psychology*, 11, 560, doi.org/10.3389/fpsyg.2020.00560 (archived at https://perma.cc/6G87-SH84)

Wieber, F J, Thürmer, L and Gollwitzer, P M (2015) Promoting the translation of intentions into action by implementation intentions: Behavioral effects and physiological correlates, *Frontiers in Human Neuroscience*, 9, 395, doi.org/10.3389/fnhum.2015.00395 (archived at https://perma.cc/B8CR-DJXP)

29

Overcoming fear

Stepping out of your comfort zone

CHRISTINE GUIRGUIS

ABSTRACT

What is it that keeps us stuck in our comfort zones, and how do we get out? The reason we stay confined within the limitations of our comfort zone is because we believe that we have control there. In our comfort we have created a routine that is predictable. Within that predictability we have a perception of control over our external environment. This gives us a false sense of security. With these walls up there is no room for growth and discovery of the greatness that lies within us. Trying to break out of our comfort zone can be uncomfortable and difficult. This chapter will you how you can help your clients overcome their fears and step out of their comfort zone to live life to their full potential.

This chapter explains the different zones through the client's journey of reaching their potential in the context of the difference between being successful and reaching one's potential. I answer what is needed to step out of the comfort zone to reach self-awareness, and how to help clients overcome the fears that hold them back from reaching their full potential.

Human potential

The *human potential diagram* (Figure 29.1) will help you as the coach gain clarity as to where your client is currently and how to help them move forward one step at a time.

There are three different zones to understand when you help your client reach their full potential. The human potential diagram helps you visualize where they

FIGURE 29.1 The human potential diagram

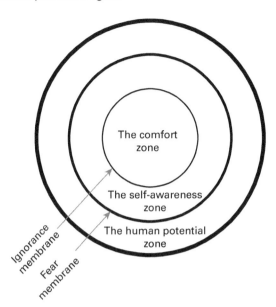

might be now and where they hope to reach. The diagram has three different zones, namely the comfort zone, the self-awareness zone and the human potential zone. Metaphorically speaking, these areas are kept intact by a membrane. To weaken and penetrate this membrane, you need its antidote.

The first membrane around the comfort zone is ignorance. Unaware of this state, things feel fine. Like they say, ignorance is bliss. To overcome the ignorance, you need its antidote; a desire to learn and grow. This will allow you to step into the self-awareness zone. Here, you gain clarity on what you want to do. However, how to get there starts to feel out of reach. The reason for that is simple – fear. To bypass the fear membrane, you will need courage.

It is important to mention that this is not a one-way street, people will keep going through these zones throughout their lives. Understanding this diagram will give you the tools you need to help your clients bypass these membranes every time you encounter them in a session.

The difference between success and reaching your potential

Most people confuse success with reaching their full potential. You can be successful, by 'attaining wealth, favor, or eminence' as stated in the Merriam Webster dictionary, but that is not the same as reaching your full potential. Reaching your full potential means attaining your goals while feeling fulfilled. This means paying attention to how you feel when you get to where you want to go and having the clarity on *why* you want to go there.

Using stress as a motivator to push yourself out of your comfort zone can be a painful process. While stress has been proven to motivate a person to reach certain levels of success as stated in the Yerkes–Dodson law (Yerkes and Dodson, 1908), it is not sustainable.

Supported by the Yerkes–Dodson law, variations of the comfort zone model depict how mental arousal (stress) can be a motivator to perform better when learning a new habit, but only to a certain point. When overly stressed, performance decreases because of how stress affects the human brain and psyche (Yerkes and Dodson, 1908). Using stress as a motivator is risky, and:

> Chronic stress, or a constant stress experienced over a prolonged period of time can contribute to long-term problems for heart and blood vessels. The consistent and ongoing increase in heart rate, and the elevated levels of stress hormones and of blood pressure, can take a toll on the body. This long-term ongoing stress can increase the risk for hypertension, heart attack, or stroke (APA, 2018, para: 13).

When stress is present, it invokes the flight or fight response (APA, 2018), which is generated by fear (Kozlowska et al, 2015). As such, habitually experiencing fear as a motivator creates constant stress, which can lead to burnout.

Our body reacts similarly when exposed to excitement or stress. So, while the Yerkes experiment helped discover that there is an optimal circumstance for us to learn new habits in a quicker time frame, arousal in the form of stress is not the answer.

Both anxiety and excitement produce an elevated heart rate, a feeling of butterflies in the stomach and generate sweat. The body is getting ready for action. The underlying difference is that excitement is connected to the emotion of joy, while anxiety comes from a different emotion, namely fear. Svetlana Whitener, a *Forbes* Councils Member, argues the importance of distinguishing these two states because 'when we operate our life from fear we are operating from a place of survival, rather than a place where we can take advantage of opportunities and possibilities, such as when we are excited' (Whitener, 2021, para 2).

So how do we reach excitement? The simple answer is to understand the driving force behind why you are doing what you are doing, and if it resonates with something meaningful to you, then you will feel excited to move forward and that can be the motivator that will get you to the next step.

Self-awareness

Once you see your client has the desire to learn and grow, they have managed to dissolve the ignorance membrane that was holding them in their comfort zone. With this membrane gone, they are in the self-awareness zone. In this zone you gain awareness of the control, or lack thereof, that exists within your internal world compared to your external world.

Control

According to converging evidence, we are in control of most aspects of our lives – a belief that is integral to our well-being (Leotti, Iyengar and Ochsner, 2010). The problem arises when we try to control our external environment. It is important to note that our external world and the outcome of any given situation is not necessarily always in our control. We need to appreciate what we can control, namely our thoughts and actions, which will influence the outcome of our lives. When we are aware of our internal state – that being our thoughts and emotions, we can choose the thoughts and actions that are in alignment with our values and desires, which are driven by self-love. By being intentional, instead of having expectations, the outcome does not have to impact your sense of self or your fulfilment. The awareness of our intentions allows us to move forward and reach our goals by taking steps out of our comfort zone.

First, as a coach, you check if your client is focusing on an aspect of life that is in their control, also identifying what their expectations are. Expectations are defined in the Cambridge dictionary as 'the feeling that good things are going to happen in the future'. With expectations, we look at the future and focus on what we think should happen in our outside world, over which we have no control. By focusing on what we thought would happen or, put simply, what we expected from others or anything outside of ourselves, we get disappointed and feel unfulfilled. Shifting our attention to our internal state by understanding our values and purpose, and being satisfied with those, we can choose an intention that is in alignment with what is truly important to us.

Getting your clients to get in touch with their internal world in order to gain control of their lives means to give them the tools to gain clarity on their thoughts and give them control over the actions they choose to take, in order to step out of their comfort zone.

To get a deeper understanding of your clients' expectations versus their intentions, you can use Table 29.1 for questions that will give you insight on whether your client has a positive intention that is driven by fulfilling their emotional needs internally or an expectation that is driven by fulfilling their emotional needs externally.

By asking your client to state their intention, you as the coach can hear where the driving factor of their actions is located. Recognizing the driving factor will allow you to help them understand if they are trying to fulfil their emotional needs from their external or their internal world. Allowing them to see that they have no control over external factors and redirecting them to find ways to fulfil their needs internally will allow them to feel less pressure to take the steps they need to move forward.

Take the example of my client. When asked what her intention was for reaching her goal, she stated 'I will be successful, and I will be remembered and the pride of my family'. When pointed to realize that this was an expectation, she realized how her family views her, or if people will remember her, was an expectation she had no control over. That brought her great awareness to the fact that she had been running on the fuel of always trying to be perfect to get the approval of others and never feeling like she was enough. With that realization she was able to form a new intention, with the internal driving factor that she would do the things that make her happy because she has the *knowing* that she is on the right path.

Beliefs

Beliefs are activated in the amygdala, a part of the limbic system that generates behavioural and emotional responses. As the processes are often subconscious, beliefs are not easily put into words (Sathyanarayana Rao et al, 2009).

Our beliefs shape our thinking, which influences our decision making and our perception of the world around us (Sathyanarayana Rao et al, 2009). So, how does this affect our choices?

When our beliefs are formed by fears, which can happen through direct experiences or indirectly through social transmission (Figure 29.1) (Olsson and Phelps, 2007), it stops us from doing things that we believe can threaten our safety. It is important to consider when a misinterpretation of a social transmission occurs.

TABLE 29.1 Steps to understanding your client's intention

Steps	Questions and actions
1. Ask your client	Why is this important to you?
2. Follow up	What would it mean to you if that was to happen?
3. Create clarity	How would you want to show up? *Give a list of values to help them find the words they need to describe their answer*
4. Write it out	Let your clients write out a list of intentions versus their expectations *Notice if an intention is really an expectation and guide them to gain a better understanding*

Most of our beliefs are created in the early stages of life. As children we pick up on cues, especially from primary caretakers and other role models, or witnessing generational expressions that we may have misinterpreted, which become an entrenched belief that will be operating our proverbial hard drive into adulthood (Connors and Halligan, 2015). These phenomena are called limiting or disempowering beliefs, which can hold you back from stepping out of your comfort zone.

Discovering your client's beliefs gives you valuable insight into the types of beliefs that are guiding their decisions and actions. By simply becoming aware of one's thoughts and emotions, the coach has a window to see clearly whether their client has empowering or disempowering beliefs that are motivating their actions. By exploring your client's triggers, emotions, needs and values, you can start building an insight into what those beliefs are. Helping your client discover these beliefs gives them the awareness they need to see what's been getting in the way of stepping out of their comfort zone.

Breaking through the fear

Now that your client has reached the self-awareness zone, the membrane separating it from the human potential zone is fear. To dissolve this membrane, the client needs courage, which is not so much about overcoming fear but accepting and letting go of it.

Understanding fear

Our human minds are wired to keep us safe by building and activating a belief system. Our minds have the capability of creating an internal representation of a threat by using emotions from repeating past events and imagination of similar future events to prompt action. This can just as easily trigger us to activate our defence systems while no real threat is being presented in our external world but is being imagined or anticipated (Kozlowska et al, 2015). These internal processes limit us from taking steps out of our comfort zone when our emotions are being triggered by perceived threats, which then influences our behaviour. 'The recurrence of a particular situation triggers the reactivation of emotion-influenced neural patterns, which biases decision-making toward choices that maximize reward and minimize punishment', argued Ronningstam and Baskin-Sommers (2013: 196). As fear and fear avoidance are important motivating factors, the trigger of fear by a perceived threat prevents you from making choices that can allow you to step out of your comfort zone.

Overcoming fears

Once we encounter something we perceive as danger, we are wired to store this information to keep us safe from any recurring similar circumstances. These internalized memories may keep us stuck in the same recurring pattern of response attached to the original fear (Kozlowska et al, 2015).

As a coach, you can use a process I created, called The Seven Keys of Discovery (Table 29.2), which will help your clients unlock the doors that have been stuck and discover what has been in the way of allowing them to reach their Human Potential Zone.

Once you have explored these questions with your client, they have a choice to be led by fear or by faith.

TABLE 29.2 The seven keys of discovery

Key	Questions and actions
Trigger	What is the trigger?
	Discover the trigger by paying attention to which point your client started feeling the discomfort in their life
Emotion	What was the emotion that they felt in that moment?
	Using the Wheel of Emotions, a visual representation of the spectrum of emotions and how they relate to each other (Maupome and Isyutina, 2013), can help get the words they are searching for to identify their emotion
Needs	What were the needs that were not being fulfilled in that moment?
	Using a list of needs, allow your client to go through and choose the words that are in alignment with the needs that were not being fulfilled in that moment
Values	What are your values?
	You can use a list of values to help your client list their values, regardless of the relevance to the situation, allow them to list all their values and find the connection between unmet needs and values
Beliefs	What is the self-limiting belief?
	By this point, you will uncover a limiting belief through questioning and understanding your client's emotions, needs and values in context with the trigger
Intention	What was your intention?
	Notice if your client's intention relates to their expectation. Help them get to the root of their intention. If the intention is not aligned with their values, ask them to change it to what they would like it to be
Expectation	What was your expectation?
	Ask your client to define and examine their expectation. Help your client see that they are not in control of the external expectations and bring their attention towards what they do have control over: their intentions.

In this context, what does faith mean exactly?

Professor of Sociology at the University of Leicester, Barbara Misztal, described faith as a 'strategic decision to take a risk in the condition of uncertainty' (1996: 15).

According to a study, firefighters build trust with each other by labelling, storytelling and evaluative standards, which guide their risk-taking decisions (Pratt, Lepisto and Dane, 2018: 5). The research found that 'firefighters take a leap of faith to move from weak evidence derived from mundane tasks and behaviors at the fire station to trust in terms of entering a burning building with other firefighters' (p 29).

These findings show that a leap of faith is required to take a step into the unknown despite our best efforts to base decisions on an analysis of our exterior world to get the best formative result. While we try to form conclusions and control by analysing external factors, we must recognize that it may be an illusion of control. The illusion is what is keeping us in the comfort zone. By gaining awareness and clarity on what we do and do not have control over, we allow ourselves to make choices that are in alignment with our empowering beliefs and values. Taking a leap of faith and stepping out of our comfort zone feels like the right thing to do when you have that kind of clarity.

Let's look at the story of a nine-year-old boy who took heroic action during a massive earthquake in China's Szechuan province. When the ceiling of his school collapsed, almost all the kids in it were killed. The boy got away, and as he was running away, he noticed two other kids struggling to get out. He ran back and saved them. When he was asked later, 'Why did you do that?' his answer was, 'I was the hall monitor! It was my duty; it was my job to look after my classmates!' (Zimbardo, 2011). Again and again, when looking at acts of heroism, people did what they believed was the 'right' thing to do. Heroic examples aside, getting your clients to discover the seven keys will allow them to move into the human potential zone with courage and make heroic choices in their own lives.

With few exceptions, no one is born fearless. We all have fears. Some people have learnt from an early age that when they put their fears aside and choose to take action, they will eventually figure it out and gain the confidence they need. Some people have chosen to cave in to their fears and not take those chances, never realizing that they could accomplish great things if they tried.

The only way to attain courage is through faith. Being uncertain of the external but having the confidence that your deepest desires are in alignment with your internal state, that is, your values, your intentions and your empowering beliefs, stimulates faith. Taking that leap gives you confidence in your ability, because the only way to build confidence is to do things repeatedly, until you reshape your disempowering beliefs.

So, eventually, stepping out of your comfort zone will not feel so scary any more, because your confidence will grow in two areas, the area you're currently facing and the area of doing ANYTHING that you desire, which might have initially scared you.

References

APA (2018) Stress effects on the body, American Psychological Association, 1 November, www.apa.org/topics/stress/body (archived at https://perma.cc/6DF6-V8YG)

Connors, M H and Halligan, P W (2015) A cognitive account of belief: A tentative road map, *Frontiers in Psychology*, 5, doi.org/10.3389/fpsyg.2014.01588 (archived at https://perma.cc/3ZN5-BR59)

Kozlowska, K, Walker, P, McLean, L and Carrive, P (2015) Fear and the defense cascade: Clinical implications and management, *Harvard Review of Psychiatry*, 23 (4), 263–87, doi.org/10.1097/HRP.0000000000000065 (archived at https://perma.cc/FLB4-AXXM)

Leotti, L A, Iyengar, S S and Ochsner, K N (2010) Born to choose: The origins and value of the need to control, *Trends in Cognitive Sciences*, 14 (10), 457–63, doi.org/10.1016/j.tics.2010.08.001 (archived at https://perma.cc/TF2Z-5DYN)

Maupome, G and Isyutina, O (2013) Dental students' and faculty members' concepts and emotions associated with a Caries Risk Assessment Program, *Journal of Dental Education*, 77 (11), 1477–87, doi.org/10.1002/j.0022-0337.2013.77.11.tb05624.x (archived at https://perma.cc/5B5B-TLXQ)

Misztal, B (1996) *Trust in Modern Societies: The search for the bases of social order*, Polity Press/Blackwell, Cambridge

Olsson, A and Phelps, E A (2007) Social learning of fear, *Nature Neuroscience*, 10, 1095–1102, doi.org/10.1038/nn1968 (archived at https://perma.cc/CGN9-4DHX)

Pratt, M G, Lepisto, D A and Dane, E (2018) The hidden side of trust: Supporting and sustaining leaps of faith among firefighters, *Administrative Science Quarterly*, 64 (2), 398–434, doi.org/10.1177/0001839218769252 (archived at https://perma.cc/3DW9-Z36D)

Ronningstam, E and Baskin-Sommers, A R (2013) Fear and decision-making in narcissistic personality disorder – a link between psychoanalysis and neuroscience, *Dialogues in Clinical Neuroscience*, 15 (2), 191–201, doi.org/10.31887/DCNS.2013.15.2/eronningstam (archived at https://perma.cc/QX6H-KMTL)

Sathyanarayana Rao, T S, Asha, M R, Jagannatha Rao, K S and Vasudevaraju, P (2009) The biochemistry of belief, *The Indian Journal of Psychiatry*, 51 (4), 239–41, doi.org/10.4103/0019-5545.58285 (archived at https://perma.cc/77AH-JAWE)

Whitener, S (2021) Anxiety vs. relaxation: Relabeling anxiety as excitement, *Forbes*, 7 April, www.forbes.com/sites/forbescoachescouncil/2021/04/07/anxiety-vs-relaxationrelabeling-anxiety-as-excitement/ (archived at https://perma.cc/L3W6-KPKS)

Yerkes, R and Dodson, J (1908) The relation of strength of stimulus to rapidity of habit-formation, *Journal of Comparative Neurology and Psychology*, 18, 459–82, psychclassics.yorku.ca/Yerkes/Law/ (archived at https://perma.cc/QRG2-QK2F)

Zimbardo, P (2011) What makes a hero? *Greater Good Magazine*, 18 January, greatergood.berkeley.edu/article/item/what_makes_a_hero (archived at https://perma.cc/X9BB-2Z4R)

PART SIX

Transforming theory into practice

Execution

30

Goal setting – be SMARTER!

PAUL SMITH

ABSTRACT

Goal setting plays a fundamental part in every coaching practice. If we do not set the right goals, we will not achieve our desired results. We must analyse and review the goals we set for ourselves as coaches and also how we work with clients to set theirs. This chapter explains just how to do that.

Shoot for the moon and even if you miss, you will land amongst the stars.

LES BROWN

Aim for blissful failure rather than constipated success.

SADHGURU

Introduction

Carlos had a dream. He wanted to set up his own restaurant chain that prepared his private recipes for home-made Peruvian food. When calculating what he needed, the total amount to fund the business was $600,000. Carlos was starting from zero with no savings and very little income from his day job. After exploring all the options to fund the business, Carlos decided after careful consideration that the best way to receive the funding was to win the local lottery. The total prize fund was just short of $1,000,000.

As part of his plan each week, Carlos would pray to God before watching the lottery numbers being announced. Weeks went by and Carlos had still not managed to win anything to fund his business.

A few months later, after feeling disappointed and depleted by the lack of progress, Carlos decided as part of his prayer to speak to God:

'God, each week I sit here and pray to you for help with funding my restaurant chain. I have promised that my food will serve the people and bring joy to many. I promise that I will put my heart and soul into preparing the food and to teach others my recipes. All I am asking is for you to help me win the lottery, just once. Why is it that you ignore me so?'

A few moments of silence passed, when suddenly Carlos got a surprising response from nowhere. He sat up excitedly as God responded to his question:

'Carlos, I have been with you all this time. I have wanted to help you with your business and to win the lottery. But my friend, you need to buy a ticket first.'

Many of us hold dreams and visions, but a dream without action is only a wish. To make our dreams reality, we must set actionable goals and work to smaller milestones. In this chapter we will explore goal setting, how to set SMART goals and discuss how we can make our goals SMARTER. We can then use the tools and exercises in this chapter both with our clients and for our own goals.

Starting with a tool – goal mind-mapping

Before diving into a description of what goals are all about, I would first like to walk you through an exercise (don't worry I'm not going to ask you to get up and do 10 star jumps). What I would like you to do is grab a pen and blank sheet of paper and begin to mind map all your current goals (try to capture 10). Spread the goals out on the sheet and circle them all. Now follow the next steps:

1 Reflecting on your goals, cross out the five least important.

2 Now review the remaining goals and when ready, put a cross through three of them.

3 With the two remaining goals, think carefully and then remove one of them.

4 Put all your focus and attention on the remaining goal.

You may find this exercise a little difficult but the first important point to consider is that if we are unable to make difficult decisions, and prioritize and review our need for our goals, we will very rarely achieve them.

ACTION

Grab a drink and work through the above exercise.

Goals, visions and wishful thinking

For us to understand goals, we must be able to distinguish them from both visions and wishful thinking. Goals are our milestones; the pit stops we take on our journey to living our desired vision. For example, you may have a dream to be a successful coach who travels the world making a difference, which forms your vision. Your goals on the road to achieving this vision could include gaining a certification or accreditation in coaching, establishing a business plan and model for your business, obtaining 20 clients and earning $2,000 a month. Each of these goals could help you reach your desired vision.

A vision, on the other hand, is the imagination of a future point or lifestyle, it is a creative view of how we wish to see ourselves and achievements unfold.

Working with visionary clients and helping clients set and reach goals are very different. Helping clients establish clarity in their vision involves a lot of visualization work, diving deep into their why and alignment with values and core beliefs. Working with goals includes an analysis of how attainable they are and what actions need to be taken to achieve them.

If we do not have a plan of action or we are not making any progress towards our goals, then we are just wishful thinking.

Goals are great milestones to help us achieve our overall vision. They give us a direction and help us track our progress. The most important point to note as a coach when working with clients is to never advise, introduce, or offer new goals. Our role is not to change the goal but to help our clients break the goal down into more achievable actions. We do this by challenging and checking how realistic and achievable the goal is for our client. For example, imagine you have a client whose primary goal is to run a marathon, but they have not trained for the past six months. They have set themselves a goal to run a marathon in two weeks. Their training plan is to run two hours every day until the event. Now, many of us will realize that this seems to be an unrealistic goal. Some of us may be tempted to tell the client that this does not look achievable and enter advice mode. However, our role is not to give advice but to challenge. In a scenario like this, we can ask the following types of questions:

1 How prepared will you be after you have implemented this plan?
2 Are there any other marathons available to run?
3 Do you see any risks with this plan?
4 Do you think this goal is achievable given the time frame?
5 Are there any alternatives available for you?

Using questions similar to the ones above, we can begin to pull out more information around how realistic the goal is for the client and how successful they believe they will be with the plan they have in place. If changes present themselves in the conversation, then we can work with the client to amend or draft a new plan of action. The aim here as a coach is to help our clients set SMART or, as I like to call them, 'SMARTER' goals, which we will explore in more detail below.

ACTION

Think of a current goal you have and ask yourself the five questions above.

Making your goals 'SMART'

SMART is a great model developed by George T Doran (1981) that is used in businesses to improve objectives and in coaching to improve clients' goals. SMART is an acronym for Specific, Measurable, Achievable, Realistic and Time-bound.

By setting goals, we provide ourselves with a target to aim for. A SMART goal is clearly defined and gives us clarity on our direction. Let us explore each of the stages below:

Specific

When a goal is 'specific', it is more attainable. When we make our goals specific, we consider the 'who, what, where, why and when'. When working with our clients to define a specific goal, we can ask the following questions:

1 Who is involved in this goal?

2 What do you want to accomplish?

3 Where can you achieve this goal?

4 Why do you want to achieve this goal?

5 When do you want to achieve this goal?

Example:

A general goal: 'I want to lose weight.'

A **specific** goal: 'I want to work out four days a week, two cardio and two strength training, at my local gym to feel healthier.'

Measurable

A SMART goal must have a measure. At this stage in the model, we can explore the criteria for measuring our client's progress. If the client has no criteria, they will not be able to acknowledge when they have attained the goal. To make a goal measurable, we can ask our clients:

1 What is an indicator of your progress?
2 How are you keeping track of your progress?
3 How many…?
4 How much…?
5 How will you know when you have reached your goal?

Example:

A general goal: 'I want to lose weight.'

A **measurable** goal: 'I want to lose 10kg.'

Building on from the 'specific' element:

'I want to work out four days a week, two cardio and two strength training, at my local gym to lose 10kg.'

Achievable

A SMART goal must be achievable. This will help us consider the journey to attaining the goal and allow us to explore alternative options. An achievable goal can be stretched (which we will discuss below) to set a challenge but still must be possible. To explore how achievable our client's goal is, we can ask questions like:

1 Do you have a clear path laid out to your goal?
2 Do you know the relevant milestones for your goal?
3 Do you have the necessary resources and skills to achieve the goal?
4 Are there any resources or skills you are missing?
5 How can you find these resources or build on these skills?

When we challenge how achievable the client's goal is, we understand the confidence our client has in attaining the goal and any obstacles that might get in the way. We can then work the conversation to reset the goal or add additional action points to obtain the necessary skills and resources.

Realistic

A SMART goal must be realistic. There must be a reasonable probability of achieving the goal with the given strategy resources, and time. Here we are looking at the client's belief and capability. We can explore this by asking questions like:

1 Is the goal realistic?

2 Is the goal within reach of your proposed time frame?

3 Do you feel like you have enough resources to achieve the goal?

4 How committed are you to achieving your goal?

5 How confident do you feel about the goal?

We can work with our clients here to strengthen their belief, confidence and commitment towards the goal. If we identify that any of these are low, we can work with them to amend the goal or strengthen their belief, confidence and commitment.

Time-bound

Finally, a SMART goal must have a specific time frame with a start and finish date. By working with our clients to set deadlines, we add urgency and priority to the goal, which makes it more likely to be attained. At this final stage of the model, we can ask questions similar to:

1 Does your goal have a deadline? If so, when?

2 When will you start taking action towards your goal?

3 When would you like to accomplish this goal by?

4 Are there any important dates or deadlines for this goal?

5 How urgent is this goal?

Using the example above we can simply make it time-bound by adding in a deadline date. This could look something like: 'I want to work out four days a week, two cardio and two strength training, at my local gym to feel healthier. I aim to lose 10 kg in three months and I will measure my weight on a frequent basis to track my progress.'

Being SMARTER with our goals

In my extensive use of the SMART model, I have found through experience that the model lacks two key ingredients: Exciting and Rewarding. I have therefore created an extension to a 'SMARTER' model that provides an addition to the framework.

Exciting

Considering the first five core parts of the SMART model, we will struggle to achieve our goal if there is no excitement. When we make a goal exciting, we are pulled to work towards it, and it becomes easier to achieve. We become inspired to attain it. So how do we make a goal exciting?

To make a goal exciting, it must contain a strong essence of the 'why' followed by an affirmation. There is power in the words we choose to capture our goals.

Example:

A general goal: 'I want to publish a book.'

An **exciting** goal: 'I want to publish a book that empowers people to take back control of their life. I want to hold my book in my hand and see it in bookstores. I want to read the positive reviews and to feel like an accomplished author.'

When working with clients to help define an exciting goal, we can ask the following questions:

1 What is really driving you to achieve this goal?
2 What will it feel like to achieve this goal?
3 Where is your inspiration coming from?
4 Are there any other accomplishments you will attain by achieving this goal?
5 What would it mean to you if you were to achieve this goal?

These questions will help tease out inspiration, positive emotions and other benefits for achievement.

Rewarding

Have you ever achieved a goal and held feelings of disappointment? After putting in all the hard work and achieving it, you still feel dissatisfied. This is generally due to a lack of consideration for the reward when we first set out to achieve our goal. For us to feel fulfilled after attaining our goal, we must ensure that it is rewarding. When working with clients we can ask questions like:

1 What difference will this goal make in your life?
2 What reward do you expect to receive?
3 How will you reward yourself on your journey?
4 What is the purpose behind this goal?
5 How does it tie in to your passion?

When we want to attain a goal, we must make it rewarding. If not, we will find ourselves giving up when we hit obstacles and setbacks, or feeling a void when achieving it.

Using the SMARTER model

We can use the SMARTER model whenever our clients are sharing their desired goal with us to help get clarity on what it is they want to achieve. Often the client's progress reflects our results as a coach, so working through the model can be key to us succeeding with the client. For example, if the client is contracted with us for coaching and the desired goal is unrealistic, if we fail to clearly define the goal and the client does not achieve it, we may find ourselves being blamed because of our coaching. Clients reach out to us for results; to succeed we must facilitate them. It is therefore important for us as coaches to add the SMARTER model to our toolkit and use it often.

Returning to Carlos

In this chapter we have explored goal setting, SMART goals and SMARTER goals. The tools explained in this chapter can be used for both our own goals and to work with clients.

Do you remember Carlos at the beginning of this chapter? The lesson we can take from his experience is to ensure that no matter how SMART or SMARTER our goals, we must take the necessary action to make our goals a reality. A goal without action is only a wish. And wishes will remain for those living in a land of fantasy. Take action and succeed!

Reference

Doran, G T (1981) There's a S.M.A.R.T. way to write management's goals and objectives, *Management Review*, 70 (11), 35–6

31

Sustaining and committing to action

VIJAYA GOWRISANKAR

ABSTRACT

Your client has a big dream, has created a vision board, a plan, and is all set to go. They start with enthusiasm, sometimes managing to meet their daily or weekly goal. Yet, they fail to meet their quarterly or half-yearly goals. The biggest challenge seems to be sustaining and committing to action over time. Where are they falling short? And how can we overcome such a sticking point?

Introduction

Supporting our client in 'taking action' is a key part of any coaching practice. As coaches, we hold space for the client. At the end of the session, the client comes up with an action plan. We offer to check-in at predefined intervals. In the next session, the client shares that they have not been able to take sustained action. The failure to take action plays on their mind. They have not been able to meet their goals in the defined time frame.

How then, as coaches, can we help our clients, through our coaching practice, to find their mantra of sustaining and committing to action?

The first step could be about **gaining self-awareness**. What question can we ask our clients to help them identify the reasons for not being able to take action?

1 What happened to derail you from your action plan? The reasons could be intrinsic, like loss of motivation, procrastination, fear, or extrinsic, like urgent work needing their attention.

2 What did you do that day instead of your planned action?

The second step could be to help the client **identify the impact** of their not taking action for a day, or other specified duration or time frame:

1 What is the impact of derailing from the plan?

2 If the client must meet the deadline, but is delayed or prevented from doing so, we can ask them 'What do you need to do to meet the deadline?'

The third step could be to ask the client, 'How can you get back on track to take sustained action?' This can help them to identify how to recover and reprioritize:

1 What can you do to meet your action plan?

2 How can you meet your action plan?

3 How can you resume your action plan?

The fourth step could be in terms of **tracking or having an accountability partner** or a support system/team that can help the client commit to and take sustained action.

This helps the client identify what is blocking them from taking action. Is it about commitment or is it about sustaining the action over time? It helps them to find the steps to move forward. Any obstacle or constraint that the client faces today can reoccur when the circumstances fall together. The coach can help the client identify these patterns and what it will take to reach their goals.

Coaching is a collaborative interaction. It is about inviting the client to act and gaining their commitment. As a coach, we invite the client to be self-aware and commit to action. There is no pressure or obligation for them to accept the invitation. It is their choice. By encouraging the clients to make commitments, we, as a coach, help them to create new patterns and behaviours that help them to achieve their desired goals.

Theory and literature review

Sustaining and committing to action can be challenging. Developing implementation intentions help to translate goal intentions into actions (Gollwitzer, 1999). They are 'if-then' plans that link situations with responses to attain goals or desired outcomes. 'If situation B is encountered, I will initiate behaviour C in order to reach goal A.' Goal intentions are instructions that people give themselves to perform particular behaviours to achieve desired outcomes. As such, goal intentions specify what the person will do when certain conditions exist. In other words, implementation intentions emphasize when, where and how the person will take action. They help people to manage the following areas: failing to get started, getting derailed, becoming rigid and overextending oneself. To form an implementation intention, the person must a) identify a response that will promote goal attainment and b) anticipate a suitable occasion to initiate that response (Gollwitzer and Sheeran, 2006). The success of implementation intentions depends on the following: self-regulation and strength of the goal intention. Forming implementation intentions should activate the mental representation of the specified cues (if component) and automate responding to these cues (as specified in the then component).

Self-determination theory delves into 'why' of behaviour (Ryan and Deci, 2000). It covers intrinsic and extrinsic motivation. It highlights three factors that enhance self-motivation, social functioning and well-being – competence, autonomy and relatedness. Motivation concerns energy, direction, persistence and equifinality – all aspects of activation and intention. Social environments can facilitate or forestall intrinsic motivation. People are intrinsically motivated for activities that hold inherent interest for them personally. Therefore, doing an activity to gain intrinsic satisfaction is initiated and sustained by intrinsic motivation, for example, learning a language because you like learning new dialects.

Extrinsic motivation is doing an activity to get a separable outcome. When you are extrinsically motivated, you do something to gain an external award that has instrumental value rather than for some intrinsic motivation, for example, a student studying for a test to make a qualifying grade for the football team. Extrinsic motivation can be divided into four types, namely external regulation, introjected regulation, identified regulation and integrated regulation.

- **External regulation** is about the need to comply with external rewards or punishments.
- **Introjected regulation** is about self-control and involves the ego as rewards or punishments are internalized.
- **Identified regulation** is about personal importance and what one consciously values.
- **Integrated regulation** is about congruence, awareness and synthesis with self. People tend to follow through on their goals to take action if they are aligned to their values and enhance their well-being.

The theory shows that the bridge between motivation and process of achievement is committed action. In other words, when an individual consistently demonstrates specific behaviours needed to result in optimal performance, they exhibit committed action (Gardner and Moore, 2007). This means that committed action is closely interlinked to values. Values-driven behaviour or committed action is easy when situation and action align to one's values. It is important for a client to become aware of and identify the barriers to value-driven behaviour, for example, fatigue, fear, overwhelm, time constraints, anxiety, weather conditions, and more. Writing down one's values, goals and specific behaviours associated with commitment can help track performance. The Mindfulness-Acceptance-Commitment (MAC)-based approach is useful to regulate emotions and increase athletic performance. This and other studies have shown that values-aligned behaviour and mindfulness support each other to enhance performance and well-being (Gardner and Moore, 2007).

Similarly, monitoring goal progress can help in goal attainment, which can be performed in six dimensions (Harkin et al, 2016). The first dimension is whether we are monitoring behaviour or monitoring outcome. The second dimension is whether the progress monitoring is public or private. The third dimension involves self-recording where information obtained from monitoring is physically recorded, or recording by a third party. The fourth dimension is about the reference value taken – a) a past reference point, b) a desired (future) target, or c) comparison with others. The fifth dimension is about monitoring the rate of progress towards a goal versus distance from the goal. The sixth and final dimension is about active monitoring versus passive monitoring. In active monitoring, the person makes deliberate efforts to attend to goal-related behaviour, and/or seeks out information about goal-related outcomes, for example, actively monitoring learning to complete a course. In passive monitoring, the person obtains the information about progress without making deliberate efforts to seek it, for example, friends commenting that a person is looking slim, or realizing that clothes feel looser than before. The review by Harkin et al (2016) observed that progress monitoring has an important role in shaping goal attainment.

The self-motives framework by Sedikides and Strube (1997) proposes interactions among four different motives – self-assessment, self-improvement, self-enhancement and self-verification. Accountability partners, accountability groups and success partners are some techniques to help in progress monitoring beyond self-recording.

CASE STUDY
Application

Ana, my client, was a successful leader in her workplace. She was holding a position of responsibility and spent 12 to 14 hours daily at work. She had been promoted two levels in the last five years. In my first coaching session with Ana, she was upset with herself for not meeting her monthly and quarterly goals. The next few sessions had the same pattern, where she had a long list of goals. She was making progress towards a few. A few were untouched.

Ana was well read. She had set her professional goals by using the SMART model, making sure that every goal was specific, measurable, attainable, relevant and time-bound. Her calendar was packed with meetings, with no room for anything else. Her work often spilled over into the weekends, consuming some portion of her weekend. The rest of her weekends were packed with engagements and commitments to her family.

In the sessions, Ana wanted to discuss her goals, more specifically why she was failing to make the progress she wanted. We used different models to streamline her work calendar like scheduling, clearing up space in the calendar, etc.

Being well read, Ana suggested that she wanted to try the GROWTH model of coaching (Acha, 2018) to help her dig deeper into her current goals:

G – Goal

R – Reality

O – Options/Obstacles

W – Way forward/Will

T – Team capabilities (who from the team or support system can help)

H – How to manage

Lack of time was one area she wanted to explore. We used the Do, Defer (Delay), Delegate and Delete (Drop) model for her to manage her time and tasks better.

She was neglecting her health and art. She loved to paint. She found pockets of time during the day and used implementation intentions to bring in changes to her eating habits and find time for painting. Some of her implementation intentions were:

If I get 15 minutes between meetings, I will go and drink a glass of water.

If I feel hungry at 11 am, I will have an apple instead of cookies.

If I do not have meetings at 8 pm on Monday, I will use the 30 minutes to paint a picture.

In a few coaching sessions, we explored deeper into her motivation for each goal. She was reluctant to drop or defer any goal. She had set high expectations for herself with no time to recharge and relax. By exploring the intrinsic and extrinsic motivation for each goal, she was able to identify *why* each goal mattered to her. Why was she holding on to the goal? For a few goals, her motivation was external regulation. She was just pursuing them to meet professional and family expectations. For a few goals, the motivation was introjected regulation, where she was punishing herself for not meeting the goals. These were goals where she wanted to prove that she was worthy. She was letting her past experiences and failures rule her. The goals related to her art and serving others were motivated by identified regulation. It gave her a sense of fulfilment and satisfaction.

As Ana had an interest in reading, she explored deeper into the self-determination theory between the coaching sessions and understood the concepts better. She created a detailed document for each goal assessing her motivation for the goals. In the subsequent coaching sessions, Ana was less upset with herself. She was more at peace. She shared that she had dropped a few goals that were seeking external validation or were driven by a sense to prove her worthiness to herself.

Ana shared that she was struggling to meet even her reduced set of goals. She showed her weekly timesheets for the past two weeks. We delved deeper to understand the barriers towards a few goals. Even though she had time, she was procrastinating and not attempting to take action towards the goals. We did an exercise to identify the values that mattered to her.

Ana wanted to do a detailed analysis for the goals that she was failing to start. She came up with these parameters in our coaching session that she wanted to explore for these goals:

- SMART description of the goal

- Desired outcome

- Values driving the goal

- Barriers to action

- Impact of not achieving the goal

- Emotions attached to the goal

- Tasks to be performed to meet the goal

TABLE 31.1 Values

Values	Value-aligned SMART goals	Emotions associated with the goal	Resistance to the goal	Committed action

We began with this table (Table 31.1). Ana added additional parameters to the goal.

This exercise helped her to be more self-aware and get started on the goal, instead of procrastinating and giving excuses to herself. She used the Mindfulness-Acceptance-Commitment-based approach to understand her emotions and resistance.

Once Ana started on her goals, monitoring the progress became a key next step. She was pursuing a lot of goals in parallel. Ana was not comfortable in having an accountability partner or group. She did not want to share her goals or progress with anyone. She created an Excel sheet to track her progress towards her goals. For a few goals like her eating habits, she chose to monitor her behaviour rather than the outcome of losing weight and having more energy. For her creative pursuits of her art, she chose to track it against past performance: how many art pieces she had created in the past quarter. She chose to actively monitor most of her goals. After three months of monitoring her progress, Ana shared the results and observations with me in our coaching session. After the session, she told me that it was one of the most impactful sessions for her. In that session, she was able to prioritize her goals by looking at the data for the past three months. She accepted that she could not meet all the goals she had set for herself. It was okay to see slow progress for a few goals. She was happy to spend time doing an activity like painting instead of setting it as a goal with strict deadlines and beating herself up over it.

Ana wanted to discuss her mindset shift towards goals in the next two coaching sessions. She opened up about how her outlook towards herself and her goals had evolved through the coaching sessions with the help of these tools. She shared that she had spent a lot of her travel time listening to the different techniques, reading about mindset and behaviour patterns, and understanding herself. All this had a cascading effect. She was less frustrated, had reduced anger bouts, and she was more accepting of herself. She was spending time journalling about what she achieved each day and what she was grateful for instead of focusing on what she had not achieved and all her failure points. She was in a better place emotionally now. She was a happier person. Her family members and colleagues were seeing the visible difference and asked her about it. She felt a lot lighter and relaxed now. She shared that the coaching sessions had really helped her understand herself better, though she was first sceptical about coaching when we had started the sessions.

Practical recommendations

Sustaining and committing to action is related to progress. It has many aspects, including goal setting, *why* the goal is important, deadlines, plan of action, progress monitoring, reprioritization, fallback plan, support system, behavioural patterns, emotional attachment and investment to the goal. Sustaining and committing to action can impact one's self-confidence, self-esteem and self-talk. It may leave a lasting impression on the person.

Goal setting and taking action requires clarity. The client must know where they want to go, how to get there, who can provide support to get there, and the belief that they can get there.

A visual way to represent these ideas to help your clients is shown in Table 31.2.

Accordingly, as a coach, we use these processes to invite the client to act and gain their commitment. We can offer to check-in and be their accountability partner. If the client fails to act or is not willing to take action, we can invite them to share what is holding them back. We can invite them to identify the goal hijackers. At times, the past may be preventing the client from moving forward. We can ask forward-looking questions like 'What would you like in your life right now?'

A client may be focusing only on failures, shortcomings and weaknesses. We can invite the client to focus on their strengths and take action based on their strengths. Delve deeper and ask the client what has worked for them in the past. Help them identify their past successes and what helped them achieve the same.

A client may show rigidity in terms of their deadlines. Asking them about alternatives in terms of dates, alternative course of action, whom they can ask for help, risks, risk mitigation plans, etc, can help them sustain and commit to action.

A client may be failing to take action or make progress due to past patterns, behaviours, or habits. Tools like visualization and affirmations can help the client to keep their focus on goals. It can take time to break patterns and build habits, and this may lead to the client failing to take action.

TABLE 31.2 Sustaining and committing to action steps

Process step	Types	Objective	Questions	Outcome
Implementation intentions	If situation B is encountered, I will initiate behaviour C in order to reach goal A	Helps to automate the chosen goal-directed behaviour	What is your goal? What behaviours can help you reach your goal? What is stopping you from reaching your goal? How can you use implementation intention to automate your behaviour?	Identified cues Formed habits Reached goals
Motivation and values alignment	Intrinsic	Helps to commit to and sustain action in absence of external requirements (e.g., job requirement) or in the face of adversity	What are your interests? If you had no constraints, what would you choose to do? If you had no constraints, what would you choose to pursue? What are your top three values? What conditions help to elicit your interests? What conditions help to sustain your interests?	Improved well-being
	Extrinsic	Helps to align to personal expectations Helps to align to professional expectations Motivates you to take action when the outcome is clear	What goal do you need to achieve? By when do you need to achieve it? What are the obstacles to achieving it? What motivates you to pursue this goal? How will your life change once you've achieved this goal?	Aligned to personal expectations Aligned to professional expectations

| Monitoring progress | Self-recorded | Helps to monitor and record behaviour
Helps to monitor and record progress
Helps to monitor and record outcome | How will you track your behaviour?
How will you track your progress?
How will you reflect on your progress?
What actions will you take based on your reflections on your progress? | Identified patterns
Identified rate of progress against plan
Identified actions to take to reach the desired outcome |
| | Accountability partner | Check-in to see progress
Prods a person towards action
Holds the person accountable to take action | Who can help to keep you accountable towards your action?
How can they help keep you accountable towards your action? | Scheduled check-ins leading to action/progress towards outcome |

Making regular (daily, weekly or monthly) progress is the key to success. Encouraging the client to break the barriers that stop them from getting started and taking regular action is important. Momentum enhances motivation and motivation keeps the momentum alive. Progress is a learning curve. Help the client choose their pace.

Sustaining and committing to action is a mindset game. What emotions and feelings do the goals evoke in the client? What do they need to keep the momentum going?

As important as it is for a client to reflect on and after the sessions, so it is for the coach. Reflecting on how the session went, understanding your client better, upskilling yourself to broaden your skills, knowledge and competency is important to serve your client better.

References

Acha, K (2018) The GROWTH model of coaching, KennethMD, 2 August, www.kennethmd.com/the-growth-model-of-coaching/ (archived at https://perma.cc/M6V3-ZLYN)

Gardner, F and Moore, Z E (2007) *The Psychology of Enhancing Human Performance: The mindfulness-acceptance-commitment (MAC) approach*, Springer, New York

Gollwitzer, P M (1999) Implementation intentions: Strong effects of simple plans, *American Psychologist*, 54 (7), 493–503, doi.org/10.1037/0003-066X.54.7.493 (archived at https://perma.cc/YW89-VT8S)

Gollwitzer, P M and Sheeran, P (2006) Implementation intentions and goal achievement: A meta-analysis of effects and processes, *Advances in Experimental Social Psychology*, 38 (6), 69–119, doi.org/10.1016/S0065-2601(06)38002-1 (archived at https://perma.cc/6V2W-4DFL)

Harkin, B, Webb, T L, Chang, B P I, Prestwich, A, Conner, M, Kellar, I, Benn, Y and Sheeran, P (2016) Does monitoring goal progress promote goal attainment? A meta-analysis of the experimental evidence, *Psychological Bulletin*, 142 (2), 198–229

Ryan, R M and Deci, E L (2000) Self-determination theory and the facilitation of intrinsic motivation, social development, and well-being, *American Psychologist*, 55 (1), 68–78

Sedikides, C and Strube, M J (1997) Self-evaluation: To thine own self be good, to thine own self be sure, to thine own self be true, and to thine own self be better, *Advances in Experimental Social Psychology*, 29, 209–69, doi.org/10.1016/S0065-2601(08)60018-0 (archived at https://perma.cc/NEM7-BWEV)

32

The discovery call

DONNA BURFIELD

ABSTRACT

The discovery call is typically the first direct opportunity coaches have to sell their service, start building rapport with a prospective client, gauge the alignment between coach and client, and explore the client readiness to benefit from the coach's approach. Thus, rather than treating the discovery call as a sample coaching session, it is all about assessing the fit between the coach and prospective client. Using a structured approach and template to guide the conversation helps achieve optimal outcomes for both parties.

Introduction

A discovery call is highly recommended for anyone who is embarking on collaborating on a business venture or, as in our case, partnering with a potential client.

For this chapter, I refer to these sessions as discovery calls, but they are also called clarity sessions, chemistry calls, sample sessions, strategy calls and breakthrough sessions, among others.

These sessions give you the opportunity to explain about your services and area of expertise, and how this will be beneficial to the potential client, appraise if they are ready for coaching, assess what their obstacles are, explore what they have tried in the past, and enquire as to why it is important for them to change their current situation now. In this chapter we are breaking down the moving parts of a discovery call:

- What a discovery call is and is not and the benefits of providing this service
- Pre-discovery call set-up
- What a discovery call looks like
- Talking logistics and closing a discovery call

What a discovery call is (and is not) and the benefits of providing this service

Depending on how many clients you have, most coaches offer this service for free or at a minimal fee. Sessions offered range from 30–60 minutes and are usually conducted online. This is where the beautiful dance of sharing information begins, such as why they have reached out to you now, why you are qualified to support them, and how your tools and strategies can help them obtain the results that are unique to their personal needs and circumstances.

Despite one's intentions for offering a discovery call, this is fundamentally where the journey and relationship is established between the coach and the client. It is the foundation on which trust, rapport, safety and empowerment are built.

Some coaches have the opinion that this is purely a sales opportunity and spend much of the time talking about themselves and upselling their services. They promise to deliver results that they cannot morally or ethically guarantee and will happily share testimonials to prove that their strategies work! This is where one's ego needs to be kept in check. This is about what is best for the client, not you.

It is important for coaches to remind themselves that every client and coaching session is unique. You will find many who will show up with a predisposed belief system that they have been carrying around with them for many years. As a result, they may not know where to start to effect change. It is our job, as their coach, to cultivate an environment in which they can be honest and vulnerable without judgement, and creative and daring so they have the courage to explore different possibilities and opportunities in all aspects of their lives. This can be achieved in several ways:

1 Adopting an inviting tone, pace and volume when speaking.

2 Actively listening to what they are saying and responding accordingly.

3 Asking thought-provoking and reflective questions that are specific to them and not merely reading off the '10 most powerful questions to ask in a coaching session'.

4 Managing your body language – does it convey warmth, trust, confidence and curiosity?

5 Setting up your environment (whether this is in person or online) – is it clean, calming and inviting?

With care and attention to co-regulating and adapting the atmosphere and environment to suit your client, a coach has the best opportunity to build trust and determine the prospects of working with this client.

Reflection exercise

Before starting a discovery call, ask yourself the following questions:

- Why am I offering this?
- What am I hoping to convey?
- What do I want the prospective client to walk away with?
- How do I want the prospective client to feel after our conversation?
- If we are not a match, what am I taking away from this conversation?
- Is this call about me or the needs and desires of the client?

A discovery call is an invitation for someone to experience the power of coaching, an opportunity for them to distinguish the differences between coaching, mentoring, therapy and consulting, how it will look for them to work with you, and sample your coaching style and techniques. Most importantly, you will be able to reassure them on confidentiality, the code of ethics and duty of care that you are obligated to uphold. For example:

- How you store their information
- The circumstances in which you would be breaking confidentiality
- The ethical and moral boundaries of the client/coach relationship
- Why a coaching agreement is drawn up and needs to be agreed by both parties before commencing
- Also, the circumstances to address when/if your client should seek support from qualified medical providers for issues such as depression, self-harm, addiction to substances, suicidal thoughts, health conditions and mental/emotional/physical abuse

Remember that the main benefit of offering a discovery call is to ascertain what their needs are, including the suitability of coaching versus therapy, and if this is a partnership that you are both willing and wanting to invest in.

Pre-discovery call set-up

Regardless of how you attract people to your discovery call session – social media, website, networking events, speaking engagements or word of mouth – it is important to spend some time on what procedures and processes you want to have in place before the initial call.

When it comes to booking a discovery call, some coaches share their email addresses and WhatsApp numbers and are happy to be contacted via these platforms, but the majority of coaches direct their audience to a calendar link that has specific days and times set aside for these sessions.

One way to filter out those who aren't in your preferred demographic is to write up a mini-questionnaire that they need to fill in when signing up. Time is a valuable commodity and you are providing a professional service, and this enables you to hone in on those who are seeking to change and move forward aligned with your coaching approach and level of expertise. This is a personal preference and not all coaches do this. I, however, do. I find it is a productive and insightful way to gather relevant and specific data before the call and it helps the prospective client to focus on why they are signing up in the first place, what struggles or obstacles they are currently facing, what would be their ideal situation and which strategies/tools they have previously tried. These questions promote reflection, awareness, curiosity and possibilities.

TABLE 32.1 Example questionnaire

Sample intake questionnaire
To prepare for our session, please take your time to reflect on the following questions and answer as honestly as possible. These questions are intended to begin the process of enquiry, reflection, learning and 'taking action' with purpose. If you do NOT feel comfortable answering any of the questions, then please feel free to leave them blank.

1. Where did you hear about me? Facebook, LinkedIn, Instagram, my website, groups, friends?
2. Have you had coaching before?
3. On a scale of 1–10, how happy are you with your life right now?
4. What makes you truly happy?
5. What is the greatest challenge you are facing right now?
6. What do you want to achieve within the next three months?
7. What makes this so important for you?
8. What are the most common obstacles that get in your way?
9. If anything was possible, what would you wish for?
10. What have been your three greatest successes to date?
11. What else would you like to tell me about yourself?

Helpful tip: In preparation for our discovery call please make sure you have as little disruption as possible (e.g., children/partner asking for your attention, pets needing let out, TV on in the background!). You will get so much more out of our time together if you are in an environment where you feel comfortable and calm.

When you read the sample intake questionnaire in Table 32.1, what came up for you? Did it promote a deeper enquiry as to why you are booking a discovery call? Did it give you an indication as to the style of questions that may be asked during the call? Did it champion forward-thinking and solution-focus possibilities? Did it bring up some of your core values without directly asking what they are? Did it bring to light some of the 'pain and pleasure' areas currently in your life? While you may have answered 'no' to some of these questions, as a coach your answers would have provided me with valuable information and how I can best serve you.

What a discovery call looks like

I genuinely enjoy discovery calls – now! At the beginning of my coaching career, I was a bag of nerves and either forgot to relay important information or the whole session turned into a casual conversation with no real purpose or direction. Do not be hard on yourself. It takes practice and then more practice to find your voice and your style. Some coaches find it beneficial to have a grounding ritual or mantra before they start a call, where they declare their purpose and intentions, open up their minds to being fully present and invite curiosity.

To help you on your way, I have included the script that I use for my discovery calls and a cheat sheet I print off to ensure I relay all the important processes and procedures, and document what was shared by the prospective client during the call.

Welcome and introductions – pleasantries, where are you calling from? Then I explain the format of the call – I like to explain the structure and process of a discovery call to give maximum impact and value.

Example: 'So, what can you expect from this call? Well, I like to break a discovery call into three parts. For the first 20 minutes or so, we are going to have an actual coaching conversation so you can experience how powerful it can be, understand the coaching process and how it will be to work with me. For the next 20 minutes I will then share with you what coaching is and is not, what you can expect from me as your coach and what a client is responsible for. I will also answer any questions you may have regarding the logistics, such as fees, confidentiality, my credentials and so forth. Once I have answered all your questions, we will discuss the next steps and if we think we would be a good match, I will ask you if you would like to hire me as your coach for which you are under no obligation. How does that sound to you?'

Mini coaching session – should you, or shouldn't you?

Again, this is a personal preference, and you have to decide what feels right for you. While a discovery call is essentially a sales call, it is also a call where you are promoting an abstract service and the only way a potential client can experience your service is by you giving them a sample session. Let's put it this way. If you are looking to buy a house you would want to view it first and check out the neighbourhood, find out where the nearest schools are and what the commute would be like for you getting to work. If you are looking for a new car the principles are the same. You ask the dealer about the mileage, any previous accidents, insurance claims, and then you would ask to take it for a test drive. For both of these examples, and I am sure you can think of many more, you are investing a lot of time and money, and both will have an effect on your life.

So, why is coaching any different? The benefits and services coaching offers can have a tremendously powerful impact on one's life; however, it requires the client to invest their hard-earned cash and time. So, morally, shouldn't we be providing a sample session before we ask the prospective client to partner with us? Some coaches have the gift of the gab and are fantastic at marketing themselves, but their coaching skills aren't strong, and they mentor or give advice. The client has the right to make an informed decision as to whether you are the right coach for them, and without experiencing your 'coaching' how can they?

Sample coaching session

During a discovery call coaching session, I like to use either the GAP or GROW model.

Example using the GAP model

The GAP model is designed to move clients from where they are to where they want to be by 1) Gathering information, 2) Acknowledging their experiences, thoughts, beliefs and perspectives, and 3) Producing structures to support change (Donlin, 2018).

- In what way is your current situation working for you?
- What are you doing well?
- What do you need to change to create a better outcome?
- What do you need to include/do to change this situation?
- What is in your current situation that may be keeping you from the change you want to make?
- What do you ultimately need to change to reach your desired goal/outcome?

Example using the GROW model

Historians claim that John Whitmore first coined the acronym GROW in his 1992 book *Coaching for Performance*. The concept presents a simple structure for goal setting and problem solving to achieve a desired outcome:

1 Goal – what do you want?

2 Reality – where are you now/what is your current situation?

3 Obstacles/Options – what is getting in the way/what are your options?

4 Will/Way forward – what will you do next/what can you do today to ensure that you are moving towards your desired goal/outcome?

Discovery call cheat sheet

A good discovery call cheat sheet (Table 32.2) is useful to organize the flow of the session and ensure that no aspect is overlooked or skimped on.

TABLE 32.2 Discovery call cheat sheet

Discovery call cheat sheet	
Date	
Name	
Email	
What coaching is	Facilitates the creation/development of personal, professional or business goals, and to develop and carry out a plan for achieving those goals
	A non-judgemental and supportive environment, which in turn stimulates the client to reflect, enquire, acknowledge, apply SMART goals and 'take action' where applicable in your life
	Confidentiality – all information about the coach/client relationship will remain strictly confidential, except in very rare circumstances whereby decreed by law. Exceptions to confidentiality relate to circumstances such as intent to seriously harm someone, child abuse, thoughts of suicide, etc. All remaining information will be kept confidential
What coaching isn't	Advice, counselling or therapy
My credentials	I am fully licensed to work as a life coach and hold XXX certification, as well as XXX accreditation. Additionally, I have been police checked, hold a current safeguarding certificate and a mental health first aid certificate

(continued)

TABLE 32.2 (Continued)

Discovery call cheat sheet	
Role of the coach	My role is to ask thought-provoking questions and create an environment that inspires you to maximize your personal and/or professional potential
	I will hold up that mirror and guide you to where you want to go. With that being said, I am not in the driving seat – YOU are.
Role of the client	Punctual to all sessions
	Takes responsibility for all decisions/actions
	Setting the agenda and topic
	Identifying your goals
	Implement the action steps agreed during the coaching session
	Complete any additional tasks that have been agreed upon
Available days/times (Make sure these are connected to your calendar for them to book directly)	Monday: 9:00, 11:00, 1:00, 3:00
	Wednesday: 10:00, 12:00, 2:00, 4:00
	Thursday: 1:00, 3:00, 5:00, 7:00
Options & fees	Four sessions a month with a three-month commitment is $XXXX
	Two sessions a month with a three-month commitment is $XXXX
	Payment link – xxxxxxxxxxxxxxx (if not linked to calendar booking)
Cancellation & refunds	24 or 48 hours' prior notice, full refund or transfer
Send out information for	Newsletter
	Facebook group
	Blog
Notes	

The importance of conveying coach credentials

Sharing personal information as a coach can be a controversial subject. But, as of now, coaching is not a regulated service industry. Every Tom, Dick and Harry are calling themselves a 'coach', often with zero training, mental health awareness, or the understanding of the ramifications to providing this service. Many coaches, especially those who are certified and accredited, believe that it is our moral and ethical duty to inform our clients and the public of our credentials and that we can practice a viable coaching business by law. Although some coaches may feel that most clients will not care less about this, nor will they even know what it means, does this make sense not to disclose qualifications or the lack thereof? However, having and informing our clients of our qualifications and documentations validate and authenticate us as professional coaches! Does this not highlight that a coach is prepared to invest in their chosen profession and be accountable for upholding the moral, ethical and legal requirements that our clients rightly deserve? By disclosing this information, we are empowering our clients to ask these questions when reaching out to other coaches or wellness providers, to benefit and safeguard all clients, coaches and the coaching industry.

Coaching falls under the umbrella of 'mental well-being/health'. During a coaching session, we ask our clients to dig deep on where their limiting beliefs lie, what their biggest challenges/obstacles are, who they need to forgive so they can move forward. They reveal things to us that they may not have spoken about in years or to another living soul. Their financial situation. Their medical history. Unconsciously they share their deepest fears and feelings of shame. This is extremely private information, and it is imperative that the client understands that there are systems in place and authorities they can contact if they feel their private information is being shared, if they are feeling unsafe or exploited.

Many coaches start their careers working with adults and then transition into working with their clients' children, collaborating with schools, after-school clubs, etc. I think you can guess where I am going with this. Isn't it our duty to educate parents and schools to ask for our credentials, whether we have first aid and safeguarding training and have been police checked, when it comes to not only working on the mindset of children but also being in the company of children?

You may never be asked what qualifications you have but that doesn't mean we can't help people to start asking the right questions.

Talking logistics and closing a discovery call

At the beginning of my discovery call conversation, I give prospective clients the heads-up that we will be covering my coaching services, fees and so forth. After completing the 20-minute coaching session, I ask them for the one most impactful 'takeaway' that they will be going away with. Then, I reiterate the steps of the call, 'At the beginning of this call I mentioned that you will be experiencing a coaching conversation, which we have just completed. I will now share with you what coaching is and is not and then I will answer any questions you may have regarding the logistics such as, fees, confidentiality, my credentials and so forth. How does that sound?'

When discussing your fees, be comfortable and confident in your pricing and delivery. I have my fees printed out so they can see me reading them out and not pulling numbers out of my hat, which increases confidence and trust! I am also very clear on the payment gateways they can use and if I accept instalments or not.

Now comes the part where many coaches feel uncomfortable. Wrapping up the discovery call.

I must make a confession here! I do not go in for the hard sale. I have set personal boundaries as to who I will and won't work with, my intentions for working with a client and if their requirements are in the realm of my level of expertise. If by the end of the discovery call, I feel that we would not be a good match due to psychological reasons I would say something along the lines of, 'Coaching is very much about assessing where you are today and moving you towards your desired goal/outcome. Right now, I feel that it would be more beneficial for you if we were to pick this up once you have got a better handle on... (addiction, depression) and if you are open to it, I am more than happy to recommend... (addiction/grief/sexual abuse/family) counsellor.' OR, if I think they would benefit from seeing another coach who has more experience in a particular field then I would be honest and transparent about this and offer them three recommendations that they can enquire about independently.

If I think we are a good fit I will simply say, 'We are nearing the end of our call and I am going to ask you if you would like to hire me as your coach?'

There are only three responses to this question, yes, no or maybe. Here are some examples of how you can respond to those answers:

- **Yes** – 'Great, I am very excited to be working with you. Why don't we look at our calendars now and book in our first session? I will then email you the onboarding welcome pack, which will include a coaching agreement. This agreement needs to be signed and returned to me 48 hours before our first session.'

- **No** (this is usually due to not being able to afford it right now) – 'That's fine, I get it, the timing is not right for you now. This is a big investment and requires commitment. When you are ready, I am here, so please, feel free to reach out at any time. In the meantime, if you would like to be notified of any workshops or webinars coming up then you can subscribe to my newsletter or follow me on LinkedIn/Facebook/Instagram.'

- **Maybe** (this is usually followed by 'I need to talk to my partner first', 'I need to sort out someone to watch the kids') – 'I understand. You need to do what you feel is best so you can come to these sessions focused and ready for action! In the meantime, if would you like to be notified of any workshops or webinars coming up then you can subscribe to my newsletter or follow me on LinkedIn/Facebook/Instagram, and feel free to share this information with your friends.'

Final words

Always remember that discovery calls take practice. The more you do, the more fluid and natural you will become. These sessions are all about connection, so have fun doing them. Whether the client signs up or not, know that for those 60 minutes you have given them the gift of being seen and heard. That's the powerful gift you can bestow, especially in today's world!

References

Donlin, A M (2018) Coaching model: Bridging the GAP, International Coach Academy, 6 October, coachcampus.com/coach-portfolios/coaching-models/ann-marie-donlin-bridging-the-gap/ (archived at https://perma.cc/CJ42-X3E3)

Whitmore, J (1992) *Coaching for Performance: The principles and practice of coaching and leadership*, Nicholas Brealey, London

33

Coaching ethics – don't be a plastic coach!

PAUL SMITH

ABSTRACT

As a consistent compass, ethics is more important in our everyday lives than rules or even values. Honouring ethics in practice is the bedrock of a responsible and sustainable coaching business. Industry membership, certification, accreditation and continuous professional development protects coaches and clients and ensures the highest standard of service and care.

Introduction

George, a coach and motivational speaker, was held in high regard by his driver who listened in awe at every event his boss presented. He was astonished by the way in which the coach answered questions about ethics so easily.

One day, feeling adventurous, the driver asked his boss if they could switch roles for a day. After a moment of thought, the coach agreed and hopped in the front seat. When they arrived at the venue, the driver handled himself remarkably well, delivering some great motivational content.

Towards the end of the talk, a gentleman at the back asked: 'Is the epistemological view of the universe still valid in an existentialist world?'

'That my friend is an easy one. In fact, it is that simple even my driver could answer the question. George, I'm going to hand this one over to you.'

Integrity sits at the heart of ethics. If we do not operate our coaching practice with honesty and strong moral principles, we run the risk of doing more harm than good in our service. In this chapter we will explore ethics in coaching, self-regulated organizations and how we can create an ethical coaching practice, with actions to take at the end of each subsection. Sound good? Let's get started.

How would you make ethics an interesting topic?

With such a dry subject and a possible temptation to skip this chapter, I would like you to first reflect on how you might write your own chapter on coaching ethics. How would you grip the reader's attention? Take a few minutes to reflect on your knowledge of ethics and brainstorm how you would approach this.

Using this as a benchmark, grab yourself a beverage and let us see if I meet can your expectations.

ACTION

Grab a drink, put your feet up and make your way through this thrilling chapter.

The obvious question – what are ethics?

So, what do we mean when we use the term ethics? What is the difference between ethics and morals? Are ethics legally enforceable?

When we talk about ethics in coaching, we refer to a set of terms or guidelines (collectively a code) that stipulates what we should and should not do as a coach. They are not legally enforceable and act only as an agreement between you (as a member of a coaching organization) and the organization itself. Concisely:

> Here are a set of guidelines you must follow, in exchange we give you this accreditation and allow you to publish it; if you breach these terms, we will take that accreditation away from you.

You can find an ethics code in most, if not all professions. However, where the profession is regulated, such as psychotherapy and counselling, the regulating body has the power by law to issue fines and penalties for non-compliance. As a non-regulated profession, there is no such power granted to any organization in coaching.

Furthermore, it is important to establish that ethics are also not morals. Morals are a set of values and beliefs we have developed within ourselves to define what we see as 'right or wrong', which acts as our compass to navigate through life (our moral compass). As such, something that may be defined as ethical by an organization may be seen as immoral to you. For example, you may find that it is not morally wrong to give people advice; however, ethically, in coaching we should not give people advice.

Where the lines blur and it can get confusing for some, is when morals, ethics and law cross over. While they are three completely different terms, they do intertwine.

You can have an ethical code that incorporates certain law. For example, an ethical code could bring in a guideline on data protection and reference the relevant legislation. A breach of this guideline would result in not only a breach of law, but also a breach of code.

With morals, you may find that you resonate more with a code because it has been built and structured on your values or beliefs. Codes based on ethics do incorporate morals, they just may not be aligned with yours.

ACTION

Think of an example of something that is legally accepted, but you perceive as morally unacceptable.

Are you a plastic or an ethical coach?

At present, coaching remains a non-regulated profession, meaning that anyone and everyone can label themselves a coach and offer what they believe are 'coaching services'. No qualifications, training or experience are necessary. If you wanted, you could go online, find yourself a $25 'coaching programme', skip through six videos and label yourself a 'certified coach'. You may be thinking, 'this is excellent' and if so, head over to Google and follow the many other plastic coaches on the web, but I guarantee your coaching practice will not succeed (if you manage to develop one). In order to become an ethical coach, you must first establish credibility, competence and confidence within your practice. All of which are achieved through an in-depth understanding of coaching ethics.

Imagine you were seeking a coach or a mentor (which I highly recommend you do) and you find yourself with a coach who has not invested in their practice or obtained the necessary skills, and is not continuously growing. Essentially, you are giving permission to someone with no experience to enter your mind and personal space. To put it into context, would you allow an unqualified surgeon to operate on you with a hammer and chisel? It may sound like an extreme analogy but as a coach we are dealing with the mind, which is a weird yet wonderful place. If we do not approach the mind with care and ethics, we run the risk of causing more damage than actual healing. Therefore, choose to be an ethical coach, not a plastic one.

ACTION

Invest in an accredited certification programme or temperature check the standards of your current coaching practice.

Certification and accreditation: how credible is your coaching practice?

The first step to becoming an ethical coach is to build credibility in your practice by obtaining certification and accreditation (true certification; not a $25 certification). If you are reading this as a certified or accredited coach, then you are already on the right track. However, it is important for us to understand the difference between the two.

Step 1: Membership to a self-regulated organization

Taking an ethical approach to your coaching begins with making the decision to join a self-regulated organization (more on these below). As a member you expand your coach network, begin to understand the standards of the profession and open yourself to a number of different events from coaches, supervisors and leaders in the profession.

Step 2: Certification with an Accredited Organization

True Certification in the coaching profession is received by completing a Coaching Program with an Accredited Organization. Here, the organization (and training program) is accredited, and you receive Certification as a coach, through their accreditation status.

Step 3: Accreditation with a self-regulated organization

Accreditation is awarded directly to you from a self-regulated organization (SRO) (more on these organizations below). However, in order to receive accreditation, there are certain requirements you must meet. One requirement is to first receive certification from an accredited organization (as explained above). There are also different levels of accreditation with SROs that you can work towards.

As an established certified or accredited coach, you should have your next steps towards building your credibility ready, whether that is working towards accreditation from certification or completing the requirements for the next level of accreditation with your chosen SRO. Building credibility is a continuous part of your coaching journey and plays a vital role in safeguarding coaches, clients and the industry from claims, penalties and disrepute.

ACTION

Draft a plan for your certification, accreditation or higher accreditation.

SROs in coaching – should I become a member?

Although the profession is non-regulated, professional coaching standards are set through a number of self-regulated organizations (SROs). To list the biggest:

1 The International Coaching Federation (ICF) (coachingfederation.org)

2 European Mentoring and Coaching Council (EMCC) (emccglobal.org)

3 Association for Coaching (AC) (associationforcoaching.com)

Accreditation with any of these three organizations will provide a high benchmark of professional standards and credibility. However, the ICF is known to be the most stringent.

There are many other SROs at both national and international levels, all with different standards and requirements for accreditation. It is important that when choosing an accreditation, you select the most credible for yourself and your clients. Here are some points to think about:

1 What level do I want my accreditation to be recognized at?

2 What resources and benefits are provided by the SRO?

3 What are the costs of membership and accreditation?

4 Which SROs are known to and valued by my clients?

5 Which SRO would I like to work with?

6 Which SRO aligns closest to my values?

Holding a membership and accreditation with an established SRO is a huge step to developing an ethical coaching practice. It provides you with higher standards of coaching, a stronger coach network and accountability for the service you deliver, and continuous development opportunities.

ACTION

Research SROs in your coaching sphere and take the necessary steps to become associated with them.

The ethics toolkit – do I possess the essential documents?

Every ethical coach should have the following documents in their toolkit (for the SRO of their choice):

1 Professional Charter for Coaching (EMCC, 2022)

2 Global Code of Ethics (EMCC, 2021)

Professional Charter for Coaching

The Professional Charter reflects the mission of SROs to promote and ensure best practice in coaching. It establishes a benchmark for ethics and is the basis for the development of self-regulation.

Global Code of Ethics

The Code aligns with the content and requirements set out in the Professional Charter for Coaching and has several signatory organizations committed to maintaining and promoting excellent practice in coaching.

Both documents are guides for the highest professional standards of coaching and highlight how we should be performing as a professional coach.

For instance, while establishing the accredited organization, Coaching Minds, I worked closely with the EMCC to embed the Global Code into a 'Professional Code of Conduct' (Coaching Minds, 2022). Our aim was to rewrite the code in a more simplified and accessible way, focusing more on an 'outcomes-based' regulatory approach (changing written rules to outcomes we should be achieving) rather than a list of regulations. This provides coaches with more of a 'results' focus rather than a 'process and action' focus. When we focus on our results rather than actions, we can measure the standard of service much better. As part of this work, we established seven Principles of the Code. I would like to share these with you for ease of remembering the contents of the Global Code:

1 Act with integrity

2 Act within the best interests of each client

3 Provide a proper standard of service

4 Maintain trust within the coaching profession

5 Comply with legal obligations

6 Run our business effectively with proper governance

7 Encourage equality and respect diversity

If we can operate our practice around these seven principles, we can run an ethical and high-professional-standard coaching practice. Let's take a look briefly at what each of these means.

ACT WITH INTEGRITY

To act with honesty and to hold ourselves accountable to moral principles. Accurately reflecting our coaching competencies, appropriately crediting work to original authors and keeping service at the heart of our coaching practice.

ACT WITHIN THE BEST INTERESTS OF EACH CLIENT

Understanding that each client is different, there is no 'one size fits all' approach. Maintaining confidentiality and being able to spot and appropriately manage any conflicts of interest.

PROVIDE A PROPER STANDARD OF SERVICE

Considering your client journey and customer experience. Following up on our promises and commitments to our client. Ensuring we always seek to improve the services we offer our clients.

MAINTAIN TRUST WITHIN THE COACHING PROFESSION

Always acting in a way that promotes success and trust in the coaching profession. Being conscious of our interactions with other coaches, members of organizations and the public.

COMPLY WITH LEGAL OBLIGATIONS

Understanding and complying with our legal obligations as a coach: data protection, tax, contract law, etc. Ensuring that we have the appropriate insurance for our business.

RUN OUR BUSINESS EFFECTIVELY WITH PROPER GOVERNANCE

Developing, publishing and upholding business policies such as refunds, cancellations, privacy and other important governance documents. Establishing a clear decision-making process.

ENCOURAGE EQUALITY AND RESPECT DIVERSITY

Treating everyone equally and respecting the differences of others. Being conscious of any biases we may hold and working to remove these. Having the courage to challenge other members of the profession who we may witness falling short of this principle.

We must understand what is required of us within these seven principles and the Global Code of Ethics, and shape our ethical coaching practice around them.

ACTION

Read and add the Professional Charter for Coaching and the Global Code of Ethics to your coaching toolkit, and identify any areas of improvement to enhance the standards of your practice.

Setting professional boundaries – what is the current standard of my coaching practice?

One of the most fundamental attributes of an ethical coach is having the ability to create, set and maintain professional boundaries with your clients. This is termed in coaching as 'contracting'. By setting clear boundaries with your client, you mitigate the risk of breaching your SRO's Global Code of Conduct. Your contracting is the foundation for your ethical coaching practice. Here are some important things to think about when setting boundaries:

1 What does my service look like as a coach?

2 How can I effectively explain the extent of my service to my client?

3 How do I make sure my client is clear on my obligations under the Global Code of Ethics?

4 How do I effectively communicate my duty of confidentiality?

5 How do I make my prices and methods of payment clear to my client?

6 How do I clearly define my methods of contact and availability?

7 What do I need in place to ensure my client is aware of the duration and number of coaching sessions?

8 What policies do I have in place for situations such as cancellations and refunds?

Setting clear boundaries based on the questions above allows you not only to ensure an ethical practice is in place but also to begin to build a better rapport with your clients. Always seek to provide maximum clarity to everyone you coach.

In addition, it is not only important to set these boundaries at the outset but also to manage stages to which 'recontracting' (where something in the verbal or written contract changes) takes place and boundaries need to be reset. A professional and ethical coach will hold the ability to recontract and reset boundaries with seamless ease.

ACTION

Consider the questions above and reflect on your coaching practice. Are there any improvements you can make to set clear and more defined boundaries with your clients?

Developing your ethical coaching practice

When we piece all of the above subsections together, we can develop a simple check-list to ensure we are on the correct path to establishing a professional and ethical coaching practice. To illustrate:

1 Understand what 'ethics' is all about.

2 Make a conscious choice to be an ethical coach rather than a plastic one.

3 Work towards certification and accreditation.

4 Select and join an SRO in the profession.

5 Build on your ethical toolkit.

6 Set professional boundaries with your clients.

When we pull all of these together, ethics will become second nature to our coaching practice.

A final thought

To close this chapter, I would like to leave you with one final ethical tip. Do you remember George's driver at the beginning of this chapter? Do not be like him. Whenever you are asked something you do not know the answer to, own it with integrity. Have the courage to say, 'I don't know' and then take it upon yourself to go find the answer. Once you understand this, you understand ethics.

References

Coaching Minds (2022) Professional Code of Conduct, September, coachingmindsglobal.com/creating-opportunities/ (archived at https://perma.cc/PKZ4-H5FZ)

EMCC (2021) The Global Code of Ethics, European Mentoring and Coaching Council, July, www.emccglobal.org/leadership-development/ethics/ (archived at https://perma.cc/2MEK-336Q)

EMCC (2022) Professional Charter for Coaching, Mentoring, and Supervision of Coaches, Mentors, and Supervisors, European Mentoring and Coaching Council, 15 July, www.emccglobal.org/about_emcc/press_releases/professional-charter-for-coaching-mentoring-and-supervision-of-coaches-mentors-and-supervisors/ (archived at https://perma.cc/D5S2-S32C)

34

Structuring the session (or not)

MONDANA HAMNIAZ

ABSTRACT

Coaches support the clients in clarifying and reaching their goals. Following a structure can be a beneficial approach for doing so, but it can also be limiting. The more rigidly we follow a structure, the more likely we are to misunderstand our client's needs. Yet, straying too far from structure can result in chaos rather than improvement. In this chapter, I show how we use listening, patience and clarity to create less-restrictive parameters and structure, thereby not losing sight of the client's individual expectations and remaining adaptive.

Introduction

Many coaching approaches incorporate sets of structures for coaches to follow during a session or series of sessions. Such blueprints, especially when they are well researched and psychologically supported, bring accuracy and legitimacy to the coaching brand, reduce risks for clients, support coaches' training and practice, and reduce legal liabilities. However, some processes are rigid and discourage adjustments based on the client's unique circumstances. For instance, when the structure does not match the client's preferred system of learning, they may find it more challenging to follow.

The question is, should the coach always stay loyal to the regiment? Is there a way to be structured but also receptive to the client's needs?

When I began coaching, I struggled with sticking to a predetermined structural model. Even then, I wasn't convinced one strategy worked for all circumstances. Therefore, I set out to answer some basic questions about structure: What is structure? Why is there so much emphasis on having structure during a coaching session? Is following structure always helpful to coaches? How do clients benefit from having structure? In what ways can we undermine our clients and the integrity of our coaching practice by staying true to a rigid predetermined structure? This chapter aims to help you answer these questions by understanding what structure is and giving you the benefits and drawbacks of both structuring and not structuring your sessions. Let's look at some of the answers I figured out.

What is structure?

The Oxford Dictionary defines structure as 'constructing or arranging according to a plan'. This definition immediately raised a question for me. If it is 'construct or arrange according to a plan', whose plan? And whose plan is more important? The coach or the client?

Coaches agree that the client's needs and expectations matter most. In fact, in my experience, giving client space to understand their needs and come to their own realizations about those needs is pivotal to the success of a coach–client relationship and coaching outcomes. While I can always observe and guide the direction of that process, I cannot prioritize my ideas and plans over those of the clients as their needs set the course and pace.

Even beyond this, however, there is a question we must ask about the nature of structure, and what it is about humanity that seeks structure in almost everything and not just in coaching. One could argue humankind has benefited from its own ability to structure. Looking at scientific research, architecture, literature, mathematics, function of human physiology or its psyche, etc, it seems most fields of study and practice hold a form of structure. Moreover, according to Sherwood, Subiaul and Zawidzki (2008), a great part of our ability to learn new skills is based on 'goal-directed actions'. This is important because it reinforces the idea that humans seem to have learnt more effectively and therefore faster when they have plans, or structures, to accomplish goals while extracting different variables, which causes more focused learning (Braun, Mehring and Wolpert, 2010). It is important to note, such systems of learning are not necessary for all types of learning. For instance, If I wanted to learn a language, I would be more likely to succeed if I had a goal to study for a certain amount of time every day and in a certain progression.

Humans, it seems, are psychologically predisposed to learn better in environments where there are both plans and intentions behind their actions. This is also true in helping clients with their own goals.

Within the context of coaching, structure is a tool, which allows clients to set their own goals, examine their own value systems and find their own solutions. The structure can also prevent coaches from convincing the clients to implement their agendas. Our responsibility is to help our clients recognize their options, the possibilities that they have available to them, and to find solutions to reach them.

Table 34.1 shows an example of a typical series of sessions based on the cognitive behavioural coaching (CBC) approach. Everything, from the session topic and goal to the outcome, tools, exercises and questions are predetermined, leading the client through a progression of steps designed by the developers of CBC and cognitive behavioural therapy (CBT), which formed the basis of CBC.

TABLE 34.1 Sample cognitive behavioural coaching structure – first four sessions

Aspect	Session 1	Session 2	Session 3	
Topic	Goals	Limiting beliefs	Thoughts and feelings	Habits and behaviours
Objective(s)	Collaboratively defining the desired outcome	Define beliefs that interfere with goal achievement	Identify thoughts and feelings that defy goals	Identify habits and behaviours that don't support your ideal outcome
Outcome(s)	1–2 SMART goal(s)	1–3 negative beliefs	1–2 patterns/ themes of negative thoughts and feelings	1–3 unhelpful habits and repetitive behaviours
Tools/exercises	Wheel of Life	Compound core beliefs questionnaire	Thought diary	Daily activity tracker
GROW: goals	What does your ideal life look like?	What would you like to believe about yourself?	When do you feel the best and which thoughts are associated with that?	Which 1–2 habits would most support your goals?
GROW: reality	What does your current life look like?	What do you believe about yourself that you don't like?	When do you feel the worst and which thoughts are associated with that?	Which habit (or behaviour) do you think is wasteful or harmful?
GROW: obstacles	What stands in your way to move towards your ideal life?	What stands in your way to change your negative beliefs (or their impact)?	What stands in your way to thinking and feeling more positively?	What makes it difficult for you to change your harmful habits or implement positive ones?
GROW: what to do	What 1–2 things can you do right now to progress?	What 1–2 things can you start doing right now to change your negative beliefs?	What are 1–2 things you can do right away to think and feel more positively?	What 1–2 things can you start doing regularly to implement a better habit?

This model supports a progressive flow of enquiry and shows how a coach allocates the topic in the first few sessions, helps identify the objectives and the desired outcome, and suggests which tools to use. It also includes the GROW model that is used in every session to determine the goals, reality, obstacles and what to do, through suggested questions. In this process, the coach uses the structure to help the clients maximize and optimize their success rate, typically within a limited time.

Factors of structure

According to Reinke, Sprick and Knight (2009), many factors need to be met to support the success of a coaching programme. The following are among the factors that are relevant to our discussion and help establish a coaching structure:

- **The role expectations of a coach** Coaches need to define their roles just as job descriptions do. We need to have clarity in our expertise. What demographic are we competent to serve? What are our specialities? Responsibilities, expectations and criteria can also impact the coaching structure. What are the evidence-based approaches that we are competent to follow?

- **The goals of the coaching programme** What does the programme promise to achieve for the individual or the organization? How is the structure relevant to the purpose of the programme? Is the programme geared toward personal or organizational coaching; an individual, group or team setting, for instance?

- **The experience of the coach** An experienced coach may set up or use the structure more intuitively, flexibly and interchangeably, with more confidence than their younger and less-experienced colleagues. In general, new coaches can greatly benefit by following structures, as they provide guidance and require less interpretation. While they are building experience, their margin of error might be higher due to lack of practice. In such cases, following a set structure can be safer and more predictable for client and coach.

- **The maturity level of the client** One of the factors that determines the success of the structure is how well the client can use the coaching content and consistently follow the steps that the structure provides. A more experienced coach is proficient in more methods and tools and has better judgement to decide which would be most helpful in any circumstance.

Benefits and drawbacks of high versus low/no structure

Therefore, using or not using a structure is not always a straightforward question. Both cases have drawbacks and advantages that a coach must consider, providing the most effective and appropriate service that is in the client's best interest while the coach is competent to deliver it.

Benefits of a structure

Conceptually, holding a structure is about creating a balance between growth and implementation, awareness and transformation, exploration and confirmation. As mentioned above, structure is a tool, a framework that supports coaches to create a system of intervention that includes learning and efficacy, aiming to increase the rate of success for both. A structure also often includes monitoring how clients progress. Knowing client improvements adds to the coach's credibility and confidence, as well as the client's satisfaction and motivation.

A structure sets bounds for our practice, to set a safe and predictable standard by preventing coaches from deviating from the norm(s) prescribed by the structure. Therefore, adhering to structure during sessions can provide the clients with psychological safety, clarity of their journey, increased focus and reasonable expectations (Sherman and Freas, 2004). For example, in my experience, structure or the sequence of the structure have the following benefits:

- Create a sense of mutual accountability, which encourages commitment to change, supported by a symbiotic coach–client relationship.
- When clients realize it is the structure that guides them in the depth of the process, not the coach, they seem more at ease for not being judged and feel more supported rather than directed to explore, reflect and focus on their growth.
- It allows the coach and client to arrive at the sessions more informed and prepared, which helps reflection and managing expectations on the client's side, while supporting the coach to better observation and effective feedback as they have more tangible bounds to work within.
- Psychological safety – structure does not allow a coach to enter the field of psychology and act as a therapist or a psychologist without having the proper training and medical expertise, which can cause confusion for the client.
- Clarity of their journey – coach and the client know what to expect next on their journey. They do not arrive to a session with a random idea and focus on unrelated issues.
- Increased focus – the objectives, outcome and time frame are determined with the client, which creates a sense of priority and therefore focus for them.
- Reasonable expectations – as clients explore the goals and their outcomes, they actually base that on their own ability to perform.

Drawbacks of a structure

Now we examine the potential downside of having structure. It is likely that you, occasionally, find yourself a few steps back after a series of sessions, feeling that much of your client's progress has disappeared. Or with a new discovery, you realize you could have used the information earlier, which would have changed your coaching approach a long time ago. Have you found yourself discouraged because the client does not follow through with your programme or homework, and the most soothing conclusion you come up with is that the client is not coachable? Or they are not ready to change?!

Over the course of ten years, from 1978 to 1987, Walter Burke and Niel Flemming created the VARK (originally VAK) model of learning: Visual, Auditory, Reading and Writing, and Kinaesthetic, (Ibrahim and Hussein, 2016: 4). The research examined different learning styles, with varying needs and expectations. Some require whiteboards, documents, visual aids, etc. The question is, if there are so many combinations and ways to learn and explore, why would we expect the same structure would be equally effective for every client? Not to undermine the benefits of having a framework and a road map, however, sticking to the same model or session structure for everyone is likely to undermine the potential of many clients. As different as our clients' strengths and limitations are, so are the unique and personalized ways to help them.

Having a structure may detract from the coach's focus on being present and observant during a session, picking up clues in a client's body language, the way they communicate, their choice of vocabulary, and the emotion behind their voice. For instance, the tone of the language they use tells us more about their state of mind or what the topic means to them. These clues help us know what to ask next, how to help them recognize their own interpretations of the issue. A structure may limit us to preset questions and methods, rendering the need to recognize nuances less important.

For instance, curiously listening to my client, Ben, who led the conversation, gave me insight into the incongruencies that came from his conflicting value system that caused him to stagnate. If I was focused on the structure and schedule, I could have missed such an important discovery, so it was imperative to first re-evaluate his value system despite what the structure prescribed.

In other words, if you always stick to a predetermined structure and lack customized and flexible planning and objectives, you are more likely to hit a roadblock with your client that you have not been expecting or prepared for. By listening, paying attention and being present, we allow the client to lead, and we take the cues from them to determine what the next step will be.

If we are adamant about holding our structure, at times we end up interrupting our clients to get back to the structure. I believe it can be highly disempowering for clients to feel they have been redirected. Disrupting the flow of the session just to meet the needs of your plan somehow contradicts the concept that the client is whole and resourceful. The same way that we have confidence that the client has the answers, we can also have the confidence in knowing that they know which problems they want to solve first and find their own way to do this.

On a few occasions, I had spent hours preparing the next session's topics as part of a set programme. However, my client needed to work on a different issue. I chose my client's needs at that moment. On at least one occasion we ended up discovering something more crucial that positively influenced what I had already prepared for them. On another occasion I had enough time left to introduce the preplanned work. I learnt that most important is to pay attention to the client's needs and balance structure around that.

Professor David Clutterbuck believes structure can sometimes be dangerous because it allows some coaches to force their own agenda onto the client (Clutterbuck and Megginson, 2011). He also found, by strictly adhering to the structure to set a goal for a session, we can easily miss what clients would like to express. While being concerned about moving from A to B and to C, during a session we may miss where the client is wanting to go (Clutterbuck and Megginson, 2011). Assuming, as coaches, we know the answer and allow our assumptions to lead the conversation, is misleading. When we stay curious and allow the clients to lead the conversation, we realize that the clients know best and are able to arrive at their own conclusions.

Benefits of no structure

In my conversation with my clients and other coaches, I realized it is most effective to first listen, get to know our clients better, and discover more about their experiences and the way they do things. How they communicate, how openly and clearly they discuss their session's agenda, and what are the roadblocks they have been facing, before we conduct any technique or structure, expecting them to perform. Among the four types of coaching Clutterbuck and Megginson (2011) observed, they highlighted the following about the 'systemic eclectic'

> The fourth, most liberating mindset is the systemic eclectic. These coaches have a very wide array of ways of working and a toolkit amassed from many sources, both within couching and from very different worlds. They have integrated this into a self-aware, personalized way of being with the client. They exhibit an intelligent, sensitive ability to select a broad approach, and within that approach, appropriate tools and techniques, which meet the particular needs of a particular client at a particular time. This relates to what Webb (2008) calls coaching for wisdom (Clutterbuck and Megginson, 2011: 303–4).

We live in an unprecedented era of information. Scientists make new discoveries, and the information is almost instantly available to the world. If we only want to rely on what we learnt last year, for instance, we are falling behind and being stagnant and ineffective in our coaching approach. Effective coaches hold a high standard with up-to-date knowledge and tools to help clients achieve their goals.

Therefore, to be a capable coach, we commit to continuously educating ourselves, being curious, learning more ways to communicate, and we use our skills in natural ways to develop rapport with our clients. If we only pledge to follow structure, it seems, we are excluding much of the client in the session, and our method in coaching could become robotic and lack personal touch. In such a case, as Clutterbuck and Megginson (2009: 74) suggest in their research, the session 'could be conducted by a machine'.

A skilful coach manages a session by asking the right questions to help the client achieve their desired outcome. Some choose not to follow a set structure meticulously and focus solely on forward progression during a session. Many coaches may have a blueprint based on the approach or methods they are competent in, which they follow in principle and concept, but they do not necessarily follow a preset plan, and allow the client to lead. In other words, the biggest benefit of having no (or little) structure, is the freedom to follow the client's direction, which can serve to empower them more and build a stronger rapport.

Drawbacks of no structure

If there are no set expectations or structure and we only show up to have an open discussion, thinking that clients will lead the way, we may end up having random

TABLE 34.2 Summary of benefits and drawbacks of high versus low/no structure

High structure – benefits	Low/no structure – benefits
• Efficiency in time	• Tailor comfort and rapport
• Ability to measure	• Niche-specific (some spiritual coaching)
• Creates accountability	• Allows freedom, client pace
• More predictable outcome	• Flexibility
• Management of expectations	• Client-focused
• Simplified coach training	
High structure – drawbacks	**Low/no structure – drawbacks**
• Limits flexibility	• Time inefficiency
• Missing important information/cues	• Lose focus, delayed outcome
• Limiting clients' learning and growth	• Develop bad habits, unpreparedness
• Reliance on assumptions	• Lack of boundaries
• Time-bound schedule	• Eclecticism needs special competency

aimless conversations, which can impede an effective process. The use of time may be ineffective since hours can be spent on storytelling, rants, and so forth, versus allocating the time to a focused objective and progression. On the other hand, since we do not have a framework to monitor the client's growth, we may not recognize progress (or the lack thereof), which can lead to demotivation, a lack of momentum, and frustration on the side of both the coach and client.

Table 34.2 highlights the main benefits and drawbacks of having a structure and having no/little structure in a quick and easy-to-read format.

Essential competencies regardless of structure

In the end, I personally believe there are three competencies that are needed regardless of whether we structure or do not structure a session. These are listening, patience and clarity, which serve to enable eclecticism and adaptability in lower-structured approaches while getting richer information to offset some disadvantages of higher-structured environments.

Listening

In my experience, the most successful session happens when clients communicate the most. I came to realize that clients can normally find their own solutions by hearing themselves speak. It helps them find the patterns that have taken them to a problem or a solution, especially with the coach's guidance to help them zoom out so they can see their situation from several perspectives and find more clarity. One of a coach's responsibilities is to tune in to realize what inspires them the most. We pick up clues, use collective knowledge about body language, listen to the tone of their voice, and to their spoken and unspoken story. Effective listening helps to support structure with information or manage a lack of structure by adapting and pivoting approaches and direction more effectively. The following actions help a coach to be present and listen:

- Face the speaker and make eye contact at a level that the client is comfortable with.
- 'Listen' to non-verbal cues like expression, posture and movement, especially when there seem to be inconsistencies or contradictions.
- Only interrupt the client to reset the direction to the agreed topic and do so gently, using a natural break in the conversation.
- Listen without judging the client or jumping to conclusions. Ask if you want to know or confirm something.

- Do not plan what to say next when the client is talking. Use your presence to follow the rhythm and flow of what the client is saying to guide your questions.

- Do not impose your opinions or solutions onto the client as they are inevitably inappropriate or unsuitable to the client's unique position. Remember, the client is the expert of their own life and can find the best answers themselves.

- Stay focused. Minimize distractions. Set boundaries and rules that you expect of the client to streamline your engagement.

- Ask open-ended, non-directive questions. Enquire broader when you want to gather information or alert your client to other perspectives. Go deeper when you want the client to explore underlying factors that they may not have thought of or discovered before.

Listening is a critical core competency in coaching and forms the basis that enables coaching effectiveness, regardless of the level of structure that a coach is employing. This has been the key point – listening and paying attention to incongruencies, thought patterns and conflicting values make it possible for a coach to turn sessions around to a great success at times. Focusing on clients is often more effective than trying to fit the structure of a predesigned programme.

Patience

In my early business negotiation training, I learnt patience revealed much more if I gave it a chance. In coaching, like negotiation, it is best to talk less than the other party. According to Herb Cohen in *Negotiate This!* (2006), when we are eager to share what we think we know, we often miss important clues or jump into unnecessary assumptions. I have implemented the same negotiation principles in coaching, and it has never fallen short of proving that patience is necessary. If clients did not find their solutions during a session, they eventually did the next time, or the next. The extra time to process allows them to increase their confidence and helps to develop ownership of their own growth, which are factors associated with successful change.

I also need to add, on rare occasions, the client's safety overwrites any structure. The only time I have intervened has been when I felt my client might be facing harm by having a completely negative understanding of the issue that required clarity, for instance. Even then, I interjected only with the client's permission, with respect, and in as neutral and natural a way as possible.

Clarity

Gaining clarity is another cornerstone of coaching. Sometimes helping our clients reach clarity is all we ought to do (Clutterbuck and Megginson, 2011). A coach helps them recognize how they think, how they process information, how they implement their findings in different situations, and help them figuratively put a mirror up to examine if their perception matches their reality.

My tools to help my clients gain clarity are to raise their curiosity, seek knowledge, examine their value systems, and find solutions. I also found the following can aid the process:

- Clients who know their value systems are in a better position to find clarity.
- Asking honest and thought-provoking questions is the key to trigger a client's curiosity to understand more.
- Examining if their actions align with their values and interests.
- Keeping a healthy lifestyle, with balanced rest, activities and eating habits provide the energy to clear the mind of mental fog.
- Prioritizing and avoiding overwhelming experiences that tend to activate the stress cycle and shut down higher thought processes.

Ultimately, my goal is to make my clients self-sufficient to find their own creative solutions at the best pace and with clarity.

Conclusion

It seems both the coach and the client can benefit from a valid, evidence-based structure as long as it does not keep the session too rigid and take away the autonomy from the clients and discretion from the coach. Additionally, we should be responsible enough to continuously develop our skills and command in our abilities to manage with flexibility, be able to comfortably help clients dig deeper, be perceptive enough to address limitations, and be efficient in supporting our clients. In *The MindBody Self*, Dr Mario Martinez (2017) reminds coaches, leaders and psychologists that our commitment to structure should not compromise our respect for our clients and their freedom to choose their direction during a session.

In the end, if the structure fulfils the client's purpose and you are competent to deliver it, it may be helpful to follow. But also recognize that it can sometimes be a disservice to limit our clients by imposing a structure on them. Ultimately, clients do not seek a coach to be interviewed or turn in homework, but they want to be empowered to find their own solutions in an environment where trust, safety and collaboration are valued most.

References

Braun, D A, Mehring, C and Wolpert, D M (2010) Structure learning in action, *Behavioral Brain Research*, 20 6(2), 157–65, doi.org/10.1016/j.bbr.2009.08.031 (archived at https://perma.cc/4W2H-ES4M)

Clutterbuck, D (2009) Coaching reflection: The liberated coach, *Coaching: An International Journal of Theory, Research and Practice*, 3 (1), 73–81, doi.org/10.1080/1752188090310 2308 (archived at https://perma.cc/L4QJ-WMYC)

Clutterbuck, D and Megginson, D (2011) Coach maturity: An emerging concept, in *The Handbook of Knowledge-Based Coaching: From theory to practice*, eds L Wildflower and D Brennan, pp 299–314, Jossey-Bass, San Francisco, CA

Cohen, H (2006) *Negotiate This! By caring, but not T-H-A-T much*, Warner Books, New York

Ibrahim, R and Hussein, D (2016) Assessment of visual, auditory, and kinesthetic learning style among undergraduate nursing students, *International Journal of Advanced Nursing Studies*, 5 (1), 1–4, doi.org/10.14419/ijans.v5i1.5124 (archived at https://perma.cc/D6NC-RWDS)

Martinez, M (2017) *The MindBody Self: How longevity is culturally learned and the causes of health are inherited*, Hay House, New York

Reinke, W M, Sprick, R and Knight, J (2009) Coaching classroom management, in *Coaching: Approaches and perspectives*, ed J Knight, pp 91–112, Corwin Press, Thousand Oaks, CA

Sherman, S and Freas, A (2004) The Wild West of executive coaching, *Harvard Business Review*, 82 (11), 82–90, hbr.org/2004/11/the-wild-west-of-executive-coaching (archived at https://perma.cc/UD6W-RARR)

Sherwood, C C, Subiaul, F and Zawidzki, T W (2008) A natural history of the human mind: Tracing evolutionary changes in brain and cognition, *Journal of Anatomy*, 212 (4), 426–54, doi.org/10.1111/j.1469-7580.2008.00868.x (archived at https://perma.cc/KL5Z-6PTM)

Webb, P (2008) Coaching for wisdom: Enabling wise decisions, in *The Philosophy and Practice of Coaching: Insights and issues for a new era,* eds D B Drake, D Brennan, and K Gørtz, pp 161–76, Jossey-Bass, San Francisco, CA

35

Questioning techniques

JOAN SWART

ABSTRACT

Asking questions is the mainstay of the coaching process and the most important competency a coach can learn and apply in their trade. Fortunately, it is a skill that can be learnt and practised. Scientific techniques such as Socratic questioning, critical thinking and cognitive interviewing provide the framework to get clients from where they are to where they want to be with the help of focused and systematic questioning.

Introduction

Communication is the main operant in any talk intervention such as therapy and coaching. It is the essential competency that drives awareness and action in the coaching process. Aside from an empathic presence and listening, questioning is the third skill that completes an effective exchange. It is the coach's main 'weapon' and, fortunately, coaches do not have to rely on informal skills or intuition but have proven and rigorous methods at their disposal that can be learnt and practised, such as Socratic questioning, critical thinking frameworks and cognitive interviewing.

Questioning as the quintessential coaching skill

We start by reviewing why we ask questions, the different types of questions to ask, and how to reflect on your questioning experience before introducing more comprehensive techniques.

Why do we ask questions?

At the most stripped-down level, we ask questions to know the answer. But beyond information gathering, questioning has other dynamics too. It can empower the recipient. Challenge, motivate, clarify, acknowledge and stimulate. But it can also undermine, lead, provoke or deceive a person, depending on the thoughtfulness, appropriateness and intent. The core purpose of coaching is to help guide a client to achieve a desirable outcome, whether a tangible accomplishment, developing a valued quality or strength, or live a more balanced, purposeful and fulfilling life. As a talking intervention, the quintessential skill of a coach is communication. Questioning and listening are two sides of this coin. We gain information and under-standing through observation and listening, which may require questions to direct and help the flow of the exchange.

As questions have a strong impact on the trust and willingness and ability of the client to share, a coach must always be mindful. **Every question must have a conscious and deliberate intention**. Ask yourself the following:

- How is the client likely to receive the question?
- What are you hoping to achieve with the question?
- Is the timing right for this question?
- Does the question move the conversation towards the session topic and objective?
- What is the likely impact of this question on the client (e.g., confidence, creativity, empowerment, reassurance, stress, emotion)?
- Does the question delve deeper or cast the net wider?

With a clear intention, and idea of the likely impact on the client, as well as how it can contribute to the coaching outcome, a coach ensures to achieve maximum value, ethical responsibility and client insight. Thereby, a balance between transactional efficiency (i.e., steps, plans, goal-achievement) and transformational substance (i.e., awareness, insight, drive) is achieved according to the client's needs and the stage of the process they are in.

Different types of questions

In any conversation, there are different types of questions. As coaching has an objective that is distinct from most other normal interactions, the question types also differ. The following question types are relevant in coaching.

1 **Open questions** The most used type of question in coaching. Usually starting with What, Why, How, Where or When, open questions invite finding out more about a person or experience and encourage critical or creative discussions. Keeping it objective and non-judgemental produces the best information as it acknowledges

and shows interest without condescension. For example, you may ask, 'Where do you see yourself in the future?' 'What is most important to you every day?' 'What would you like to achieve from this session?'

2   **Probing questions** Useful for gaining clarification and encouraging deeper information sharing. Probing questions aim to find a deeper understanding of underlying issues and avoid misunderstandings. Consider whether the client is ready to share the information. 'Why do you think that is?' 'Could you tell me more about…?' 'What is preventing you from…?'

3   **Hypothetical questions** These questions are meant to stimulate the client's creativity and imagination by thinking of new ideas and solutions. It encourages proactive rather than reactive approaches. For instance, 'What would you do if…?' 'What would happen if…?'

4   **Paraphrasing questions** Coaches use this question type to check that their understanding of what the client has said is accurate. They reflect the client's answer back using different words and ask for confirmation. For example, 'I'm hearing you say that… Am I understanding this correctly?' Paraphrasing acknowledges what a client has said and shows an interest in understanding them, thereby empowering the client.

5   **Funnel questions** Related to probing questions, a coach uses a funnel effect as follow-up to broader questions to narrow the discussion to a specific, important point and get deeper information. 'When did it start?' 'Can you give an example of what you mean by…?' By asking a series of progressive questions, the client can be helped to relive an experience or recall a memory in greater detail if they are ready to do so safely.

6   **Closed questions** These are generally avoided in coaching unless asked with a deliberate intent, for example, getting a quick answer or confirmation, leading into a further discussion, reinforcing a point, or introducing a new direction. 'Are you happy?' 'Have you thought of…?' 'Are you satisfied with…?'

7   **Leading questions** These are designed to lead the client to a conclusion or realization by implying a specific answer and are also steered clear of in coaching, as a process led by the client. For example, 'How ashamed did you feel when your boss criticized you in the meeting?' leads the client to accept that they felt shame without reflecting on the true nuance of the feelings that they experienced. Instead, 'How did you feel…?' pushes the client to think deeply and vocalize a more nuanced answer. However, used very sparingly (and subtly), leading questions can be used to guide a conversation in a positive direction or motivate the client to pursue a desired outcome. Examples are, 'So, would it not have been better to…?' 'Do you think you should not have…?' This should be a gentle influence to reinforce a client's point rather than implying a 'correct' answer.

After receiving an answer, do a reflection-in-action before asking the next question. Did you get the information you intended? Was the client's reaction as you expected? Do you need clarification? Would a deeper or broader follow-up be more useful? Always consider your intention in line with the objective of the session and, of course, the safety of the client.

When you do your reflection-on-action after the session, ask yourself, could you have asked your question(s) in a better way? Did the client misinterpret your words? Was the type of question appropriate? How was the flow of the session in the context of the objective and outcome? Did any question have a noticeable effect on trust, emotions, openness, etc? In the light of your reflections, consider what you could have changed to create a more efficient, safe and fulfilling experience for the client (and you).

Socratic questioning

The disciplined practice of Socratic questioning stems from the Greek philosopher Socrates, who used thoughtful questioning to help students examine and challenge the validity of ideas. The teacher assumed an ignorant and questioning mindset while students engaged in critical thought to explore contradictions and reformulate inaccurate or incomplete ideas. The premise is that thinking – as in the acquisition of knowledge and understanding – is based on structured logic. Therefore, systematic questioning is effective to guide the process.

Much later, the most widely used psychotherapy approach, cognitive behavioural therapy (CBT) incorporated Socratic questioning as a method to help achieve cognitive restructuring – a process of identifying, disputing, defusing from or reframing maladaptive thoughts and beliefs (David, Cristea and Hofmann, 2018). Through progressive questioning, the therapist guides the client to uncover the assumptions and interpretations that underlie thinking patterns linked to dysfunctional behaviour and emotions (Beck, 2020; Clark and Egan, 2015).

Socratic questioning has also become indispensable in coaching. According to Neenan (2009), good Socratic questions are more effective than relying on intuitive questions to increase awareness, stimulate reflection, and enhance problem-solving. Socratic questions stem from a logical base to systematically formulate and order questions rather than suffering from intuition bias. Kirkebøen and Nordbye (2017) pointed out that a reliance on intuition causes personal experience to 'leak' into choices about questions, which blocks sound analytic enquiry. This is important as the coach is fully present and curious but not personally invested, recognizing that the client is in charge of the direction. A good coach asks questions with intent to help the client make discoveries to aid their specific journey. While coaches avoid becoming 'stuck' in Socratic questioning mode, it is an effective line of enquiry to produce a depth of understanding. As such, it is a 'guided discovery approach' (Neenan, 2009).

Neenan suggested the most effective Socratic questions are 1) **concise** – maintain focus, 2) **clear** – no jargon and ambiguity, to avoid confusion and misunderstanding, 3) **open** – inviting maximum information and reflection, 4) **purposeful** – definite reasons for every question, 5) **constructive** – facilitating insight and action, 6) **focused** – on the client's current concerns, 7) **tentative** – not assuming or expecting an answer, and 8) **neutral** – not leading or directive reflecting the coach's viewpoint or expectation.

Therefore, each question has a deliberate purpose, and a series of questions flows in the direction of overall intent, for instance, the client's objective for the session. Paul and Elder (2019) identified six types of Socratic questioning:

1 **Questions for clarification** Unpack and unravel the client's statements and experiences to get to the roots while ensuring that the coach and client are on the same page. For instance, 'What does that mean to you?' 'Could you tell me more about…?' 'How does that relate to…?'

2 **Questions that probe assumptions** Clients are asked to think about the unquestioned beliefs and presuppositions that underlie their argument or experience. 'What evidence do you have for that assumption?' 'What would a more helpful or accurate belief be?'

3 **Questions that probe reasons and rationale** Digging deeper into the rationale for a decision, behaviour, feeling or belief rather than assuming it is fixed. 'How is your reason related to the situation or context?' 'Why is that happening?' 'How do you justify your decision?'

4 **Questions about viewpoints and perspectives** Most arguments and experiences are seen from one viewpoint. Ask the client to explore other possible positions and perspectives that may be valid. 'Is there another way to look at…?' 'What would you tell your best friend if they were in the same position?'

5 **Questions that probe implications and consequences** Ask questions that identify and analyse outcomes that the client may not have considered. 'What are the unintended consequences of…?' 'What can happen that you did not think about?' 'How will it matter 5–10 years from now?'

6 **Questions about the question** Ask a client what they think a question means. Why did they think you asked the question.

Being curious, analytical and neutral are strong qualities that support effective Socratic questioning. Stay in the moment and focus on only asking open-ended questions with intent. Keep your client's objective in mind when sequencing questions. When the direction strays into unhelpful or irrelevant areas, gently nudge the conversation back on track, using closed questions when appropriate to refocus the client, for example 'Let's get back to what you said a few moments ago. Did you think about…?' followed by Socratic questions in the resumed direction.

Promoting critical thinking

Critical thinking allows coaching clients to rise above their assumptions, biases and fixed mindset (e.g., giving in to frustration, resisting change, avoiding feedback and limiting their potential) and achieve clarity and new ideas with confidence. Critical thinking is a disciplined way to analyse facts, arguments, evidence and observations to arrive at a rational and clear conclusion or decision. In the coaching context, questions help the client examine their assumptions and alternative perspectives, as well as encourage the development of healthy scepticism (Cox, 2013).

Perhaps the most widely known and supported method to promote critical thinking in education and learning, Bloom's taxonomy of thinking, can also be applied in coaching, using the following steps progressively by asking questions relevant to each stage (Figure 35.1).

1 **Knowledge** The coach asks the client questions to help them obtain and organize all information that is relevant to their goal or objective. It may require the client to find new information on their own or the coach may point the client towards topic and sources or even teach the client – as long as it is brief, in the client's best interest, and contracted for. The client must appreciate that the coach has their 'teaching hat' on for the moment. The coach tests the client's knowledge with questions such as 'What is…?' 'How do…?' 'How do you explain…?' 'What is the definition of…?'

2 **Comprehension** The coach helps the client to understand the meaning of the information that they have learnt or discovered. How is this knowledge relevant to the client's goals? Can it help achieving those goals or provide clarity on why the goal is important? Possible helpful questions are, 'What do the new facts or ideas show you?' 'How can you explain the new knowledge in the context of your goal?' 'How can it help you reach your goal?'

3 **Application** The coach asks questions to transition the client from having and understanding new information to formulating new ideas and solutions and applying them in pursuit of their goals. Questions to ask include, 'How would you use…?' 'How would you solve _____ with what you have learnt?' 'Is there another way you can…?'

4 **Analysis** Stephen Covey has said, 'To learn and not to do is really not to learn. To know and not to do is really not to know' (2004: 12). Now that the client has trialled their new ideas in practice, it is time to evaluate the new information in this context. What were the outcomes and consequences? Were there gaps and limitations in the information that impeded the performance of its application? With the help of the coach, the client examines the information-application process critically by looking at smaller parts or steps where possible. The coach asks, 'What conclusions do you reach?' 'Why do you think…?' 'Why does _____ work/not work?' 'What are the pros and cons of…?'

5 Evaluation In this step, the client makes a judgement on the merits of the idea, solution or action, based on the criteria they have set (e.g., contribution to goal, consequences, doability). The coach critically questions the client to help them reach a conclusion of how to move forward. The coach asks, 'If you repeated the action, how would you predict the outcome?' 'What alternatives or changes can make the process or outcome better?' 'What new information do you need?'

6 Creation Now that the coach and client have completed steps 1–5 of the critical thinking process, the client explores their options of how to use the new information effectively and consistently in the future. The coach reinforces the process so that the client completes the next cycle – perhaps with a new goal, new information or new application – more effectively and smoothly. Questions that are often helpful are, 'How would you improve…?' 'How could you adapt…?' 'What would you suggest to someone else with a similar issue or goal?'

In coaching, Bloom's taxonomy offers a useful framework to move the client from knowledge and ideas to a workable solution. The method is semi-structured and

FIGURE 35.1 Bloom's taxonomy in the coaching context

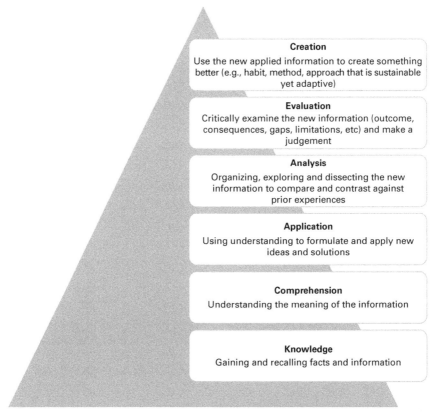

Creation
Use the new applied information to create something better (e.g., habit, method, approach that is sustainable yet adaptive)

Evaluation
Critically examine the new information (outcome, consequences, gaps, limitations, etc) and make a judgement

Analysis
Organizing, exploring and dissecting the new information to compare and contrast against prior experiences

Application
Using understanding to formulate and apply new ideas and solutions

Comprehension
Understanding the meaning of the information

Knowledge
Gaining and recalling facts and information

SOURCE Adapted from Anderson and Krathwohl (2001)

supported by questions to allow the client to be creative, critical and analytical throughout the process, which will allow them to find the most appropriate, workable solution for their situation, as well as repeat the steps in other areas.

Cognitive interviewing

Traditionally a custodial interviewing technique used to enhance witness memory and accuracy, cognitive interviewing (CI) is a technique that can also be useful in coaching. Also based on similar guidelines as in most coaching exchanges, CI requires conversation management based on client–coach rapport, intentional questioning, client autonomy and coach guidance (not dominance). Similarly, a session is conducted in five major sections, namely 'introduction and rapport building, open-ended narrative, review, and closure' (Shepherd et al, 1999: 118). The application of CI is useful to enhance memory recall of past events to challenge erroneous assumptions and reframe the experience, using any of four mnemonics or systems (Eisenberg, 2019):

1 **Report everything** The coach asks the client to report everything that they can remember, especially including the emotions they felt, and sensory awareness (i.e., see, hear, touch, smell, taste). Any association with feelings and senses improve recall. The client withholds no information, even if they do not think it is useful or relevant, which gives the coach a more complete picture.

2 **Mental reinstatement** Remembering something can be more detailed and accurate when the context of the experience is restated (Eisenberg, 2019). For instance, when a person is in the same or similar environment, or has the same feelings or sense, information becomes more easily available. The coach can create a mental picture by having the client describe their feelings and senses during a past event and connecting it with what happened.

3 **Recall events in different orders** By asking the client to recall events in a reverse order, for instance, may help to retrieve things that they have not remembered before (Eisenberg, 2019). It helps to separate things that usually happened in the same circumstances and emotional interference from real events. In this sense, the prefrontal cortex and episodic memory are activated while semantic memory and emotion perception are deactivated (Macoir et al, 2019).

4 **Change perspectives** Although people usually report their experiences from their own perspective, using a perspective from another person (real or imaginary) can free them from their previous assumptions, beliefs and defences (Memon et al, 1996).

When conducting a cognitive interview and going through one (or more) of the systems, there are a few important considerations for a coach to consider:

• Trust and rapport are critical enablers of complete and accurate information. The best foundation is to:

- o treat the client from the beginning with respect and compassion
- o check your biases and do not make assumptions
- o acknowledge and accept the client
- o value their autonomy
- o be consistent
- Continuously ask open-ended questions
- Link emotions and senses to statements
- Be observant. Listen to the words of the client but also notice their body language. Is it consistent with what they are telling you?
- The client's safety comes first:
  - o If the client shows signs of distress – emotions or behaviour that are unexpected, severe or uncontrollable, create space, cease your questioning, step back, or suspend the session
  - o If a client has been traumatized in the past, exposure to the same memories can retraumatize them – if there may be memories that are repressed or the trauma still has a marked effect on the client's current functioning, avoid CI unless you have specialized training
- Finally, if you are unsure about anything, ask the client

If done correctly by a trained practitioner, cognitive interviewing is an effective method with which to recall and reframe memories. For a coach, the most important thing to remember is the importance of linking emotions and senses felt in the past to an event to make it more vivid.

Final thoughts

Coaching is about facilitating the growth and enhancement of a client in areas they choose. Communication is the most important cornerstone of the process that requires effective listening and questioning. Focused presence, curiosity, acceptance and empathy are the enablers of good questions. Developing an analytic mindset in conjunction, applied in a deliberate and systematic way through a series of mostly open-ended questions produces the most effective and sustainable coaching outcomes. Socratic questioning, critical thinking frameworks and cognitive interviewing provide rigorous methodologies that are invaluable to clients and set great coaches aside from decent ones.

References

Anderson, L W and Krathwohl, D R (eds) (2001) *A Taxonomy for Learning, Teaching, and Assessing: A revision of Bloom's taxonomy of educational objectives*, Longman, New York

Beck, J S (2020) *Cognitive Behavior Therapy: Basic and beyond*, 3rd edn, The Guilford Press, New York

Clark, G I and Egan, S J (2015) The Socratic method in cognitive behavioral therapy: A narrative review, *Cognitive Therapy and Research*, 39, 863–79, doi.org/10.1007/s10608-015-9707-3 (archived at https://perma.cc/7LT8-268M)

Covey, S R (2004) The 7 Habits of Highly Successful People: Powerful lessons in personal change, Free Press, New York

Cox, E (2013) *Coaching Understood: A pragmatic inquiry into the coaching process*, Sage, Thousand Oaks, CA

David, D, Cristea, I and Hofmann, S G (2018) Why cognitive behavioral therapy is the gold standard of psychotherapy, *Frontiers in Psychiatry*, 9 (4), 1–3, doi.org/10.3389/fpsyt.2018.00004 (archived at https://perma.cc/39NN-JYEW)

Eisenberg, P (2019) The cognitive interview and enhanced cognitive interview in financial forensics and investigations, *Journal of Contemporary Research in Social Sciences*, 1 (1), 55–64

Kirkebøen, G and Nordbye, G H H (2017) Intuitive choices lead to intensified positive emotions: An overlooked reason for 'intuition bias?' *Frontiers in Psychology*, 8 (1942), 1–11, doi.org/10.3389/fpsyg.2017.01942 (archived at https://perma.cc/6X6A-9CZ4)

Macoir, J, Hudon, C, Tremblay, M, Laforce, R and Wilson, M A (2019) The contribution of semantic memory to the recognition of basic emotions and emotional valence: Evidence from the semantic variant of primary progressive aphasia, *Social Neuroscience*, 14 (6), 705–16, doi.org/10.1080/17470919.2019.1577295 (archived at https://perma.cc/SV7M-HM67)

Memon, A, Cronin, Ó, Eaves, R and Bull, R (1996) An empirical test of the mnemonics components of the cognitive interview, in *Psychology, Law, and Criminal Justice: International developments in research and practice*, eds G Davis, S Lloyd-Bostock, M McMurran and C Wilson, pp 135–45, Walter de Gruyter & Co, Berlin

Neenan, M (2009) Using Socratic questioning in coaching, *Journal of Rational-Emotive & Cognitive-Behavioral Therapy*, 27, 249–64, doi.org/10.1007/s10942-007-0076-z (archived at https://perma.cc/499B-XXQM)

Paul, R and Elder, L (2019) *The Thinker's Guide to Socratic Questioning*, Rowman & Littlefield, New York

Shepherd, E, Mortimer, A, Turner, V, and Watson, F (1999) Spaced cognitive interviewing: Facilitating therapeutic and forensic narration of traumatic memories, *Psychology, Crime & Law*, 5 (1–2), 117-43, doi.org/10.1080/10683169908414997 (archived at https://perma.cc/4FGK-7HCQ)

PART SEVEN

Special niches and target groups

36

Leadership and executive coaching

ROB HALLOTT

ABSTRACT

Leadership and executive coaching cover areas as wide and deep as the uniqueness of all individual leaders, and the systems and organizations within which they lead. Coaches are uniquely placed to help leaders and can draw from a range of simple and powerful models to help leaders lead through an increasingly complex world.

Leadership and coaching

Leadership is fundamentally different to management, and its nature requires particular skills and ways of being where the coach is uniquely placed to assist. As per Kotter (1990), management is about creating order and some stability through activities such as planning and budgeting, organizing and controlling, while leadership is about motivating and inspiring individuals to energize them to overcome barriers to change, aligning them behind a clear vision, and creating productive change that enables the organization to achieve its ambitions.

Given the more complex, demanding and influential role of a leader, coaches have a particularly valuable role: 1) with a coach, a leader can speak entirely freely without needing to be concerned about confidentiality, or how they are perceived; 2) by asking reflective questions, facilitating creativity, and questioning existing thought, beliefs and perspectives, a coach can stimulate the highest-quality thinking; 3) by the coach creating a space safe for vulnerability, leaders can own their emotional state, rather than unconsciously project their anxieties, fears and doubts onto others; 4) leaders may be inhibited by insufficient challenge within the organization, whereas '… a healthy challenge, when delivered from a relationship of trust and mutual respect, serves to stretch people's thinking and drives them to dig deeper into the reality of their situation and the true potential of the future' (Blakey and Day, 2012: 2).

The range and depth of skills and approaches required by leaders are therefore considerable, particularly in an increasingly complex world. Within this wide landscape, an understanding of some leadership models, styles and types of issues that arise in leadership coaching can help provide frameworks within which coaches can help leaders thrive.

Leadership models

There are a considerable number of different leadership models that can assist leaders and coaches alike. Models are not, however, in themselves, either 'the answer' or of universal applicability. 'The best leaders select from a wide palette and make informed choices about their interventions and the approaches that suit the individuals, the culture and the specific situation' (Passmore, 2015: 6). The skill is to develop that palette and the ability to discern the most valuable approach. I set out two such models below.

Transactional and transformational leadership

Bass's 'full range of leadership' references transactional and transformational leadership styles (1998). In a transactional style, leaders influence by reinforcing positive or negative behaviours. These include positive feedback, promotions and salary rises where expectations are met, or negative feedback and withdrawal of privileges where they are not.

A transformational style potentially has a greater positive impact. It can transform followers to 'perform beyond expectations' and create a greater emotional bond by arousing enthusiasm for a common vision (Kearney, 2008).

The four transformational components of Bass's leadership model are:

- **Idealized influence** – behaving in ways that the leader is admired, respected, trusted and therefore emulated.

- **Inspirational motivation** – behaving in ways that provide meaning, optimism and enthusiasm.

- **Intellectual stimulation** – encouraging people to question assumptions, and to be creative and innovative.

- **Individualized consideration** – actively developing people's potential by creating new opportunities for development – encouraging, rather than monitoring efforts.

The key to the models is to understand the appropriate balance of their complementary effectiveness, which will be different for different businesses and situations. Operationally focused sectors may tend to have a more transactional style, and more creative and developmental sectors may tend to be more transformational. Research by Bass et al (2003) suggests the greater the complexity, the more the transformational style is effective.

It is therefore important to understand more about the organization and context within which the leader is working. While developed in the 1980s, the models remain relevant today, particularly in complex organizations and sectors, and where employees are increasingly being asked to do more with the same resources.

Authentic leadership

Lee and Roberts (2015) express the tension between 'personal authenticity' and 'social authenticity' at the heart of leadership. A leader needs to be true to themselves, drawing on their core character strengths, and at the same time tune in to others, the environment and be able to apply approaches according to the context.

They describe authentic leadership as character strengths and organizational goals being creatively attuned. The positions either side of this are 'defiant leadership' (where the leader focuses on their own strengths and goals, with limited attunement to others), and 'compliant leadership' (where the leader focuses on the qualities and needs of others, the organization, with limited self-expression).

This can be a powerful model to help leaders reflect on where their focus is, and needs to be, between 'self' and 'other', both generally in their leadership style, and in particular situations and contexts. 'Leadership is what is co-created in the space between the leader and the led' (Lee and Roberts, 2015: 16).

The key to authentic leadership is therefore the ability to reflect with curiosity and courage on the mental states of self and others, and then to use that reflection to enter insightful dialogue to help shape how best to lead different individuals and groups.

This simple model has profound foundations. Lee and Roberts (2015) make connections between the traits of compliant and defiant leadership, and attachment theory (Bowlby, 1973). Avoidant attachment, where parenting is experienced as unresponsive and rejecting, may lead to the child and adult being more emotionally 'cut off' from others, and therefore a more 'defiant leadership' style. Ambivalent attachment, where parenting is experienced as inconsistent and the child is alert to the caregiver's state of mind, can lead to children and adults being 'needy' for recognition, keen to please others, and therefore a more 'compliant' leadership style.

At its core, the authentic leadership model requires courageous and skilled reflection to help leaders understand themselves, others and their organizations better, to be able to lead with effective authenticity.

Leadership styles

Each leader is unique. While leaders are unlikely to fall neatly into a specific type, it can be helpful to have a frame of reference for different clusters of types and styles of leadership (Goleman, 2000). This can help leaders become aware of their predominant style or styles, and widen their range and ability to apply different styles and approaches. The following are six such styles, with the strengths and potential limitations of each.

Commanding

In commanding leadership, the leader makes most decisions and sets clear expectations and roles. This approach can be efficient and can reduce an individual's stress by the leader making decisions quickly, and individuals not needing to think outside of their specific role.

The commanding approach can also mean that individuals become demotivated and disempowered. It can stifle creativity, collaboration and diversity in thought, and can be highly stressful for the leader, who may feel disproportionate personal responsibility for results.

Visionary

A visionary leader understands the big picture and can set and communicate a long-term direction for the organization. This can inspire people to work towards the vision and create energy and empowerment to steer through change.

Visionary leaders could be too concerned with the bigger picture and the future, and so need to also become comfortable dealing with details and the 'now' or ensure they get someone around them who is.

Affiliative

An affiliative leader focuses more on people and relationships, helping people to connect with their organization and each other, and to feel they are 'in something together'. This approach can achieve stronger teamwork, personal bonds and well-being.

Overused, an affiliative approach can result in fear of conflict, and low accountability, where team harmony is privileged over productivity and results.

Democratic

With democratic leadership, people are empowered to be part of decision making and to bring forward ideas and suggestions. This can produce effective ideas generation and wider commitment to a plan or direction.

The desire for consensus within this leadership approach can also cause resentment where views are not perceived as having been considered, decisions are not made swiftly, or people expect to be included in all decisions, even when it is not appropriate.

Pacesetting

The pacesetting leader focuses on performance goals, standards and results, and leads by expecting the same (or more) from themselves. This approach can help lead teams that need little direction or coordination and can inspire high performance and pace, particularly where short-term progress is needed.

The pacesetting approach can be detrimental for longer-term employee engagement and motivation. Individuals may feel stressed, overwhelmed, and that they receive little or no feedback or development, which can lower staff morale when goals are not achieved.

Coaching

A coaching leader coaches team members to develop themselves in the long term as individuals and professionals. A coaching leader is skilled in spotting and nurturing talent, and improves performance through higher commitment, trust and empowerment.

A coaching approach requires skilled time investment and may not be appropriate where swifter results are required, or where people are less open to change and development.

Understanding leadership style is important

A coach can help a client understand their natural leadership style, and how to strengthen and develop further to widen their range and seek out complementary skills and styles to become a more effective leader.

Themes in leadership coaching

The areas that may come up in leadership coaching are as diverse as the width and depth of leaders themselves. It can be helpful to be aware of topics that may be discussed but they are far from exhaustive:

- **Leading change** – creating a clear vision, energizing others, understanding culture, addressing resistance and building momentum.

- **Virtual leadership** – developing effective communication, empowerment and collaboration, and maximizing effectiveness of the operating model.

- **Conflict resolution** – effectively resolving conflicts to develop trust, collaboration and solutions.

- **Imposter syndrome** – ability to experience and work through anxiety, doubts and low self-confidence.

- **Communication** – developing an effective range of communication styles for different situations.

- **Delegation** – effective empowerment of others.

- **Building trust** – understanding the importance of trust for the success of the organization, and developing different ways to build trust, including the ability to be vulnerable.

- **Board/team dynamics** – understanding the importance of teams and developing ways to build high-performing teams (see 'Team coaching' below).

- **Significant decisions** – understanding the context, obtaining appropriate diverse stakeholder input and ensuring high-quality thinking.

- **Improving productivity** – understanding and addressing obstacles, increasing motivation and the impact of different leadership styles.

Even if there is a principal focus, coaching is likely to include multiple and overlapping areas. The key is the quality of exploration of both the surface issues, and the more impactful issues underneath.

Team coaching

The effectiveness of teams is essential for the success of organizations, and so team coaching is an important component of leadership coaching. Models relating to the functioning of teams can be helpful to provide a frame of reference for coaching teams to develop their effectiveness.

One such model is by Lencioni (2002), which focuses on the five dysfunctions of a team (with the counterpoint for each):

1 **Absence of trust** – team members need to be vulnerable to each other about weaknesses, mistakes, fears and behaviours.

2 **Fear of conflict** – team members can passionately dialogue with, challenge and question each other to discover truth and make the best decisions.

3 **Lack of commitment** – the team achieves genuine buy-in to decisions, given the robustness of their debate and consideration.

4   **Avoidance of accountability** – teams hold one another accountable for decisions and standards as peers.

5   **Inattention to results** – 'Teams that trust one another, engage in conflict, commit to decisions, and hold one another accountable are very likely to... focus almost exclusively on what is best for the team... and the collective results that define team success.' (Lencioni, 2005: 7)

The central principle to the model is that 'no quality or characteristic is more important than trust' (Lencioni, 2005: 13). Trust is developed through the vulnerability and courage of individuals to admit the truth about themselves, and be comfortable and open around their failures, weaknesses and fears.

Lencioni's model provides a powerful frame of reference for team coaching, and steps to work through, with trust being the critical starting point.

Executive coaching

In executive coaching, the coach typically interfaces with the organization as well as the individual, and so it is important to be aware of the potential implications and develop ways to navigate the stakeholders and process.

Who is the client?

Where the organization is involved in the coaching arrangements, it is essential to be absolutely clear who the client is. It will often be the organization. They are paying the fee, they are the ones who want the outcome, and it is your job as coach to help deliver it. Alternatively, it could be the coachee, as the role of the coach is to help the person in front of you. It is important to be aware of the difference, and the different implications (e.g., reporting, goal setting, confidentiality), and to address this through the contracting stage. This is likely to centre on who sets the outcome for the coaching.

ORGANIZATION AS CLIENT

Where the organization sets the goal, the coach works on that goal with the coachee. As with any coaching relationship, the work will be wider and deeper than the goal set, but the goal needs to be clear. The organization may monitor the achievement of the goal, during or at the end of the contract. Stakeholders may be brought into the process and feedback sought. Where the coachee wishes to challenge or change the goal set by the organization, the coach should address that with the coachee. For example, the coachee could be asked to address this with the manager, or they could agree for this to be raised with whomever is monitoring the outcome on behalf of the organization.

A tripartite contracting process, when the contract is agreed by three parties, can be very helpful for the coach. Having the commissioner/client, coachee and coach in the same room can give the coach significant insight into the work, the relationships and system around the coachee. It can help deepen the understanding of the outcome (being clear on the 'return on investment' is often a vital part of the process) and reinforce everyone's respective responsibilities to achieve it.

COACHEE AS CLIENT

Where the organization offers coaching, but without requiring that the organization sets the outcomes, the focus of the coaching work is decided by the coachee. This needs to be clear for all concerned that these are the parameters. The organization must respect the coachee's confidentiality, and the coachee must take responsibility for setting the goal.

360-Degree feedback

It is helpful for both coach and coachee that the coachee receives feedback, which can be used as part of the coaching. A 360-degree evaluation involves obtaining feedback on a range of areas from a variety of people, including managers, peers, people they manage and supervise, and clients. The 360-degree feedback request could be part of the general appraisal process, or bespoke to the person, and even informed by the coach. The feedback could be repeated at the end of the process, as part of evaluating a 'return on investment' based on a quantified before-versus-after comparison.

Conflicts

It will often be the case that, over time, the coach coaches more than one person in the organization. The coach needs to be highly alert to issues of confidentiality and objectivity. They will learn tangible information, and also develop views on the system and culture. This will be more pronounced for internal coaches, who will have significantly more information regarding the people and system. The internal coach needs to be aware of the strength of the insight and awareness they have, and the risks associated with being part of and complicit in the very system they are helping the coachee navigate.

The principle of transparency is essential here, and it may be appropriate to inform both parties relevant to any conflict and request their consent to continue. The role of the coach supervisor is particularly important here, to help the coach navigate situations, and there will be occasions when the coach may need to decline or terminate the contract.

Remedial coaching

Executive coaching can cover any and more of the areas referred to in the 'Themes in leadership coaching' section above, but one area worthy of particular note is that of 'remedial' coaching, given the potential ethical dilemmas that a coach may be exposed to.

The organization needs to be clear where they perceive the gap to be, and what performance improvement looks like from their perspective. The coach may need to challenge the organization to provide this clarity, and this can be a healthy part of the process as it may help the organization itself to become clearer.

Where it appears to the coach that the organization may be using coaching to show it has tried everything before justifying an exit, the coach should challenge this. The outcome of performance improvement needs to be a genuine one, with the organization playing its part to help achieve it. An effective coach clarifies the specific ways the organization will commit to help the improvement, and what will happen if the intended improvement occurs. It may be appropriate to refuse work where there is insufficient transparency and ethical foundation for the outcomes and the commitment to help achieve them.

Emotional intelligence

Emotional intelligence is a thread running through leadership coaching. Goleman's model (1996) focuses on 'emotional intelligence' as consisting of five areas:

1 **Self-awareness** Knowing one's emotions, strengths, weaknesses, drives, values and goals, and recognizing their impact on others.
2 **Self-regulation** Managing or redirecting one's disruptive emotions and impulses and adapting to changing circumstances.
3 **Social skill** Managing relationships, influencing others' emotions to move people in the desired direction.
4 **Empathy** Recognizing, understanding and considering other people's feelings.
5 **Motivation** Developing drive to improve and achieve, commitment to goals, optimism and resilience.

Emotional intelligence is therefore essential for developing awareness of a leader's predominant leadership style, as well as valuing other styles and the ability to increase and adapt their range of styles. It is essential for the awareness of self and others in the authentic leadership model. It is inherent in 'transformational' leadership, in making emotional connections that transcend tangible reward. A leadership or executive coach works with their client to develop their emotional intelligence by focusing on taking other perspectives, knowing and eliminating blind spots (e.g., biases, stereotyping and assumptions), and acknowledging emotions in your coaching conversations, as well as reflecting on 360-degree feedback to identify gaps and development areas.

CASE STUDY

The use of leadership styles and value of drawing on a range of models is illustrated in this case study.

Esther was the successor in an organizational leadership role where the previous leader had been successful, but whose style Esther believed had created unhelpful dependencies on the leader that inhibited performance. Esther was charismatic, with a clear vision and view on what she considered needed to change. While she noted the success of the previous leader, she considered the style too 'soft', without provision for sufficient structure and clear performance standards. She was ambitious for the organization and wished to increase the pace of change.

Esther's aim was for less dependency on the leader, with managers taking more responsibility for their areas. Her style had worked for her local team, so she proposed adopting the same style to other teams in the organization.

Esther set out structures and expectations for people and made clear she wanted each manager to take responsibility for their team, without coming to her for solutions.

Esther found that, even though she had apparently taken a markedly different approach to the previous leader, she was having some similar issues, and in fact people were actually taking less responsibility and performing less well than they had previously.

We discussed her leadership style, and she considered herself a pacesetter and visionary. I asked how she reconciled being a pacesetter when standards apparently have dropped. She talked about the people 'not being up to it', and I reflected back that many were the same people who had previously been performing well (trying to strike the balance as coach between support and challenge).

Esther was becoming increasingly frustrated with the team, and (as a visual person) we developed images of 'pacesetting leadership' – one image where the pacesetter was running way ahead and shouting back at the group with a loudspeaker to 'speed up', and one image where the pacesetter was running at the front of, but within the pack. Esther recognized that her frustration meant she might be demotivating the team, and paradoxically slowing them down. We recognized that this might be more pronounced given the move to virtual working, which had exacerbated the distance between herself and the organization.

Esther's frustration was partly because she could see the potential of the organization and wanted it to move faster to get there. She explained her vision, which was inspiring, and I asked how she communicated this to the organization. She said she had talked about it at times, but because productivity had dipped, she felt she needed to focus there, before talking about 'grand visions'.

We discussed the transactional and transformational models. I speculated whether her vision could be part of bringing a transformational dimension to her leadership. The energy that came from Esther when she expressed her vision was palpable. I reflected back to Esther that her energy levels when she was frustrated were very noticeable to me too and might be what the organization was experiencing. Likewise, I expressed how inspiring she could be when expressing her vision. This was a good example of how the coach can reflect back to the leader how the organization might be experiencing them, and how drawing on both leadership styles and models can be effective.

She was very frustrated about the dependency on her, and why people appeared not to be taking the initiative, even though she was giving them space to do so, and she was making clear she expected more responsibility. She did not understand why the previous team she led 'got it', and the wider organization did not.

We discussed the authentic leadership model, and how she may have seen the previous leadership model as 'compliant leadership', where the leader was keen to please and support others, and 'took on' many of their problems. I speculated as to whether Esther had introduced 'defiant leadership'. By being more 'cut off' (again exacerbated by the shift to virtual working), people had begun thinking less for themselves. This had resulted in equivalent dependency, with the added challenge of people struggling to contend with a marked shift in style. Esther had focused on imposing her own style, in the same way she had successfully used it for her team, but without sufficient focus on the 'social authenticity' of understanding the new teams she was overseeing.

Over time, Esther shifted her leadership style so that she spent more time collaborating with people, so she could share her vision more, and work with people to find solutions. She went into the office more, and encouraged others to do so, recognizing the psychological distance created by virtual working (contrary to her previous view that it improved productivity, given less time for people 'chatting'). She recognized the importance of understanding the teams she was now leading, and tuning in with that, rather than imposing her style. She is beginning to experience a shift in the organization, where there is increasing energy and productivity. Significantly she is also more energized herself, feeding off the energy of others rather than feeling 'everything' was down to her.

As well as demonstrating the value of drawing on (rather than imposing) leadership styles and models, this case study also shows the considerable impact on leadership caused by the increase in virtual working.

Conclusions

While there is no universal model for leadership and executive coaching, an understanding of different models and leadership styles can be extremely helpful in providing frames of reference within which to explore complex situations, people and systems.

Courage, vulnerability and reflective ability in relation to both the leader and system they are seeking to influence are themes at the heart of leadership work.

These themes universally require great emotional intelligence, from both coach and leader alike.

While this chapter focuses principally on leadership within organizations, leadership is relevant for all areas of life. Brown (2012: 185) says:

> A leader is anyone who takes responsibility for finding the potential in people and processes and has the courage to develop that potential. Leadership is not about titles or the corner office. It's about the willingness to step up, put yourself out there, and lean into courage.

References

Bass, B M (1998) *Transformational Leadership: Industrial, military, and educational impact*, Lawrence Erlbaum Associates, Hillsdale, NJ

Bass, B M, Avolio, B J, Jung, D I and Benson, Y (2003) Predicting unit performance by assessing transformation and transactional leadership, *Journal of Applied Psychology*, 88 (2), 207–18, doi.org/10.1037/0021-9010.88.2.207

Blakey, J and Day, I (2012) *Challenging Coaching: Going beyond traditional coaching to face the FACTS*, Nicholas Brealey Publishing, London

Bowlby, J (1973) *Attachment and Loss, Volume 2: Separation, anxiety and anger*, Hogarth Press, London

Brown, B (2012) *Daring Greatly: How the courage to be vulnerable transforms the way we live, love, parent, and lead*, Avery, New York

Goleman, D (1996) *Emotional Intelligence: Why it can matter more than IQ*, Bantam Books, New York

Goleman, D (2000) Leadership that gets results, *Harvard Business Review*, March-April, hbr.org/2000/03/leadership-that-gets-results

Kearney, E (2008) Age differences between leaders and followers as a moderator of the relationship between transformational leadership and team performance, *Journal of Occupational and Organizational Psychology*, 81 (4), 803–11, doi.org/10.1348/096317907X256717

Kotter, J P (1990) *A Force for Change: How leadership differs from management*, Free Press, New York

Lee, G and Roberts, I (2015) Coaching for authentic leadership, in *Leadership Coaching: Working with leaders to develop elite performance*, 2nd edn, ed J Passmore, pp 15–32, Kogan Page, London

Lencioni, P (2002) *The Five Dysfunctions of a Team: A leadership fable*, Jossey-Bass, San Francisco, CA

Lencioni, P (2005) *Overcoming the Five Dysfunctions of a Team: A field guide*, Jossey-Bass, San Francisco, CA

Passmore, J (ed) (2015) *Leadership Coaching: Working with leaders to develop elite performance*, Kogan Page, London

37

Coaching and mental health

JOAN SWART

ABSTRACT

With about one in four people experiencing diagnosable mental health problems each year in the US and UK (and one in nine globally), and numbers continuing to rise, coaches are highly likely to encounter affected clients. The central premise of all helping professions is to do no harm, therefore it is a coach's professional duty to acquaint themselves with basic mental health knowledge and tools to make an informed decision whether to refer a client to a mental health professional and/or whether it is in the best interest of the client to provide coaching that is within their boundaries of competence (McManus et al, 2009; SAMHSA, 2020).

Introduction

The scope of this chapter is not to differentiate between coaching and counselling or therapy but to give coaches practical guidelines to feel more confident in navigating the boundaries of mental health within a structure to ensure the safety and well-being of clients and themselves. While some trainers and institutions maintain a traditional view of coaching that avoids exploration of a client's past and dealing with emotional distress, for instance, such an orientation is much too simplistic, impractical and limiting. Emergent coaching practices, and increasing maturity of systems, frameworks and practitioners are making a difference, but there is still much work to be done.

Although the core premise of coaching is to collaborate with a client in a non-directive way to pursue their goals, and that they are naturally creative, resourceful and whole to find their own best solutions, people are complex and fluid as they respond to constantly changing worlds. Today's circumstances, specifically, are brittle, anxious, nonlinear and incomprehensible, colloquially abbreviated as BANI, which increase stress individually and collectively. Coupled with concerning social trends such as cancel culture, bullying, fearmongering, destabilizing identity and breaking down functional social organization, mental unwellness has accelerated to unsustainable levels over the past few years. As a result, mental health services are overwhelmed and support with first-line defences are desperately needed.

The coaching profession has shown phenomenal growth in the same period, with exciting developments at industry bodies to oversee its quality and responsibility. Coaching and mental health have traditionally been seen as mutually exclusive but, in reality, such a view is misguided. Any coach, whatever their level of experience or setting, is likely to come across clients struggling with their mental health, temporarily or otherwise.

Furthermore, with knowledge of how to recognize signs and symptoms of mental health struggles and to make the best-informed decision of what to do next, whether it is a referral to another professional or not, coaches are better equipped to deliver an effective service and extend their skills to other populations and settings where it may be valuable.

Basic mental health education is still lacking at many coach training schools and programmes. Many coaches, especially newbies, are hesitant and anxious when exposed to mental health issues – if they recognize the signs at all. As a result, they may make assumptions, which invariably leads to wrong decisions that do not serve the client (and themselves) well.

With this chapter, I aim to provide a rough guideline to decide when (and why) to refer a client to another professional – a therapist, counsellor or coach with the needed specialization. The process is not definitive. Variables such as the 1) coach's competence, capacity and capability, 2) coach–client relationship, 3) client expectations, 4) severity, chronicity and impact of a mental health symptom, and 5) specific client situation (e.g., environment, support, risk factors) can all play a decisive role. However, four core (and non-negotiable) principles exist in ethical coaching – beneficence, nonmaleficence, autonomy and justice (Varkey, 2021).

1 **Beneficence** The coach must act in the client's best interest.

2 **Nonmaleficence** The coach must take all reasonable measures not to harm their client.

3 **Autonomy** With a few exceptions (e.g., clear and imminent risk of harm to the self and others, illegal conduct, mental incompetence), clients have the power to make rational decisions and choices, including terminating coaching and not participating in an exercise. The umbrella of autonomy also covers informed consent, confidentiality and disclosure, which the coach must respect.

4 **Justice** The coach must provide fair, equitable and appropriate care within the bounds of competence.

Therefore, when contemplating the mental health of a client, a coach is responsible for ensuring that these requirements are met within their best ability as determined by professional standards set by the industry. An important part of this process is to determine and consider the client's mental health status and, more specifically, the impact it has on the coaching process and outcome, which is to pursue a safe and positive result.

Mental health as a continuum

The mental health status of an individual is rarely clear-cut simple, and conclusive. In addition, most coaches are not equipped to make clinical decisions. Therefore, coaches should, at the minimum, have the knowledge, awareness and process in place to make informed referral decisions. This does not mean shying away or avoiding discussions about trauma in the past, intense emotions or suicide ideation, for instance, but recognizing signs that fall outside their competence and situations that warrant specialized support.

Mental health is a continuum where everyone is in flux over time. Important considerations are severity, chronicity and risk of harm. Severity (acuteness) refers to the client's level of distress and the impact on their life at any moment. Chronicity points to the stability of their struggle over time, for example, grief is usually more contextual and has a shorter duration than major depression. Whether a struggle is trigger-related, improving or deteriorating it is all relevant because it suggests a movement on the continuum scale (Figure 37.1). People on the healthy end of the scale generally feel happy, and are goal-oriented, balanced and stable. As they move to the right, they may react to something negative and start showing signs of distress. When the stress becomes more pervasive, their behaviour becomes more dysfunctional and (often) co-morbid, which means that the negativity permeates through many more areas in their life (e.g., activities, performance, relationships, health). At this stage, are sufficiently acute to become acontextual, i.e., not relating to specific, isolated situations and events any more. If not properly treated by a professional, the impact is likely to be devastating and deteriorate even further.

A competent coach works on noticing and understanding when (and why) a client moves into the reacting and injured stages and what it likely means for the coaching process. In the injured zone, they will likely seriously consider a referral, whereas being watchful in the reacting zone for any lasting or worsening effects outside of a single context.

To inform the process, I suggest following a best-practice protocol such as represented in Figure 37.2. Starting with the formation of the coach–client relationship in the chemistry call and contracting phase to manage the client's expectations of the coaching objectives, the coach's watchfulness and enquiry continue by constantly assessing the client's status.

FIGURE 37.1 The mental health continuum model

HEALTHY	REACTING	INJURED	ILL
Normal fluctuations in mood	Nervousness, irritability	Anxiety, anger	Excessive anxiety
Takes things in stride	Sadness, overwhelmed	Pervasive sadness,	Panic attacks
Good sense of humour	Displaced sarcasm	tearfulness, hopelessness,	Easily enraged, aggressive
Consistent performance	Procrastination	worthlessness	Depressed mood, numb
Physically and socially active	Forgetfulness	Negative attitude	Cannot concentrate
Confident in self and others	Trouble sleeping	Difficulty concentrating	Inability to make decisions
Drinking in moderation	Low energy	Trouble making decisions	Cannot fall asleep/stay
	Muscle tension, headaches	Decreased performance,	asleep
	Missing an occasional class	regularly missing	Constant fatigue, illness
	or deadline	classes/deadlines, or over	Absent from social
	Decreased social activity	work	events/classes
	Drinking regularly or in	Restless, disturbed sleep	Suicidal thoughts/intent
	binges to manage stress	Avoidance, social withdrawal	Unusual sensory experiences
		Increased use of alcohol	(hearing or seeing things)
		hard to control	Alcohol or other addiction
Nurture support	Recognize limits, take	Tune into own signs of	Seek professional care
systems	breaks, identify	distress	Follow
	problems early, seek	Talk to someone, ask for	recommendations
	support	help	
		Make self-care a priority	
		Don't withdraw	

Excel	Adapt	React	Struggle	In crisis

SOURCE Chen, Chang and Stuart (2020: 2)

FIGURE 37.2 Referral decision steps

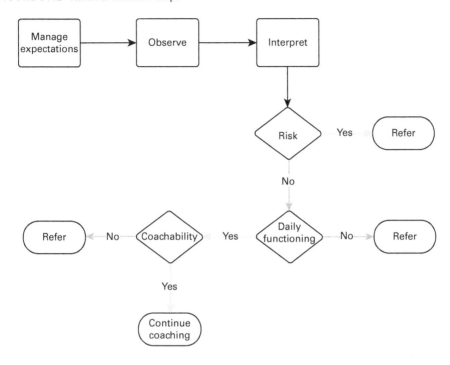

Manage expectations

From the beginning, but also throughout the coaching relationship, the coach ensures that the client is informed about the process and what coaching is (and is not). Coaching is a non-directive approach that relies on the creative input and insight from the client. Clients understand that they find and apply their own unique solutions to problems, which require development of a conscious competence (and willingness) to address issues and blocks.

Therefore, a necessary starting point, in addition to a trusting coach–client relationship, is their ability to pursue change with a goal-oriented approach. Coaches manage these expectations through information and openness while staying true to the spirit (and intent) of coaching as a guide rather than a leader or advisor.

Observation

When an interviewer asked me recently what I believe is the most important skill for a coach, I did not hesitate to answer. Knowing how to observe. Meaning, observing with understanding, to be more inclusive. In this scope, observing covers multiple facets usually mentioned in competency frameworks. Presence, listening, questioning, having empathy all come to mind.

While many contemporary experts and practitioners question Mehrabian's well-known 7-38-55 communication model (all communication is done through 7 per cent verbal, 38 per cent tonality of the voice and 55 per cent body language), published in the late 1960s, the exact numbers are beside the point (Mehrabian, 1981). The message is undisputed. Body language (e.g., facial expressions, movement and posture) and tone of voice (e.g., dimension – humour, respectfulness, formality, enthusiasm – frequency and intensity) transmits a significant portion of the meaning of a speaker's message. Consistency with their spoken words reinforces the message while inconsistencies and discrepancies invalidate it.

By looking carefully at non-verbal cues, coaches acquire rich and valuable information (Swart, 2022a). Combined with active listening, an empathetic and non-judgemental presence, and avoiding distractions, including biases and assumptions, we unlock the full power of observation. We can use this information to gain clarity, confirm our observations and obtain deeper information. Clients value our interest. When they have the assurance that they do not have to answer or share if they feel uncomfortable, and feel trusted and acknowledged, they rarely decline an opportunity to open up.

Interpretation

With the information obtained through observation, verbal information, active listening and questioning, we can learn to recognize patterns, gaps and inconsistencies. We can then practise through reflection-in-action (analysis in the session) and reflection-on-action (reflection after the session). Further information can be obtained by paying attention to strong cues such as metaphors, narratives and unintended communication, such as leakages, slips and omissions.

Try to find the underlying reasons for the patterns, gaps and inconsistencies that you noticed. If you are unsure or need clarification, ask the client. 'I noticed that you seem upset. Did I get that right? Can you tell me more?' Clarifying your gut feeling, intuition or interpretation greatly increases the value of the conversation and puts the coach and client on the same page.

Rich and thorough information shows changes over time, groupings of events, experiences, and behaviours, as well as cause-and-effect relationships. Trends and clusters can tell you a lot about the different stages of a client's story. Remember that mental health is expressed as a continuum. Often the client may share something, having had suicidal thoughts at some time, for instance, but if you interpret the experiences closely enough, you may find that it does not influence them as much today any more. They may have recovered from their distress, be in remission, or have processed past experiences. This way, a coach can separate the past and present better to be able to focus on what matters (and what can be changed) now. Therefore, with all the information, the coach considers the client's daily functioning to build a clearer, qualified idea of the client's mental health status.

Risk of harm

An important consideration that may trump everything else, including most struggles of daily functioning as it could require priority attention, is the risk of harm that a client presents to themselves or others. Suicidal (or violent) ideation in the present is a warning sign. While most people who think about suicide do not progress to plans or an attempt (Nock et al, 2008), due diligence should be given at any time a client expresses such a thought. About 9 per cent of adults have a lifetime prevalence of suicide ideation, which means that just more than 1 in 10 people think of suicide in their lifetime (Nock et al, 2008). Of these, about 15 per cent attempt suicide without a prior plan, while having a plan raises the rate significantly. These findings are valuable for coaches as they help guide the risk assessment.

- While an indication of suicidal thoughts always represents a red flag, a competent coach can assess and triage risk and, frequently, if not most often, result in not having to refer the client. Follow up by asking the recency, intrusiveness, repetitiveness of these thoughts, and whether they have the commitment and means to enact a plan.

- Question whether one or more risk factors are present. These include a previous attempt, a psychiatric disorder – most often clinical-level depression, anxiety, substance abuse, bipolar disorder, post-traumatic stress disorder (PTSD) and schizophrenia – feelings of hopelessness and worthlessness, and childhood adversity (Sareen et al, 2005).

- Having social support and family connectedness protects against suicide (Goldsmith et al, 2002).

- If you, as a coach, have a suspicion that your client may be at risk of suicide, or they indicate suicide ideation, plans, previous attempts, have an existing treated or untreated psychiatric disorder, or present any of the risk factors, do not hesitate to ask about your concerns. Talking about suicide does not increase the risk – on the contrary, it acknowledges the client's struggles and shows empathy and support, which counters the isolation and hopelessness that the client is likely feeling (Swart, 2022b). If the client confirms one or more of these risk factors, refer them to a mental health professional.

- If you have any indication of intent, refer the client without any delay. Also provide information of resources, such as their local helpline, support groups, literature, etc.

Therefore, treat any signs of present suicidality or violence as a clear warning sign. Explore the risk in the current session and do not let the matter go unresolved until the next session. If you are unsure or uncomfortable in any way, refer the client immediately and strongly encourage them to heed your advice.

Daily functioning

A client's daily functioning provides a coach with valuable information about the lack or presence of struggles in many areas. The Global Assessment of Functioning (GAF) is used by mental health professionals to rate the daily social, occupational and psychological functioning of a patient on a scale that ranges from 1 (severely impaired) to 100 (extremely high-functioning). Although the measure has been replaced in the DSM-5 with a new tool, the GAF remains useful as a robust, practical scale to assess daily functioning (Gold, 2014). Despite some limitations, including a lack of distinction between different areas of functioning, conceptual and subjective rating, and blurring symptoms and functioning (Aas, 2010; Dimsdale, Jeste and Patterson, 2010), knowledge and application of the concept of daily functioning in a qualitative way is useful to coaches to assist with referral decisions.

To demonstrate the concept and scales, refer to Table 37.1. With almost no exception, people seeking coaching fall in the upper half of the ratings, with anyone considered to be below 60 a good candidate for referral to a mental health professional as their functioning and symptoms are a more sustained impairment on their everyday functioning. Coaching may be appropriate when any issues or problems are mild (or, of course, absent), transient, and linked to a stressor or root cause.

The GAF ratings are very subjective but best estimated in clinical settings by utilizing a variety of sources, including self-report, semi-structured questions, psychological tests, health and police records, observations, and third-party sources like family, friends, colleagues and health personnel (Aas, 2014). Nevertheless, a well-sourced and interpreted idea of daily functioning is helpful to guiding decisions about the help needed. Questions that are helpful for coaches to use are.

- How often are you engaged in activities that you consider socially useful, such as work, study, volunteering, housework? How do you feel about these?
- How much time do you spend with friends and family? How do you feel about this?
- What do you do for self-care? How do you feel about this?
- Do you engage in any behaviours that concern you? What are the impact of these?

TABLE 37.1 Global Assessment of Functioning scales

Rating (0–100)	Symptoms
90–81	Absent or minimal symptoms with good functioning in all areas – occupation, work, personal life, education. Socially active and involved in a wide range of social activities. Generally satisfied with life. Only (minor, temporary, contextual) everyday issues and concerns
80–71	If social or occupational functioning or symptoms are present, they are isolated, transient and linked to identifiable stressors. Functioning well with only slight, occasional impairment
70–61	Mild symptoms or some difficulty in social and occupational functioning. Still generally functioning well with some meaningful relationships
60–51	Moderate symptoms or moderate difficulty in social and occupational functioning that are more intrusive in multiple life areas
50-41	Serious symptoms and/or serious impairment in social and occupational functioning (e.g., unable to keep a job or friends)

SOURCE Adapted from APA (2000: 36)

Although these questions require much careful consideration, the better you know your client and the stronger the coach–client trust, the more meaningful will your conclusions be about the daily functioning of your client in these main areas.

Figure 37.3 provides another way to visualize the consideration of referral based on daily functioning and severity (acute and chronic). I demarcated four quadrants, which are more conceptual than quantifiable.

1 **Disordered** – high severity of symptoms and low functioning. Coaching will (most likely) not be beneficial as a positive outcome is very unlikely and the risk of harm is high.

2 **Tension** – high severity of symptoms and high-functioning. The person is either suppressing, hiding or compensating for their symptoms but continues to perform well in most or some life areas. An example is a high-performing alcoholic. However, it is a precarious balancing act destined to fail when control slips for whatever reason. A coach could focus on the high-performance aspects, but the client may require professional care to reduce their symptoms.

3 **Blocked** – low severity of symptoms and low-functioning. Despite having no discernable (or minimal symptoms), the person is low-functioning in one or more areas. Coaching may focus on finding and understanding the root cause(s) of these struggles so that they can be 'unblocked' with appropriate changes.

4 **'Normal'** – low severity of symptoms and high-functioning. Coaching focuses on elevating performance, achievements and satisfaction even higher.

FIGURE 37.3 The functioning–mental health quadrant

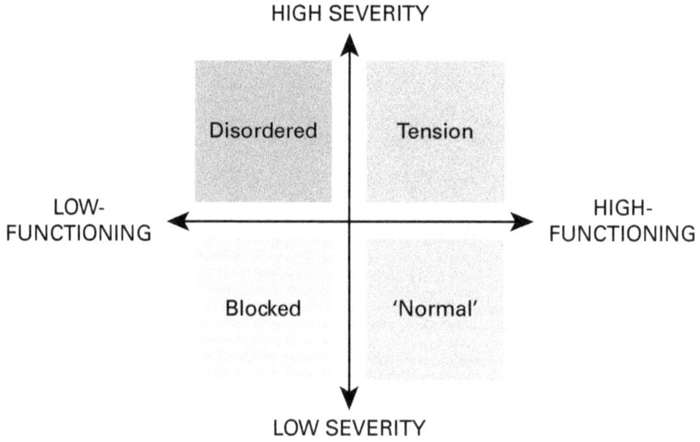

The functioning–mental health quadrant is a useful representation of how to approach a client, what to focus on, and whether to refer them. It is not definitive but provides a guideline to use in understanding where a client is at, their difficulties, what blocks them, and how to pursue their best interest.

Coachability

Coachability refers to those qualities that contribute to a higher probability of achieving a positive outcome. These include self-awareness, openness to feedback, motivation, accountability and a willingness to learn and change (Swart, 2022a). Aspects that block coachability are significant distress and suffering, an inability to adapt to or interact with one's environment, and behaviour that is uncontrolled and unpredictable, irrational, and/or violates important social norms (Świeży, 2022).

A client may have (relatively) normal functioning in their daily lives with no discernible mental health issues, or sub-clinical symptoms, and still be considered not coachable. In other words, they perform at or around their baseline at work, home, socially and in college or school, and have no perceptible issues other than contextual ups and downs (see Figure 37.3). For example, despite the coach and/or client investing significant efforts, there is no visible progress. The client may be denying having any problems, despite evidence to the contrary, actively avoiding acknowledging or confronting these. They become defensive or aggressive when receiving constructive feedback. They may consistently not implement actions agreed on (Świeży, 2022). More enquiry and exploration are needed to uncover obstacles and impediments.

Sometimes, the coach's decision is clear but, many times, it may not be so obvious and relies on your gut feeling and instincts. If a client triggers unwanted and/or disturbing thoughts or feelings in their coach, it more often than not proves the best not to take them on. If you are a coach, trust your gut intuition about a client. Most times, you would have been right, and placed yourself and the client in jeopardy to pursue the relationship against your better judgement. At best, you will waste valuable time and emotional and energy resources, become frustrated, and question yourself. The worst case is that your frustration projects onto the client, who loses hope and confidence, ending up in a worse position than before coaching – a lose–lose situation for both.

Final thoughts

I have provided multiple concepts and tools to help guide coaches to consider their client's mental health situation and make the best decision for them. Do not hesitate to refer clients. Do it in an empathetic manner while acknowledging their struggles as a part of life that affects many people. Remember that clients often seek a coach because they feel less stigmatized and have more access to coaching compared to mental health services. Also, they have likely built a powerful rapport and trust with you, which they have come to rely on. Therefore, they may want to continue seeing you even after being referred (or come to see you when already in therapy). If in their best interest, such an arrangement may be workable if you avoid conflicts of approach and clearly demarcate your focus while managing their expectations.

References

Aas, I M (2010) Global Assessment of Functioning (GAF): Properties and frontier of current knowledge, *Annals of General Psychiatry*, 9 (20), 1–11, doi.org/10.1186/1744-859X-9-20 (archived at https://perma.cc/7X3C-59EC)

Aas, I M (2014) Collecting information for rating Global Assessment of Functioning (GAF): Sources of information and methods for information collection, *Current Psychiatry Reviews*, 10 (4), 330–47, doi.org/10.2174/1573400509666140102000243 (archived at https://perma.cc/L8SF-FH58)

APA (2000) *Diagnostic and Statistical Manual of Mental Health Disorders – Revision IV-TR* [DSM-IV-TR], American Psychiatric Association, Washington, DC

Chen, S, Chang, W and Stuart, H (2020) Self-reflection and screening mental health on Canadian campuses: Validation of the mental health continuum model, *BMJ Psychology*, 8 (76), 1–8, doi.org/10.1186/s40359-020-00446-w (archived at https://perma.cc/CR8Q-LWAG)

Dimsdale, J E, Jeste, DV and Patterson, T L (2010) Beyond the Global Assessment Functioning: Learning from Virginia Apgar, *Psychosomatics*, 51 (6), 515–19, doi.org/10.1176/appi.psy.51.6.515 (archived at https://perma.cc/89SV-CHCR)

Gold, L H (2014) DSM-5 and the assessment of functioning: The World Health Organization Disability Assessment Schedule 2.0 (WHODAS 2.0), *Journal of the American Academy of Psychiatry and the Law*, 42 (2), 173–81

Goldsmith, S K, Pellmar, T C, Kleinman, A M and Bunney, W E (eds) (2002) *Reducing Suicide: A national imperative*, National Academies Press, Washington, DC, www.ncbi.nlm.nih.gov/books/NBK220939/ (archived at https://perma.cc/Q8GL-DRL8)

McManus, S, Meltzer, H, Brugha, T S, Bebbington, P E and Jenkins, R (2009) Adult psychiatric morbidity in England, 2007: Results of a household survey, NHS, London, doi.org/10.13140/2.1.1563.5205 (archived at https://perma.cc/7RES-8M9X)

Mehrabian, A (1981) *Silent Messages: Implicit communication of emotions and attitudes*, Wadsworth, Belmont, CA

Nock, M K, Borges, G, Bromet, E J, Alonso, J, Angermeyer, M, Beautrais, A, Bruffaerts, R et al (2008) Cross-national prevalence and risk factors for suicide ideation, plans, and attempts, *British Journal of Psychiatry*, 192 (2), 98–105, doi.org/10.1192/bjp.bp.107.040113 (archived at https://perma.cc/UE5K-H52N)

SAMHSA (2020) Key substance use and mental health indicators in the United States: Results from the 2019 National Survey on Drug Use and Health (HHS Publication No PEP20-07-01-001, NSDUH Series H-55), Rockville, MD: Center for Behavioral Health Statistics and Quality, Substance Abuse and Mental Health Services Administration, www.samhsa.gov/data/ (archived at https://perma.cc/S3JT-HYEN)

Sareen, J, Cox, B J, Afifi, T O, De Graaf, R, Asmundson, G J, Ten Have, M and Stein, M B (2005) Anxiety disorders and risk for suicidal ideation and suicide attempts: A population-based longitudinal study of adults, *Archives of General Psychiatry*, 62 (11), 1249–57, doi.org/10.1001/archpsyc.62.11.1249 (archived at https://perma.cc/EWG4-6ASE)

Swart, J (2022a) Good coaches learn and apply basic diagnostic skills, ethically (and supervision plays a vital role), International Conference on Coaching Supervision, Oxford Brookes University, 5 May, Oxford, UK

Swart, J (2022b) The value of diagnostic skills for coaches and supervisors, *Coaching Perspectives*, 35, 54–5

Świeży, M (2022) *Psychology for Coaches: Key concepts and findings to ground your skills*, Routledge, New York

Varkey, B (2021) Principles of clinical ethics and their application to practice, *Medical Principles and Practice*, 30, 17–28, doi.org/10.1159/000509119 (archived at https://perma.cc/4MF6-YZDN)

38

Coaching 'difficult' personality types

JOAN SWART
CHRISTINE GUIRGUIS

ABSTRACT

Obtaining information from a client is a vital link in the coaching process. Not to diagnose or stereotype clients, but to build a collaborative and trusting relationship, and build plans based on accurate data. As some personality and behaviour traits can interfere with coaching, a coach able to recognize these is in a stronger position to manage or work around any resistance or lack of insight. This chapter explores narcissistic, psychopathic and borderline personality traits, providing insight on presentation, impact, how to recognize the signs, and what to do when faced with a 'difficult' client.

Introduction

Personality is one of the most significant factors in coaching as it influences the coaching relationship, the readiness of the client to discover blind spots, their natural resilience, their needs, and their attitude to change. Personality is defined as the combination of characteristics or qualities that form an individual's distinctive character. As such, it contains sets of baseline behaviours, thoughts, emotions and beliefs that are unique to each person. Therefore, personality determines a person's motivation and psychological interaction with the environment and others. As it evolves from all their genetic, biological and environmental factors, and experiences they have been subjected to, personality becomes settled and ingrained by adulthood.

Hence, personality traits are consistent across different situations and stable over time. Based on a person's genetic predisposition and experiences, they make meaning of how to relate to the world with the best outcome. Personality is relatively hardwired but can be shaped to better adapt to changed circumstances, for instance.

Observing and understanding your client's personality characteristics are important for a coach as they determine the likely relationship, how they may cope under stress, knowing what they value and feel comfortable with, and help to anticipate potential issues. Usually, an adaptive personality can shape responses somewhat to different demands. They may be willing to compromise; be compliant when usually dominant, be mindful of people's needs when naturally task-oriented and provide support when commonly independent. In the context of coaching, I consider a 'difficult' personality type those who are not adaptive, do not recognize that their responses do not match the situation or expectations, and are blind to their own role and responsibility in the outcome or consequences.

Considerations of coachability

For coaching to be optimally effective, the key premise of the client as sufficiently and naturally creative, resourceful and whole to discover their own answers must apply. Although coaching is a technique to reveal, shape and utilize the inner resources of the client, not all clients are equally coachable all the time. Orange and red flags may become apparent in the coaching interaction that impact the client motivation, client–coach relationship, and intrapersonal stability and insight needed to explore potential. The following present warning signs for the observant coach:

- Poor grasp of reality
- Unmanageable instability (emotions, behaviour)
- Mention of recent suicidal intent
- Unprocessed trauma that affects daily functioning
- Unwillingness to be accountable
- Lack of or unstable boundaries
- Pathological lying and manipulation

When there are any symptoms that seriously affect daily life (e.g., social, work, mood, judgement, communication, inappropriate behaviour), the coach must be extra attentive and consider whether the client is more suitable to receiving specialist guidance. Some of these presentations and traits are linked to personality types that are considered difficult to coach, primarily because of innate poor interpersonal relationships, a significant lack of insight and accountability, dependence on external validation, and a manipulative and callous nature. Ultimately then, we are looking for qualities of openness to feedback, self-awareness, accountability, dedication, motivation, and a willingness to change and learn in our clients to be of best service to our clients.

Navigating 'difficult' personalities in practice

For the scope and purpose covered here, I limit my exploration to three personality types that I, and many other helping professionals, consider challenging to work with. These are narcissistic, psychopathic and borderline personality types. They share similar features in lacking insight of their responsibility, having an external locus of control, having little regard for the needs and rights of others, and are generally impulsive with poor emotion and behaviour regulation.

Narcissistic personality traits

As we start to look at the first type of a potentially 'difficult' client, namely those with narcissistic personality features, a few words of caution are in order.

In recent years, more and more people have started to label and informally diagnose people with mental health disorders, from politicians and celebrities to CEOs. Unless you are a trained and accredited mental health provider, such judgements are outside your limits of competence and, therefore, unethical. As we all know, unofficial labels stigmatize people undeservedly and are often part of a selfish agenda of the broadcaster.

Second, diagnosing or labelling someone with a recognized mental health disorder requires that they satisfy a rigorous diagnostic process and set of behavioural criteria. These standards include experiencing the symptoms consistently over a specified number of months and a significant struggle with normal daily functioning.

It is common to encounter antagonistic people who fall within the Five Factor Model of Personality Traits, which considers openness to experience, conscientiousness, extraversion, agreeableness and neuroticism, especially with a low level of agreeableness (Sleep et al, 2021). Whitebourne (2020) describes the seven factors of antagonism as such:

- Callousness: being cruel and lacking sympathy for other people.
- Grandiosity: having an unrealistic view of being superior to others.
- Aggressiveness: expressing behaviour that is directed to harming others verbally or physically.
- Suspiciousness: unreasonably lacking trust in other people.
- Manipulation: influencing or swaying someone to benefit your needs.
- Domineering: assuming the role of superiority and the right to control others.
- Risk taking: experiencing thrills through risky behaviour that is likely to negatively impact one's health or others' safety.

Antisocial or narcissistic personality traits often feature high antagonism accompanied by one or more factors (Whitebourne, 2020).

The Diagnostic and Statistical Manual of Mental Disorders, or DSM-5, characterizes a person with narcissistic personality disorder, or NPD, as exhibiting a grandiose sense of self-importance, a constant need for admiration and praise, and a lack of consideration and empathy for others that has typically started in early adulthood (American Psychiatric Association, 2013). Sometimes, despite a lack of evidence, they exaggerate and believe their capabilities and accomplishments are superior to others. Therefore, they feel entitled to, and may demand, constant respect and recognition. The narcissist personality believes they are much more unique and special compared to others. Only high-status people deserve their time and effort.

Studies show that environmental (childhood upbringing, cultural and peer influence, etc.) and genetic factors (genes, personality, proneness to violence, addiction, etc.) contribute to NPD (Pedersen, 2021). Interestingly enough, though people with narcissistic traits present these characteristics, they inherently suffer from fragile self-esteem. As a result, they are desperately trying to prove their worth to themselves and others to feed their narcissistic supply, or psychological addiction to constant attention and admiration (Brummelman et al, 2015).

Their relationships at work and home suffer because they take advantage of others to achieve their goals and feed their narcissistic demand for praise. They are arrogant and can be cruel if they think a person is not deserving of their attention. They lack the ability to recognize the feelings or needs of others.

A person with narcissistic features is often dissatisfied or distraught when others do not constantly recognize or admire them. They may go to unreasonable measures to fulfil this excessive need. They feel envy towards others that they may think do not deserve attention and rewards and they believe others are envious of them.

In a nutshell, the narcissistic executive is completely self-absorbed, often makes decisions based on their own interests, and ignores the feelings and needs of colleagues and subordinates, especially if they are not as nearly as 'special' as they are.

They want to be popular rather than efficient and do not attend well to details. When crossed, they become petty and resentful, becoming vengeful to punish and teach their 'rival' a lesson. They will try almost anything to get their way, including manipulation, deceit, threats, blackmail and gaslighting.

Gaslighting is a form of psychological control where the person manipulates the environment of another person to cut them off from support, options and resources so that they are forced to rely on the perpetrator or unable to oppose them.

The recipient of narcissistic behaviour typically feels isolated, lacks options, becomes anxious and distressed, and their productivity suffers. Together with their intent on following self-interest that distracts their focus and decisions, these effects on people in their workplace make narcissists a liability for organizations.

So, when a suspected narcissist enters your coaching practice, which approaches could you try? When we recognize narcissistic traits in a client, how do we best approach them?

When you suspect or realize a client has narcissistic features, know that their sense of self is delicate, and they have a pathological need to be admired. Although narcissists appear to be very confident, it is a coping mechanism to hide a deep vulnerability and sense of inadequacy. Therefore, here is what you, as their coach, could do:

- Do not question or attack the client's self-esteem and accomplishments they claim.
- Rather try to stabilize the foundations of their confidence.
- Respect your client and acknowledge their need to be recognized.
- Do not accentuate weaknesses or reinforce grandiose notions.
- Show empathy to gain trust as the narcissist views it as you being their ally.
- Start by identifying small problems that cause them distress, such as perceived disrespect from others or not getting the credit they believe they deserve. Ask how they think their behaviours and beliefs may limit them and block their potential.
- Set small and concrete goals to improve these issues.
- Your narcissistic client will likely try to please you – use this tendency to build the working relationship.
- Narcissists are typically very ambitious – acknowledge their ambitions without fuelling their grandiosity and show how you can help them achieve it.
- Slowly aim to build empathy for their colleagues and ground them in reality.

As narcissistic tendencies are also deeply embedded in a person's psychology, they naturally tend to regress to their old behaviours after a while. Therefore, it is important to stabilize and follow up on them over time, remembering that, while narcissistic tendencies are deeply entrenched, they are not always permanent (Raypole, 2020) and tend to decrease with age (Wetzel et al, 2020). Change is always possible but must be led by the client.

Psychopathic personality traits

Although you are unlikely to find someone with psychopathic features seeking personal coaching, such a client may be part of a company-sponsored coaching programme, especially among senior managers and board-level executives. Research found approximately 1 per cent of the general population have clinically significant levels of psychopathic features, while as many as 30 per cent may have reduced empathy, higher risk taking and greater self-regard compared to the general population (DeAngelis, 2022). In his book, *The Wisdom of Psychopaths: What saints, spies, and serial killers can teach us about success*, British psychologist Kevin Dutton (2012) places CEOs, lawyers and salespeople among the top 10 careers that attract the most psychopaths. These jobs are all cut-throat, require risk taking, utilize power and control, attract a measure of deceit and manipulation, and favour those with low social inhibition to get ahead. It's important to note that not all psychopaths are serial killers.

A psychopath is born with a higher inclination to develop psychopathic tendencies. Research found neurological differences such as a bigger striatum and fewer connections between the ventromedial prefrontal cortex (vmPFC) and the amygdala. The striatum is a brain structure involved in reward processing, which a psychopath vigorously pursues, excessively engaging in impulsive, stimulation-seeking behaviour with deficient decision-making (DeAngelis, 2022; Glenn et al, 2010). The vmPFC is responsible for feelings of empathy and guilt, while the amygdala processes fear and anxiety. The reduced functional connectivity between the vmPFC and amygdala means that psychopathic behaviour is prone to callousness and a disregard for prosocial norms when making decisions (Motzkin et al, 2011).

While a psychopath cannot easily change, being a threat to society can be prevented. Rather than 'curing' the underlying tendencies, interventions that are multimodal and address inappropriate behaviour through, for instance, impulse control or anger management programmes have proved to reduce risk (Felthouse, 2015). Hyde et al (2016) wrote that early parent-focused intervention could also minimize the risk of future antisocial behaviour. Therapeutic approaches such as schema therapy have also shown promising results among offenders and other forensic patients by moderating the innate temperament of the inner child to their existing situation, including current norms, responsibilities and unfulfilled needs (Bernstein et al, 2021; Dadomo et al, 2016).

Hervey Cleckley (1988) introduced the characteristics of a psychopath in his seminal work, *The Mask of Sanity*. He believed that they are adept at hiding behind a mask of normality to hide the disorganization, amorality and deceitfulness that are present in their strive to dominate. Originally listing 16 features, Robert Hare later expanded the traits, dividing them into four factors, which are 1) manipulativeness, 2) unreliability and a lack of focus, 3) callousness and insensitivity, and 4) intimidating and aggressive (Mathieu et al, 2013).

The 20 different features are as follows. The first factor, being manipulative, consists of:

- Ingratiating themselves into positions of power or favour
- Being glib
- Using charm
- Claiming expertise that is questionable or false
- Rationalizing mistakes and failures

The second factor, being unreliable and having a lack of focus, includes:

- Not being loyal
- A lack of planning
- Not having a consistent or the right focus
- Being impatient with a lack of progress, results, or perceived subordination
- Being unreliable, especially when something does not suit them

The third factor, being callous and insensitive, refers to:

- Rarely showing emotions
- Being insensitive to others' feelings and needs
- Appearing to be 'cold inside'
- Showing little or no remorse
- Showing no empathy

And, the fourth factor, being intimidating and aggressive, consists of:

- Acting in ways that are construed as intimidating
- Frequently appearing to be angry
- Asking harsh questions
- Threatening other workers
- Being dramatic

As a coach, you may come across a 'psychopath lite', to use a term coined by Professor of Leadership Development and Organizational Change at INSEAD, Manfred Kets de Vries (2012). A typical psychopath lite fits in, and thrives in organizational settings, where they use their gamesmanship, risk-taking, calmness under pressure, domination, competitiveness and assertiveness to their advantage. They have better emotion regulation and behavioural control than their lesser successful counterparts.

These clients are likely to adopt one or a combination of three approaches in coaching. The first is a passive-aggressive type of resistance masquerading as disinterest, or a more aggressive stance questioning the value of coaching. The second, milder but related approach, is to try to get the coach on their side against the people who forced them to receive coaching. The third approach is trying to impress the coach to try to gain something from a positive relationship and feedback. In most cases, they will mirror what you say and ask them to do, and, if it will benefit them, claim to make positive progress.

It is important to note that a psychopathic personality will, for all practical purposes, not change, unless the consequences of their behaviour are so dire that it presents a sufficiently compelling reason to accept some responsibility, at least, an awareness that is a necessary precursor for change. The characteristics are, at least partly, hereditary, and are deeply embedded in their belief, coping and behaviour systems. The best thing a coach can do is to:

- Work with them to find task-oriented ways to achieve the outcomes that will benefit them, and hopefully the organization too
- Stay away from confrontations and arguments
- Stay objective and factual – the psychopathic personality does not respond to empathy or emotions
- Keep to small and concrete action-based goals
- Try to relate any people-related or relationship issues directly to their goals
- Set and keep strict boundaries
- Avoid being pulled in or manipulated to anything you feel uncomfortable with

Know that you will feel uneasy and perhaps vulnerable in a coaching relationship with an executive with psychopathic features. They are masters at control and manipulation. When you feel psychologically unsafe or triggered in the process, end the relationship, if possible, as it is not worth compromising your values and health for a client.

Furthermore, leaders with psychopathic tendencies often cause problems – relational and operational, including a culture of exploitation and bullying – causing distress, anxiety, absenteeism, turnover, lower productivity and a decrease in creativity in an organization. When you, as a coach with an organizational sponsor, observe these effects, you may consider speaking truth to power within the boundaries of your contractual and confidentiality arrangements. This may mean confronting authority, calling out injustices and demanding change. Keep your own safety and professionalism protected, but do not compromise values for fear of speaking out or losing a client.

Borderline personality traits

Treating or coaching a client with borderline personality features is notoriously challenging as there are several typical blocks that prevent change, including a lack of insight, unstable moods, fearing rejection and internalizing criticism (O'Connor and O'Donovan, 2022). Borderline personality types are defined by the following difficulties in personality and interpersonal functioning, and/or personality traits, according to the DSM-5 (American Psychiatric Association, 2013):

1 **Identity:** markedly impoverished, poorly developed, or unstable self-image, often associated with excessive self-criticism; chronic feelings of emptiness; dissociative states under stress.
2 **Self-direction:** instability in goals, aspirations, values or career plans.

3 **Empathy:** inability to recognize the feelings and needs of others associated with interpersonal hypersensitivity (i.e., prone to feel slighted or insulted); perceptions of others selectively biased towards negative attributes or vulnerabilities.

4 **Intimacy:** intense, unstable and conflicted close relationships, marked by mistrust, neediness, and anxious preoccupation with real or imagined abandonment; close relationships often viewed in extremes of idealization and devaluation and alternating between over-involvement and withdrawal.

5 **Negative affectivity:** emotional liability, anxiousness, separation insecurity, depressive.

6 **Disinhibition:** impulsivity, risk taking.

7 **Antagonism:** hostility, which is easily excitable and quick to arise.

8 Difficulties are relatively **stable over time** and consistent across situations.

9 It cannot be normalized in the individual's **developmental stage or socio-cultural environment,** or due to effects of substance use or medical conditions.

Many of these symptoms impair the mental and emotional stability of a person to the point where they struggle with relationship interactions and trust. Small things become crises and they make devastating assumptions about their self-worth and valuation from others.

If you, as their coach, notice signs that a client may have borderline personality traits that impact their functioning and relationships, including the coach–client relationship and ability and willingness to change, here are some helpful things to be mindful of:

- **The victim role** People with borderline personality traits often thrive in a victim role. Be mindful that they do not manipulate you by pushing you into a rescuer role. As in Karpman's drama triangle (2014), the codependence between the victim and rescuer roles are negative and unhealthy as it traps both parties into their respective roles with little incentive to change.

- **Suicidal thoughts** Borderline personalities often catastrophize experiences and may be prone to suicidal thoughts and intent. Do not hesitate to explore these thought processes and determine the imminent threat or risk involved. Consider a 'contract' with your client to commit to their own safety. When in the best interest of your client and/or outside your level of comfort, refer them to a mental health professional.

- **Boundaries** Set appropriate boundaries, rules and structures to safeguard your client and you. These may include modes and times of communication, handling of emergencies, intolerance of aggressive or demeaning behaviour, and taking time off to regain stability.

- **The darker side** As they oscillate between hope and despair, rather than emphasizing positivity, performance, strength and action, take time to acknowledge and reflect on the darker side of the client's lived experiences to help discover new meaning and thinking.

- **Transference** As a coach, be mindful of the impact you have on the thoughts, emotions and behaviour of your client and vice versa. At any time when you notice new or different sensations arising, you are probably touched by transference. Transference happens when a client projects their feelings or beliefs about someone else onto the coach, whereas countertransference is when the coach transfers their feelings onto the client. For example, you may feel disgusted about something the client said they did because it reminds you of something someone else did to you and display these feelings towards the client. If this happens, reflect on the meaning and origins of your feelings and what triggered them.

- **Direction** Promote and encourage the client to practise self-respect, treat others with care and validation, be assertive, and regulate unhelpful emotions and behaviour.

When working with borderline personality types, ultimately, always consider the safety and benefit of the client, coach and others in the client's life. Prevent acting and making decisions on unfounded assumptions. If you feel you are stuck in an endless spiral, or every step forward is followed by a step or two back, accept that referral, termination or suspension of coaching may be the best option at the time.

Conclusion

Having the knowledge necessary to recognize any issues that may interfere with coaching is important, including personality traits linked to a lack of self-awareness, responsibility, empathy, stability and regulation. Although the idea is not to diagnose or label your client, knowing how to deal with a difficult client is necessary to provide effective coaching, including when to step away and refer them to a trained professional.

References

American Psychiatric Association (2013) *Diagnostic and Statistical Manual of Mental Disorders*, 5th edn, Washington, DC, doi.org/10.1176/appi.books.9780890425596 (archived at https://perma.cc/D4G5-P6HW)

Bernstein, D P, Keulen-de Vos, M, Clercx, M, Vogel, V, Kersten, G C M, Lancel, M, Jonkers, P P, Bogaerts, S, Slaats, M, Broers, N J, Deenen, T A M and Arntz, A (2021) Schema therapy for violent PD offenders: A randomized clinical trial, *Psychological Medicine*,

53 (1), 88–102, doi.org/10.1017/S0033291721001161 (archived at https://perma.cc/NH65-6JFX)

Brummelman, E, Thomaes, S, Nelemans, S A, Orobio de Castro, B, Overbeek, G and Bushman, B J (2015) Origins of narcissism in children, *PNAS*, 112 (12), 3659–62, doi.org/10.1073/pnas.1420870112 (archived at https://perma.cc/G9V6-JZGF)

Cleckley, H (1988) *The Mask of Sanity*, 5th edn, Emily S Cleckley, Augusta, GA

Dadomo, H, Grecucci, A, Giardini, I, Ugolini, E, Carmelita, A and Panzeri, M (2016) Schema therapy for emotional dysregulation: Theoretical implication and clinical applications, *Frontiers in Psychology*, 7, 1987, doi.org/10.3389/fpsyg.2016.01987 (archived at https://perma.cc/2LKY-FE8M)

DeAngelis, T (2022) A broader view of psychopathy, *Monitor on Psychology*, 53 (2), 46, www.apa.org/monitor/2022/03/ce-corner-psychopathy (archived at https://perma.cc/8859-2S3E)

Dutton, K (2012) *The Wisdom of Psychopaths: What saints, spies, and serial killers can teach us about success*, Scientific American/Farrar, Straus, and Giroux, New York

Felthouse, A R (2015) The appropriateness of treating psychopathic disorders, *CNS Spectrums*, 20 (3), 182–9, doi.org/10.1017/S1092852915000243 (archived at https://perma.cc/5BZ2-QCV3)

Glenn, A L, Raine, A, Yaralian, P S and Yang, Y (2010) Increased volume of the striatum in psychopathic individuals, *Biological Psychiatry*, 67 (1), 52–8, doi.org/10.1016/j.biopsych.2009.06.018 (archived at https://perma.cc/9FSZ-6R5C)

Hyde, L W, Waller, R, Trentacosta, C J, Shaw, D S, Neiderhiser, J M, Ganiban, J M, Reiss, D and Leve, L D (2016) Heritable and nonheritable pathways to early callous-unemotional behaviors, *The American Journal of Psychiatry*, 173 (9), 903–10, doi.org/10.1176/appi.ajp.2016.15111381 (archived at https://perma.cc/J5U2-JDXL)

Karpman, S B (2014) *A Game Free Life*, Drama Triangle Publications, San Francisco, CA

Kets de Vries, M (2012) The psychopath in the C Suite: Redefining the SOB, *SSRN Electronic Journal*, doi.org/10.2139/ssrn.2179794 (archived at https://perma.cc/G5L4-KQGL)

Mathieu, C, Hare, R D, Jones, D N, Babiak, P and Neumann, C S (2013) Factor structure of the B-Scan 360: A measure of corporate psychopathy, *Psychological Assessment*, 25 (1), 288–93, doi.org/10.1037/a0029262 (archived at https://perma.cc/N3HF-6EM6)

Motzkin, J C, Newman, J P, Kiehl, K A and Koenigs, M (2011) Reduced prefrontal connectivity in psychopathy, *The Journal of Neuroscience*, 31 (48), 17348–57, doi.org/10.1523/JNEUROSCI.4215-11.2011 (archived at https://perma.cc/43E5-YFW2)

O'Connor, M and O'Donovan, H (2022) *Coaching Psychology for Mental Health: Borderline personality disorder and personal psychological recovery*, Routledge, New York

Pedersen, T (2021) What causes narcissistic personality disorder? *Psych Central*, 29 March, psychcentral.com/disorders/what-causes-narcissistic-personality-disorder (archived at https://perma.cc/ZY6M-3FF4)

Raypole, C (2020) Can narcissistic people change? *Healthline*, 16 January, www.healthline.com/health/can-a-narcissist-change (archived at https://perma.cc/EZ8G-3AS5)

Sleep, C E, Crowe, M L, Carter, N T, Lynam, D R and Miller, J D (2021) Uncovering the structure of antagonism, *Personality Disorders: Theory, Research, and Treatment*, 12 (4), 300–11, doi.org/10.1037/per0000416 (archived at https://perma.cc/FQ23-CWE5)

Wetzel, E, Grijalva, E, Robins, R and Roberts, B (2020) You're still so vain: Changes in narcissism from young adulthood to middle age, *Journal of Personality and Social Psychology*, 119 (2), 479–96, doi.org/10.1037/pspp0000266 (archived at https://perma.cc/FEB6-V56F)

Whitebourne, S K (2020) Seven basic personality ingredients of difficult people, *Psychology Today*, 1 December, www.psychologytoday.com/us/blog/fulfillment-any-age/202012/7-basic-personality-ingredients-difficult-people (archived at https://perma.cc/BF9B-WBJ4)

39

Empowering women to overcome cultural barriers

MADHVI TAILOR

ABSTRACT

Cultures inform how we see the world, interact with other people, make decisions and take action towards our goals. With the rapid increase in multiculturalism and diversity, cultural competence would unarguably be valuable for coaches. Considering that culture is a complicated and complex concept, what is the possibility of acquiring some cultural competence, let alone mastering it?

Introduction

I am a 2022 TechWomen100 award winner; born and raised in Kenya to second-generation immigrants from India, educated in the UK and working within the male-dominated technology and financial sector – I am frequently asked 'where are you from?' A polite yet inquisitive conversation starter aroused by one's curiosity regarding my identity, background and what differentiates me from other people. The mix of cultures that I have grown accustomed to and assimilated with, have made me who I am today. Consciously overcoming the cultural barriers to become more of who I authentically want to be rather than who I was born to be, has made it possible for me to guide, support, encourage and motivate others to do the same.

Using a simple step-by-step coaching approach, I share with you how to help the client become aware of their cultural identity by embarking on a journey of self-exploration and forming a picture of their values-based identity. During this the client will learn the importance of self-care and self-love, by intentionally embedding it in their daily life through practice.

As coaches, we keep a forward momentum by uncovering limiting beliefs and blind spots, guiding the client to build deeper relationships and step out of their comfort zone. We want the client to stop seeking external validation and look internally to what is in their control and can be changed. To transform the 'lack mindset' of never being enough coupled with the fear of failure into a mindset of abundance, where excitement enables them to embrace new opportunities by going beyond their comfort zone.

This chapter introduces coaches to some approaches and tools to empower clients to overcome cultural barriers. As the client's coach and thinking partner, we start with a blank canvas and build awareness of the cultural aspects that they have been exposed to. We want to encourage our clients to embrace the cultural aspects that flourish their values-based identity and let go of the ones that no longer serve them. This practice enables the client to consciously gain awareness on who they want to be, the goals they hope to achieve and the motivation required to achieve them. The client feels in control and able to make positive changes throughout their life.

A review of the concepts and theories

Due to globalization and the growing presence of the digital world, most of us find ourselves exposed to multicultural environments. An individual is influenced by their parents' or guardians' culture as well as a plethora of other factors, such as place of birth, origin of family, tradition, language, physical appearance, accent, gender, religion, profession and childhood experiences. These cultural aspects play an important role in the construction of an individual's identity, goals, values and beliefs.

'While formerly scholars assumed identification with cultural groups to be obvious and stable, today most view it as contextual and dependent upon temporal and spatial changes' (Chen, 2014). In multicultural environments, is it possible to define cultural groups, types, categories or characteristics? Can one easily associate oneself to a specific cultural group or type? Culture is a way of life. Cultural identity is a sense of belonging to a cultural group. In a study conducted by Holliday (2010) with a group from diverse national backgrounds, all acknowledge the complexity of their cultural realities, and refused to be pinned down to specific cultural types. One example was a married woman who did not have children yet. Her husband was in charge of domestic duties such as shopping and meals, while her focus became pursuing her passion and studying to help further her career. She expressed feeling out of place among women her age where she lived.

Collectivistic cultures value personal interdependence. This is usually observed in non-Western spheres where the traditional focus has been on humility, respect, security, conformity and obedience. As evidenced in the case study above, individuals within such a culture may feel anxious or confused when complying with their cultural obligations while attempting to pursue their individual goals, due to limited time and energy, and expectations from others. Individualistic cultures value personal independence. This is typically observed in Western cultures where the traditional focus is based on values such as power, achievement, and the pursuit of assets and pleasure. Individuals within this culture have the freedom to find and define their self-identity. However, having an abundance of choice may lead to decision fatigue and confusion.

What is cultural identity?

Identity is who we see ourselves as. We are not born with an identity; we develop one and it is dynamic (Kirova, 2021). Our background, family, upbringing and environment where we were raised are all factors that contribute to our identity; moulding and making us into who we are today. In childhood, our cultural identity is formed by internalizing our parents' or guardians' personal and cultural values, which are later influenced by our experiences, environment and media.

Why is it beneficial to understand our values-based identity?

When we understand our values and live by them, we become confident to make the best decisions in complicated circumstances. In turn, we develop a powerful identity based on our chosen values, which leads to high self-esteem and self-worth.

Why is it important for us to belong, fit in, blend in with the crowd?

We are social creatures with a deep desire to connect with others. A sense of belonging is a universal human need (Baumeister and Leary, 1995). It is a key support component for the physical and mental health (Hale, Hannum and Espelage, 2005). Once we have a sense of belonging in a group, or fit in with one, then we may feel more comfortable to blend in rather than stand out and draw attention.

Why is it okay to be different?

The understanding of the importance of diversity and inclusion in the workplace and its benefits have attracted much attention in the media over a number of years. It's also gained a prominent spotlight in the education system. 'It's okay to be different. You are special and important just because of being who you are' (Parr, 2009). There are a number of children's books that convey the message that it is important to accept and celebrate all the different qualities we have as individuals that make us unique. We want to go a step further and include the physical qualities that are visible on the surface as well as those that are invisible, hidden beneath the surface.

CASE STUDY

The following case study illustrates the process of accommodating cultural priorities and values and beliefs by creating awareness, identifying gaps and conflicts, and challenging limiting beliefs.

Irina had always prioritized her duties and obligations as a mother, wife and daughter before considering her own wants and needs. She had paused her university degree for her marriage. However, this momentary pause lasted much longer than she anticipated as her son was born. Considering herself fortunate to have a husband with a sufficient income to support the family, Irina continued to fulfil her cultural role. This was centred on serving her husband, children and parents as the primary duty and value of her existence. As time went on, she felt a sense of emptiness as though there was something missing in her life and started her search for the missing piece. Was it completing her university degree or something else?

Irina decided to do a coaching certification, with a goal to start her own coaching business. The balance in time and energy required to fulfil her cultural expectations, her own goal and maintain her well-being was a struggle. If she spent time on herself, she would feel guilty that she was not doing enough as a mother nor was she a perfect wife. As a result of this, Irina experienced an array of negative emotions such as internal anger, anxiety, resentment and frustration.

Longing to achieve her goal, she embarked on coaching sessions for herself. To empower herself, and make decisions to progress towards her goal, Irina had to understand the juxtaposition between her cultural priorities versus her values and beliefs. She had to work through her emotions, understand the messages that they were sending her, review her options, make decisions, and take action.

To illustrate the principles and process of overcoming cultural barriers and incorporating personal identity and values, I have outlined the main breakthrough moments in Irina's coaching journey.

Pursuit of identity

I am not what I think I am, and I am not what you think I am. I am what I think you think I am.

CHARLES COOLEY

Who am I? This is the question that Irina asked herself in our first coaching session. Most of us may have pondered over this question at some point in our lives. Our identity, our understanding of it, and its alignment with our goals, beliefs and values is of great importance. This rules our daily lives and determines what we do, how we react, how we see ourselves, how we think others see and identify with us.

In childhood, we are exposed to the culture that our parents or guardians were a part of. However, the same cultural aspects may not work with our generation because the challenges we face are different to the ones our parents faced. The available opportunities, interpersonal exposure, our goals, beliefs and values are different. This may lead to cultural differences between generations and to us questioning our cultural identity.

Our parents or guardians may have operated with a mindset that suited their needs in their situation. For instance, they may have been the first-generation immigrants or lived through a war or political unrest, leading them to have a safety, scarcity or anxious mindset for survival, which worked for them. It is often different now, in a multicultural modern world, most of us have opportunities to thrive, not just survive. We are encouraged to have the mindset to question, not silently accept. This creates generational and cultural gaps, leading us to become disoriented if our cultural identity does not align with our values-based identity.

'People internalize social norms and seek a favorable self-image by conforming to the expectations of others' (Wrong, 1963). To get closer to our identity, we want to understand who we are when we are not fulfilling a cultural role and its expectations, for example, in Irina's case, her role as a mother, wife or daughter. This awareness raises our self-belief, self-worth and self-esteem; enabling us to set our own expectations that we want to fulfil, create healthy boundaries and make informed decisions when faced with others' expectations.

According to Maio (2016), values are relevant to everything we do, our choices and decisions. Values are the core beliefs that govern our life. As children we pick up the values of close family members and friends. We also adopt values that help us to earn approval and receive care and love from the adults around us. Some examples of values are freedom, equality, achievement, learning, individuality, independence, generosity, helpfulness, security, tradition and peace.

As a coach, we want to guide our clients through their journey of self-discovery to understand who they are now and their values. This awareness is key to their starting point towards becoming who they want to be and the life they want to lead. 'Who am I outside the expectations of others?', 'What are my values?', 'Who am I now?', 'Who do I want to be?', 'What makes me feel alive?', 'What makes me feel free?' are essential questions that our clients need to answer to live a meaningful and fulfilling life.

Journey of self-discovery

An awareness of our inner child can help us think back to lighter, carefree, playful and fun years. In some cases, there may be feelings of neglect, sadness or emotional pain, which we may have buried to protect our burgeoning self. These buried feelings often surface in our adult life. They may transpire as feeling distressed in personal relationships, neglecting our own needs, having low self-esteem, finding it difficult to make decisions or not getting enjoyment out of life.

Working to heal your inner child can help us address some of these issues; however, Irina was concerned that her mind went blank during a guided meditation that asked her to converse with her inner child. According to Heath (2017), memories create our world view. Irina's mind went blank; this indicates that she may have consciously or unconsciously blocked and buried her memories. Together, we embarked on a journey of self-discovery with the intention of helping Irina unblock and recover her childhood memories. It would later prove to help her have a better understanding of her world views and great awareness of her past in order to empower her to move forward and make present and future decisions that are more in alignment with who she is. I used the tools 'Sentence completion' and 'Every picture tells a story' to facilitate this process.

'Sentence-completion is a deceptively simple yet uniquely powerful tool for raising self-understanding, self-esteem, and personal effectiveness' (Branden, 1997). This tool requires a conversation with our inner self. It allows us the precious opportunity to withdraw from the outside world and explore our inner world of thoughts and feelings. It has a list of sentence stems like 'Living consciously to me means…', 'The happiest time…' and 'What annoys me…'. We ask the client to complete these in a session or on their own. I suggested that Irina find some quiet time on her own to do the 'Sentence completion' exercise.

Additionally, while on the self-exploration journey, we explored the notion that 'Every picture tells a story' in a coaching session. This tool works on the principle that we all have our own individual world view based on our personality, beliefs and experiences. The client picks a picture/image from a selection, one that evokes the most intense feelings and vivid thoughts. Together with powerful questioning and active listening, we encourage the client to explore their world view or perception of the image by describing the present situation depicted, the preceding events, thoughts and feelings of the character(s) – as well as anything projected to their own – and what could happen next.

Both the tools enabled Irina to connect with her inner self and gain valuable insights. With this newly gained awareness, she was able to understand what is important and valuable to her now. When we are in tune with our values-based identity we are better empowered to manage our thoughts, show up fully and set boundaries. We have the courage and confidence to overcome difficulties and challenges, to be the best version of ourselves, and live a life that is aligned to our values and true self.

Importance of self-nourishment

Anger was directed at the self when a woman felt she lacked energy or competence to accomplish all that she expected of herself.

THOMAS (2022)

Irina felt that she had become an angry person and reminisced about times when she was energetic and happy. Our emotions, both positive and negative, are important. Each has a message that needs to be deciphered and processed, using powerful questioning and active listening techniques.

In cultures with patriarchal hierarchy, females are expected to be selfless, giving and serving (Varshney, 2020). Girls are taught housework and cooking during their teenage years. They are often told to take care of their younger siblings. These females may believe that self-nourishment in the form of self-love and self-care is low priority and is pushed down their to-do list. They have seen their female role models around them do the same and consider it the norm without questioning it. However, as the cup and saucer analogy tells us: we must all fill our own cup first before we are able to give to others from the overflow in the saucer; otherwise we may feel anger, resentment, frustration or fatigue. These were the troubling emotions experienced by Irina.

To get to the root of why Irina was getting angry, I used a visualization technique. I asked her to talk me through her ideal day, in which she prioritized tasks that she valued; we then compared it to her usual current day. To explore further, I asked her questions on each of the differences to dig deeper into the reasons why her current day did not align with her ideal day. Irina discovered that she wanted some reading and exercise time. She anchored this to her existing morning routine by waking up earlier. This was a small step but significant towards her well-being and in turn towards achieving her big goal.

Overcoming limiting beliefs and stepping out of the comfort zone

Most people hold limiting beliefs, such as I could never do that or I am not good enough. It's almost as if we have been mandated to accept certain beliefs and principles. We need to acquire our own beliefs and principles.

AMS (2014)

Our world view may be partly made up of the beliefs stored deep in our subconscious mind that we are unaware of. These may be passed on to us by our parents or other role models through conditioning, or we may have learnt them from our experiences. A limiting belief is a story you tell yourself that keeps you in your comfort zone. It may have once worked as a defense mechanism or a safety net but is now holding you back. When a client is stuck, we want to help them figure out why and what action they must take to become unstuck and make progress. A client may have low self-esteem and believe that they will not be able to add value so they do not want to attempt the task, or they may have a low self-efficacy image, believing that they do not have the ability to do the task. See Table 39.1 for a list of questions to challenge and transform limiting beliefs.

As Irina worked through her coaching certification, she wanted to read her study material at least twice. She believed this was necessary for her in order to retain the information, however, it was placing constraints on her limited time and energy. She was not making progress nor was she enjoying studying. Through several layers of replies to my 'Why?' questions, she discovered she had always done this since her earliest childhood memories of studying for exams because her father had told her to do it. Her father's voice in her head was conditioning this belief in her when she was a child. This may have worked for her father's learning, competitiveness and survival cultural aspects, but not necessarily for someone else with different abilities, preferences and situations. My question: Was it working for Irina or was it holding her back? She tried and tested different ways of reading through her study material. She realized that she was more effective when she studied earlier in her day than later in the evening when she was tired. She made notes and used highlighters to help her focus. As a result of these simple changes, she was able to let go of her limiting belief and trust her ability, which empowered Irina to make positive progress towards her big goal and also enjoy her study experience.

Towards the end of Irina's coaching certification course, after completing the theory, she had to start her practice sessions with practice clients. She had a block and was stuck. Irina said that she did not feel that she would live up to the practice client's expectation. I asked her what she thought their expectation was. She said that her client would want to gain something out of the session. Naturally, I asked her 'why do you feel that you wouldn't be able to help them gain something?' Unconfidently, she whispered she did not know. When a client says, 'I don't know,' I would immediately ask her, 'what does she not know?' and keep asking targeted questions to un-layer, diagnose and discover the assumption or feeling or limiting belief. I asked her if it was a fact or a feeling and she replied, 'It's not a fact, it's just a feeling.' My next question is 'how much value do you give to this feeling compared to a fact, on a scale from 1 to 10?' After a little thought and silence, Irina said, 'I can't because I don't know, I might be an effective coach, or I might be an ineffective coach.' As Irina's coach, I have created cracks in her limiting belief, which is the start of the process of uncovering and replacing a limiting belief with a self-belief in her ability.

Practical recommendations

What frequently goes unnoticed is the fact that without the participation of women, patriarchy would be impossible. The participation, however, is not completely voluntary or intentional. It is fundamentally enabled by conditioning women to succumb to patriarchy from their early childhood through learning and internalizing their supposed inferiority.

POLÁKOVÁ (2021: 10)

TABLE 39.1 Questioning techniques to explore and challenge limiting beliefs

Goal	Questions	Key points
	What makes you say that?	Is it fear of failure or a limiting belief?
	Is that a fact, belief, feeling or assumption?	This could be a voice in the client's head, so we need to uncover where it is coming from
Creating cracks in a limiting belief This is when the client says: I can't do xyz.... I will not live up to the expectation of ... I am not good enough ... I will not succeed ... I need to do xyz	If it's a fact, then ask further questions relating to the fact	This could be a past experience that needs to be explored and any emotions that arise will need to be processed
	If it's a belief, then ask further questions to understand where the belief originates from	This may be a conscious or unconscious limiting belief; both need further exploration
	If it's a feeling, then ask the client how much value they place on this feeling on a scale of 1–10	This will trigger the client to think about the value that this feeling is adding. If the client places a value greater than 5, then explore the feeling further
	If it's an assumption, then ask what it is based on. If a past experience, then what is the probability of it repeating?	Assumption is something we think will happen. The client may be assuming that something will happen again if it has happened in the past. There is no proof
Uncovering a block This is when the client says: I don't know...	What don't you know?	The client can't answer a question. so they say 'I don't know...'. They may not want to answer or they may not know the answer. Keep asking further questions because this is giving us a clue that there's more beneath the surface
	And what else? Tell me more...	These are powerful questions after a period of silence that has allowed the client to process what was discussed or think of more

As a coach, create a safe and open space that allows the client to share vulnerably and form a trust-based relationship. To achieve this, one should be non-judgemental, self-aware, fully present, curious and empathetic. Remind the client that the coaching sessions are confidential and they are in a safe space. Don't make assumptions, validate your observations and interpretations by using phrases such as 'what I hear you saying is...', 'what I am learning about you...', 'I understand that...', 'it looks like…', 'my perception is…'. Although we may never fully understand our client's unique cultural world view, we have the tools to empower them to understand it (and the consequences) for themselves. The coaching tools that I have used in Irina's sessions are powerful questioning, active listening, visualization, silence, curiosity, being present, un-layering to discover the root cause, 'Sentence completion' and 'Every picture tells a story'.

In a world where most people listen to fix and give solutions, as a coach our greatest tool is active listening with an intent to learn, compassion, and full attention while being fully present. When the client has stopped talking, ask them 'What else?' or 'Tell me more…' Then, be comfortable with silence, which gives the client space to reflect. The silence allows the coach to take in the information and come up with the next powerful question.

To guide the client to interpret and process their emotions, there is no other way besides going through each emotion step by step. They may start off with confusion, anger, resentment, hurt or sadness. We want to guide the client to find peace, acceptance, purpose, joy and fulfilment.

Emotions have a reason for surfacing. We cannot go over them nor can we go under them, we have to go through them to process and manage them. We need to ascertain what is triggering these emotions, understand the message they are giving us, un-layer, and get to the root cause. This creates the awareness that empowers us with the knowledge, ability and courage to confidently step through the emotion, leave it behind, close the door behind us and unlock the door ahead of us.

> You've always had the power, my dear, you just had to learn it for yourself. Glinda, *The Wizard of Oz*

References

Ams, S (2014) *Transformation in Action: Breaking through limiting beliefs to live the life of your dreams*, Balboa Press, Bloomington, IN

Baumeister, R F and Leary, M R (1995) The need to belong: Desire for interpersonal attachments as a fundamental human motivation, *Psychological Bulletin*, 117 (3), 497–529, doi.org/10.1037/0033-2909.117.3.497 (archived at https://perma.cc/99PH-XT7R)

Branden, N (1997) *The Art of Living Consciously: The power of awareness to transform everyday life*, Simon & Schuster, New York

Chen, V H (2014) Cultural identity, *Key Concepts in Intercultural Dialogue*, 22, 1, centerforinterculturaldialogue.files.wordpress.com/2014/07/key-concept-cultural-identity.pdf (archived at https://perma.cc/V5NR-2XHC)

Hale, C J, Hannum, J W and Espelage, D L (2005) Social support and physical health: The importance of belonging, *Journal of American College Health*, 53 (6), 276–84, doi.org/10.3200/jach.53.6.276-284 (archived at https://perma.cc/TE2S-2FDW)

Heath, C (2017) Your memories make you who you are, *Psychology Today*, 8 August, www.psychologytoday.com/gb/blog/psychoanalysis-unplugged/201708/your-memories-make-you-who-you-are (archived at https://perma.cc/26WL-KDJC)

Holliday, A (2010) Complexity in cultural identity, *Language and Intercultural Communication*, 10 (2), 165–77, doi.org/10.1080/14708470903267384 (archived at https://perma.cc/4ZKY-PNE5)

Kirova, D (2021) How values shape identity, Values Institute, values.institute/how-values-shape-identity/#The_Importance_of_Individual_and_Group_Identity (archived at https://perma.cc/6BKC-XURJ)

Maio, G R (2016) *The Psychology of Human Values*, Routledge, New York

Parr, T (2009) *It's Okay to be Different*, Little, Brown and Company, London

Poláková, D (2021) Patriarchal gender roles in the poetry and essays of Adrienne Rich, Master's thesis, Univerzita Karlova, dspace.cuni.cz/bitstream/handle/20.500.11956/125779/130301439.pdf (archived at https://perma.cc/2MER-56TJ)

Thomas, S (2022) Women's anger, aggression, and violence, *Health Care for Women International*, 26 (6), 504–22, doi.org/10.1080/07399330590962636 (archived at https://perma.cc/PEB3-FPYJ)

Varshney, R (2020) Patriarchy begins at home: Understanding gender roles within the family, *Youth Ki Awaaz*, 8 April, www.youthkiawaaz.com/2020/04/gender-and-politics-of-care-in-family (archived at https://perma.cc/Y8A3-DPB2)

Wrong, D H (1963) The oversocialized conception of man in modern sociology, in *Personality and Social Systems*, eds N J Smelser and W T Smelser, pp 68–79, John Wiley and Sons Inc, New York

Conclusion

MARIE FAIRE

Maybe you are one of those people who read a conclusion to see if a book is worth reading; if so, rest assured it is! If you have read it already, then you will know that. As Jeannette said in the Foreword, whether you have read the whole thing or dipped into different chapters as and when your interest has been piqued, I am certain that you will have found hope, inspiration, challenges and insights.

This is an extraordinary and unique collection of chapters – written, in the most, by new coaches, for new coaches, although the wisdom and food for thought that exists within these pages will be as useful to those who count their experience in thousands of hours as to those just starting out.

In preparation for writing this conclusion, I did a quick search about what makes for a 'good' conclusion. The general advice appears to be to keep it short, to summarize the learning, and tie it all together. For this book, that is an impossible task. There is so much learning in every chapter, and so many chapters. I will therefore endeavour to meet two out of the three criteria; to keep it short and offer my observations by way of an overview (if not entirely tying it all together).

The coaching profession is still a relatively new profession and with each passing decade it is evolving and maturing. The breadth and depth that is offered by the authors bears testament to this fact.

It is refreshing and enlightening that chapters that develop core coaching skills (that are in every professional body's competency list) sit alongside wisdom from across the globe, from other professions and many ideologies. Each author has, it seems, embraced the desire to offer, as Oliver Wendell Holmes put it, 'simplicity on the other side of complexity' (Condeluci, 1996: 97).

Edna Murdoch, a pioneer in coach supervision, often used the maxim, 'who you are is how you coach' (McLean, 2019: 156), and certainly there is plenty of evidence for that in the wonderful diversity and individuality expressed by the authors. Who are you as a coach? What is your philosophy and approach? I encourage you to read those chapters, if you haven't already, that challenge your opinions as well as those that support it.

If this conclusion were a form of punctuation, it would be a comma, or at the most a semi-colon, not a full stop. Whoever you are as a coach today, I hope that you will be a different one in the years to come and will continue to delve into this book and learn.

References

Condeluci, A (1996) *Beyond Difference*, CRC Press, Boca Raton, FL

McLean, P (2019) *Self as Coach, Self as Leader*, John Wiley & Sons, Hoboken, NJ

INDEX

NB: page numbers in *italic* indicate figures or tables

CPSIA information can be obtained
at www.ICGtesting.com
Printed in the USA
JSHW040149180623
43357JS00004B/19

9 781398 610491